Handbook
of
Data Communications

'My department is in possession of full knowledge of the details of the invention [the telephone], and the possible use of the telephone is limited'

Engineer-in-Chief, British Post Office, 1877

'One day, every town in America will have a telephone'

Mayor of a small American town, circ. 1880

PUBLISHED BY NCC PUBLICATIONS

British Library Cataloguing in Publication Data

Bleazard, G.B.
  Handbook of data communications.
  1. Data transmission systems.
  1. Title
  001.64   TK5105

  ISBN 0-85012-363-1

© BRITISH TELECOMMUNICATIONS, 1975

© THE NATIONAL COMPUTING CENTRE LIMITED, 1982

First published in 1982 by:

NCC Publications, The National Computing Centre Limited, Oxford Road, Manchester M1 7ED, England.

Reprinted in 1984

Typeset in 10pt Times Roman and printed by UPS Blackburn Limited, 76-80 Northgate, Blackburn, Lancs.

ISBN 0-85012-363-1

Acknowledgements

This book contains British Telecommunications copyright material copied, under licence, from the Handbook of Data Communications. We should, however, make a disclaimer to the effect that, excluding material reproduced without modification, the final responsibility for factual correctness at the time of going to press, and for any opinions which are expressed, rests with The National Computing Centre Ltd.

We also gratefully acknowledge the assistance of the following: PACTEL (PA Computers and Telecommunications), who contributed a substantial amount of the material; David Wheeler and Malcolm Payne of the Centre's Training Division, who made a number of helpful suggestions; and other Centre staff whose published and unpublished work was frequently referred to (these and other authors are acknowledged by name in the bibliography). Thanks are also due to the NCC typists who coped, often in difficult circumstances, with a considerable body of work.

Bernard Bleazard of the Centre's Office and Communications Systems Division undertook responsibility for overall supervision of the work, including the structure and assembly of the text, and also contributed a significant amount of new material.

Finally, the Centre acknowledges with thanks the support for this project provided by the Electronics and Avionics Requirements Board of the Department of Industry.

Introduction

This book draws heavily on an earlier NCC book with an identical title, first published in 1975. The material of the earlier book was prepared by staff at Post Office Telecommunications (as it then was) and was published on behalf of the PO by The National Computing Centre. In the seven years which have elapsed since it first appeared, the book has enjoyed considerable success both in the UK and overseas.

Two factors prompted the decision to produce this new book. In the first place, in the intervening period there have been dramatic changes in computing and communication technology and concepts, and the original book is clearly out-of-date in a number of respects. Secondly, there was the equally compelling reason that stocks of the book were nearing exhaustion, whilst there was strong evidence of a continuing demand for the publication.

These considerations encouraged us to the view that a new book should be produced: the present volume is the result. Before embarking upon the task we discussed the proposal with British Telecom, who kindly gave their blessing to the venture, subject to satisfactory arrangements regarding copyright on material which has been reproduced from the earlier book. British Telecom also indicated that on this occasion, for reasons which we accept and respect, they did not feel able to participate directly in the task. Therefore, apart from the material reproduced from the earlier volume, The National Computing Centre assumed responsibility for preparing and assembling new material and for any restructuring of the book.

It is not a trivial task to compile a book such as this, covering a subject area which has experienced such rapid changes in recent years – a process that can be expected to continue throughout the next decade. Inevitably, the ideal solution would have been to completely rewrite the book, but this would have had two major disadvantages: the timescale would have exceeded what we considered reasonable; and the result would itself in turn fall a victim to technological change. We elected for a compromise approach based upon the following guiding principles.

First of all, for reasons that will be shortly explained, we decided to retain the broad structure and balance of topics of the original. Secondly, we decided to retain those parts of the original which had stood the test of time and remained valid; this includes the basic principles and much material which is not easily accessible elsewhere. We nevertheless considered it proper to amend this retained information either in the interest of increased clarity or for stylistic reasons. And finally, we felt it essential to take account of the major technological and conceptual changes which have occurred and which are now exerting a significant influence on data transmission, on the future shape of telecommunications networks, and on the role of data communications generally.

We shall first of all briefly review those topics where major revision is indicated. But before doing so, it is worth quoting a paragraph from the preface to the earlier book:

'Computer and telecommunications technologies are becoming increasingly convergent and the UK Post Office, in conjunction with The National Computing Centre Limited, has produced this Handbook as a contribution to a greater understanding of their interdependence by students of both disciplines'

The phenomenon of convergence is now a commonplace, but its recognition in 1975 in the above context can now be seen to have been remarkably prophetic. Looking back over a distance of seven years we are also reminded of the major technological changes and trends which are bringing about its realisation. These were then either non-existent or barely discernible.

The underlying common thread is digitisation – of transmission and switching, and the representation and storage of information. Although in the mid-1970s digital transmission of speech using PCM was beginning to be applied in the world's telephone networks, the UK Post Office, in common with other PTTs, was still at the stage of formulating its long-term network modernisation plans. Now, most PTTs are committed to digitisation of speech and data throughout their networks, and in the UK in particular this is beginning to take shape in the form of System X, and private circuit digital services, culminating in the Integrated Services Digital Network.

The present book therefore gives far greater prominence to *digital* transmission technology, as opposed to *analogue,* than did its predecessor.

In the mid-1970s, Packet Switching was starting to be considered as an alternative to circuit switching for data transmission in public switched networks. However, the bulk of experience was largely in the academic and research environment, although the UK PO had decided to launch the Experimental Packet Switched Service; this was touched upon in the earlier volume. Since then there has been rapid progress both in the UK and internationally. In the UK we have a fully operational public packet switched service (PSS); other national telecommunications administrations are introducing similar services, and these are all being progressively interconnected through national gateways. This is an area which obviously requires an expanded treatment.

Major changes are also occurring in the nature of the transmission vehicles. Whereas, in the early part of the 1970s, coaxial cable was the favoured vehicle for terrestrial circuits, and was fast displacing the traditional multistrand copper cables, now optical fibres are set to displace coaxial cable, with satellite transmission opening up totally new dimensions.

Data communications can only achieve its full potential if, in principle, any device (such as a computer or a terminal) can readily access and communicate intelligently with any other device. The eventual goal is to achieve the potential universality of intercommunication for data communications as exists in the world's telephone network. Although the electrical interface standards specified by CCITT and implemented by the PTTs have provided an essential and solid foundation for data communications, a substantial hierarchy of additional standards and protocols is also required.

In the last few years there has been substantial progress in the development and adoption of new protocols, such as HDLC for line control and X25 for packet switched networks. A deeper understanding of the conceptual framework has also emerged. Because of these developments we have restructured and almost completely rewritten this part of the text, and we have been able to do this within a framework which we hope is a little more systematic and more coherent than has been customary.

These developments have required the formulation and agreement of a complex hierarchy of standards for attaching equipment, and formalised rules governing intercommunication.

With regard to the broad structure, some explanation may be in order for the newcomer unacquainted with the earlier book but who has already read other texts on the subject. Such a reader may be struck by the increased coverage given to the public network and its operation, compared with other texts. The reason is that the original handbook arose as a by-product of courses on data transmission jointly organised and operated by the Post Office and The National Computing Centre. The courses were aimed at two categories of people: the telecommunications specialists who wished to expand their knowledge of computer communications, and the dp professionals who wanted to find out more about the transmission and telecommunications area. It is this background that largely accounts for the unique flavour of the original, and which we decided to retain in the present volume. The decision has been amply justified by the comments we have received and our experience in running courses. Whilst it is certainly *not* essential for the dp professional to have a particularly detailed knowledge of the telecommunications infrastructures, many have found it rewarding to gain an insight into what lies beyond the modem interface. This insight has often resulted in a vastly increased respect for the achievements of telecommunications engineering. For the telecommunications engineer traditionally preoccupied with voice requirements, and who is now having to get to grips with the world of data communications, information technology, the electronic office, etc, the book also contains some familiar landmarks on the road to finding out more about data communications.

The book is organised so that roughly the first half is concerned with transmission and switching theory and hardware. It starts with a discussion of basic principles, then moves on to describe the public switched telephone network. Identification of the limitations of the analogue telephone network provides the transition to data transmission and its requirements, and how these are met under analogue transmission, and the enormous improvements brought about by conversion to digital transmission and switching technology. This part of the book concludes with a review of British Telecom's network modernisation strategy and plans.

From this point, the text moves into the area of data communications proper. It commences with an overview of *data communications systems* as assemblages of various components such as transmission circuits, modems, multiplexers and the like. The subject is discussed in terms of the physical arrangements for linking the various elements together, and the functional or conceptual architectures necessary to ensure that the system as a whole operates in a disciplined and coordinated manner.

Following this, there is an extended discussion of data communications standards, protocols, and error control procedures. This is perhaps the most abstract part of the book, but a vitally important one and an area in which there have been major developments in the last few years. In the literature the topics covered are not always presented in a clearly understandable and logically coherent manner, and this we have tried to remedy.

Data communications systems can never be completely left to themselves: faults have to be detected and remedied, performance monitored and so on. In short, the system has to be managed, and the penultimate chapter discusses in general terms some of the more important topics which come under this heading.

Data communications, comprising the whole body of principles and techniques described in this book, results from the marriage of telecommunications and computing technology. The computer is a fairly recent innovation but telecommunications goes back much further; to 1837 in fact, when Wheatstone invented the electric telegraph. Together, these disciplines provide the basis for the Information Technology Revolution which is now underway. In the final chapter, 'Into the Future', we try to offer a glimpse into this new world by describing the main technological driving forces, the expanding and novel opportunities that are emerging and the potential impacts on society.

In the process of preparing the book a major problem was in deciding what parts of the original text to leave out. It was impossible to include everything in addition to the new material.

Portions of the text were discarded for a variety of reasons, including: present-day relevance, expediency, it being considered simpler to rewrite rather than to merge fragments of text, and several other practical considerations. In particular, it should be noted that we have omitted detailed descriptions of specific UK and international telecommunications services which had their own separate chapters in the original version. Because of the rapid changes which are occurring, and the speed at which new services are being introduced or expanded, this information very quickly becomes out-of-date, and we decided that it would be prudent to exclude it.

We have already indicated the kind of mixed audience to which the earlier version was directed, and we feel that this still applies, with one or two qualifications. There is some significance in the use of 'Handbook' in the title. Whilst the book could usefully serve as a textbook – and we would not wish to dissuade the reader from using it is this way – we feel that a complete newcomer would gain added benefit if the book were supplemented by a more basic text. Above all, the book serves as a reference text, to be dipped into as the occasion requires; either to refresh the memory, or to supply information not always easily accessible.

In conclusion we hope that the book turns out to be a worthy successor to its predecessor and enjoys a similar success.

Bernard Bleazard
Senior Consultant
NCC Office and Communications
Systems Division

Contents

1 Origins and Basic Concepts

ORIGINS

One of the historical measures of man's progress has been his ability to communicate information between people, primarily over distance but also through time. Efficient recording and dissemination of information was a major problem until William Caxton developed the printing press in 1473. However, although this allowed more efficient preservation of records, communication over distance still included physical travel. The faithful horse, succeeded by the steam engine, governed the speed of information travel until the advent of true 'telecommunications'. Whereas physical transport of hard copy information is still used to this day, it is to other early methods of communication over distance that we owe today's sophisticated communications systems.

DEVELOPMENTS IN TELECOMMUNICATIONS

Our inability to make our voices heard beyond a very limited distance is something we all learn as children. Most of man's attempts at rapid communication beyond voice range have therefore necessitated using some form of telegraphy, which means the conveyance of messages using signalling symbols or codes. Fiery beacons, for example, used to be a very popular method of indicating danger. Homer, describing the fall of Troy in the 11th Century BC, spoke of a chain of flaring beacons which brought the news to Argos. In 1588, warning of the Spanish Armada was given by a chain of beacons throughout the length and breadth of Britain. Smoke signalling was used widely by the North American Indians.

How much information could be conveyed accurately by such means obviously depended on weather conditions and it is reasonable to conclude that the Indians had a few error control problems! The tom-tom is one of the most ancient methods employed and is still in use today by the natives of Africa, South America and Polynesia. Little is known about the codes used but it is interesting to reflect that such primitive peoples, by inventing suitable codes and the means to transmit and relay information, have communicated effectively and rapidly over considerable distances since before the time of Christ.

In more recent history, signalling systems have been developed using the movements of human or mechanical arms (semaphore) or reflected light (heliograph) and these systems are still effective today where no alternative form of communication is possible. Since electrical telegraphic communication began in 1837 there have been many ingenious machines using various codes and signals. Although the first reliable machine for sending letters and figures was invented by Wheatstone in 1840, we owe much to Baudot, Hughes, Morkrum and others for their pioneering work in electrical telegraphy.

Since the telephone was invented by Bell in 1876, two completely different but complementary methods of fast communication over distance have developed, both reaching a high level of sophistication. The telephone effectively removed the problem of the limited range of the human voice: apart from the enormous social benefits and changes it has brought, it has also enabled man to advance more rapidly by breaking down the main barrier to the exchange of ideas over distance.

Telegraphic communication, through telegram services, privately-rented telegraph circuits and the dialled Telex, has developed more modestly to enable the rapid worldwide communication of graphic information or of information which is to be printed. It may be regarded as remote typewriting using teleprinter machines: the transmission speed of telegraphy is closely allied to the keying speed of teleprinter operators. Telegraphic communication is normally used for messages rather than for conversation and provides a faster alternative to the postal services.

A third major thrust, in the second and third quarters of this century, has been the rapid expansion of data communications. These communications, generally at much higher speeds than telegraphic applications, are closely associated with the development of the electronic computer.

THE ELECTRONIC COMPUTER

Charles Babbage's nineteenth-Century work, now regarded as the real precursor of modern computing, lay dormant for nearly a century until the technology emerged for the construction of the first automatic computer. In 1937 Claude Shannon first demonstrated the parallel between switching circuits and the algebra of logic. He also defined a universal unit of information, a 'bit' being the amount of information needed to remove the uncertainty between yes and no (or between on and off).

Data and Information

The modern history of digital computers began in 1939 with the efforts of Howard Aiken and his associates at Harvard University. Work on their electromechanical Sequence Control Calculator began in 1939 and was completed in 1944.

The second key development was the construction of the ENIAC (Electronic Numerical Integrator and Calculator) as a joint project between the University of Pennsylvania and the United States Army. This machine, which was completed in 1946, used thermionic valves rather than electromagnetic relays and was the forerunner of the first generation of electronic digital computers. Until the discovery of the germanium transistor in 1947, electronic computers consumed enormous amounts of electrical power, generated much heat, and were unreliable. The early machines using valves were employed mainly for scientific and experimental work. There was then little desire to add to the problems of computing by passing information remotely over telegraph and telephone lines.

The next generation of electronic computers emerged in the mid-1950s. These were 'stored program' machines, holding programming instructions in the main memory of the computer rather than externally on punched cards or tape. They used transistors instead of valves, had more efficient storage and consumed less power; they were faster and more reliable than their predecessors. Work at Birkbeck College, London, in the development of magnetic drum storage, contributed to this area of development. This reflected earlier contributions by Cambridge University and J Lyons & Co Ltd who introduced LEO (Lyons Electronic Office, 1951), the first computer for commercial use. Because they could store and rapidly process large amounts of information, computers were increasingly being developed for commercial data processing. When information for processing originated at sites remote from the central computer, the source documents were usually sent by post to the computer centre: here the information was converted into a machine-readable coded form and held on punched paper tape or punched cards for processing at some later time.

In the later 1950s, as the volume of information grew and as jobs became more time critical, people turned towards the existing telegraph circuits and the Telex system as faster alternatives to the post for collecting information 'off-line'. By the 1960s and 1970s, as the demand for remote processing grew, slow-speed circuits could not cope with the volumes of data, and requirements emerged for lines capable of higher speeds. Networks, involving many users and computers, developed – locally, nationally and internationally. Future networks are expected to carry data at speeds ranging from hundreds to millions of bits per second (Mbit/s).

COMMUNICATING WITH COMPUTERS

Complementing the development of computer systems has been the utilisation of communications to extend the power of the computer beyond the computer room, thereby allowing the benefits of the system to

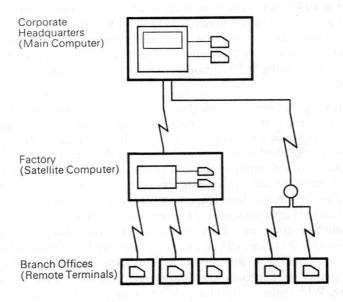

Figure 1.1   Simplified Configuration of a Business Data Communications Network

be more widely available geographically. This mixture of computers and communications gives the benefits of computer facilities at one's finger-tips regardless of location whilst preserving on one site the expertise needed to operate the system. A simple example is where a person dials a connection over the telephone network to interconnect a terminal with the facilities available at the computer.

A typical involvement with data communications is shown by the example of a large firm with numerous branch offices and several factories (Figure 1.1). Each of the factories could have its own medium-sized computer which would be linked to terminals within the factory and also at adjacent branch offices. Further communications links could exist between these machines and a larger machine at the corporate headquarters. The individual terminals would be used for the collection and dissemination of the user data, with the 'satellite' computer collating and editing this data and carrying out much of the local minor data processing. Major computation and corporate matters would be passed into the large machine at headquarters.

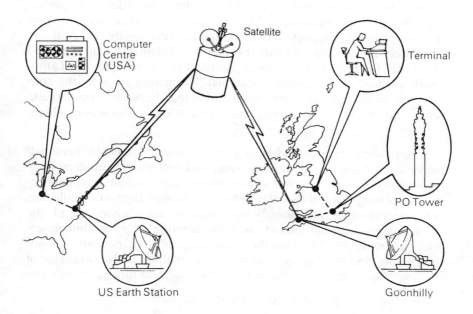

Figure 1.2   International Data Communications Connection

This blend of computers and communications is now taken for granted in a rapidly growing proportion of business organisations. Even the most unsophisticated of users may unconsciously be using very complex systems. For example, a small business in Manchester, England, may have a fairly simple terminal which is connected, via a local telephone call, into a computer service bureau to use one of the facilities offered by that bureau.

Unknown to the user, however, his local call takes him a very long way from home (Figure 1.2). The connection is to a small communications computer in Manchester which concentrates the data along with that from other local users and passes it to a larger computer in London. Here, because of the particular services being used, it is passed via a communications satellite in orbit above the Atlantic, to the service company's main computer centre in the USA. The results come back over the same links giving the user the impression that the bureau is just next door.

TELEMATICS

In the late-1970s and 1980s, many other applications of data communications have been developed, and it is reasonable to expect the growth of communications support for Information Technology to continue unabated. At the heart of this revolution is Telematics (an anglicised version of the French 'Telematique', applied to the combination of automatic control and telecommunications). Telematics involves the convergence of voice and data communications, together with computers and office automation, into an integrated approach to information technology.

The primary impetus had been given by developments in 'personal/ office computing' (eg word processing, desk-top microcomputers, business minicomputers) coupled with the moves towards digital communications, as exemplified by digital telephone exchanges, digital facsimile, etc. The opportunities are now being seized to take advantage of the economies of scale and added cost-efficiency offered by combining services wherever possible. Thus the convergence of voice, computers, word processors, and message systems is being capitalised to the advantage of the user. No longer will a business manager have to turn separately to:

—   the DP department for computer services;

—   the PABX for phones;

— the typing pool for document preparation;

— a secretary for messages;

— the mail room for document transmission.

The technology of telematics in the automated office will offer such services as:

— distributed computing;

— multi-feature digital telephones;

— word processing with remote communications;

— voice and electronic mail.

Data communications is used to link the systems, both locally and throughout the networks. In a sense, data communications is something of a misnomer since, with the change from analogue transmission to digital transmission now underway, it will be possible to transmit information in all its principal forms with equal facility. These include speech, numerical information, text and images, whether facsimile or video.

COMMUNICATING INFORMATION

As you read these lines, you are forming part of an information system; the author being the message source (transmitter), the publication the message medium and yourself the receiver. This is an example of a 'simplex' system, communication being in one direction only. In a telephone conversation, people do not generally speak at once but exchange roles as transmitter and receiver, maintaining a check on the understanding and accuracy of the messages they are each receiving. This type of information system where messages are transmitted in both directions but not at the same time is termed 'half-duplex' and again we find the three essential parts of an information system – a message source, a message medium (the telephone line) and a receiver. A great deal of information can, of course, be exchanged in both directions at the same time by two people gazing into one another's eyes. In their attempts to describe this simultaneous transmission of messages, poets have surprisingly failed to recognise that this is simply a 'duplex' information system.

It is only recently that communication itself has been studied, man throughout the ages having concentrated on the *methods* of communicating. The study of communication theory has provided a better understanding of the factors which limit the rate at which information can be transferred. To the communications theorist, information is 'any organised signal'. This, of course, presupposes that these organised signals have some meaning which is understandable to a receiver. In speech conversation within a room, information in this sense would consist of the complex sound waves 'organised' by the vocal chords, pharynx and tongue of the speaker (transmitter) being transmitted via the medium of air to the listener (receiver). Information on a telephone circuit may consist of a series of tones, a group of tones, direct current pulses or any other signals which are organised. Collectively, the information constitutes the message. Noise also has a precise meaning in communication theory and can be defined as 'any signal which interferes with the message being sent'. Music, no matter how beautiful, could therefore be regarded as noise by two people wishing to talk to one another during a concert.

In addition to the problem of noise, the communication channel must have sufficient capacity for the intended purpose. Analogous to the transmission of a fluid down a pipe, a communications channel does have a finite capacity. This is not readily apparent in speech conversation, where the primary concern is with intelligibility, but it has very important implications for information transmission in its general sense. From this discussion it is evident that there are a number of concepts and principles which require a closer examination and a more precise definition.

THE NATURE OF DATA COMMUNICATIONS

Data and Information

The term 'data' can be defined as 'any representation, such as a figure or a letter, to which meaning can be ascribed'. 'Information' has a number of meanings; to the communications theorist, for example, it means 'any organised signal'. Generally, however, the term is understood to describe something which is meaningful. Throughout this book we shall tend to use the terms interchangeably, bearing in mind that information can assume various significant forms meaningful to the user, as we have noted earlier.

Data Transmission

Data transmission can be defined as the movement of information over some physical medium, using some form of physical representation appropriate to the medium. Thus, we include: electrical signals carried along a wire; radio waves propagated through space; optical signals transmitted along a wire; and thermal or infra-red signals transmitted through space from a laser source.

Data Communications

'Data communications' has a much wider meaning than data transmission and embraces not just the electrical transmission but many other factors involved in controlling, checking and handling the movement of information in a communications-based computer system. For example, it includes: the physical transmission circuits and networks; the hardware and software components required to support the data communications functions; procedures for detecting and recovering from errors; standards for interfacing user equipment to the transmission network; and a variety of rules or protocols for ensuring the disciplined exchange of information.

TRANSMISSION CONCEPTS

Transmission Codes

The power of digital electronic computers lies in their ability to do simple tasks at very high speed. To help computers achieve high processing speeds, data is fed into computers in a logical and simplified form using binary digits. A binary digit or bit can be defined as 'the amount of information derived from the knowledge of two equiprobables' and can be represented mathematically by a 1 or 0 or electrically by two differing conditions +ve or −ve, on or off.

The use by computer systems of binary notation has required coding systems to be developed to convert alpha and numeric characters (letters and numbers) into binary notation. In this way it is possible to convert information and data which is easily recognised by humans to a form acceptable by computers. To express numeric information only four binary digits are required; and to represent alpha (letter) information a further two bits must be used. A coding system that will give a full numeric and alpha character set is the Binary Coded Decimal (BCD) system with 36 characters.

An extended character set is usually required for data communications. In addition to the need to communicate letters, figures, punctuation marks, etc, a considerable number of control characters may be required. These control the transmission of data, manipulate the format of a message, separate information and switch on or off devices which are connected to the communications line.

The Extended Binary Coded Decimal Interchange Code (EBCDIC) is an extension of BCD code and uses eight bits instead of six. This code is useful where an application calls for a large number of different characters. Although there are only 109 assigned meanings, there are $256(2^8)$ possible combinations. The code is used mainly to transmit the eight-bit bytes[1] of some computers and obviates the need for the code conversion which is often necessary between the transmission code and the code used by the computer.

International Alphabet No 5

Because of the proliferation of data transmission codes throughout the world, serious attempts have been made to standardise the codes used. The International Telegraph and Telephone Consultative Committee (CCITT), the International Organization for Standardization (ISO) and national bodies have given much thought to a problem which had become increasingly serious as the need grew to communicate between devices of different manufacturers and between different countries.

The International Alphabet No 5 (IA 5) is a 7-bit code which has been developed to satisfy the need for a standard code which will allow both sophisticated telegraphic and data communication. The new alphabet originated from a proposed American Standard Code for Information Interchange (ASCII) put forward by the American Standards Association (now the American National Standards Association) in 1962. This was developed by the CCITT and the ISO and was subsequently ratified by them.

Standardisation too early can adversely affect progress by impeding the introduction of new and better ideas. This argument is recognised by CCITT and ISO and the IA 5 code allows for a certain amount of flexibility enabling users to 'escape' from the normal conventions of the code by the use of special characters. Examples of the control characters used in IA 5 code are given in Appendix 3.

---

[1] A byte is 'a group of consecutive binary digits operated on as a unit by a computer'. Although the eight-bit byte is common, the number of bits in a byte may vary between computers of different manufacturers up to sixteen- or thirty-two-bit bytes.

Telegraph Codes

A number of computer-based data communications systems still make use of the long established telegraph codes. In telegraphy, the need to transmit plain language text predominates and fewer characters are needed than in data communications. Separate characters for all decimal figures and letters of the alphabet (though not necessarily capital letters and small letters) must be available, which gives a required minimum of 36 characters. Although punctuation marks, 'space', etc, could be indicated in words or combinations of these characters, this would be cumbersome and tedious for both the operator and the reader. Separate characters are therefore provided in practice for these and other purposes. Figure 1.3 shows the keyboard of a traditional teleprinter which provides for the entry of 58 different characters. The code, or alphabet, used is the five-bit International Alphabet No 2 (IA 2) shown in Appendix 4 which has been widely employed for telegraphy throughout the world since it was ratified by the International Telecommunications Union (ITU) in 1932.

The number of different characters which can be derived from a code having two different states is normally given by a 2^n where n is the number of different units in the code; a five-unit code would therefore give 2^5 or 32 characters. However, IA 2 uses two 'shift' characters to extend the capacity of the code. The depression of a 'figures' key results in a unique character being reproduced which when transmitted informs the receiver that the characters which follow are to be interpreted as 'figures' or other 'secondary' characters. Similarly, 'letters' indicates that the following characters are to be letters or other 'primary' characters. In this way IA 2

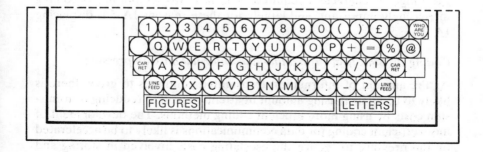

Figure 1.3   The Keyboard of a Traditional Teleprinter

offers 52 graphical (ie printable), two shift, three functional and one unallocated characters.

Efficiency of Codes

The efficiency of a two-condition code can be expressed by the formula:

$$E = \frac{\log_2 N}{M}$$

where   E = the efficiency of the code;
        N = the number of characters or symbols required;
        M = the number of bits in the code.

Let us assume that in a particular application 64 different characters are required and a seven-bit code is to be used. Applying the formula we have:

$$E = \frac{6}{7} = 86 \text{ per cent.}$$

If an eight-bit code were to be used then the efficiency would be 6/8 or 75 per cent.

Examined in this way, the telegraph codes such as IA 2 which employ 'letter shift' and 'figure shift' characters to extend the character set seem to be very efficient. IA 2 is only a five-unit code, yet 55 different characters are available to the user. Assuming that all these characters are required this gives a coding efficiency of approximately 116 per cent.

However, in practice a balance has to be struck between efficiency, ease of use within the system, acceptability to the human operator, and the range of characters required. The last two factors are becoming increasingly important, and largely for these reasons IA 5 is displacing IA 2.

Coding by Statistical Probability and Information Compression

As the amount of information transmitted continues to grow, there is likely to be an increasing amount of attention paid to reducing transmission costs by using more efficient coding methods. The development of more efficient coding for data communications is likely to be accelerated by the pressure to reduce the escalating costs involved in storing and controlling the vast and ever increasing quantities of information held on computer files.

Already, considerable advances have been made in this area, and one application which is worth mentioning is the use of information compression techniques to reduce the bandwidth (see below) requirement for transmitting video signals. The techniques used either rely upon a coding scheme which reflects the statistical probability of occurrence or merely avoids transmitting information which is in some sense redundant. Examples of the latter are blank areas in printed text; and those parts of a video image which remain static within a given sampling interval.

Physical Transmission

In order to be transmitted, the coded representation must be converted into a physical representation or signal. This can be illustrated by reference to telegraphy or telex.

The method of entering information on a teleprinter is normally a keyboard, and the basic unit of information entered is a 'character'. To arrange information entered by the keyboard into a form suitable for transmission, the depression of a key results in the conversion of a character into a code comprising a combination of five separate units. Each unit represents one or two possible conditions termed 'mark' or 'space'; these are equivalent to the binary symbols '1' and '0' respectively.

The code must be converted into electrical signals in order to be transmitted over a line. In practice, telegraph signals are transmitted 'serially' or one element at a time. Also, because a disconnection can provide a false signal if 'space' is represented by no current flow, the 'mark' and 'space' conditions are indicated by current flowing in different directions.

The teleprinter signals transmitted to line when the R or 4 key is depressed are shown in Figure 1.4. The signals transmitted are 'digital', ie they are transmitted at predetermined discrete levels; in this case 80 volt positive or negative, the polarity or direction of the current flow depending on whether a 'mark' or a 'space' condition is to be transmitted.

Transmission Signal Attributes

For telecommunications purposes the transmitted signal, and its behaviour during transmission, has three fundamental attributes. These are frequency, amplitude and phase. These are perhaps most readily appreciated in relation to sound or auditory signals.

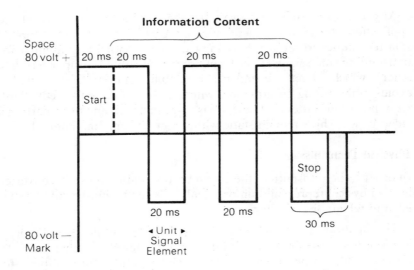

Figure 1.4   Signals Transmitted to Line from Teleprinter

Sound

Sound is the physical disturbance of air (or some other medium) which when received by the ear can be transmitted to the brain by the nervous system. Sound is produced by vibrations which cause compression and rarefaction of the air. The air vibrates with the sound source and the diaphragm of the ear will, if it is within range, vibrate in sympathy. The variations of air pressure which produce sound can be plotted graphically against time as shown in Figure 1.5.

In this example the wave form is sinusoidal or 'pure'. Only one complete variation between compression and rarefaction is shown; this is termed a 'cycle'. In mathematical notation this would be represented by a trigonometrical function – the example is in fact a sine wave. To complete a full cycle requires a complete rotation through 360°.

Frequency or Pitch

In music, notes are often referred to as being 'high' or 'low'. Perhaps this is because of the position of the notes on a musical scale or the tendency of some tenors to 'reach' for a note by standing on their toes! The fact is that

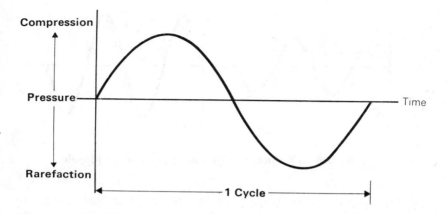

Figure 1.5   The Pure Sound Wave

so-called 'high' notes have a greater number of cycles in a given time than do 'low' notes. Middle 'C' at concert pitch for example has a frequency of 270 cycles per second (270 Hertz), while the 'C' above middle 'C' has a frequency of 540 Hertz (Hz). The relationship between pitch and wavelength can be best illustrated by an example. If in Figure 1.5 the cycle shown took 0.001 of a second to complete and were to be continually repeated, a note of 1000 cycles per second (1000 Hz) would be produced. If this took place at normal room temperature, the velocity of sound would be 340 metres/s; the 'length' of each cycle would therefore be 340/1000 or 0.34 metres; the 'wavelength' of a 1000 Hz note therefore would be 0.34 metres through air at room temperature.

Amplitude or Volume

Volume or loudness is determined by the 'amplitude' of the waveform or the height of the peaks of compression and rarefaction. In Figure 1.6, the two soundwaves have the same frequency or pitch but B has a greater volume than A.

Tone

A person who is tone deaf might have difficulty in hearing or reproducing correct pitch. This is a fairly common malady which in no way affects the

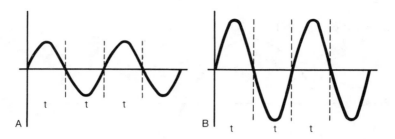

Figure 1.6   Frequency with Two Levels of Amplitude

afflicted person's ability to speak or sing. Indeed tone deaf people are usually blissfully unaware of any problem and seem gifted with painfully robust voices. In contrast, the vast majority of people are able to distinguish between the characteristic sounds of say a dinner gong and a violin, or a male and female voice. This ability to tell the difference between 'tones' is of more fundamental importance to human beings for it is only in doing so that we are able to communicate.

Differences in the quality of sound are produced by variations in the fundamental waveform (the pitch). These variations are produced by the introduction of additional frequencies known as 'harmonics' or 'overtones'. For example, if a middle 'C' is produced by a piano, the fundamental frequency is caused by the middle 'C' string vibrating 270 times a second. However, the outer edges of the string, the frame and wooden components also vibrate at different frequencies to produce harmonics providing the characteristic tone, not only of the type of instrument, but of the particular piano being played.

Phase

Figure 1.7 shows two sinusoidal waveforms in which B lags behind A. Each is said to be out of phase with the other. Whether one lags or the other leads depends upon the point chosen for the time origin. In the diagram, 0 is regarded as the origin and B therefore lags A by 90° since the amount of lag corresponds to a quarter of a revolution.

Phase is particularly important for modulating theory, and is the basis of several commonly used modulation techniques discussed in a later chapter.

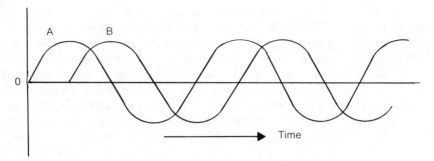

Figure 1.7

Digital and Analogue Transmission

Although less fundamental from the foregoing in terms of providing a complete description of the signal, whether it is digital or analogue constitutes a very important qualitative difference.

Digital computers and associated equipment generate digital signals, and the distinction assumes significance when we have to consider the feasibility and efficiency with which digital signals can be transmitted through a network which is designed primarily to transmit analogue signals exemplified by the traditional telephone network.

The telegraphy example above illustrates the form of digital signals and the figures accompanying the discussion of frequency and amplitude illustrate the essential character of analogue signals. The distinguishing feature is that digital signals are discontinuous, and the analogue signals are continuous.

Noise and Attenuation

Noise

In our earlier discussion we noted that the quality of communication can be impaired if some concurrent extraneous communication interferes with it. This introduces the problem of noise.

Gardeners are well aware of the fact that man's view of orderliness does not coincide with that of nature. Reversion to nature is not a problem exclusive to gardeners, however, and all man's attempts to impose his own version of order are opposed by nature's. This strong natural force is evident in the oxidisation of metals and is most familiar in the form of rust. This force is at work on telecommunications channels in opposition to organised signals (information), producing weakening and distortion of the signals. It also manifests itself in the background noise which can sometimes be heard as a hiss on telephone or radio channels. This type of 'white noise' (or gaussian noise) is inevitable on telecommunications channels, being produced by a natural movement of electrons which varies with temperature. The term 'white noise' is used because just as white light contains all the colours in the spectrum, white noise is purely random and can be of any frequency. Impulsive noise is also a serious problem in the transfer of information on telecommunications links. This can often be heard as clicks in a telephone conversation and is less of a natural phenomenon, being produced as a result of interference from other telephone circuits.

The full impact of noise depends upon whether speech or data is being transmitted. With speech communications, we are primarily concerned with intelligibility. Intelligibility can be defined as 'a percentage of simple ideas correctly received over the system used for transmitting or reproducing speech'. There are problems in measuring intelligibility; this is due to the fact that the human brain has an error correction capability and, although we may miss sections from words or sentences in a telephone conversation, our brains have the ability to fill in some of the gaps and interpret the meaning. Let us assume that the following sentence is spoken during a telephone conversation – 'Now is Tom foot all goot men toot compt taid party'. This sentence would probably be corrected by the listener without too much difficulty and perhaps unconsciously into the familiar sentence – 'Now is the time for all good men to come to the aid of the party'. Many interesting tests have been made using 'logatoms' which are specially constructed sentences using words or syllables which contain no information whatsoever but are extremely useful in measuring intelligibility.

The intelligibility of the human voice is contained within the harmonics produced; most of the intelligence in human speech occurs from between 125 and 2000 Hz – a 'bandwidth' of about 2000 Hz. The CCITT recommend a circuit responding to frequencies between 300 Hz and 3400 Hz as being adequate for the purposes of telephony, giving a high degree of speech intelligibility.

Considering information (or data) to be processed by a computer or where content is not immediately meaningful to a human being, the situation is rather different. As far as the physical representation of the signal is concerned, a major effect of noise is to distort the shape of the signal; and the information received following transmission could either be complete gibberish or contain errors which are not necessarily readily apparent.

Whether noise does interfere significantly with information is obviously connected with the power of the signal relative to the power of the noise and to the sensitivity of the receiving apparatus. This leads us into the topic of attenuation.

Attenuation

It is a fundamental physical fact that a signal loses power during transmission, and this loss of signal strength is referred to as attenuation. The extent of the loss depends upon the transmission medium, and for a specific medium is generally a function of distance.

For example, an audible sound very quickly becomes inaudible in still air, and the same applies to electrical signals, although to a much lesser extent. Other factors, such as frequency, also affect attenuation, and these are discussed in later chapters.

In practice, it is therefore necessary when attenuation reaches a certain level to restore the power of the signal by amplification. However, in the case of analogue channels this has an adverse side effect, in that besides amplifying the signal, the power of the noise is also increased at the same time. This problem does not arise with digital transmission. Although the digital waveform or pulse eventually loses power, and its shape may be disturbed due to noise, a different technique is available for restoring the quality of the signal. Since the pulse corresponding to the binary value can be standardised in advance, all that is necessary is to introduce at intervals a much simpler device which, instead of amplifying the signal, compares it with the reference signal and reshapes the transmitted pulse accordingly.

Data Transmission Rates

There are a number of different ways in which the rate of transmission can legitimately be expressed: 'modulation rate', 'data signalling rate' and 'data (or information) transfer rate'. A great deal of confusion can be caused by the misuse of these terms and they are explained separately below.

Modulation Rate

This is a term used by the communications engineer to describe the performance of a circuit in terms of the rate at which changes in the condition of the circuit can be made in a given time. More precisely it is the reciprocal of the duration of the unit signal element. The unit used in expressing modulation rate is the 'baud' which is equal to one unit signal element per second. For example, in Figure 1.8, each unit signal element is 20 ms in duration. The modulation rate is therefore:

$$\frac{1}{0.020} = 50 \text{ baud}$$

It should be noted that the expression of modulation rate in bauds does not necessarily indicate the rate at which data is transmitted.

Data Signalling Rate

The data signalling rate is used to express the rate at which information can be transmitted.

It is expressed in bits per second (bit/s) and for serial transmission it is defined as:

$$\left(\frac{1}{T}\right) \log_2 n$$

where T = the duration of the unit signal element in seconds and n = the number of signalling conditions.

Again referring to Figure 1.8 the data signalling rate would be:

$$\left(\frac{1}{0.020}\right) \times 1 = 50 \text{ bit/s}$$

It would, however, be wrong to conclude from this that a baud is the same as 1 bit/s, for if more than two signalling states (multi-state signalling) were used we would have completely different answers.

Multi-state signalling can be explained by using a simple analogy.

Suppose the following data has to be passed between two persons in the same room without speaking or using written communication: 100001011001. There are, of course, many ways in which this might be achieved using two 'signal states', eg a white flag could be waved to represent binary '1' and a red flag for binary '0'.

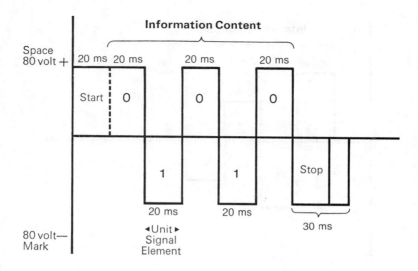

Figure 1.8   Data Signalling Using Two Voltage Levels

However, if four different coloured flags were to be used, say white, red, green and yellow, further possibilities would be available. There are only four different ways of combining two binary digits, ie 00, 01, 10 and 11, therefore the white flag could be used to represent 00, the red 01, the green 10 and the yellow 11. Thus in the example, the data 100001011001 could be sent using flags in the following order: green, white, red, red, green, red. It will be seen that with this 'four-state signalling', the number of signals necessary to transmit the information is only half that necessary with two-state signalling. Eight different coloured flags could be used to convey three bits of information at a time (there are eight different ways of combining three binary digits), sixteen flags for four bits and so on. Theoretically an increase in the number of flags used should result in more information being transferred with the same number of signals. There is, however, an obvious problem with coding and decoding which progressively increases; there are also technical problems which increase with the number of different states employed when multi-state electrical signalling is employed for data transmission.

Figure 1.9 shows a simple four-state signalling system, each 20 ms unit signal element representing two binary digits. The data signalling rate would therefore be:

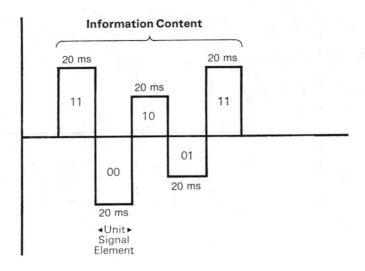

Figure 1.9   Data Signalling Using Four Voltage Values

$$\left(\frac{1}{0.020}\right) \log_2 4 = 50 \times 2 \text{ or } 100 \text{ bit/s}$$

Note that the modulation rate is still 1/0.020 or 50 bauds.

Although serial transmission is most common in telegraphy and data transmission, parallel transmission is sometimes used, complete characters rather than separate bits being transmitted at the same time. If the simple hypothetical example in Figure 1.10 is considered, it will be seen that the data signalling rate in bit/s transmitted will be a summation of the bits transmitted on each transmission path or 'channel'.

$$
\left.
\begin{array}{cc}
1 & 0 \\
0 & 1 \\
1 & 0 \\
0 & 1 \\
1 & 0
\end{array}
\right\} \rightarrow
$$

Figure 1.10   Serial Transmission

The data signalling rate in a parallel system can therefore be expressed by:

$$\sum_{i=1}^{i=M} \frac{1}{T_i} \log_2 N_i$$

where M is the number of parallel channels

T_i is the duration of the unit signal element in the ith channel in seconds

and N_i is the number of signalling conditions of the modulation in the ith channel.

If in Figure 1.10, there were only two signalling conditions for each of the five channels and if the duration of each signal element were again 20 ms, we would have:

$$\frac{1}{0.020} + \frac{1}{0.020} + \frac{1}{0.020} + \frac{1}{0.020} + \frac{1}{0.020} = 250 \text{ bit/s}$$

Data (Information) Transfer Rate

Unlike data signalling rate which is used to describe the rate at which data is transmitted, 'data transfer rate' describes the rate at which data actually arrives after transmission. It is defined by CCITT as 'the average number of bits, characters or blocks per unit time passing between corresponding

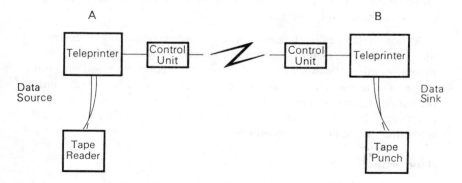

Figure 1.11 Automatic Tape Transmission

equipments in a data transmission system. It is expressed in terms of bits, characters or blocks per second, minute or hour'.

Frequently the corresponding equipments referred to in this definition are a 'data source' and a 'data sink'. Consider the example of an automatic paper tape transmission between two teleprinters, A and B (Figure 1.11). For the purposes of this example, we will regard the tape reader at A as the data source and the tape punch at B as the data sink. We know from an earlier example that the data signalling rate is 50 bit/s but bits are not received at the same rate at the data sink. Assuming continuous error-free transmission, 400 five unit characters would be received at the tape punch in one minute, a total of 2000 bits and an average of $33\frac{1}{3}$ bit/s. The difference is accounted for by the $2\frac{1}{2}$ unit signal elements used for start/stop during transmission but which are of no use later; one third of the signals transmitted are therefore redundant.

In this example we could define data transfer rate as:

$$DTR = \frac{N}{T}$$

where DTR = the data transfer rate in bit/s
       N   = the number of information bits accepted by the data sink
and   T   = the time required (in seconds) to transmit N bits.

However, as will be seen in Chapter 11, the calculation of information transfer rate is not usually as simple as this and will depend upon the error rate on a particular transmission, the type of error control and link protocol employed and not only the number of bits but the number of complete characters which are redundant.

Although data transfer rate is a much more accurate way of describing the movement of usable information in a data communications system than any other, it cannot be stated without calculation based on knowledge of a particular system. A line or a piece of equipment cannot therefore be said to have a data transfer rate of a certain number of bits per second. For this reason, bit/s in this book will be used to indicate data signalling rate unless stated otherwise.

Bandwidth

The bandwidth of a channel is the major determinant of the channel's information-carrying capacity. The bandwidth has a precise definition: it is the range of frequencies that the channel is capable of transmitting. There is therefore an intimate relationship between bandwidth and frequency, and as we have already seen, a signal in general can be analysed into a number of component frequencies. The analysis is performed using the technique of Fourier analysis. (Fourier analysis and its associated principles play a fundamental role in communications theory.)

The use of range in the above definition is important because not only are a number of frequencies present – so that the signal has a frequency spectrum – but the lowest frequency to be catered for is likely to be something different from zero, and the higher frequency can be either finite or theoretically infinite, as we shall see. Thus, the PSTN is designed to transmit frequencies in the bandwidth 300-3400 Hertz. Therefore, a number of the higher frequencies or harmonics present in the human voice are not transmitted, and this is the reason why people's telephone conversation often sounds 'flat' and relatively low-pitched.

With speech conversation the main problem is conveying intelligibility, and the bandwidth provided is generally adequate for the purpose. Also the rate at which analogue speech information is transmitted is not usually constrained by the telephone channel but by the natural rate of the conversation.

However, bandwidth is a major constraint on the rate at which digital information can be transmitted. This can be seen more clearly if we examine the capacity of the human ear, with a maximum bandwidth of 20,000 Hz, to accept digital information. We often receive what might loosely be described as digital signals and an example of this can be heard whenever we sit in a railway compartment. The typical two-state di-di-di-dum sound rises with the speed of the train. The pitch of this sound continues to rise with speed and if the train were to travel fast enough, the frequency of the signal would rise to a point where we could no longer hear it. The relationship between the rate at which information can be transmitted and bandwidth can perhaps be seen more clearly if we examine a telegraph type signal, ignoring for convenience the usual start/stop elements. We can see from Figure 1.12 that this 50 baud signal would carry 50 bits per second of information. However, it is also apparent that the fundamental frequency produced by sending this information would vary between 0 Hz (when all ones or zeros were transmitted) to a maximum of 25 Hz if alternate zeros and ones were transmitted. One bit of information is therefore represented in each half cycle of the 25 Hz

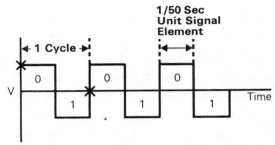

50 Baud = 50 Unit Signal Elements/Second

Minimum Frequency   = 0 Hz (All 1s Or All 0s)

Maximum Frequency   = 25 Hz (Alternate 1s and 0s)

Data Signalling Rate   = 50 Bits Per Second

Figure 1.12   Relationship between Bandwidth and Information Rate

square waveform. Nyquist[1] showed that, in a channel without noise, a signal with no frequencies greater than W could carry 2W voltage values. This means that in the idealised situation of a noiseless channel and using only two voltage values serially (to represent '0' and '1') the maximum theoretical capacity of the channel C would be 2W, where W is the bandwidth of the channel.

If more than 2 voltage levels were used, the maximum frequency would be unchanged. Figure 1.13 shows a system employing four states.

In this example, we again have fundamental frequencies which may vary between 0 Hz and 25 Hz (varying over a 25 Hz bandwidth), but two bits of information can be derived from each half cycle.

We can, therefore, extend the theoretical channel capacity in the absence of white noise to include provision for multi-state signalling:

$$C = 2W \log_2 L$$

where   C = the channel capacity in bit/s

W = the bandwidth

and   L = the number of states

Eg: bandwidth (W) = 2000 Hz

number of states (L) = 8, then

$$C = (2 \times 2000) \times (\log_2 8)$$
$$= 4000 \times 3 = 12,000 \text{ bit/s}$$

[1] Nyquist, H 'Certain Factors Affecting Telegraph Speed' (1924) and 'Certain Topics in Telegraph Transmission Theory' (1928). Trans. AIEE

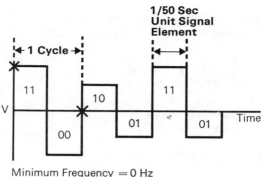

Minimum Frequency = 0 Hz
Maximum Frequency = 25 Hz
Data Signalling Rate = 100 Bits Per Second

Figure 1.13   Signalling Using 4 Levels

It would seem from this that channel capacity could be increased *ad infinitum* by increasing the number of signalling levels. Unfortunately, this is not true in practice; although these formulae are useful in showing the relationship between bandwidth, signalling levels and channel capacity, there are very real snags:

— There are no telecommunications channels which are completely free of white noise or other disturbances. However, fully-digital transmission of speech or data, combined with solid state electronics, is having a significant impact on noise reduction.

— The number of states that can be used is limited by the power available to transmit the signals, the problems of encoding and decoding and the sensitivity of the receiver to interpret the different signalling levels.

There are three main factors which determine the amount of information which can be transmitted on a channel:

  (i) the bandwidth available;
  (ii) the power level of the signal;
  (iii) the power level of the noise present on the channel.

The work of Claude E Shannon[1] is of fundamental importance in proving mathematically that a communications channel has a finite capac-

---

[1] 'Mathematical Theory of Communication', Bell Systems Technical Journal (July and October 1948).

ity. The Shannon/Hartley law is now recognised as representing the theoretical maximum capacity of a channel in the presence of white noise and is given by:

$$C = W \log_2 \left(1 + \frac{S}{N} \right)$$

where C = channel capacity
W = bandwidth

$\frac{S}{N}$ = signal to noise ratio

NOTE: It is important to remember that the noise referred to here is 'white noise'. Other forms of disturbance, which are present in practice, include 'impulse noise', or noise peaks which are critical in determining the error performance of a channel.

Applying this formula to a fairly good quality speech channel with a bandwidth of 3000 Hz and a signal to noise ratio of −30 dB we have:

$$C = 3000 \log_2 \left(1 + \frac{1000}{1} \right)$$

C = 30,000 bit/s

This is very much more than could be achieved in practice with a circuit of this kind. The actual rates achieved on analogue channels are not solely dependent on the channel but on the modems used. Although much ingenuity has gone into the design of modems, and the introduction of microprocessor technology has enabled remarkable levels of sophistication and performance to be achieved, it is most unlikely that they could be designed to approach closely the theoretical maximum capacity of a channel.

Bandwidth Requirements for Digital Transmission

We have discussed bandwidth in fairly general terms, and we should now look more specifically at the bandwidth requirements for transmitting a typical digital signal along an analogue channel. In doing this we should present the Nyquist theorem more formally.

The digital data signal generated by a typical data terminal is a square wave, like the one depicted in Figure 1.14. This actually shows a *polar*

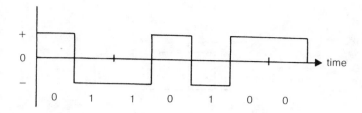

Figure 1.14   Polar Binary Signal

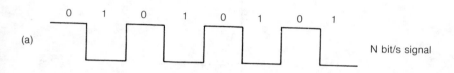

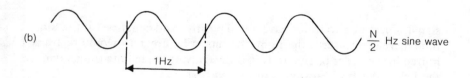

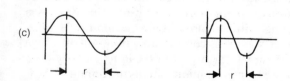

Figure 1.15   (a) Square Wave, Alternate 0s and 1s
                (b) Sine Wave Equivalent
                (c) Risetime of Waves of Different Frequency

(a)

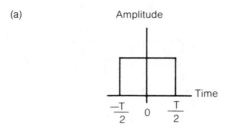

(b)

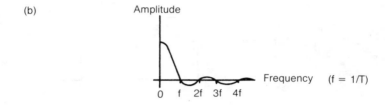

Figure 1.16   Single Square Pulse (a), and its Fourier Transform (b)

signal, since the two states have equal positive and negative values. Since time increases towards the right, the bits in Figure 1.14 would be transmitted in the order 0, 1, 1, 0, 1, 0, 0. By convention in data transmission, the low-order bit is always transmitted first.

As we noted earlier, the greatest rate of change of information in a binary signal occurs when alternate 0s and 1s are transmitted. If the bit rate is N bit/s, it can be seen from Figure 1.15 that the binary signal 0 1 0 1 0 1 . . . carries information at the same rate as a sine wave of frequency N/2 Hertz. However, if we were to transmit this data as a square wave through a channel with an upper frequency limit of N/2 Hz, we would find that the square wave was considerably rounded off. If we look at the wave forms in Figure 1.15(c) we can begin to see why. The time taken for the signal to rise from its minimum to its maximum value is shown as 'r'. The higher the frequency of the wave, the shorter 'r' is. Now a square wave changes state almost instantaneously (ie r is small), and this implies the presence of very high frequencies. In fact a full analysis of a continuous square wave reveals that it is composed of a whole series of

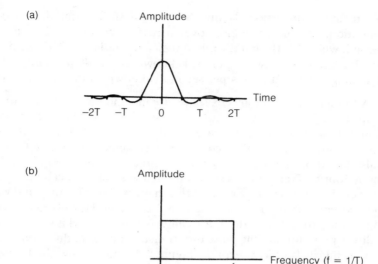

Figure 1.17   (Sin x)/x Pulse (a), and its Fourier Transform (b)

harmonically related sine and cosine waves of differing amplitudes. Such a series is known as a Fourier series. Thus, to transmit a true square wave, ie one with vertical edges, a channel of infinite bandwidth would be required.

Fourier also dealt with the analysis of a *single* square pulse. In this case the component frequencies are not a series of discrete frequencies, but a continuous spectrum. The amplitude of each component frequency is given by the Fourier Transform of the pulse. The Fourier Transform of a single square pulse is a curve of the form (sin x)/x, as shown in Figure 1.16. This curve gives the amplitude of all the component frequencies of the pulse. Note that for a pulse of duration T, certain frequencies, at f, 2f, 3f, etc, have zero magnitude (f = 1/T).

Suppose, however, we had started not with a square pulse, but with one of (sin x)/x shape (Figure 1.17(a)). What would be the component frequencies of that pulse? It turns out that the Fourier Transform of a (sin x)/x pulse has a spectrum with a sharp cut-off at one particular frequency, as shown in Figure 1.17(b). Since our transmission channels always have a finite bandwidth, this would seem to be the ideal pulse to use to avoid distortion. Nyquist's theorem shows that the maximum repetition rate of such pulses over a perfect channel is 2f pulses per second, where f is the bandwidth of the circuit in Hertz. The period 1/2f, which is the time between pulses, is known as the Nyquist interval. The signalling rate of 2f pulses per second is known as the Nyquist rate.

Although pulses of (sin x)/x shape are ideal in theory, there are other shapes which are more tolerant of the deficiencies of practical transmission systems. One of these is based on the spectrum of what is known as a raised cosine pulse. A raised cosine pulse is sketched in Figure 1.18(a). A pulse based on the spectrum of the raised cosine pulse (Figure 1.18(c)) has a Fourier Transform as shown in Figure 1.18(d). It can be seen that the penalty paid in using a pulse of this shape is that twice the bandwidth is needed compared to the (sin x)/x pulse shape. However, one of the important properties of this pulse shape is that the level is only above the halfway point for half the pulse duration, and pulses of duration T can be sent at intervals of T/2 seconds. Figure 1.19 shows how the bit pattern 0 1 1 0 1 0 0 would look in raised cosine spectrum form, together with the sampling instants.

These more sophisticated pulse shapes are not seen at the output of a data terminal, but may be generated by the modem or other transmission equipment.

Digital Transmission of Speech

The Nyquist theorem is sometimes referred to in the technical literature as the sampling theorem. This is because the Nyquist rate of 2f pulses/ second gives a lower bound to the frequency at which a continuous waveform must be sampled to enable the original waveform to be reconstructed with an acceptable accuracy, from the discrete sample values.

This has an important application to the digitisation of speech using Pulse Code Modulation (PCM). Thus, if we take the bandwidth for speech to be 4000 Hertz, the signal must be sampled at a rate of 8000 times/ second before transmission in digital mode. At the receiving end, the discrete values are then converted to speech signals of acceptable quality. This forms the basis for the CCITT recommendation for PCM.

Miscellaneous Definitions

There are a number of concepts and definitions which are briefly explained in the glossary, but the following are noted here.

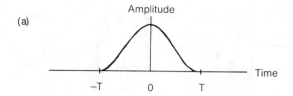

(a)

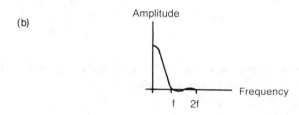

(b)

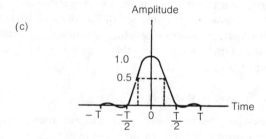

(c)

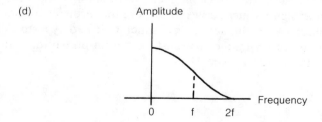

(d)

Figure 1.18 (a) Sketch of Raised Cosine Pulse; (b) its Fourier Transform; (c) Pulse Based on FT of Raised Cosine Pulse (b); and (d) its Fourier Transform

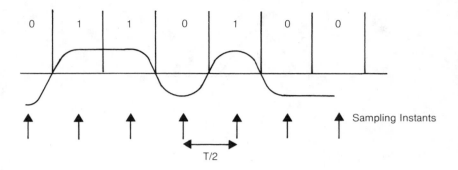

Figure 1.19   Binary Waveform using a Pulse Shape based on the FT of a Raised Cosine Pulse

Simplex, Full-Duplex and Half-Duplex Transmission

In simplex transmission, communication is in one direction only. Full-duplex working involves transmission and reception in both directions simultaneously. In half-duplex, transmission and reception are possible in both directions, but not at the same time; the circuit can only accept traffic in one direction at a time.

Synchronous and Asynchronous Working

In synchronous transmission, the receiver is kept continuously in step (in synchronism) with the transmitter throughout transmission by the use of electronic clocking devices independent of the data characters. In asynchronous or start/stop transmission, each information character is preceded by a start signal which serves to prepare the receiving mechanism for the reception of the character. This is then followed by a stop signal which brings the receiving mechanism to a stop in preparation for the reception of the next character.

2 Telephony and Transmission Principles

INTRODUCTION

Twenty or so years ago, when people first considered the possibility of communicating with computers using remote transmission, it was natural for both economic and technical reasons that they should investigate the potential of the telephone network.

The telephone network was designed specifically for transmitting speech and this, together with the use of analogue transmission, imposes limitations on the transmission of data. It is finely tuned for the purpose for which it was designed and any attempt to enhance the performance beyond certain limits would have undesirable consequences for speech transmission and possibly also for data. There is greater scope for performance improvement with leased circuits, partly because they are isolated from the public networks. However, in order to overcome the inherent limitations of the technology, the designer has to resort to increasingly sophisticated and costly engineering, particularly as the transmission speed is increased. Nonetheless, the telephone networks of the world have been adopted successfully to carry digital data; although not the ideal medium for the purpose, their widespread availability has enabled a variety of on-line computer applications to be developed.

It is because speech and data are really incompatible in analogue circuits, and because of the overwhelming advantages of digital transmission, that many PTTs including BT are in the process of converting their networks from analogue to digital transmission. They will then be capable of handling speech and data with equal facility.

In this chapter we review the development, construction and operation of the transmission systems from the traditional analogue through to the digital approach but concentrating in the main on voice telephony.

In the next chapter we examine the use of the telephone network for transmitting data; and subsequent chapters discuss such topics as switching and signalling principles and the UK network modernisation plans.

A TELEPHONE SYSTEM

A telephone system consists of the following main elements:

— terminals (typically telephones);

— transmission links;

— exchanges;

— signalling.

The system enables a telephone connected to one exchange to be connected to any other telephone either in its own country or on a system of another country.

The public system in the United Kingdom, with the exception of Hull, has been operated exclusively by British Telecom (BT), formerly the Post Office, since January 1st, 1912.

The first public telephone service in the UK was provided in 1879 by the Telephone Company Ltd, who installed exclusive point-to-point private circuits using telephones fitted with Graham Bell transmitters and receivers. In August 1879 the company opened the first telephone exchange in Coleman Street in the City of London giving service to seven or eight telephone renters. By the end of 1879 two more exchanges were opened and the number of 'subscribers' to the service had grown to 200.

The Telegraph Act of the 1860s had given the Post Master General the monopoly of the public telegraph system, and in 1880 the Crown challenged the right of a private company to operate a telephone service on the basis that a telephone message was encompassed by the Telegraph Act. The results were that the telephone companies:

— had to be licensed;

— were required to pay an annual royalty;

— were confined to areas of two to five miles in radius;

— could not construct lines between towns.

The licence restrictions meant that it was not uncommon for a person to be a subscriber on each exchange in a town; in 1884 the restrictions were relaxed to allow companies to operate anywhere in the UK and to construct lines between towns. Problems were however still encountered by private companies in obtaining 'wayleaves', ie rights of way, for underground circuits, resulting in the development of an almost wholly overhead external wiring system.

On 1st May 1889 the majority of private companies amalgamated to form the National Telephone Company (NTC). However, wayleave difficulties continued to be experienced and these, together with the extensive trunk network operated for its telegraph system, resulted in the Post Office taking over the trunk system in 1892.

In 1898 a House of Commons Select Committee recommended that the Post Office, and several local authorities, be allowed to provide telephone facilities in competition with the NTC. The licences issued to private companies expired on 31st December 1911 and, with the exception of the municipal authorities at Hull and Portsmouth, the whole of the UK telephone system came under the control of the Post Office. The Portsmouth system was taken over in 1914 but Hull is still operated independently.

In 1969 the Post Office became a Statutory Corporation with monopoly powers – for the provision of telecommunications and mail services in the United Kingdom – which it had previously exercised as a Department of State.

The British Telecommunications Act of 1981 set up a new public corporation, British Telecom (BT), to run the telecommunications and data processing business of the Post Office. The Act also permits the Secretary of State to license other organisations to provide telecommunications services and such a licence was granted to Cable and Wireless, BP and Barclays Bank to provide transmission services via the system known as Project Mercury.

The global telephone network as we know it today has evolved over a period of about 100 years, into what is now one of the largest and most complex man-made systems in the world. The magnitude of the achievement is perhaps not fully appreciated by the majority of people, although the statistics themselves are impressive. For example, at the end of 1981 there were approximately 29 million telephone instruments in place in the UK, and worldwide the number was about 425 million. Within the UK about 98% of subscribers could direct dial (via STD) other subscribers in 100 countries throughout the world.

Telephone Local Line Distribution

In the UK, there are about 18 million telephone customers connected to over 6000 telephone exchanges or switching points. In the early days of the UK telephone system, the pairs of wires needed for each customer were provided by overhead wires carried on telegraph poles and connected to derricks on the roof of the exchange building. Later, cables were carried by the same poles – each cable serving a number of customers connected at a 'distribution point'.

Today the most common method of connecting a customer to a telephone exchange is shown in Figure 2.1.

The telephone exchange location is carefully selected to minimise the cost of cabling and to ensure that there are no disproportionately long lines. The exchange area is divided up into a number of 'cabinet' areas, each cabinet area simplified by using a cabinet and pillar system rather than a number of underground cable joints. The system is flexible in that spare line capacity can be more simply diverted to those locations in a telephone area where it is most needed. If a fault does occur in an underground cable, say between a cabinet and a pillar, a spare pair of wires can be allocated quickly by simple wire strapping. The faulty pair of wires in the cable can then be repaired later when it is convenient and economic.

It is now common to connect a customer's premises by an underground feed rather than overhead wires. Although this is more costly to provide, the fault liability of the 'local end' is reduced considerably. Many large business premises have internal distribution points within their own premises.

TRANSMISSION

Frequency Response

A transmission line is a conductor or group of conductors used to transfer energy from one point to another, the energy being transmitted in the form of electromagnetic waves travelling at speeds approaching the speed of light in free space. The electrical signals originating from a telephone, or any other device, are attenuated as they are transmitted along a circuit. This loss, or attenuation, is caused by dissipation of the electromagnetic energy of the electromagnetic waves in the:

— series resistance of the wires (R);

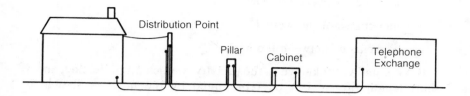

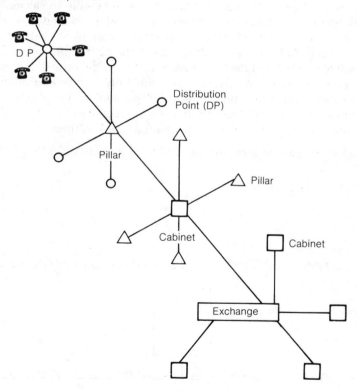

Figure 2.1   Telephone Connection to Exchange

— leakance between the wires (G);

— inductance of the wires (L);

— capacitance between the wires (C).

R, G, L and C are known as the primary coefficients of the line, and a short length of line can be represented by the network shown in Figure 2.2.

Further attenuation or loss of signal is introduced by the telephone instruments themselves, switchboard connections, automatic equipment, etc. The communication engineer needs to know the loss of power introduced by each element of a complete circuit to be able to calculate the overall loss of a connection, the nominal loss of an exchange or circuit being measured at 800 Hz (this figure being taken in the early days of telecommunications as the mean speech frequency). Although it would be possible to represent the loss of each section by the ratio of power sent to the power received, the overall loss could only then be determined by complicated and time-consuming multiplications. In practice, the logarithms of ratios are used so that the aggregate effect of a series of items may be arrived at by simply adding them together.

The loss or gain in a circuit, or section of a circuit, can be given by:

$$N = \log_{10} \frac{P1}{P2} \text{ Bels,}$$

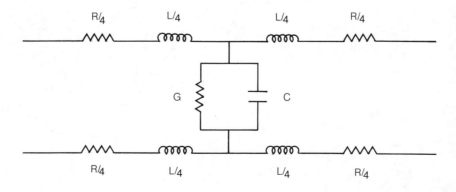

Figure 2.2

where: N = the number of Bels,
       P1 = the power sent,
and   P2 = the power received.

In practice, the Bel is an inconveniently large unit and the decibel (dB) or one tenth of a Bel is used so that loss or gain (in decibels) equals:

$$10 \log_{10} \frac{P1}{P2}$$

If the received power (P2) is greater than the power sent (P1), as for example when an amplifier is used, then the logarithm of P1 over P2 will be negative; if P1 is greater than P2 the logarithm will be positive. If the received power measured on a circuit was only a thousandth of the power sent then:

$$10 \log_{10} \frac{P1}{P2} = 10 \log_{10} \frac{1000}{1} = +30 \, dB$$

There are always losses in telephony and a 'zero loss' circuit is one in which the gains from amplifiers in the circuit are adjusted exactly to counter balance losses due to the line and apparatus.

The decibel is not an absolute unit, but is the logarithmic expression of a ratio. It can be used, as we have seen, to describe overall loss in terms of the ratio between the power sent and the power received in a circuit; similarly, it can be used to express the ratio between the signal and the noise on a line – there must, however, always be some reference level.

Table 2.1 shows power ratios corresponding to various decibel losses.

dB	Power Ratios (power sent to power received)	dB	Power Ratios (power sent to power received)
+3	2:1	+23	200:1
+6	4:1	+26	400:1
+9	8:1	+29	800:1
+10	10:1	+30	1000:1
+13	20:1	+33	2000:1
+16	40:1	+36	4000:1
+19	80:1	+39	8000:1
+20	100:1	+40	10000:1

Table 2.1

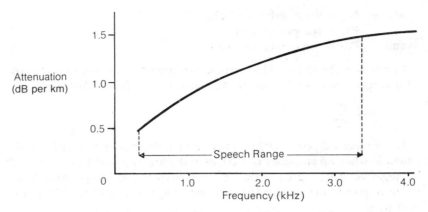

Figure 2.3   Attenuation/Frequency Curve – 0.9 mm Cable

The ability of a particular telephone circuit to 'carry' or respond to different frequencies is referred to as its 'frequency response'.

Higher frequencies will generally be attenuated to a greater extent than lower frequencies. Figure 2.3 shows the attenuation introduced at various frequencies by a type of 0.9 mm paper-covered cable, commonly used in the UK (0.9 mm refers to the diameter of each copper conductor).

In considering the transmission of a complex speech type waveform, it will be apparent that over long distances the higher frequencies will be very much more attenuated than the lower frequencies, and if this effect is severe, intelligibility will suffer. Some examples of the limiting distances over which speech can be transmitted using ordinary two-wire circuits in cables are given in Table 2.2.

Loading

The power of a signal at any point in a circuit expressed in milliwatts (mW) can be calculated by multiplying the voltage and the current.[1]

Power (mW) = Voltage × Current × 1000

---

[1] In an AC waveform, the values of current and voltage are constantly varying. Although peak values are shown for simplicity in figures, the effective or 'RMS' value is normally used. This is defined as the square root of the mean (average) value of the square of the instantaneous values taken over one complete cycle.

With a 'pure' or sinusoidal waveform, the RMS value is 0.707 times the peak value. For example, an AC wave with a peak value of 325V has an RMS value of 230V.

Diameter of Copper Conductor	Limiting Distance for Satisfactory Speech
0.63 mm	9.5 km
0.9 mm	14.5 km
1.27 mm	20.0 km

Table 2.2

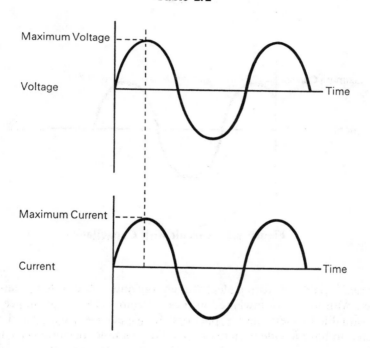

Figure 2.4 'Resonant' Circuit

This is best illustrated using a simple AC waveform as shown in Figure 2.4. When the voltage is at its peak the current is also at its highest giving maximum power. In these circumstances the circuit is said to be 'resonant'.

In telephone cables and on overhead routes, telephone wires run over long distances in close proximity. The effect of this is that a circuit

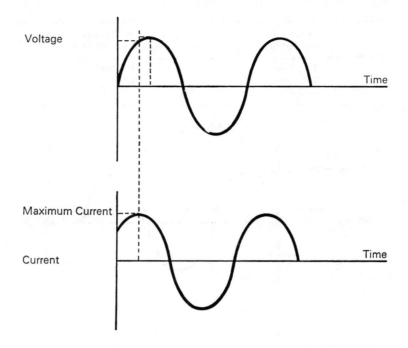

Figure 2.5   Circuit with Capacitance

becomes capable of storing electrical energy and is said to have 'capacitance'. Although it is unwanted in these circumstances, capacitance can be a valuable property and 'capacitors' are especially designed and constructed to have a wide variety of uses. For example, because capacitors can be charged, store electrical energy for long periods and discharge very quickly when required, they are used in flash photography, the 'flash' being provided by the rapid discharge of a capacitor. These properties of a capacitor are highly undesirable when they occur uninvited on a telephone circuit. The line itself becomes a capacitor which can store and discharge electrical energy. This means that the current flowing at any time in a circuit with capacitance is to some extent independent of the electro-motive force (the voltage) applied. In these circumstances, the current and the voltage become out of phase and the current is said to 'lead on the voltage' as shown is Figure 2.5. It follows that at any instant

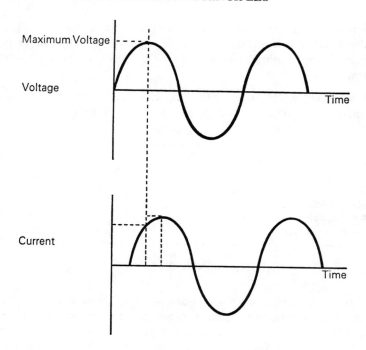

Figure 2.6   Circuit with Inductance

the product of the voltage and the current is less than maximum which results in a loss of power.

An opposite effect to capacitance is present in circuits which have coils of wire as relays or electric motors. Whenever the current value changes in a coil, self-induction occurs causing an electro-motive force or 'back EMF' to oppose the flow of current. When alternating current or fluctuating direct current flows in a circuit with inductance, the current is always in a state of change and the build-up of current is slowed so that it 'lags on the voltage' as shown in Figure 2.6.

In telephony, inductance is often added to counteract the effect of capacitance and so reduce the power loss in a circuit; this activity is known as 'loading'. In practice, loading is normally effected by induction coils housed in iron cases, either buried direct in the ground or located in manholes at appropriate distances along the cable route. 'Loading pots' can also be used with aerial cables and are then fitted on telephone poles. Typically 88 mH loading coils are inserted at 1.8 km intervals on junction or trunk routes.

With maximum loading, the limiting distance for satisfactory speech transmission can be increased to the figures given in Table 2.3.

	Limiting Distance for Satisfactory Speech	
	Unloaded	Loaded
0.63 mm conductors	9.5 km	35 km
0.9 mm conductors	14.5 km	67 km
1.27 mm conductors	20.0 km	112 km

Table 2.3

Although loading serves to counteract the power losses due to unwanted capacitance in a circuit, it has also an adverse effect on the 'bandwidth', or range of frequencies which the circuit can effectively carry. The frequency response of a circuit loaded in this way is illustrated in Figure 2.7 and it will be seen that there is a sharp 'cut-off' beyond which frequencies cannot be carried.

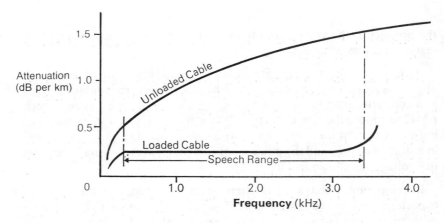

Figure 2.7   Loaded Circuit (Frequency Response)

CABLE DESIGN

The spill-over of information from one circuit to another, which on telephone circuits can lead to overhearing, can be caused by capacitive coupling between wires in a cable. This is referred to as crosstalk and is minimised by cable design.

If a single wire was used to provide a connection between a telephone and an exchange it would pick up:

— capacitive hum from overhead power lines;

— capacitive crosstalk from adjacent wires in the same cable.

This would be caused by capacitive interference between the wires. To overcome this, each connection to the exchange is made with a pair of wires in close proximity to one another so that any interference will be picked up by both wires and hence there will be no interference *between* them. The pair is then said to be balanced. To maintain symmetry as far as possible and further reduce crosstalk the pairs are twisted together and adjacent pairs are given different twist lengths within the cable. The twisting of pairs within cables also reduces inductive hum and inductive crosstalk.

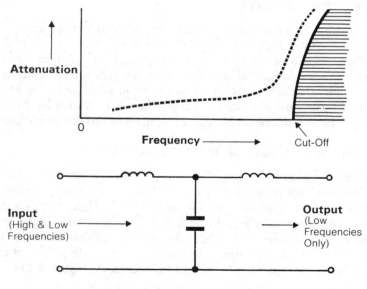

Figure 2.8   Low-Pass Filter

FILTERS

Artificial circuits can be designed (comprising in their simplest forms inductance and capacitance) which have a 'cut-off' at any frequency desired. Exact values can be calculated mathematically and modern design techniques are producing filters which have a sharper 'cut-off' than their predecessors. Figure 2.8 shows a 'low-pass' filter which allows all frequencies below the cut-off to pass almost without attenuation whilst blocking all frequencies above the cut-off.

Figure 2.9 shows a high-pass filter which allows the higher frequencies to be passed whilst greatly attenuating lower frequencies.

A band-pass filter, as illustrated in Figure 2.10, allows a band of frequencies to pass whilst cutting off the higher frequencies above the band and the lower frequencies below the band.

It will be seen from Figure 2.7 that loss is independent of frequency over the range 300-3400 Hz and beyond 3400 Hz transmission loss increases rapidly. The effect of loading has been to make each conductor pair behave like a low-pass filter.

AMPLIFIED CIRCUITS

The majority of junction and trunk circuits provided within a network are designed for the transmission of audio (speech) signals in the range or 'band' of frequencies 300-3400 Hz. The plant over which the circuit is routed can vary considerably, with a trend towards smaller and smaller gauge cable, due in no small part to the rapid increase in the price of copper. The limiting distance for transmission, even for loaded pairs, has therefore been reduced so that many circuits now require amplification.

Two-Wire Amplification and Hybrid Transformers

The main function of an amplifier is to provide a large signal output in response to a small input, referred to as 'gain', to compensate for losses in a given length of transmission line. Although a single pair of wires is capable of transmitting equally well in both directions, amplifiers are traditionally unidirectional. Therefore to provide amplification on a two-wire circuit two amplifiers are required and the directions of transmission must be separated by hybrid transformers (Figure 2.11).

The two-wire transformers are provided with balance impedances to provide a low-loss path from the two-wire to transmit, a low-loss path

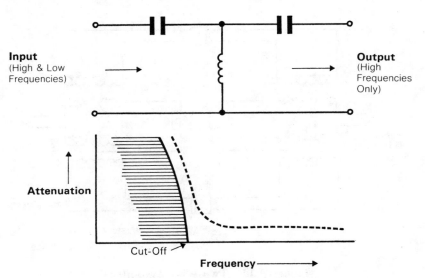

Input
(High & Low
Frequencies)

Output
(High
Frequencies
Only)

Attenuation

Cut-Off

Frequency ⟶

Figure 2.9   High-Pass Filter

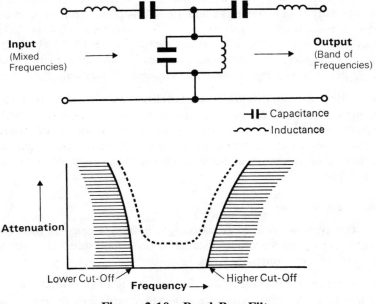

Input
(Mixed
Frequencies)

Output
(Band of
Frequencies)

⊣⊢ Capacitance
⌇⌇⌇⌇ Inductance

Attenuation

Lower Cut-Off   Frequency ⟶   Higher Cut-Off

Figure 2.10   Band-Pass Filter

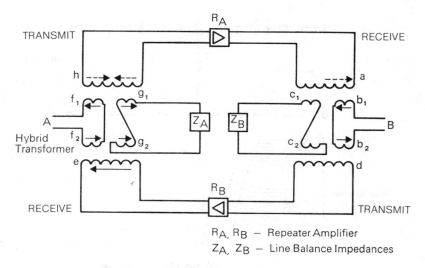

R_A, R_B — Repeater Amplifier
Z_A, Z_B — Line Balance Impedances

Figure 2.11   Two-Wire Amplifier

from receive to two-wire and high-loss from receive to transmit pair. Theoretically the low losses should be 3 dB ($\frac{1}{2}$ power) but in practice it is 3 to 4 dB because of transformer losses. The high receive to transmit loss, although theoretically infinite, is in practice 30 dB (1:1000) to 35 dB because of imperfect balance, and is required to maintain circuit stability and so prevent 'singing' caused by each amplifier driving the other.

An alternative and more economical method of providing two-wire amplified circuits is to use a device known as a Negative Impedance Repeater which amplifies both directions of transmission simultaneously. The repeater circuit is considerably more complex than a traditional amplifier and consists of an active symmetrical network having a gain of up to 12 dB.

Four-Wire Working

The effectiveness of two-wire working is limited because of problems of maintaining stability on long-distance circuits. The solution to the problem is to provide four-wire working.

Four-wire circuits (Figure 2.12) were originally provided over audio line plant for the whole distance, no matter what length was required.

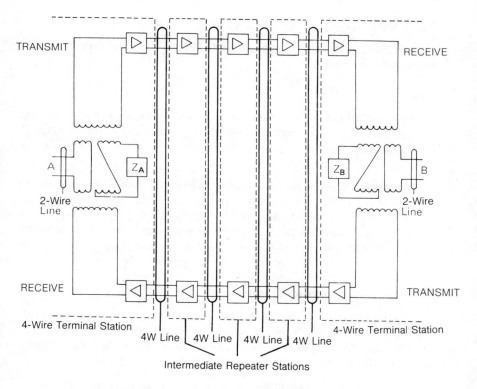

Figure 2.12   Four-Wire Circuit Arrangement

However, modern practice is to provide the major part of the circuit over channels of carrier or coaxial line systems. By whichever method the circuit is provided, the ends are normally provided as two-wire connections to the switching equipment.

Amplification must be provided at regularly spaced intervals because:

— if amplification was only provided at the receiving end of a circuit the signal would be swamped by noise picked up over the length of the circuit;

— if amplification was only provided at the transmit end of a circuit, to compensate for losses along the line, the output required from the amplifier would be so high as to be impractical.

TRANSMISSION IMPAIRMENTS

Before continuing, it would be useful to review the main types of transmission impairments.

Sidetone

Sidetone is defined as the reproduction in a telephone receiver of sounds picked up by the associated transmitter. It provides a 'live-sounding' connection allowing a speaker to adopt a normal conversational speaking level.

Too much sidetone causes a speaker to lower the voice, thus diminishing the receive level at the distant end. Too little sidetone causes a speaker to raise the voice, thus giving abnormally high signal levels at the receive end. Not only does the receiver hear speech levels in an incorrect manner, but he will also adjust the speech level accordingly, eg if speech received is loud the receiver will tend to speak softly on replying.

Insertion Loss/Frequency Distortion

This is the variation of loss with frequency relative to the 800 Hz level, within the range 300-3400 Hz. One method of compensating for frequency distortion is to introduce equalisation, this being particularly relevant for carrier and coaxial working (to be covered later).

In order to make transmission loss independent of frequency over a band of operation, an electrical network, known as an equaliser, is introduced into a line where the equaliser has the inverse attenuation/frequency characteristic to that of the line. Figure 2.13 shows how the inclusion of an equaliser results in the combined losses of line and equaliser being constant across the frequency range. The loss can then be compensated by an amplifier.

An alternative, as shown in Figure 2.14, is to have an amplifier with a gain/frequency characteristic which is a replica of the loss/frequency characteristic of the line.

Noise

Any noises, whether induced from outside sources (power lines, etc) or due to circuit defects (component noise, bad joints, etc) are naturally amplified with transmitted speech. The repeater stations must, therefore,

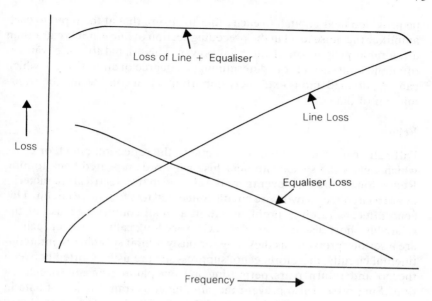

Figure 2.13   Line Equalisation

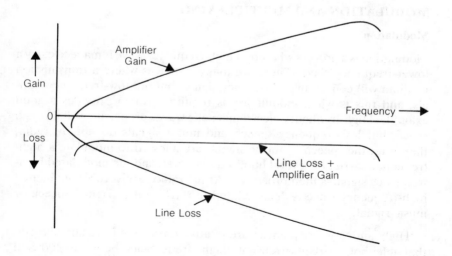

Figure 2.14   Amplifier Gain/Frequency Characteristic

be provided near enough to each other to ensure that at the input to each amplifier the noise level in the preceding section of line is not greater than a tolerable proportion of the total power. This 'signal to noise' ratio is often the limiting factor in determining the degree of amplification which can be obtained and is extremely important when considering the transmission of data.

Echo

Difficulty can arise on long circuits due to the reflection effect, or echo, which causes the speaker to hear his own words repeated back to him. Reflection occurs whenever there is a change in the electrical characteristics of a circuit, eg a two-wire circuit connected to a four-wire circuit. This echo effect is rarely a problem within a small country because of the relatively short distances involved. On very long calls, however, echoes are a serious problem, as they may seriously inhibit speech. On intercontinental circuits, therefore, echo 'suppressors' are usually fitted between the 'go' and 'return' pairs, permitting only one pair to transmit speech at a time. Suppressors also prevent the simultaneous transmission of data in both directions and if this is required then devices have to be introduced to 'disable' the echo suppressors.

MODULATION AND MULTIPLEXING

Modulation

Modulation is a process whereby a high-frequency wave is made to carry a lower-frequency wave. There are many instances where a transmission medium will convey high-frequency signals but not low-frequency signals, and this is when modulation is required. Radio provides a good example. High-frequency electromagnetic waves propagate well through space, but low-frequency speech and music signals do not. In radio, therefore, the speech or music signals are allowed to modulate a high-frequency carrier of several hundred kilohertz, and the modulated high-frequency signal is then broadcast. At the radio receiver this modulated high-frequency wave is demodulated to retrieve the original speech or music signal.

'High' and 'low' frequencies are relative terms. We have already seen that telephone circuits transmit 'high' frequencies between 300 and 3400 Hz, but not 'low' frequencies below 300 Hz. Data signals contain low-frequency components less than 300 Hz, and thus modulation is required if these signals are to be transmitted over telephone circuits.

A

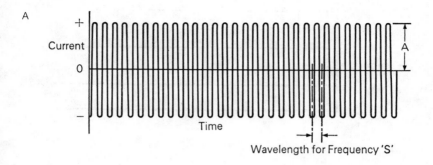

Wavelength for Frequency 'S'

B

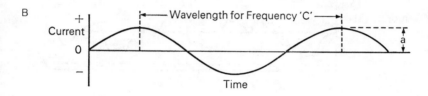

C

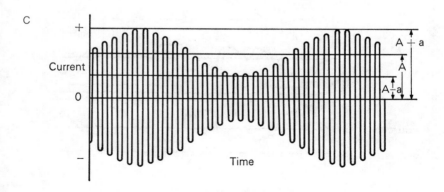

Figure 2.15 The Principle of Modulation

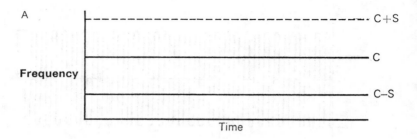

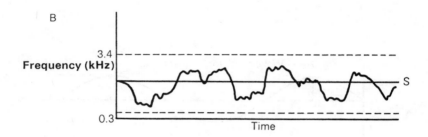

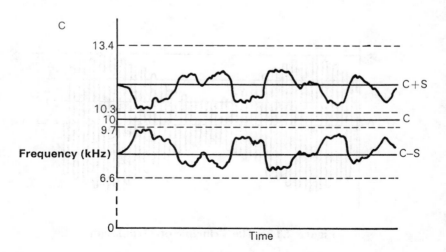

Figure 2.16   Modulation by Speech Wave

Various modulation techniques are available and these can be classified depending upon which characteristic feature of the carrier is modified. Thus, the three main categories are amplitude, frequency and phase modulation. These techniques and some of their variants will be described in this chapter and the one following.

Figure 2.15 illustrates the effect of a speech wave modulating a carrier when the technique of amplitude modulation is employed.

The typical 'envelope' shown in the lower part of the diagram is in fact a compound of three frequencies:

c   the original 'carrier' frequency

c + s   the sum of the 'carrier' and modulating frequency

c – s   the difference between the carrier and the modulating frequency.

It is therefore more convenient to plot frequency against time graphically rather than amplitude against time, as in Part A of Figure 2.16. Part B of Figure 2.16 illustrates a typical speech waveform. Part C illustrates the complex waveforms after modulating the 10 kHz carrier 'C'.

It will be seen that the intelligence now lies both in the upper 'sideband', 10.3 to 13.4 kHz and also in the lower sideband, 6.6 to 9.7 kHz. It is common practice to transmit only the lower sideband, the carrier being suppressed in a modulator which is of special design and the upper sideband being suppressed by the use of a low-pass or band-pass filter. In this way, power requirements are reduced and the number of channels which can be accommodated in a given frequency range is increased. At the receiving end, a locally generated carrier, of the same frequency and in the same phase relationship as the original carrier, is introduced (to restore the conversation to the original speech frequencies). This technique is know as 'demodulation'. The demodulator works on the same basis as the modulator in that three frequencies will be produced:

$$c \quad\quad = c$$
$$c+(c-s) = 2c-s$$
$$c-(c-s) = s \text{ (the original speech frequencies)}$$

The third frequency is the original speech frequency (or band of frequencies); it may be filtered off by means of a low-pass filter and amplified as required. The principle of lower sideband suppressed carrier working is shown in Figure 2.17.

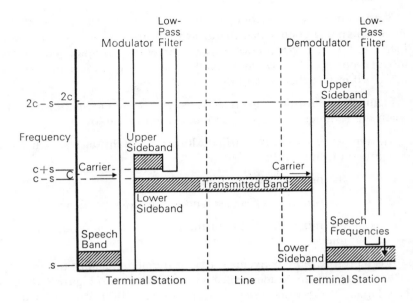

Figure 2.17   Principle of Lower Sideband Suppressed Carrier Working

The technique of modulation, as described, is the basis of Frequency Division Multiplexing (FDM) which is a system widely used to gain line economies both in speech and data transmission.

Multiplexing and Carrier Systems

If, whilst a circuit is carrying one conversation at normal speech frequencies, another conversation is lifted into a higher band of similar width, both conversations can be carried over the same circuit. The technique to achieve this is multiplexing, a technique for dividing circuit capacity into several independent channels.

In the public network, arrangements are made to allow circuits to be split into several voice frequency channels, and for these to be multiplexed together into circuits of increasingly wider bandwidth, so that the multiplexing has a hierarchical structure.

A carrier system employing carrier frequencies between 64 to 108 kHz is shown in Figure 2.18; only the lower sideband is transmitted for each of

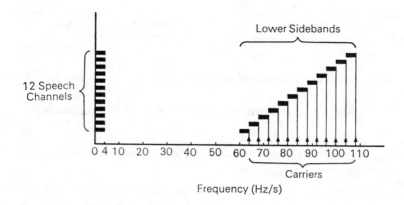

Figure 2.18   12-Channel Carrier System

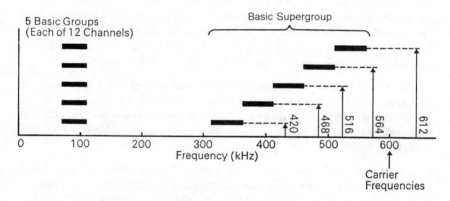

Figure 2.19   60-Channel Carrier System

the twelve speech channels which are derived. Improvements in cable design have made it possible to introduce a carrier system providing 60 channels. A 60-channel group is formed by combining five 12-channel groups (Figure 2.19). Each 12-channel group, after assembly in the range 60 to 108 kHz is arranged to modulate one of the carrier frequencies 420 kHz, 468 kHz, 516 kHz, 564 kHz and 612 kHz. The lower sidebands are selected in each case and, when combined, occupy a frequency band 312 to 552 kHz. This complete band, termed a 'supergroup', then mod-

FREQUENCY/kHz	TRANSMISSION LOSS dB/km
12	0.6
252	2.2

Table 2.4   Attenuation in Carrier Pair (Low Capacitance)

ulates a carrier frequency of 564 kHz and the lower sideband of 12 to 252 kHz is transmitted to line.

The construction of carrier cables required precision manufacture. For example, to avoid signal degradation, a quad, consisting of two pairs of cable for transmit and receive directions of transmission, had to be cut from the same roll of copper wire and the paper insulation had to be cut from the same roll of paper. Even the identification markings, in ink, on the insulation were spaced so that equal amounts of ink were placed on each conductor. Although it was theoretically possible to provide 120 channels on a carrier system, Table 2.4 shows that, at frequencies of 252 kHz, transmission loss on low-capacitance cable was high.

The repeater spacing would have to be reduced to much less than the 20 km required for a 60-channel system to overcome the attenuation and permit higher frequency working. This was not economic in practice, but fortunately it was found possible to increase system capacities by using 'coaxial' cables.

In a coaxial cable, the conventional pair of wires forming the conductors is replaced by a solid copper rod running concentrically in a copper tube (see Figure 2.20). The space between the conductors should, ideally, be filled with air, but it is necessary of course to provide 'spacers' at intervals to keep the conductor rod central in the tube.

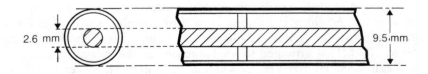

Figure 2.20   Coaxial Tube (9.5 mm Outer, 2.6 mm Centre Conductor)

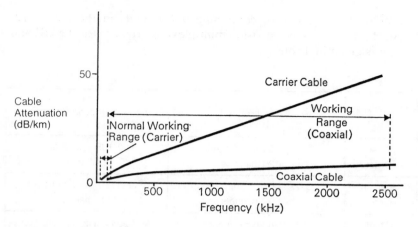

Figure 2.21 Comparative Attenuation of Carrier and Coaxial Cables

At very high frequencies, current flow takes place mainly near the surface of the conductors and in a coaxial tube the current flow is concentrated near the inner surface of the tube and the outer surface of the rod. External high-frequency influences on the cable will mainly affect the outer surface of the tube and hence interfere very little with the transmission. The comparative attenuation of carrier and coaxial cables is illustrated in Figure 2.21.

The transmission characteristics of a coaxial tube are dependent on the ratio of the inner and outer conductors which is typically 1:3.6. The two main sizes of cable used in the UK are:

1.2/4.4 tube for FDM systems up to 12 MHz (2,700 circuits)

2.6/9.5 tube for FDM systems up to 60 MHz (10,800 circuits).

The first figure represents the diameter of the inner conductor and the second figure is the diameter of the outer conductor. All figures are in millimetres. One tube is required for each direction of transmission and to compensate for line losses equalisers and repeaters for the 60 MHz system are spaced at 1.6 km intervals.

The provision of coaxial cables with better transmission characteristics than was available with carrier cable resulted in the introduction of a third stage of modulation and the provision of hypergroups. A hypergroup consists of 15 supergroups containing 900 circuits in the band 312-4028 kHz. The frequency division multiplexing structure for the UK and Europe is given in Table 2.5.

Multiplexing Level	UK	Other European Countries
First Order	60-108 kHz Group 12 Channels	60-108 kHz Group 12 Channels
Second Order	312-552 kHz Supergroup 60 Channels	312-552 kHz Supergroup 60 Channels
Third Order	312-4028 kHz Hypergroup 400 Channels	812-2044 kHz Mastergroup 300 Channels
Fourth Order		8516-12,388 kHz Super Mastergroup – 900 Channels

Table 2.5　Multiplexing Structure

Pulse Code Modulation

In the mid-1960s the Post Office (now BT) was faced with the problem within large conurbations that both audio pair-type cables and cable ducts were reaching exhaustion. In addition telephone traffic growth was increasing so rapidly that there was a need to quickly augment existing circuit capacity in an economic manner that would not require major roadworks and hence disturb road traffic in cities.

Earlier we saw how frequency division multiplexing using carrier or coaxial line systems could be used to make more economic use of line plant. Although economic over long-distance (trunk) routes, and even this is now changing, carrier systems are much less economic over the shorter-distance (junction) routes, particularly in large metropolitan areas. The ideal solution to the problem was provided by pulse code modulation (PCM) transmission. PCM was first invented by an Englishman, A H Reeves, in 1938 but it was only the availability of the transistor and other semiconductor devices that enabled large-scale development

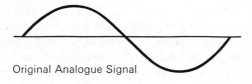

Original Analogue Signal

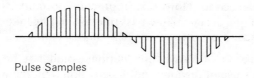

Pulse Samples

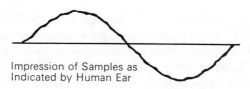

Impression of Samples as
Indicated by Human Ear

Figure 2.22

and implementation of PCM systems to take place in the 1960s. The basis of PCM is to sample a message signal at regular intervals, convert this sample to a series of pulses or code and then reverse the process to recover the original signal.

Pulse Amplitude Modulation

Figure 2.22 shows a pulse amplitude modulation (PAM) process with:

— a sinusoidal wave;

— pulse samples of that wave whose amplitude is proportional to the sample value;

— recovery of the original signal by passing the pulse amplitude samples through a low-pass filter.

It can be seen that the recovered signal is not a perfect reproduction of the original signal, but in the example shown the small variations between the transmit and receive signals would be unnoticeable to the human ear. To ensure that integrity of the signal is maintained, the minimum rate of sampling is specified by a sampling theorem which states that any signal of bandwidth B Hz can be represented by 2B independent samples per second. In following this theorem the telephony speech spectrum of 300-3400 Hz should be capable of being characterised by sampling at 6200 samples a second. However, in practice, to make signal recovery easier with a simple design of low-pass filter, sampling takes place at 8000 samples per second or once every 125 microseconds.

The transmission of PAM information would not be a practicable proposition because of the amount of distortion that the pulses would be subject to when transmitted to line as well as the interference such pulses would cause to other systems. A solution is to code the PAM signal into a digital signal.

To overcome problems of interference and distortion Pulse Code Modulation (PCM) is used whereby the message sample is sent to line as a code formed by a pattern of binary pulses. On receipt of the information, decoding logic at the receiver recognises the coded sample and reconstitutes an amplitude signal at the required level. Figure 2.23 shows a simple diagram of such a system.

The low-pass filter on the input reduces the level of any component above 4 kHz arising from preceding equipment or crosstalk from other high-frequency services.

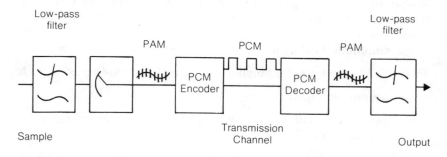

Figure 2.23

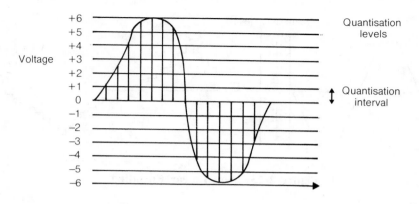

Figure 2.24

Quantisation

Ideally the exact value of each PAM signal should be given its own code. However this is not practicable as it would lead to a requirement for a large code to represent each PAM value and an increase in the information transmitted to line. Instead, each analogue pulse is represented by a discrete value or quantum by a process termed quantisation. Figure 2.24 shows the sample values of a message signal with equally spaced quantum levels.

A result of using a finite number of quantisation levels is that a PAM signal may be allocated a quantising level that is slightly higher or lower than the actual signal level and hence some error is introduced to the signal. This error is called quantisation error and the effect of a succession of quantisation errors is referred to as quantisation noise. The more quantisation levels used the less will be the noise.

Companding

Increasing the number of quantum levels decreases quantisation distortion but increases the information passed to line. If we consider that an information rate of Nbits per second requires a minimum bandwidth of N/2 Hz it can be seen that an increase in the number of quantisation levels will require an increase in the amount of bandwidth. The use of uniform or linear quantisation levels means that the signal to quantisation noise

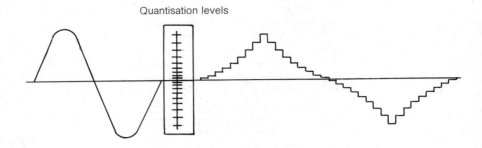

Figure 2.25   Non-Linear Encoding

ratio will be the same irrespective of the amplitude of the signal. As the range of speech signal level from different talkers on a telephone is 30 dB, the signal to noise ratio will be worse at low amplitudes and quieter speech will be encoded based on a smaller number of quantisation levels than for louder speech. To obtain a signal to noise ratio that is sensibly constant over the whole range the intervals between quantisation levels at the lower levels are reduced (Figure 2.25).

This compression of the low level signals can be achieved with a compressor amplifier inserted before a linear encoder and after decoding the signal at the receive end it is fed into an expander amplifier (Figure 2.26). Such a system is know as companding.

An alternative to the above would be to use a non-linear encoder and non-linear decoder.

The ideal companding law would have all the quantum levels spaced in a logarithmic form, but a more practical method in terms of amplifier

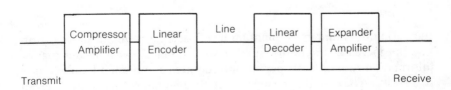

Figure 2.26   Companding System

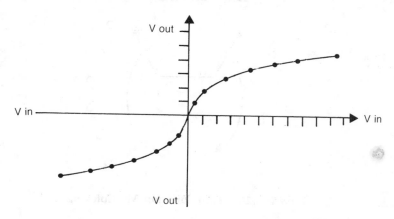

Figure 2.27 Compressor Amplifier Characteristic

design is to make the quantum levels into thirteen linear segments that approach a logarithmic form (Figure 2.27).

PCM systems now being installed by BT, and most other telephone administrations, use a compression characteristic, based on an approximation to a logarithmic law, known as CCITT 'A-Law'. The encoder, sometimes called an analogue to digital converter, codes each PAM sample into a word 8-binary digits, or bits, long. In each word one bit identifies the polarity of the signal and seven bits provide information on the signal amplitude. The number of quantisation levels used, for each sign, is 2^8 which is 256 levels.

The bit rate for one channel provided via such a system can be calculated from:

sampling rate per second x bit rate per second =
$$8000 \times 8 = 64,000 \text{ bit/s} = 64 \text{ kbit/s}$$

Time Division Multiplexing

We have stated that PCM was the answer to the problems of cable pair congestion. However, it cannot on its own provide the solution but must be used with time division multiplexing (TDM). Time division multiplexing and frequency division multiplexing have the same basic aim in that each maximises the number of message signals that can be transmitted over a transmission link.

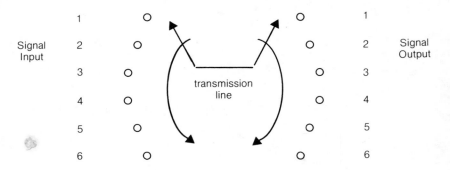

Figure 2.28   Time Division Multiplexing

We have seen that by sampling at 8000 times a second a signal is examined once every 125 μs and a PAM signal results. Where the length of this pulse is short in comparison to the sampling time then the pulses from other PAM signals can be interleaved in the time interval between pulses of this first signal. This is known as time division multiplexing (TDM).

This is shown in a simplified form in Figure 2.28 where six different input signals are time division multiplexed together.

To ensure that transmit input 3 is only received by receive output 3, the input multiplexer and output de-multiplexer must be synchronised.

PCM Over Junction Circuits

We have seen how loading of circuits with inductors:

— counteracted power losses and distortion up to 3400 Hz;

— produced a rapid frequency cut-off above 3400 Hz.

By removing the loading coils, an attenuation-frequency characteristic for 1.8 km of twisted-pair cable as shown in Figure 2.29 is obtained.

The major advantage of digital transmission is that the difference between its signalling states (1 and 0) can be discerned, with a low probability of error, even when significant noise interference is encountered. Therefore, remembering that a minimum bandwidth of N/2 is half the bit rate, digital signals with a bit rate of about 2 Mbit/s can be tolerated

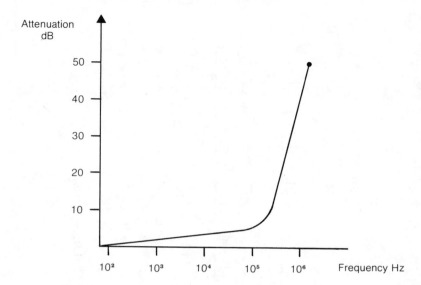

Figure 2.29   Frequency Response of 1.8 km of Unloaded Twisted-Pair Cable

before attenuation of the signal, and subsequent distortion by noise, becomes unacceptable. At this point it is therefore convenient to remove the loading coil and fit a regenerator which, unlike an analogue amplification, will reshape, retime and restore the signal to its original undistorted state.

As with conventional amplifiers, regenerators are unidirectional devices. Therefore each PCM system requires a separate pair for transmit and receive. This is considered to be very economical, and meets the original requirements, as each double pair of wires caters for a 32-channel 2.048 Mbit/s PCM system, consisting of 30 traffic channels, one channel for synchronisation and one channel for signalling.

30-Channel PCM System

Each 30-channel PCM system now being installed by BT, and which supersedes the original design of 24-channel systems, consists of terminal multiplex equipment and an associated digital-line system.

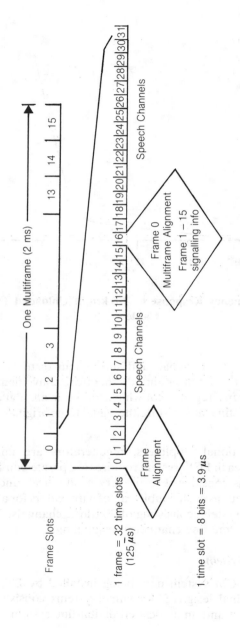

Figure 2.30 PCM Frame and Multiframe Format

The audio channel input is sampled at 8000 times a second and this, together with samples from 29 other channels, is referred to as a frame. Each frame contains 32 time slots designated TS0-TS31, with TS0 used for synchronisation and TS16 for signalling. Each time slot contains 8 bits therefore:

time slot signalling rate = 8000 x 8 = 64 kbit/s
line signalling rate = 8000 x 8 x 32 bit/s

TS16 contains signalling information for all 30 channels. As there are only 8 bits in TS16 it is sub-multiplexed over a period of 16 frames (0-15), ie a multiframe (Figure 2.30). During frames 1-15, frame 0 being used as a start signal, 4 bits of signalling information are transmitted for each of the 30 channels. As each multiframe is repeated every 2 ms this corresponds to a signalling rate of 2 kbit/s for each channel and is more than enough to meet its requirements.

A block diagram of the transmit terminal of a 30-channel system is shown in Figure 2.31. The function of the receive terminal is to perform the exact reverse operations to those carried out by the receive terminal.

High Density Bipolar 3

It can be seen in Figure 2.31 that a code converter is inserted between the PCM highway and the line. This converter changes the binary code to line code HDB3 (high density bipolar 3) so that every other pulse is given negative polarity. This removes the large-DC and low-frequency components that would arise with the transmission of a long series of pulses of the same polarity. False signals are also injected into defined positions in the pulse train so that the maximum number of consecutive zeros transmitted is limited to 3. This avoids loss of timing control of the system when long sequences of zeros are transmitted. Thus, HDB3 provides a high density of marks in the line signal, irrespective of the composition of the applied binary signal (Figure 2.32).

Higher Order PCM Systems

In addition to the cost benefits and improvement in transmission performance that accrue with the use of digital transmission, digital transmission also has the advantage that it can be used for all services: for example, telegraphy, data transmission, television and telephony.

For these reasons, and because of the move by BT towards an Inte-

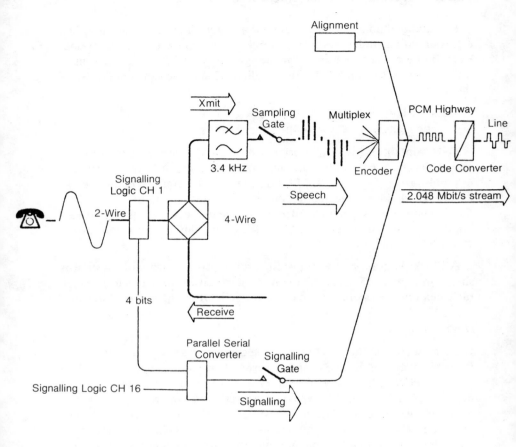

Figure 2.31   30-Channel System Block Diagram

grated Digital Network (IDN) using a family of exchanges termed System X, high-capacity PCM systems will be constructed to totally replace the analogue trunk network by the mid-1990s. These systems will be constructed by assembling together primary blocks of 30 channels of 2.048 Mbit/s in a hierarchical fashion which is analogous to the FDM groups, supergroups and hypergroups. The digital hierarchy which has been recommended by the CCITT is given in Table 2.6.

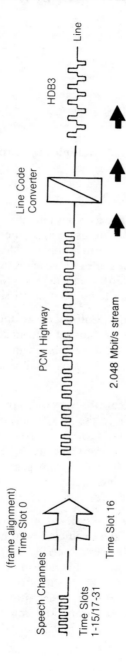

Figure 2.32　High Density Bipolar 3

Multiplexing Level	Bit Rate	Number of Channels
First Order	2.048 Mbit/s	30
Second Order	8.448 Mbit/s	120
Third Order	34.368 Mbit/s	480
Fourth Order	139.264 Mbit/s	1920

Table 2.6   Digital Multiplexing Structure

FIBRE OPTIC TRANSMISSION

Light waves, like radio waves, are a form of electromagnetic energy and the idea of transmitting information using light energy is not new. Over 100 years ago the 'Photophone' was invented by Alexander Graham Bell in an attempt to carry voice messages on a beam of light. However the practical use of light waves had to await the development of a suitable light source and detector, and a low-loss transmission medium.

Laser beam development and photodetection techniques resulted in experiments in the early 1960s to transmit information using laser light. The attempts were not successful because transmission through the atmosphere is limited to line-of-sight paths and is also severely limited by fog and bad weather.

The potential for using optical fibres, which are thin strands of pure glass, was discovered in Britain in the late 1960s at the research laboratory of Standard Telephones and Cables, a subsidiary of ITT. However, it was not until 1970, when Corning Glass in the US developed a glass fibre with an attenuation of 20 dB/km, that practical optical telecommunications became possible. Since that time, attenuation figures of less than 0.3 dB/km have been achieved.

Optical fibres work on the principle of internal reflection of light waves, each fibre being a fine glass rod clad with a glass layer of lower refractive index. The inner glass core acts as a light pipe which traps parallel rays of light emitted from a light emitting source, eg laser or light emitting diode (LED) which travel down the fibre and are detected by an avalanche photo diode. Information is transmitted as binary digits and must conform to line coding requirements similar to those used for standard digital line systems.

Three types of optical fibre are now available:

— Step Index Fibre where light waves are reflected at different angles and which then travel in a non-uniform manner and hence is only used for short distances;

— Graded Index Fibre which causes most of the light to curve through glass of graded refractive index in a uniform manner thus ensuring minimum distortion of the light signal;

— Monomode in which one ray of light only passes straight down a very narrow glass core 5×10^{-6} in thick. This fibre is the hardest to manufacture but can carry more information, with greater distances between repeaters.

Low-loss optical fibre transmission has a number of desired features and benefits when compared to audio, carrier or coaxial cable:

— *Large Bandwidth* The use of lasers which can emit an intense beam of light in the visible or infra-red region opens up a part of the spectrum when frequencies are 10,000 times higher than the highest radio frequency. This provides the potential of carrying information at a rate of 10^{14} bit/s;

— *Low Loss* With low-loss characteristics, repeater spacings can be increased;

— *Electromagnetic Interference* No electromagnetic interference can be picked up by the fibre and conversely no interference or information is radiated from the fibre;

— *Physical Size* Substantial size and weight advantages accrue compared to conventional cable.

SATELLITE COMMUNICATION

No mention of transmission would be complete without consideration of the satellite. Satellite communication has the advantage of increasing network flexibility and diversity over cable systems by being able to 'bounce' communications signals transmitted from one part of the earth to a receiver at another location on the earth.

To obtain an orbit that from the ground appears to be stationary (geostationary), a satellite must orbit the earth once every 24 hours at an altitude of 35,600 km with a velocity of 2,600 metres per second. At this synchronous altitude above the equator, a satellite can see about 42% of the earth's surface. It provides line-of-sight communication whose clarity and cost are not affected by transmission distance.

In the case of a purely national system, it is possible to focus satellite radio frequency radiated power into a beam shape to cover a single country. As a result the power received on the ground is increased and the size, and therefore the cost, of earth stations is decreased.

National systems can be used for a diversity of communications services, including:

— commercial services;

— radio and TV;

— data processing services;

— military applications;

— air traffic control and maritime communications;

— meteorological services.

Some earth stations are configured according to other specific applications. Antenna sizes can vary accordingly, from 3 to 12 metres in diameter, with the smaller sizes being utilised for small transportable stations or where a large number of earth stations is required. In international applications an earth dish antenna of up to 30 metres diameter is used.

July 1962 marked the date of the launch of Telstar, an experimental telecommunications satellite, that was the forerunner of the present day geostationary satellite operated by Intelsat. Since the launching of the first commercial satellite, Intelsat I (Early Bird) in 1965, development of satellite systems has been very rapid (Table 2.7). Included within these developments have been methods of achieving multiple access.

The power and bandwidth of a satellite repeater may be used either undivided, to carry a single signal at a maximum bit rate, or may be divided using multiple access to carry a number of independent, slower signals simultaneously. Two multiple access techniques are available: time division multiple access (TDMA) and frequency division multiple access (FDMA).

With TDMA each signal is compressed into a short, high-speed, high-

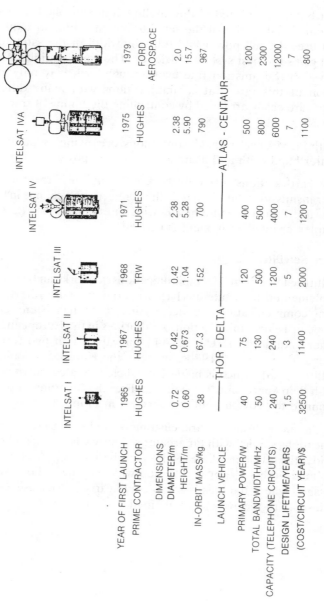

	INTELSAT I	INTELSAT II	INTELSAT III	INTELSAT IV	INTELSAT IVA	INTELSAT V
YEAR OF FIRST LAUNCH	1965	1967	1968	1971	1975	1979
PRIME CONTRACTOR	HUGHES	HUGHES	TRW	HUGHES	HUGHES	FORD AEROSPACE
DIMENSIONS DIAMETER/m	0.72	0.42	0.42	2.38	2.38	2.0
HEIGHT/m	0.60	0.673	1.04	5.28	5.90	15.7
IN-ORBIT MASS/kg	38	67.3	152	700	790	967
LAUNCH VEHICLE	THOR - DELTA			ATLAS - CENTAUR		
PRIMARY POWER/W	40	75	120	400	500	1200
TOTAL BANDWIDTH/MHz	50	130	500	500	800	2300
CAPACITY (TELEPHONE CIRCUITS)	240	240	1200	4000	6000	12000
DESIGN LIFETIME/YEARS	1.5	3	5	7	7	7
(COST/CIRCUIT YEAR)/$	32500	11400	2000	1200	1100	800

Table 2.7 Technological Progress in Intelsat Satellites

(Reproduced from Satellite Communications in the 1980s and After, by B I Edelson and R C Davis, *Communications in the 1980s and After*, London Royal Society, 1978) power burst transmitted to the satellite at a controlled time so that the different signals arrive at the satellite one at a time in sequence. Each signal uses the full power and full bandwidth of the satellite repeater, which gives the best system efficiency. The earth stations must work at full system transmission rate even though each may only use a small fraction of this rate, but communications with many different earth stations are easily arranged by controlling the timing of transmitted and received signals.

With FDMA each signal is continuous, occupying a separate part of the repeater bandwidth and using a share of the power.

The earth stations need only work at the bit rate corresponding to their own transmissions, but to change the connections a change in frequency is necessary, and to communicate with more than one, other terminal multiplex channel equipment is needed.

Future Satellite Use

The future terrestrial telecommunications network can be expected to be complemented by a satellite-based overlay network offering advanced digital communications services. Agreement has been reached with European Telecommunications Authorities in the European Space Management Authority (EUTELSAT) for capacity in two future satellite systems from the mid-1980s; namely, the European Communications Satellite (ECS), which is being constructed by a consortium headed by British Aerospace, and Telecom 1, a French Government project which is planned to provide domestic services in France.

In the more distant future, customers are likely to require a telecommunications service with far greater mobility where a telephone number will identify a caller wherever he may be located. A universal pocket telephone accessible over a nation-wide mobile-radio system can be envisaged where the businessman could carry a briefcase data terminal and display to receive electronic mail.

3 Data Transmission and Modulation

DATA TRANSMISSION USING ANALOGUE CHANNELS

We have already observed that the telephone network was designed primarily for speech communication, and in particular to transmit frequencies in the bandwidth of 300-3400 Hertz. The original design objective and the analogue technology employed impose severe constraints on the transmission of data originating in a digital form. It is important to recognise that the limitations are inherent properties of the analogue technology employed, and of the network components.

In Chapter 1 we considered the typical square wave output of a computer or similar piece of electronic equipment and showed that this had a theoretically infinite bandwidth, so that in practice a square wave signal would contain frequency components appreciably higher than the fundamental or basic repetition frequency. In addition we should note that square wave signals have no even harmonic components of the basic signal frequency to provide synchronisation or timing information.

On the other hand, as we have seen, the telephone network is designed to transmit a continuous signal, and contains various components – such as capacitances, inductances, and amplifiers – which modify and constrain the signal, and themselves function in an analogue fashion.

It is a sobering thought that in the early days of data transmission, a major challenge was to find a way of transmitting information at 110 bits/sec, such as might be generated by a standard teleprinter.

In this case, the maximum rate of change of information occurs when the bit stream is alternate 0s and 1s, equivalent to a frequency of

99

55 Hertz; the minimum rate of change occurs when the terminal is idle, equivalent to a frequency of 0 Hertz or direct current. Somehow the modem has to take this 'baseband' signal of 0-55 Hertz and shift it up into the 300-3400 Hertz speech band.

In order to transmit digital signals along analogue circuits, it is therefore necessary first of all to convert them to a form which is acceptable to the circuits which are provided. In Chapter 1 we observed that the 'raised cosine pulse' provides a suitable basis for reshaping the digital signal to remove some of the higher frequencies which are present. The effect is to 'round off' the corners of the square wave.

This is the role of the modem, whose chief functions are: to match the channel bandwidth provided; to provide information within the transmitted signal stream for synchronisation purposes; to modulate the signal onto a higher frequency carrier; and finally to compensate for a variety of other factors which might impair quality of transmission.

Whilst the modem plays an essential part in improving transmission performance, the choice of circuit and circuit quality also has an important bearing.

In the beginning, the user had only one choice of circuit, namely the PSTN, and no matter what level of ingenuity is employed in the modem, the scope of the PSTN is eventually limited by the need to protect the interests of other users of the network, particularly speech users. For this reason, the opportunities to improve network capabilities by modifying its construction, are very restricted.

Over the years, increasing demands placed upon data transmission led to the provision of private circuits. These are created by constructing 'through' routes through the switching exchanges and isolating them from the remainder of the switched networks. By this means it became possible to modify the properties of the circuit in such a way that, in combination with a suitable modem, improved data transmission characteristics could be achieved. The various properties and characteristics are specified in a series of Schedules.

The distance covered by a circuit can also influence performance, since if it is sufficiently short, it may avoid distance-dependent distortions, and also network components required for speech but which could impair data transmission performance.

MODULATION SYSTEMS FOR DATA TRANSMISSION

There are three types of modulation used in data transmission:

— amplitude modulation;

— frequency modulation;

— phase modulation.

Amplitude modulation is not often used because large variations of amplitude, caused by fluctuating losses in the transmission network, make detection extremely difficult. However, to complete the picture, and because amplitude modulation can be combined with phase modulation, all three methods of modulation are examined in this section.

Amplitude Modulation Using Digital Signals

Figure 3.1(b) illustrates a carrier wave modulated in amplitude by the binary data shown in Figure 3.1(a). A special case of amplitude modula-

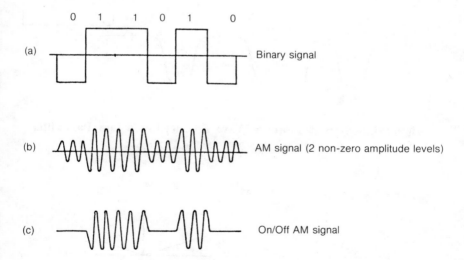

Figure 3.1 Amplitude Modulation with Binary Digital Modulating Signal

tion is when the lower of the two amplitude levels is reduced to zero; the modulation process then reduces to switching the carrier on and off (Figure 3.1(c)). However, the variation in transmitted energy makes this technique unsuitable for data transmission over telecommunications networks.

A square wave like the one in Figure 3.1(a) contains high-frequency components, and in a practical AM system the data signal would be passed through a low-pass filter prior to modulation. This rounds off the square wave (Figure 3.2), but does not affect the information content of the data signal. The output of the modulator contains frequencies as shown in Figure 3.3. Note that because the binary data signal extends

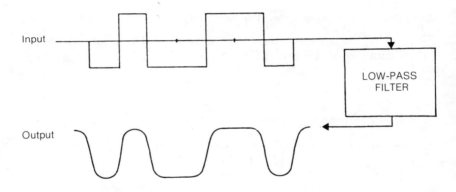

Figure 3.2   Rounded Square Wave Produced by a Low-Pass Filter

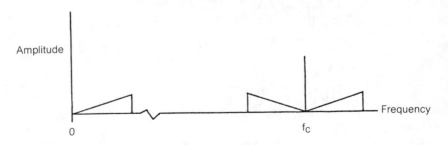

Figure 3.3   Sidebands in an AM Signal with Baseband Modulating Waveform

down to zero frequency, the upper and lower sidebands actually meet at f_c. This makes it difficult to suppress the carrier, or to suppress one sideband and the carrier, without affecting the other sideband. What can be done to reduce the bandwidth of the modulated signal is to suppress most of one sideband, leaving only a vestige of it near the carrier frequency (Figure 3.4). There is no loss of information since the lower sideband merely duplicates the information in the upper sideband. The technique is called vestigial sideband (VSB) modulation.

With clever filter design it is possible to suppress the carrier in VSB systems. It leads to part of the upper sideband being suppressed, but the vestige of the lower sideband which remains supplies the missing frequencies.

True single-sideband amplitude modulation with a digital modulating signal can only be achieved by scrambling the original data (ie randomising the bit stream) in order to remove low-frequency components caused by long strings of 1s or 0s. This has the effect of separating the sidebands from the carrier (Figure 3.5), thus making it feasible to filter out one sideband and the carrier.

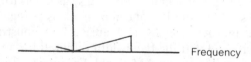

Figure 3.4   Vestigial Sideband AM

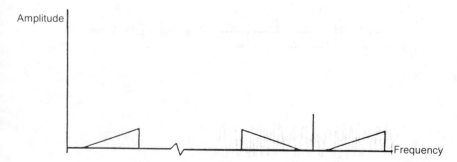

Figure 3.5   Sidebands in an AM Signal with Scrambled Baseband
Modulating Signal

Pulse Amplitude Modulation (PAM)

Pulse amplitude modulation, when used with a digital modulating waveform, provides a means of coding more than one bit per baud, by encoding the binary data signal as a signal with more than two levels (sometimes called an m-ary signal).

For example, the bits of a binary data signal could be sampled in pairs. There are four possible combinations of a pair of bits, and thus each pair could be encoded as one of four amplitude levels. The encoded 4-level signal has half the baud rate of the original data signal, and can be used to amplitude-modulate a carrier in the usual way.

Frequency Modulation

In frequency modulation (FM) systems, the *frequency* of the carrier is altered in sympathy with the modulating waveform. Systems in which the modulating waveform is a binary signal, so that the carrier is switched abruptly from one frequency to another, are referred to as frequency shift keying (FSK) systems. Figure 3.6 illustrates a binary data signal and the corresponding frequency-modulated carrier.

Analysis of an FM signal is not as easy as it was for an AM signal, but one of the simplifications that can be made is to regard the FM signal as the sum of two AM signals, as Figure 3.7 demonstrates. It is not then surprising to find that the bandwidth required for an FM signal is up to twice that required for an AM signal. Frequency modulation is superior to amplitude modulation in terms of its tolerance to certain of the

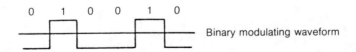

Binary modulating waveform

FM signal

Figure 3.6   Frequency Shift Keying (FSK)

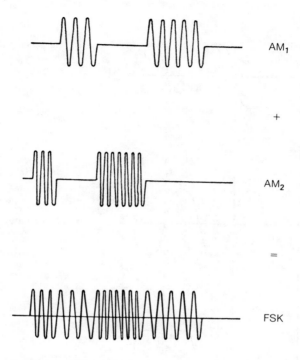

Figure 3.7   FSK as the Sum of Two AM Signals

impairments found on the telephone network, and so it tends to be used at low data rates where the limited bandwidth available is not a serious restriction.

Consider the simple low speed FSK system known as Datel 200. With this system binary 1 is represented as 980 Hz and binary 0 as 1180 Hz. The data rate is 200 bits per second. Duplex, or two-way working, is provided by means of a second channel operated in the reverse direction on the same link using two different frequencies, 1650 Hz for 1 and 1850 Hz for zero.

Phase Modulation

The simplest type of phase modulation is known as phase shift keying, by analogy with the FSK system just described. Imagine two oscillators both

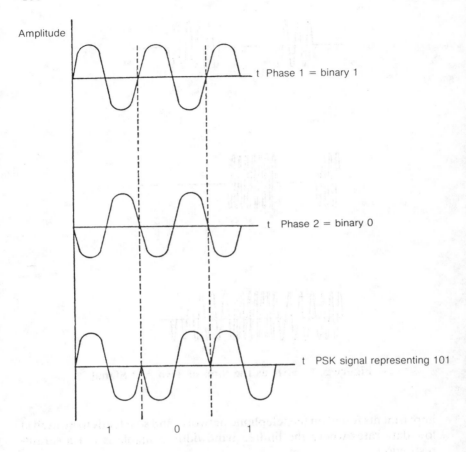

Figure 3.8   Phase Shift Keying

generating a sine wave at the carrier frequency, but 180° (half a cycle) out of phase. One oscillator is connected to line whenever there is a 0 in the data signal, and the other whenever there is a 1. The waveforms are shown in Figure 3.8.

If the receiver has a reference carrier against which to compare the phase of the incoming signal, it will be able to demodulate the signal. However, the receiver must be given some indication at the start of transmission as to which phase represents a '0' and which a '1'.

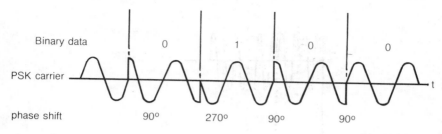

Figure 3. 9   Differential 2-Phase Encoding

A modulation system in which a carrier is generated locally at the receiver and used to demodulate the incoming signal is known as a *coherent* system. The phase modulation system just described is a coherent system. It is also known as fixed reference phase modulation.

Another technique is differential phase modulation. Each bit in the data signal is coded as a phase change relative to the previous phase of the carrier. For example, a '0' bit could be coded as a 90° phase change, and a '1' bit as a 270° phase change. Figure 3.9 shows what the modulated waveform would look like.

By comparing the phases of adjacent signal elements in the incoming signal and determining whether the phase change is 90° or 270°, the receiver can reconstruct the original data signal unambiguously. No fixed reference phase is needed in this system, but in fact some differential coding systems do use a reference signal to give improved performance.

Phase modulation using a binary modulating signal can be considered as the difference between an amplitude-modulated wave and an unmodulated carrier, as Figure 3.10 demonstrates. Put another way, a phase-modulated signal is equivalent to a suppressed carrier double-sideband amplitude-modulated signal. Phase modulation thus requires twice the bandwidth of the original data signal.

Multi-Phase Modulation

Two-phase modulation as described above codes one bit of data per phase change. With more than two phases, it would be possible to code more than one bit per phase change, and thus to increase the bit rate without altering the modulation rate. To code two bits per phase change,

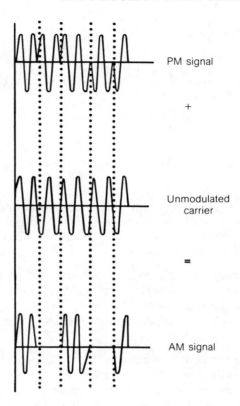

PM signal

+

Unmodulated
carrier

=

AM signal

Figure 3.10   Relationship between PM and AM

for example, we would need four possible phase changes to represent the four combinations of two bits (00, 01, 10, 11).

Using differential modulation, the technique would be to divide the data signal into pairs of bits ('dibits'), and to shift the phase of the carrier signal in one of four ways, according to the dibit combination. Table 3.1 shows one possibility.

The phase changes shown in Table 3.1 are phase shifts relative to the previous phase of the carrier. Figure 3.11 gives an example of a carrier modulated in this way.

Dibit	Phase change
00	0°
01	90°
11	180°
10	270°

Table 3.1   Coding of Dibits

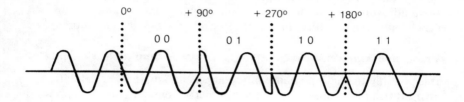

Figure 3.11   4-Phase Modulated Signal

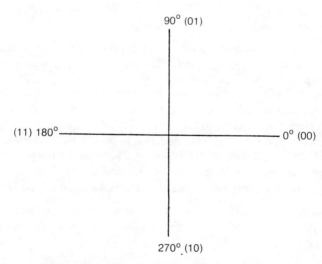

Figure 3.12   Phase Diagram Showing Phases in 4-Phase Modulation

An alternative method of presenting the information given in Table 3.1 is to use a type of phase diagram showing the possible phase shifts (Figure 3.12). A diagram of this sort provides a very convenient method of illustrating the states that a transmitted carrier can occupy, especially for the more complicated phase- and amplitude-modulation techniques.

We have already seen that, for a binary modulating signal, two-phase modulation is equivalent to double-sideband suppressed carrier (DSB-SC) amplitude modulation. Four-phase modulation is equivalent to two DSB-SC waves with carriers 90° out of phase with each other, being transmitted simultaneously, and can be considered as a special type of quadrature amplitude modulation (QAM). Phase modulation is a synchronous modulation method, requiring a clock in the modem.

Phase- and Amplitude-Modulation (Quadrature Amplitude Modulation)

It is possible to combine phase modulation and amplitude modulation to give a further increase in the number of bits per baud. Figure 3.12 showed the possible phase shifts in one type of 4-phase system coding two bits/baud. If now the amplitude of the carrier was allowed to adopt one of two possible levels for each of these phase shifts, there would be eight possible states which the carrier could adopt each baud period (Figure 3.13). This would allow three bits per baud to be carried.

Multicarrier Amplitude-Phase-Modulation

One of the newest amplitude-phase-modulation techniques relies on the simultaneous transmission of multiple carriers. One particular implementation employs 48 carriers, separated by 45 Hz spacings. By a combination of phase- and amplitude-modulation, each carrier can occupy one of 32 discrete states each baud period, permitting five bits per baud to be carried. Thus the 48 carriers can carry 5 x 48 = 240 bits per baud. For operation at 9600 bit/s, the modulation rate need only be 40 bauds; such a slow rate is very tolerant of the phase and amplitude hits so common on the telephone network. The actual bandwidth used is 2240 Hz. Modulation and demodulation are all performed digitally, in a microprocessor.

The technique illustrates the extent to which cheap electronics now makes it possible to realise ideas that would never have been practicable a while ago.

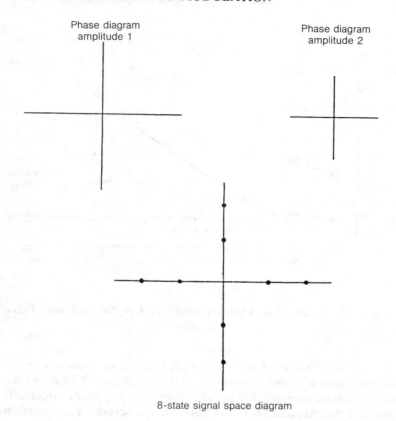

Phase diagram
amplitude 1

Phase diagram
amplitude 2

8-state signal space diagram

Figure 3.13   Phase-Amplitude-Modulation (4 phases, 2 amplitudes)

CIRCUIT CHARACTERISTICS

Circuit Characteristics – Private and PSTN

It is not possible to be precise when describing the characteristics of PSTN connections as the telephone plant used for each call is selected on a purely random basis. However, estimates of likely performance are available, based on results of network surveys.

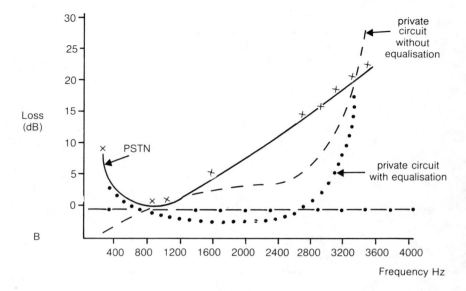

Figure 3.14   Attenuation Characteristics of UK Network and Private Circuits

The two main factors of a circuit which affect data transmission are bandwidth limitations and group delay distortion. Figure 3.14 shows the attenuation characteristics of the PSTN compared to private circuits. It can be seen that frequencies above 2500 Hz are severely attenuated in comparison to the two private circuits and this sets the limit on the maximum usable frequency for PSTN switched data services.

If component frequencies of a given signal are transmitted with varying velocity, the received phase relationships will differ from the sent phase relationships, ie the received signal will not be a replica of the sent signal. This type of distortion is known as group delay distortion and although it cannot be detected in speech signals by the human ear, it can severely impair the performance of data transmission systems as well as facsimile and television signals. Figure 3.15 compares the group delay characteristics of PSTN connections, a private circuit, and a private circuit with delay equalisation.

The Datel 200 system outlined in the section on frequency modulation is suitable for slow-speed input/output devices such as the teletypewriter.

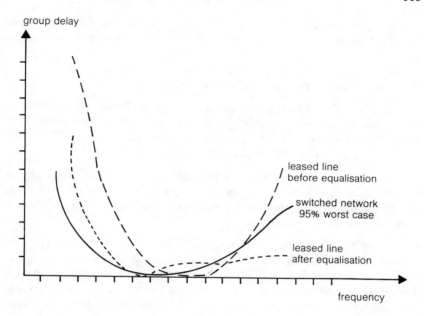

Figure 3.15   The Group Delay Curves

High-speed peripheral devices such as video displays require a much higher bit rate for satisfactory operation. For this reason, FSK systems operating up to 1200 bit/s were developed using signalling frequencies F_0 and F_1, whose spectral components lie within the range 1500 to 2000 Hz.

Table 3.2 shows the frequencies used to represent the signalling states for 600 bit/s services.

The 600 bit/s data rate is used on PSTN links that cannot achieve the 1200 bit/s rate, whereas the 1200 bit/s rate should be possible via a

Data rate (bit/s)	F_0 (Hz)	F_1 (Hz)
600	1700	1300
1200	2100	1300

Table 3.2

suitable grade of private circuit. Where even higher signalling rates are required, phase modulation techniques, as outlined previously, must be used.

Private Circuits – Published Characteristics

As we have seen, a 1200 bit/s signalling rate via the PSTN is dependent on the random choice of various components throughout the public network. To improve the likelihood of obtaining signalling rates of 1200 bit/s or higher a private circuit is generally used.

There are different grades of private circuit and although circuit specifications for them may seem daunting they are, in fact, not difficult to understand. An attempt will be made in this section to explain the key factors as simply as possible.

Table 3.3 gives the specifications, or schedules, for some typical private circuits provided by BT. Schedule D in this list is virtually the same as the CCITT specification M102 for a high-quality circuit suitable for data transmission and this schedule will be used to explain, step by step, the meaning of each of the terms used and their significance to data transmission.

Note: in all cases + means more loss

Insertion Loss

Insertion loss, sometimes known as overall loss, is the loss in decibels between one end of a circuit and the other at a stipulated frequency; in the UK 800 Hz is the common test frequency. If, therefore, a circuit were to be described as having an insertion loss of +3 dB this would express the ratio of the power of a transmitted 800 Hz signal to the power of a received 800 Hz signal in decibels.

$$10 \log_{10} \frac{\text{Power sent}}{\text{Power received}} = + \, 3 \, \text{dB}$$

In other words if an 800 Hz signal was transmitted on a line with an insertion loss of + 3 dB the received signal would be half the power of the original signal.

Loss/Frequency Response (Relative to 800 Hz)

Loss/frequency figures quoted are in decibels (dB) and are relative to the

	Schedule A	Schedule B	Schedule C	Schedule D
i) Loss/frequency response (dB relative to loss at 800 Hz – Note that + means more loss)				
300-500 Hz	−7 to +12	−3 to +10	−2 to +7	−2 to +6
500-2000 Hz	−7 to +8	−3 to +6	−1 to +4	−1 to +3
2000-2600 Hz	Not specified	−3 to +6	−1 to +4	−1 to +3
2600-2800 Hz	Not specified	−3 to +10	−1 to +4	−1 to +3
2800-3000 Hz	Not specified	−3 to +10	−2 to +7	−2 to +6
ii) Group Delay/frequency response (μ secs relative to minimum delay)				
500-600 Hz	Not specified	Not specified	Not specified	3000
600-1000 Hz	Not specified	Not specified	Not specified	1500
1000-2600 Hz	1250	1000	1000	500
2600-2800 Hz	Not specified	Not specified	Not specified	3000
iii) Random circuit noise (dBm0p)	−42	−42	−42	−45
iv) Impulsive noise No more than 18 Impulse Noise counts to exceed the threshold limit in any period of 15 mins.	Threshold Limit −18 dBm0	Threshold Limit −18 dBm0	Threshold Limit −18 dBm0	Threshold Limit −21 dBm0
v) Signal to quantising noise ratio (dB)	22	22	22	22
vi) Maximum frequency error (Hz)	2	2	2	2
vii) Transmit to receive crosstalk ratio. 4-wire presented circuits measured at 2000 Hz (dB)	Not applicable	45*	45	45
viii) Signal to listener echo ratio (dB). 2-wire presented circuits	16	20	20	20

*This parameter is not specified for omnibus circuits.

Table 3.3 Parameters of Scheduled Circuits

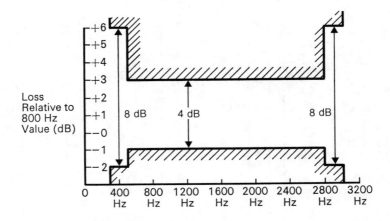

NB + Means more loss

Figure 3.16   Limits for Loss/Frequency Characteristics of a Schedule D Private Circuit

insertion loss at 800 Hz. In Table 3.3 the figures for Schedule D show that frequencies transmitted within the band 300-500 Hz would not vary outside the limits of 2 dB greater (stronger) and 6 dB less (weaker) than the power of a signal at 800 Hz.

The limits can be seen more clearly in Figure 3.16. This is a good-quality circuit and the variation in loss is limited to 4 dB (sometimes known as 'spread') over the range 500-3000 Hz. At the extremities of the band the limit of variation is much wider (up to 8 dB). The loss/frequency response of Schedule B is shown in Figure 3.17.

A Schedule B circuit is of lower quality – and therefore lower cost – than a Schedule D circuit. If, for example, the insertion loss at 800 Hz was +3 dB, then the frequencies in the range 500 Hz to 2600 Hz could vary between + 6 dB weaker and –3 dB stronger in relation to it.

Group Delay/Frequency Response

The condition which causes some frequencies to be slower than others is known as delay distortion. In data transmission, information is transmitted through rapid changes in the signal state and the term group delay/

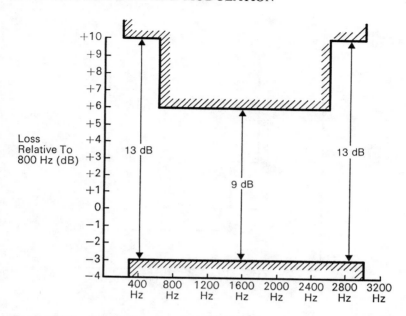

Figure 3.17   Limits for Loss/Frequency Characteristics of Schedule B Private Circuit

frequency response refers to a time measurement of a change in signal at different frequencies through a system.

It is the difference in delay of frequencies within a group which is important and on a circuit with limits such as those given in Table 3.3, a change in the signal phase would not be delayed more than the figures shown relative to the minimum delay. The minimum delay cannot be stated because this will depend on the type of telephone plant used. The limits are shown graphically in Figure 3.18.

The effect of delay distortion of a few milliseconds is not significant in speech telephony as the human ear is a fairly slow device which requires sounds to exist for at least a fifth of a second for them to be recognised. The effect of group delay distortion on data transmission will depend on the transmission techniques used. When parallel transmission is employed, the effect of the different frequencies, which make up a character, arriving at different times can obviously create problems. More serious is

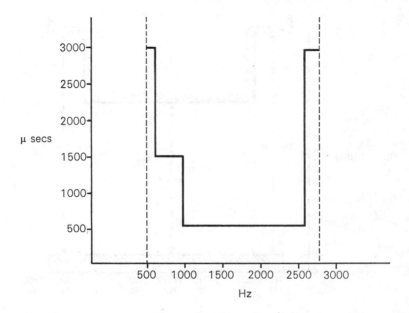

Figure 3.18   Group Delay/Frequency Limits of Schedule D Circuits

the effect on higher speed modems which rely on the selection of one of a number of conditions of the line signal for efficient operation.

The main reason for group delay distortion is the presence of filters in a telephone channel. The band-pass filters, for example, which are used in carrier telephony for multiplexing, increase the delay at the upper and lower frequency extremities of each channel. The use of loading on long junction routes effectively creates a low-pass filter which increases the delay of the higher frequencies.

Equalisation for group delay on private circuits is not a simple matter. Delay equalisers are used when necessary, which in effect slow down the faster frequencies and so reduce the difference in delay; the slight increase in total propagation delay which results from this is not important. However, the main aim in providing circuits to the high quality demanded by Schedule D is to reduce group delay distortion by careful selection of line plant.

Random Circuit Noise

Random circuit noise, or 'white noise', is an important factor in determining the maximum data signalling rate which can be achieved on a circuit. It can be of any frequency and when it is severe can be heard as a hissing sound. In Table 3.3, the figure for random circuit noise in Schedule D is −45 dBm0p. dBm0 refers to the ratio (expressed in decibels) of the noise power to the test level at a particular point in a transmission path known as the relative zero level point. The p shows that the measurement is taken using a psophometer – a device which measures only significant noise. On a circuit to the specification in Schedule D we have:

$$10 \log_{10} \frac{\text{noise power at a relative zero point}}{\text{test power at a relative zero point}} = -45 \, \text{dBm0p (maximum)}$$

The test level is 1 milliwatt and if the transmission system is close to the target there will be no loss at the relative zero point. The maximum level of random noise will, therefore, be approximately −45 dB relative to 1 mW, ie about 0.04 microwatts or 40,000 pico watts.

More important than the actual power of the random noise is its power relative to the actual signal power – the signal/noise ratio. The maximum permissible signal power level is −10 dBm0 so that with a maximum random circuit noise of −45 dBm0p the signal to noise ratio will be in the order of 35 dB, ie 3300 to one.

Impulsive Noise

Impulsive noise is the main factor which determines the error rate of a circuit. It is measured using an impulsive noise measuring instrument complying with CCITT Recommendation V55.

Signal to Quantising Noise

Quantising noise, or quantising error, only occurs on PCM links. It is caused by the process of coding and decoding an audio signal. Although the majority of private circuits will not be routed over PCM links for many years, manufacturers of equipment must assume that any 'wires only' private circuit may include PCM sections. Signal to quantising noise must, therefore, be taken into account in the manufacture of private equipment and the limits are quoted for the convenience of manufacturers.

Maximum Frequency Error

Carrier systems used in multiplexing telephone channels may introduce slight changes in the frequencies of signals transmitted. This is known as frequency error or frequency offset and the specified limit of ± 2 Hz is recommended by CCITT.

Transmit to Receive Crosstalk

On a poor telephone connection, we may occasionally hear another faint conversation in the background. This is crosstalk which is caused by induction between telephone channels. In Table 3.3 reference is made to the transmit to receive crosstalk attenuation on four-wire presented circuits. It means that if a signal is transmitted in one direction the induction or crosstalk arising from it in the other channel should not be less than 45 dB relative to the transmitted signal, eg 40,000 to 1. Transmit to receive crosstalk of very low levels such as this is not significant in data transmission.

Signal to Listener Echo Ratio

Signal to listener echoes can cause errors if they are of a sufficiently high order and were discussed earlier.

Variations with Time of the Insertion Loss at 800 Hz

The insertion loss of a circuit will vary over time so that a circuit in Table 3.3 with an insertion loss of + 10 dB at 800 Hz may vary between +7 and +13 dB. BT will take this into account when the maximum tolerable insertion loss is quoted by a customer.

4 Control Signalling in Public Networks

INTRODUCTION

Signalling is often referred to as the glue which holds a network together. It consists of the instructions which originate from the telephone user in the form of lifting a handset in order to make a call, the transmission of dial pulses generated by operating the dial, and replacing the receiver at the end of the call. Instructions are also signalled by the exchange in the form of dial tone, ringing tone, etc, to indicate the progress of the call. In addition, without the knowledge of the user, inter-exchange signalling takes place between exchanges when a call is set up, to control exchange operations and check on circuit availability.

Although these signalling procedures were developed in the context of telephony, data transmission over public circuits must take cognisance of the procedures, particularly those which apply end-to-end between subscriber apparatus. For example, the signal which causes a telephone to ring will be recognised by the modem and this will activate one or more 'Interchange Circuits' and cause the modem to respond to signals from the network and also to initiate signalling to the attached terminal or other equipment. More detailed information on the Interchange Circuits and their function is presented in Chapter 9.

Part of the procedure for establishing a dialled telephone call is outlined in the flowchart in Figure 4.1. This flowchart is very simplistic as it ignores what must happen if the calling party clears down at any time before the connection is made. However, it outlines the logical procedure involved in setting up a call, and the reader may wish to develop the diagram to outline the actions of clearing down the connection and what should happen when the line is tested and is not free. The rest of this

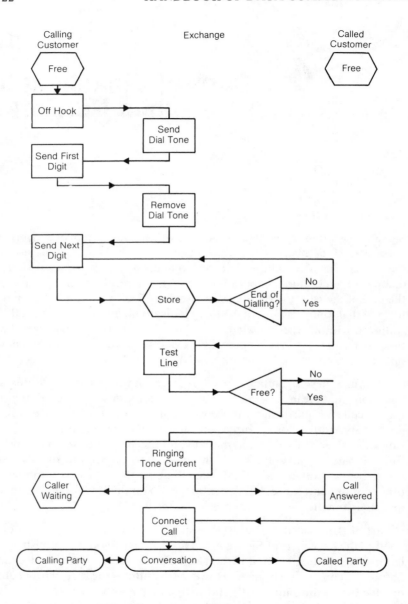

Figure 4.1   Start Transmission Diagram

chapter will briefly review signalling arrangements in the public network concentrating on the requirements of the voice network.

THE TELEPHONE INSTRUMENT

The transition from the acoustic world of man to the electronic world of telecommunications is achieved by the telephone instrument itself.

Each telephone instrument, in a simple telephone network, is normally connected by a 2-wire circuit to the nearest switching unit or exchange. Originally each telephone was provided with a local battery to power the instrument; however, the present method uses a 'central battery' to provide the DC power for the exchange and associated customers' telephone instruments.

The telephone consists of two 'transducers', ie power-transforming devices inserted between electrical, mechanical or acoustic points of a communications system, which convert the air pressure waves of sound to electrical impulses (the transmitter) and vice versa (the receiver). The standard transmitter used within the UK is the carbon granule microphone (see Figure 4.2) comprising a diaphragm which vibrates in sympathy with sound waves and causes variations of electrical pressure on carbon granules contained in a capsule. These pressure variations alter the electrical resistance of the granules so that the current from the central battery at the exchange varies in sympathy with the sound. The result is an AC signal superimposed on the DC line which is an analogue

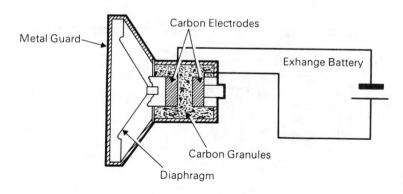

Figure 4.2   Telephone Transmitter

of the sound waveforms. The carbon granule microphone is robust, cheap and does not require an amplifier in the telephone. It does, however, have a number of disadvantages including:

— non-linear characteristics, with a lower sensitivity to lower sound levels than higher ones, resulting in signal distortion;

— sensitivity increases with increasing feed current, giving greater output on short lines;

— a wide spread of characteristics, which also change with time;

— generation of noise, which increases with age and use.

Major studies have been taking place for some time by British Telecom and other administrations to seek a replacement for the carbon microphone. A strong contender is the electret microphone, an electret being a material which, after receiving an electrical charge, retains that charge or a proportion of it. The variable pressure of sound waves on a diaphragm alters the distance between the electret material and a conducting plate in the microphone which in turn varies the electrical output from the device.

In reverse, variations in electrical current in a line are passed through small magnetic coils in the receiver (Figure 4.3) which vary the magnetic attraction of a diaphragm. This vibrates in response, generating pressure waves in the air which are a sound analogue of the electrical waveforms.

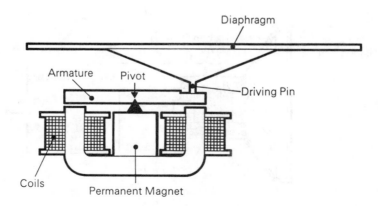

Figure 4.3   Telephone Receiver

The Telephone Dial

The telephone dial is a signalling device which simply makes and breaks the line current, or exchange loop, and sends pulses of direct current to the exchange. The pulses generated by the pulsing springs of the dial are used to control the operation of exchange equipment to establish a connection between the caller and called subscriber.

Relay A in Figure 4.4 will be operated for the duration of the time that the pulsing spring contacts are closed. When the dial is operated, say, for digit 3, the spring will make and break three times as the dial returns to the normal, and relay A will accordingly release and re-operate 3 times. The dial is arranged to generate pulses at a speed of 10 pulses per second; no pulses are sent during the forwards action (winding up) of the dial. The signalling, known as loop-disconnect, is 'anisochronous', ie the make and break signals have different durations – $33\frac{1}{3}$ millisecond 'make' and $66\frac{2}{3}$ millisecond 'break'. There must be a delay between the series of pulses (pulse trains) so that the switching equipment at the exchanges is given time to operate. This 'inter-train pause' (of some 700 milliseconds) is made up of the time it takes for the user to select the next digit and rotate the dial and also an inbuilt or 'lost motion' period in the dial mechanism.

The Pushbutton Telephone (PBT)

The Push Button Telephone has a keypad to replace the conventional dial. Although more convenient to use, it does not reduce the time

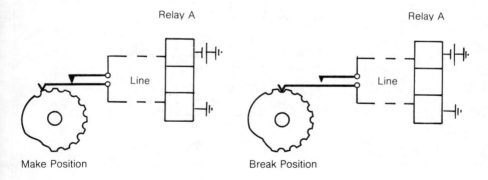

Make Position   Break Position

Figure 4.4

involved in setting up a call because it simply stores the keyed digits and retransmits them to line as standard loop-disconnect pulses with an inter-train pause between each digit. A user must wait several seconds after keying information while the store and forward circuitry in the keypad pulses out the information to the exchange.

Multi-Frequency (MF) Telephones

One method of increasing the rate of information transfer is by use of a multi-frequency (MF) telephone signalling to exchanges which are capable of high speed operation, eg Crossbar and Electronic and System X. The keypads use an international standard for layout and signalling codes (Figure 4.5). A '2 out of 8' signalling system is used based on the following frequencies:

Group 1:   697, 770, 852, 941 Hz

Group 2:   1209, 1336, 1477, 1633 Hz.

Depression of a key will transmit the two tones for the row and column in which the button lies. For example, if key 5 were pressed, frequencies 770 Hz and 1336 Hz would be transmitted to line, detected at the exchange and the digit determined. The typical duration of a signal, which

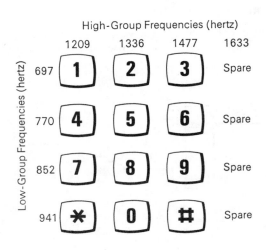

Figure 4.5   Multi-Frequency (MF) Keypad Layout

can be heard simultaneously in the receiver, is 33 ms. The tones are generated in the telephone by oscillators powered from the local line feed from the exchange.

The * and # are extra codes which may be used to increase the signalling repertoire from the telephone to the exchange for the provision of special services. These buttons are now commonly used with electronic Private Automatic Branch Exchanges (PABXs) to provide extension telephone facilities such as:

— short code dialling;

— call diversion;

— transfer;

— pick-up, etc.

SIGNALLING

Signalling is the transfer of control information from an interface at one end of a transmission line to an interface at the other end. The interface can be a terminal instrument (telephone) or an exchange relay set.

The basic information required to control a connection comprises:

— seize (or call);

— answer;

— clear (terminate).

In addition, routeing information (dialling) can be passed over a transmission link.

Different methods of signalling are used throughout a network, depending on:

— terminal apparatus;

— the transmission plant used;

— the economics of one signalling method compared to another.

The original distinction on terminal apparatus was whether it was manual or automatic. The original manual boards used a form of signalling called 'generator' signalling because the signalling was affected by the hand operation of an AC generator to supply ringing current. The original manual signal lines even required a 'ringdown' signal to be generated by the operator at the end of a call. All signalling systems within the UK network now use 'automatic' signalling, the necessary signals to set up and release a circuit being provided automatically by the exchange equipment.

The simplest forms of automatic signalling and hence the most economic, are termed direct current (DC) signalling. More complex signalling systems use alternating current (AC) or separate channel signalling.

DC Signalling

This type of signalling, like the signalling from a telephone to the exchange, relies on the provision of a discrete metallic path through the transmission link itself, the metallic path being provided by a pair of wires in a cable.

Loop-disconnect signalling is the standard system used in the local network. Seizure is carried out by applying a 'loop' across the line to operate an 'A' relay in the exchange relay set. Routeing information is

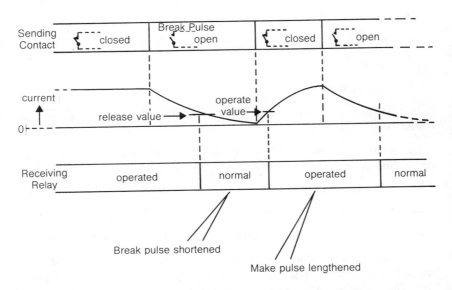

Figure 4.6   Loop-Disconnect Pulse Distortion

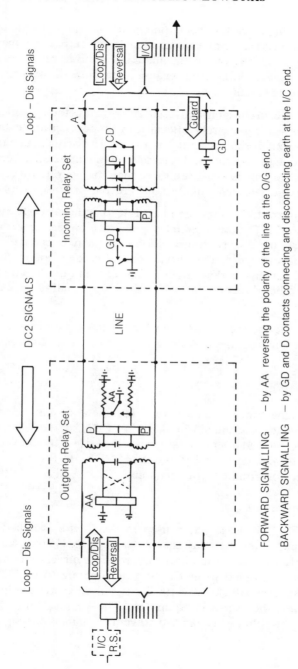

FORWARD SIGNALLING – by AA reversing the polarity of the line at the O/G end.

BACKWARD SIGNALLING – by GD and D contacts connecting and disconnecting earth at the I/C end.

Figure 4.7 DC2 Signalling

sent by transmitting loop-disconnect pulses at the rate of 10 pulses per second. The system is used either for terminal to exchange or exchange to exchange signalling. This type of signalling is limited to relatively short lines, for inter-exchange signalling, because of the pulse distortion caused by line capacitance (Figure 4.6).

Line capacitance, in charging and discharging, delays the operation and release of the pulse receiving relay. Because the impedance at the sending end is a short-circuit during the 'make' period and a disconnection during the 'break' period, the operate and release times are affected differently. In fact, the release time is increased more than the operate time, which results in the pulse rate being altered, ie it results in pulse distortion.

Signalling System DC2 is the standard UK long distance DC pulsing system (Figure 4.7). The outgoing relay converts loop disconnect pulses into double-current pulses for transmission over the line, and the incoming relay set converts the double current pulses back to loop-disconnect pulses. Double current working signifies 'current in one direction' and 'current in the other direction' instead of the loop signalling of 'current' and 'no current'.

The pulse repetition elements employ Carpenter polarised relays which are very sensitive and introduce very little overall distortion into the system.

AC Signalling

In-band AC signalling is used where a DC metallic path cannot be provided within the transmission link, eg on FDM systems. Signalling information is conveyed in sinusoidal tones injected into the transmission channel. Systems can be provided as either 2VF or 1VF versions, 1VF being preferred for simplicity and economy.

Signalling System AC9

AC9 is a 1VF (2280 Hz) system used in the 2-wire switched trunk network. Circuits enter the relay sets in 4-wire form (Figure 4.8). The 2280 Hz signals are transmitted in the appropriate direction to activate the VF receiver, designed so that it does not operate to the 2280 Hz contained in speech, which converts the signal to corresponding DC signals to operate the exchange equipment. The VF receiver also has a buffer amplifier to split the line and so prevent VF signals passing via the

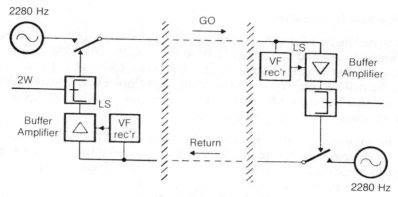

Figure 4.8   1VF Signalling

2-wire exchange connection to the next link of a multi-link connection. The buffer amplifier also isolates the VF receiver from 2-wire noise during signalling.

Signalling System AC11

AC11 is the 1VF (2280 Hz) system used in the 4-wire switched transit network. The main difference between AC11 and AC9 is that with AC11 pulsing information is not transmitted, as routeing information takes place between registers using MF2.

Multi-Frequency (MF) Signalling

Details of the MF2 signalling system are contained in a Chapter 6.

Out-Band AC Signalling

This form of signalling conveys information by tones transmitted outside of the speech band (300-3400 Hz). It is used mainly on older types of FDM transmission using a tone of 3825 Hz. As signalling and speech are separated (by filtration) out-band signalling arrangements are simpler than in-band and do not have to guard against speech interference problems.

Although out-band signalling is 'separate' from its speech channel (but still within a 4 kHz channel) it requires, like all the other signalling systems mentioned, separate relay sets for each channel.

Time Slot 16 Signalling

A signalling unit for a PCM system provides an interface between telephone exchange equipment and a PCM multiplexer. The PCM signalling unit may simply extend a speech circuit equipped with an in-band voice VF signalling system, or it may additionally process and extend any associated DC signalling activity. (The frame structure of a 30-channel PCM system was described in Chapter 2.)

Signalling information is conveyed in TS16, each 8 bits being allocated to 2 channels (4 bits for each channel). To cater for the signalling requirements of all 30 channels, TS16 is sub-multiplexed over a period of 16 frames (0-15), the period being known as multiframe. The 8 bits within TS16 are transmitted at the 2.048 Mbit/s rate so that each channel has an overall signalling rate of 3 kbit/s.

Separate Channel Signalling

The requirement to provide a separate signalling interface for each transmission channel in a network is an expensive overhead. It can represent up to 25% of the total cost. The provision of a signalling system which overcomes the need for channel associated signalling is economically (and technically) attractive.

Common Channel Signalling

Common Channel Signalling, as used on System X, is a method of signalling in which a single link carries the signalling information for many traffic circuits (typically 960 circuits). The information is carried by labelled messages in a signalling link between exchange processors (Figure 4.9). The advantages of such a system are:

—   it is efficient in use of exchange processor power;

—   there is an increase in signalling repertoire capability, leading to an increase in customer facilities;

—   high-speed signalling reduces post-dialling delay;

—   inherent flexibility of processor control allows alterations to be undertaken to cater for future signalling requirements;

—   there is a greater independence between the signalling and transmission systems;

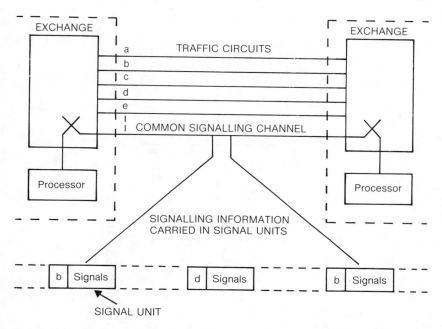

Note: Each signal unit carries a number of signals and the identity of the traffic involved

Figure 4.9   Common Channel Signalling

— error correction can be built into the system;

— it is very economic on large routes.

The fundamental principle of the structure of the signalling system is the division of functions into a common message transfer part and separate user parts for different users. This is illustrated in Figure 4.10.

The overall function of the message transfer part is to serve as a transport system providing reliable transfer of signalling messages between the locations of communicating user functions.

A user part defines the functions and procedures of the signalling system that are particular to a certain type of user of the system. The extent of the user part functions may differ significantly between different categories of users of the system.

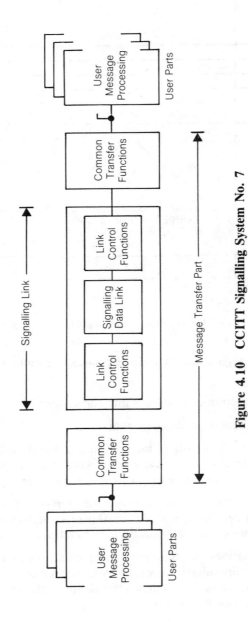

Figure 4.10 CCITT Signalling System No. 7

Flag	Retransmission Control	User Identity	Label	User Information	Check Bits	Flag

Figure 4.11

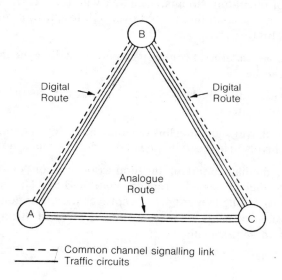

- - - - Common channel signalling link
———— Traffic circuits

Notes: Traffic circuits A-B and B-C served by associated signalling. Traffic circuits A-C served by quasi-associated signalling via B, which acts as a signal transfer point.

Figure 4.12   Associated and Quasi-Associated Signalling

Messages generated by user parts of an exchange, typically call processing, are queued by the Message Transfer for transmission over a common signalling link. Each message is therefore labelled to identify the particular route and circuit to which it belongs. Messages are transmitted in the form of signal units (Figure 4.11) and because the user information element is variable the length of each signal unit will vary and must be delimited by 'flags'.

Each signalling unit contains check bits to allow the receiving terminal to detect errors, caused by any disturbances in the signalling data link, at which point a request for retransmission is made.

The system operates at 64 kbit/s using the total signalling capability of TS16 of a 32-channel PCM system. The TS16 cannot then be used for the channel-associated form of signalling.

As the 64 kbit/s link has the capability to carry signalling messages for hundreds of telephony circuits, each link will, for security purposes, be backed up by a second link routed over a different transmission link to that of the first.

The flexible routeing of common channel signalling means that signalling links can be:

—   installed directly between 2 exchanges, ie associated with the traffic route, or

—   passed over signalling links in tandem via intermediate exchanges not involved in the switching of the traffic route, ie non-associated.

The intermediate point of the non-associated or 'quasi-associated' mode is termed a Signal Transfer Point (STP). The use of quasi-associated signalling (Figure 4.12) improves the utilisation of signalling links between exchanges and can also be invoked during congestion conditions on an associated path.

5 Switching Principles

INTRODUCTION

A basic requirement in a communications network connecting a number of users or devices having a need or the potential to communicate with one another is to provide this interconnection or switching capability. This applies equally to telephony and data communications.

In this chapter we examine various ways of achieving this. The most familiar form of switching, and the one with the longest history, is circuit switching employed in the PSTN.

The discussion starts with this, reviewing in the process the two major trends in circuit switching technology: the move from manual to automatic operation and from electromechanical to electronic and stored program exchanges.

In the latter part of the chapter we discuss switching principles in somewhat more generality, and describe two other approaches which differ significantly from circuit switching. These are message switching and packet switching.

CIRCUIT SWITCHING

The simplest method of providing interconnection economically between a number of points is to provide some form of circuit switching. The PSTN and the Telex networks are both examples of this type of switching whereby circuits are connected together for the duration of a call and then released.

The economies to be gained by this method are fairly obvious and it will

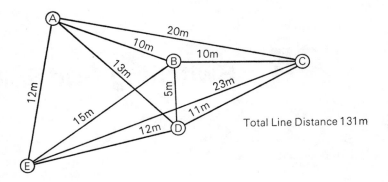

Total Line Distance 131m

Figure 5.1 (a)   Point-to-Point System

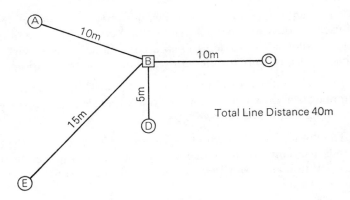

Total Line Distance 40m

Figure 5.1 (b)   Circuit-Switched System

be seen from Figure 5.1(a) and (b) that line costs can be saved in this way even in small networks.

There is clearly a trade-off between the saving in line costs and the costs of switching. However, total savings can be considerable where many points are to be connected over long distances. A major disadvantage of circuit switching is the poor circuit utilisation – particularly where single circuits are used. A good deal of personal and circuit time may be wasted trying to establish a connection, particularly in busy periods. For example, in Figure 5.1(b), A may have a number of messages for C but may have difficulty getting through, having no indication when C becomes

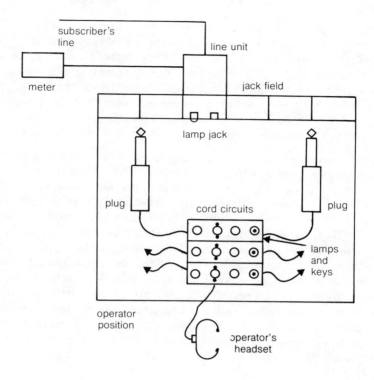

Figure 5.2   Manual Position

free. Indeed, while A is trying to reach C, C might be trying to call A; circumstances which are familiar to all telephone users. An advantage of circuit switching is that once a call is established, instant communication can be given between operators for the duration of a call.

We shall now review the evolution of circuit switching and the techniques employed.

Manual Switching

At a manually operated telephone exchange, subscribers' lines, or junction lines to other exchanges, were terminated on jacks on a switchboard. In addition to the jacks, the switchboard was equipped with indicators, plug-ended flexible conductors, terminal cords, and keys to enable an operator to interrogate and control subscribers' lines on that board. The call control, ie the operator, was able, at the verbal request of the calling subscriber to connect the appropriate jacks together by the cord circuits to establish the required connection. An associated counting meter was used to record the number of local calls connected so that a subscriber could be charged accordingly (Figure 5.2). With early exchanges the number of telephone users was such that a switchboard with one or two operators' positions was sufficient.

The operating procedure was simple because all jacks and indicators were within sight and reach of each operator. Complications arose as the telephone system grew and extra positions were added to accommodate the increasing number of subscribers. The problem of completing a connection between two subscribers at opposite ends of the switchboard was initially resolved by means of 'transfer circuits' between positions, but this arrangement was soon found to be inefficient in use of operators and equipment and to be extremely cumbersome. The major advance in switchboard design was the provision of the multiple system where each subscriber's line was connected to a number of jacks, one of which was associated with the calling indicator and a label on which was engraved the subscriber's number. The remaining jacks, known as multiple jacks, were positioned around the switchboard so that at least one of them was within reach of any operator (Figure 5.3).

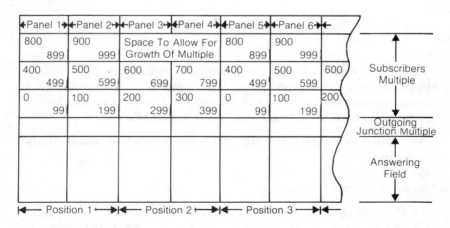

Figure 5.3 Switchboard Multiple

In terms of control features and user facilities, the manual system was almost ideal:

— operators could be varied to suit traffic conditions;

— communication including numerical information from subscriber to exchange and vice versa was verbal, thereby giving minimum inconvenience to the subscriber;

— interpretation of commands was carried out by human operator who, although when first 'installed' was slow and cumbersome, had enormous learning, translation and self-development capabilities;

— connection of calls was physically carried out, by means of plugs and jacks, by the operator who instinctively tested circuits, avoided faulty connections and re-routed calls as required;

— where congestion or blocking of the system occurred through busy connections, 'delay working' was employed whereby the operator recalled the calling subscriber once the connection could be completed;

— in large exchanges a supervisor's position controlled and upgraded other parts of the system, ie the operators, to ensure smooth functioning of the exchange.

Obviously the performance of the exchange was heavily dependent on the ability of the central control operators but it was reasons of security and cost that led to an early desire to replace operators.

Automatic Telephone Systems

In order to replace a manual system with an automatic system it is important to consider the basic features that have to be incorporated:

— apparatus must be provided at the exchange to respond to signals from the subscriber's instrument;

— the exchange apparatus must select free equipment and route the call to the required connection;

— a signal (ringing current) must be applied to the called instrument to ring the subscriber's bell;

— when the called subscriber answers, the ringing current must be disconnected, a circuit completed for conversation, and the calling subscriber's meter operated so that a charge may be raised for the call;

— the automatic apparatus required for the speech path must be held in position during the setting-up period and throughout the period of conversation;

— an engaged line must be guarded against intrusion to prevent 'double connections';

— at the end of the call, the automatic apparatus must be released in order that it may be used by other subscribers.

Such a system, which permits two-way transmission between terminals when the call has been established, is said to be circuit-switched.

Strowger

The first true automatic switching system to be commercially practicable was patented in 1879 by Almon Brown Strowger, a gentleman of original mind and unorthodox habit who was at that time an undertaker in Kansas City. It is alleged that he discovered that local telephone operators were diverting his calls to other undertakers, thus losing him business, and he wished to devise a system that would not be so misused. The first Strowger exchange was installed in 1892 with much of the credit for the success of the Strowger switch belonging to those who developed the original idea to a workable form.

The Uniselector

The Uniselector is a selector in which the wiper assembly moves in one plane only and includes wipers which rotate about a central shaft and wipe over a series of contacts set radially in a bank. The bank may consist of from 3 to 10 rows of contacts and each row is provided with individual contacts equally spaced over the arc. Figure 5.4 shows a 10 contact uniselector.

The uniselector provides a cheap concentration stage for connecting subscribers to the first set of two-motion selectors.

The Two-Motion Switch

The two-motion switch is the basic unit of the Strowger System.

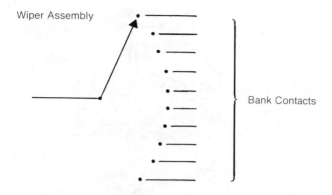

Wiper Assembly

Bank Contacts

Figure 5.4   10 Contact Uniselector

The two-motion selector is a typical intermediate or 'group' selector and can, as the name implies, be moved in two planes. Vertical motion is controlled by digits transmitted from a dial, and horizontal 'hunting' over the 'dialled' level, to select a free outlet to the next switching stage, occurs during the inter-train pause. As each switch is controlled individually by digits transmitted over the speech pair from the subscriber's dial this system is often referred to as dispersed control. The call progresses step-by-step as each selector in turn is activated by the routeing information sent by the subscriber. At no time could the route selection process take account of the possibility of encountering busy at a later selection stage.

Figure 5.5 shows one bank of a simple two-motion selector which consists of ten semicircular 'levels' each with ten contacts or 'outlets' giving a total of 100 outlets. The capacity of the switch may be doubled to 200 outlets by providing each level of the selector bank with double contacts at each outlet separated by insulation material, so that the wiper will hunt over odd and even outlets for the respective upper and lower wiper contact.

Director Systems

As the telephone system expanded, routeing of calls through step-by-step Strowger exchanges in metropolitan areas became very complex. The destination exchange routeing code could vary depending on the originat-

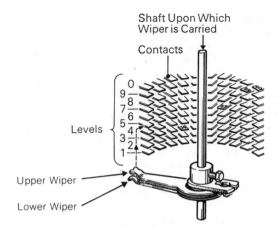

Figure 5.5   Two-Motion Selector (Strowger)

ing point of the call. In some of the largest cities of the UK – London, Birmingham, Edinburgh, Glasgow and Liverpool – the non-director system became impracticable and uneconomic for the then Post Office because of the large number of exchanges required (263 in London) and the complex junction network required to provide a linked numbering scheme.

The Director system was installed to overcome these difficulties and provide linked numbering scheme working by introducing a degree of intelligence into the exchange that would translate the digits dialled by the subscriber into a number that would efficiently complete the connection.

The translation function varied from exchange to exchange so that the dialled number was standard and independent of the origin of the call and greater flexibility was possible in the junction network. The original version of the equipment incorporated in step-by-step Strowger was termed a Director, or register translator system.

The Director equipment was only involved during the setting up and routeing of the call and not for the duration of the connection. The equipment was therefore referred to as short holding time equipment as it was released after the last numerical digit was transmitted and thereby became available for routeing other calls.

Director equipment was, as with the non-director systems, not capable of taking account of the possibility of encountering busy at a later stage of selection as it still employed dispersed control for the step-by-step routeing of a call. Improvements in this area did not come about until the introduction of common control.

COMMON CONTROL

Crossbar Exchanges

Crossbar systems, like the Strowger system, employ electromechanical technology and space-division multiplexing. In a space-division exchange each call is connected via a physical path which is maintained for its exclusive use for the duration of the call. The term space-division is derived from the spatial separation of each connecting circuit.

The crossbar switch, which is in effect a multiple relay, was developed from a 1916 American patent by Reynolds, with the first public crossbar exchange in Sweden being opened in 1926. Development in America resulted in crossbar exchanges being opened in Brooklyn and Manhattan in 1938, and subsequently being standardised for large metropolitan areas.

The UK Post Office in the late 1950s expected to progress directly from Strowger to electronic-based systems. This did not happen and as a result crossbar systems were installed in quantity in the 1960s as an intermediate technology between Strowger and electronic exchanges, to provide greater reliability and improved quality of service within the telephone network. Common control also marked the beginning of the return to a standard of service previously provided by manual systems by using faster operating equipment and more centralised control features than used in Strowger.

Crossbar Switch and Exchanges

The crossbar switch uses fixed precious metal contacts and has advantages over the sliding base metal contacts used in Strowger, including absence of microphonic noise, greater reliability and faster operation. The interconnecting network or switching matrix of a crossbar switch can be represented diagrammatically by a series of horizontal and vertical lines (Figure 5.6). The corner of each square represents a crosspoint at which a horizontal inlet can be connected to a vertical outlet if required.

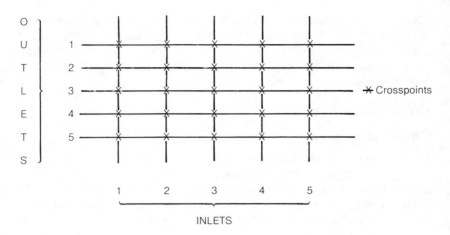

Figure 5.6

To connect inlet (2) and outlet (4) of the matrix the crosspoint is operated where the inlet and outlet wires cross one another at co-ordinate (2,4).

A multi-switch can enable any one of, for example, 22 inlets to be connected to any one of 28 outlets by means of 22 vertical switch assemblies each fitted with 28 spring sets (see Figure 5.7).

The principle of operation is that the horizontal select bar operates first to prime the required outlet by moving the select finger in front of the lifting spring, followed by the operation of the vertical operating bar associated with the inlet, which traps the select finger causing the spring-set of the crosspoint to make. The horizontal bar is then released, leaving the spring-mounted select finger trapped in position and, thus, allowing the second outlet associated with the horizontal bar to be used in conjunction with another inlet. The crosspoint contact, although open to the atmosphere, is established between precious metals and, because of its physical design, is more reliable than the Strowger system.

The much simpler design of the crossbar switch generates little mechanical vibration. Its comparatively fast switching ability allows the established path to be tested, which enables repeat attempt facilities to be provided.

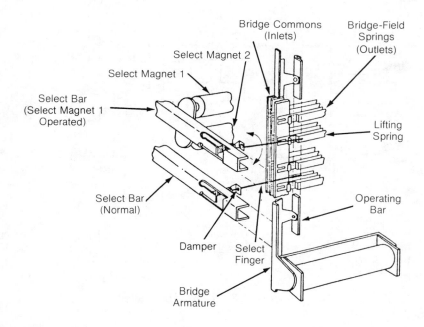

Figure 5.7 Principle of Operation of Crossbar Switch

Crossbar switches are expensive and various trunking techniques have been devised to economise on contact provision. The interconnection of the various stages of switches does not take place in a step-by-step, or stage-by-stage, sequence, but instead a common control quickly interrogates the paths through the various stages using 'by-path' or 'information highways', and establishes a connection having monitored and assessed the system state.

The control equipment is provided on a common basis in order to:

— reduce the overall cost;

— make more effective use of short hold equipment which is only used for call set-up;

— centralise control.

However, by centralising the equipment it becomes a reliability hazard in that any malfunction in common equipment can seriously affect a large

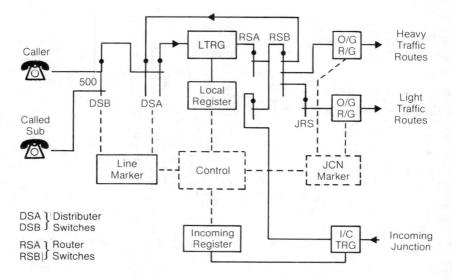

Figure 5.8   TXK 1 Exchange

number of calls. Great emphasis is therefore placed on system reliability which is independent of component reliability by constructing each crossbar switch and associated relays as self-contained units and using the self-steering method of control. During the setting up of a call, if a faulty component or outlet is met in a part of the system, the effective switch train is immediately released, the call is automatically set-up again over an alternative path, and the faulty connection is logged.

Figure 5.8 shows the switching arrangements for a crossbar TXK 1 exchange manufactured by Plessey.

Each crossbar switch consists of 10 inlets x 26 or 28 outlets. Exchanges are built of line distributor groups each serving up to 500 subscriber lines and main routes each carrying up to 100 Erlangs of traffic.

Note: An Erlang (E), is a dimensionless measurement of telecommunications traffic where E = ah. The value of a is taken to be the rate at which calls are connected and h is the mean holding time of calls.

The transmission relay group (TRG) provides:

— a transmission bridge;

— battery feed to subscribers;

— tones, ringing and supervisory signals;

— connection to a register for setting up a call.

A caller, on an own exchange call, is connected through the DSB and DSA switches to a Local Transmission Relay Group (LTRG) under the control of the Line Marker. The LTRG obtains a free Local Register which connects dial tone to the caller and receives his dialled digits. When all digits are stored the Local Register obtains a Control equipment and signals the wanted numbers to it. The Control seizes the appropriate Line Marker and through it tests the called subscriber's line which: if busy, Control returns busy tone; if spare number unobtainable, (NU) is returned; and if free, Control marks the Called Subscriber's DSB outlet and the DSB marks all its available inlets to DSA. This 'self-steering' process continues from DSAs to RSBs and from RSBs to the primed RSA. The path is then switched and tested, the Control and Local Register released and ringing, ringing tone and metering are effected from the LTRG.

TXK 3 Crossbar

Since the late 1960s local director exchanges have been expanded and modernised with ST & C large crossbar (basic switch 22 inlets x 28 outlets) equipment coded as TXK 3. This is a common control system using common highways for the fast transfer of information within the system. Exchange units of up to 20,000 directory numbers are possible.

Reed-Relay Exchanges

The British Post Office in the 1950s and 1960s devoted considerable time and effort to developing electronic circuits employing valves, cold-cathode tubes and semiconductors for certain control functions in Strowger and crossbar exchanges. It was not until the development of the transistor and the reed relay that an electronic controlled exchange system became a practicable and economic proposition. The attractions of an electronic exchange are:

— with the exception of the sophisticated electromechanical reed relays there are no moving parts; therefore the equipment is not subject to mechanical wear, nor does it require lubrication and/or mechanical adjustment;

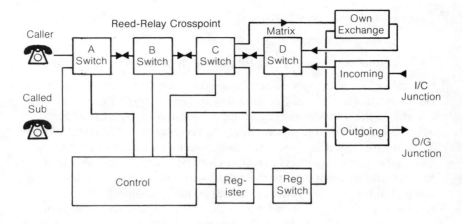

Figure 5.9   TXE 2 Trunking

— electronic equipment can take up less space than equivalent electromechanical systems;

— sophisticated control equipment can offer an increased range of
   facilities to users and the telephone administration;

— increased reliability by using solid-state components;

— high speed operation.

TXE 2

The small electronic exchange TXE 2 was introduced from 1966 in
non-director areas for use as a local exchange with a self-contained
numbering scheme or as a satellite exchange in a linked numbering
scheme. The exchange capacity is between 2000-40,000 subscribers.
Figure 5.9 shows the main components and trunking of a TXE 2
exchange.

For an own exchange call, a caller is initially connected via A, B and C
switches to the most often used supervisory relay set, eg outgoing. A free
register is connected to the supervisory relay set via the Register Switch,
dial tone is returned to the caller who dials the first digit which is stored in
the Register. This digit is recognised as an own exchange call and during
the inter-digital pause the supervisory relay set is changed from outgoing

to own exchange type. The caller dials the rest of the number into the Register which asks Control to set up a path through the D, C, and A switches to the called number. When the connection is made and tested the Control and Register release.

The control equipment can only deal with one call at a time but such is its speed of operation that this is no limitation on a small exchange. This element is however crucial to the operation of the exchange and is therefore duplicated to guard against failure.

TXE 4

The preferred system for replacement of local directory exchanges is the large TXE 4 reed electronic common control exchange. This exchange shown in Figure 5.10 is a space-division system catering for up to 40,000 directory numbers and:

— uses scanners to detect change of status and signalling on subscribers' lines and junction circuits;

— controls the matrix switching of the reed relays by following a logic which is pre-set or 'wired' within the control circuitry.

During development of the TXE 4 system it became obvious that, with changing technology, there were possibilities for cost reduction and sys-

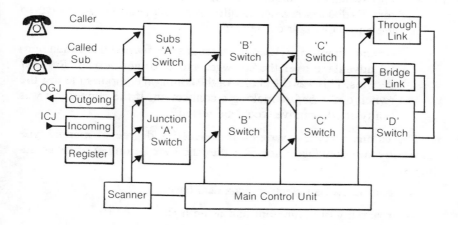

Figure 5.10   TXE 4 Trunking

tem enhancement. The result of further development was the production of the TXE 4A system which amongst other features uses large-scale integration MOS shift registers and RAM/ROM stores compared to basic threaded wire stores of the TXE 4.

Stored Program Control

It would be fair to say that ever since the first automatic systems were introduced into a telephone network all subsequent developments have been leading to a return to the flexibility and central control features available with a good manual operator system. It would of course be foolish to believe that a manually controlled telephone network could meet the demands of the large public network systems now installed throughout the world. However, to prove the point about the manual system a review of the switching techniques already covered would be useful:

— manual systems provided great flexibility, used the spoken word for signalling, had inbuilt learning capability and a high degree of intelligence;

— Strowger used dispersed control under the direct influence of the customer signalling to each switching stage by means of a dial;

— register control permitted a degree of intelligence to be introduced into switching. Unique exchange codes transmitted by the customer's dial to a register resulted in translations to route the call to the correct distant exchange;

— common control, as used in crossbar systems, had one fundamental advantage over the Strowger and Strowger-derived Register systems. This was the ability of the common equipment to test the switch outlet *before* making a connection. If the connection was faulty an alternative would be tested.

The common control systems introduced a degree of manual-type flexibility into exchanges; however they did have a number of disadvantages:

— control had an electromechanical base;

— reliability of equipment had to be high;

— fault location could be complex;

— system flexibility was not perfect, particularly where changes to routeing translations were required;

— exchange growth could not be catered for in an economic manner.

A first step in overcoming these problems was to introduce a control system and switching mechanisms using the high-speed capabilities of electronic circuits. The switch mechanisms used a reed-relay matrix and registers were controlled in groups by electronic 'processors' containing the necessary thinking power. Translations of routeing information were obtained at high speed by the processors, on behalf of registers, from common translators. The translations and control used a wired logic array to carry out the functions, a translation change being made by altering only one or two wires in the whole of the exchange. Electronic scanners associated with the processor provided continuously updated information regarding performance at all the exchange terminations.

The wired logic processor was a vast improvement over common control but still suffered from degrees of inflexibility. The ability to base exchange control on computer logic is a further improvement.

The control functions setting up a call within an exchange follow clearly defined actions as outlined by the flowchart at the beginning of Chapter 4 (Figure 4.1). Every customer action requires an exchange response which is dependent on the:

— actions that have preceded it;

— type of equipment used;

— service required;

— actions allowed by the exchange administration.

In other words there is a logical sequence to controlling, setting up and clearing down calls within an exchange. It is therefore possible to hold the sequence of operations and instructions as a 'program' within a computer memory. This is the basis of stored program control (SPC).

The stored programs and their associated data are collectively termed 'software' in distinction to the 'hardware' which consists of printed circuit boards, racks, etc. The benefits of SPC are that new or modified facilities can be provided by software changes without recourse to hardware redesign or rearrangement. The range of facilities given to customers can be greatly increased, especially with the advent of inter-processor signalling, and closely approaches the facilities of manual systems, with the provision of features such as call diversion, follow-me, ring back when free, etc. An additional major advantage is the ability of the SPC equipment to routinely check itself and all major functions within an exchange to minimise call failures.

Of course all these features cannot be obtained without some penalties, the main one being that although the computer performs relatively simple processes it has to carry out the processes involving large numbers of inputs under very severe 'real time' constraints. Reliability, duplication, changeover and processor architectures must all be investigated and taken account of in the design of an SPC exchange.

DIGITAL SWITCHING

The cost per channel for transmission equipment has shown a continual decline as new technology, and the move to time division multiplexing, has allowed more and more circuits to use the same transmission medium. In contrast, telephone exchanges, even with the advent of SPC, have remained primitive in the way in which the routeing of a call requires the exclusive use of a set of switches and contacts for the duration of the call. The development of digital techniques, and low cost crosspoint devices, now offers the ability to move from space switching techniques to time switching techniques.

Digital Crosspoints

For many years the reed relay was the only cost effective device that could be employed as a crosspoint in electronic exchanges. Various electronic components were tested for crosspoint use in analogue space switching exchanges but all encountered the same problems:

— electrical linearity is required of a crosspoint to keep harmonic distortion of an analogue signal to a low level;

— semiconductors must have a very high 'off' resistance value, to prevent accumulative signal leakage through thousands of contacts in a switching matrix appearing as a high noise level;

— crosspoints must allow 50 volts DC to pass to feed the transducers in the telephone instrument and 75 volts AC to ring the telephone bell.

However, the use of semiconductor devices as crosspoints has become more attractive to exchange designers due to the availability of low-cost, large scale integration (LSI) devices and the economic benefits of integrating digital transmissions with digital switching systems. Digital switching systems can use electronic crosspoints because the analogue voice signals are converted to binary digital signals and switched digitally using time-sharing techniques. Linearity and off resistance are no longer important because there are only two signal levels.

Terminations on a Digital Switch

A digital switch must provide a capability to terminate both analogue and digital (2.048 Mbit/s) junction and trunk circuits. In addition it must also provide an analogue/digital interface, and termination, for the telephone loop circuit. This can be a significant part of the total exchange costs as the termination must perform what is called the 'BORSCHT' functions which are:

— battery feed;

— overload protection;

— ringing for the telephone;

— signalling;

— clocking;

— hybrid (2- to 4-wire conversion);

— test access.

The digital switch must also provide filtering and digital conversion of functions.

Time Switching

Figure 5.11 is a simple representation of a time division switch. It consists of an analogue to digital converter and digital multiplexer with 6 connections, a delay circuit, or time slot interchanger, and a de-multiplexer with digital to analogue conversion.

Each circuit termination is allocated a time slot on the TDM highway. The switch is required to connect transmitted information from A on circuit 1 to circuit 5(B) and information from B on circuit 5 to circuit 1(A).

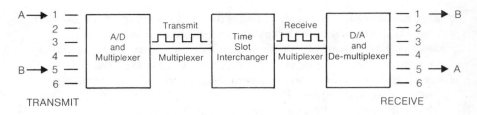

TRANSMIT   RECEIVE

Figure 5.11   Time Division Switching Principles

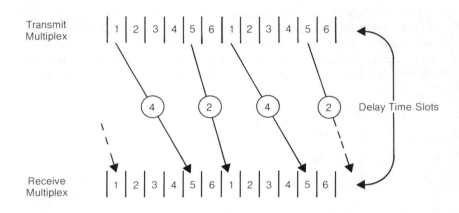

Figure 5.12   Time Slot Interchanging

The time slot interchanger delays time slot 1 by four time slot intervals to correspond with time slot 5 on the receive multiplex (Figure 5.12). Similarly B is delayed by two time intervals to transfer information from termination 5 to 1. Thus a 4-wire transmission path is established between terminations 1 and 5.

The actual delay introduced by a switching stage is not noticeable to the human ear until a number of TDM switches are connected in tandem, at which point the cumulative delay may become noticeable as echo. Careful network planning overcomes the problem.

The single stage time division switching network of Figure 5.12 had an equal number of time slots and terminations. Such a network would ensure non-blocking. ('Blocking' occurs when a free path is not immediately available between the required pair of inlets and outlets.) However, with a constant sampling rate the time interval for each time slot is inversely proportional to the number of terminations. A sampling rate of 8000 times a second means that each termination is examined once every $125\mu s$. With 10,000 terminations the duration of each time slot would be:

$$\frac{125 \times 10^{-6}s}{10,000} = 12.5 \times 10^{-9}s$$

Such a short interval would place severe constraints on memory access time for the delay circuit and tight delay controls would be required through gates and cables. The timing requirements can be reduced by increasing the number of stages in the network, and as a two-stage network is virtually as complex and expensive as a three-stage network, most large switch architectures use three or more stages.

Three-Stage Switching Structure

The choice of switch structure to be adopted with a digital exchange depends on:

— the circuit technology available;

— component power consumption;

— space required;

— the complexity of interstage connections;

— the digital transmission capacity of internal highways.

None of the above factors can be taken in isolation, but the trend in switching structures has been to use a combination of time and space switching.

TST

A time-space-time structure is shown in Figure 5.13 using, for simplicity, three digital channel inputs from two 30-channel PCM systems.

Each of the 30 incoming time slots places its 8-bit information into a buffer store in strict rotation. The contents of each buffer of the incoming time switch are then removed during a later time slot and passed down a highway to the space switch. During the same time interval, one electronic crosspoint is operated in the space switch and the information is

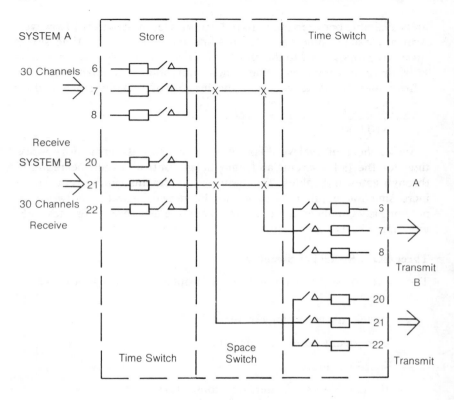

Figure 5.13   TST Network

transferred to the required outgoing time switch, and hence outgoing PCM system, where another electronic switch is operated to transfer the information into the buffer of the required outgoing time slot. At the correct time slot this information is then read out of store to the required time slot on the transmit highway of the PCM system.

The space switch crosspoint is only operated for a few microseconds during the time necessary to pass the information from the incoming to outgoing time switches. In the time interval between passing further information for the same call, the space switch will be used for interconnecting other inputs and outputs, thereby time-sharing the space switch.

A switching structure based on a space-time-space (STS) architecture can also be used; however the comparative component costs, physical layout, recent developments in LSI memories and the potential of future cost reductions tend to favour the time-space-time (TST) structure. Such a structure has been adopted by BT within their family of digital switching units embraced under the generic description of System X.

System X

Following the development of electronic exchanges (TXE 2, TXE 4) and SPC, on-going studies by BT and UK equipment suppliers highlighted a need for systems that would provide greater telecommunications facilities at an economic price. As a consequence, a new family of switching systems, under the family name System X, was defined, using:

— microelectronic technology;

— digital switching;

— SPC;

— common channel signalling;

— modular design.

System X is the central feature of an overall strategy to convert the whole of the existing analogue trunk network to digital by the early 1990s, thus paving the way for an expanding range of facilities and services for customers. During the same time frame a major programme to replace all large Strowger exchanges with System X will take place.

The System X Family

The exchanges of System X will be provided as a 'family' (Table 5.1). The family concept enables each member of the family to share common:

— equipment practice;

— technology standards;

— software standards;

— documentation and data base control schemes.

By adopting a modular approach to system architecture, each switching system can be assembled from a range of modular 'building bricks'. The

	Termination Capacity	Switch Capacity (switched erlangs)	Processing Capacity (busy-hour call attempts)
Multiplexer	24 or 30	4 or 5	
Concentrator	2,000	160	8,000
Small local exchanges	2,000	160	8,000
Medium local exchanges	10,000	2,000	80,000
Large local exchanges	60,000	10,000	500,000
Medium trunk exchanges	8,000	2,000	80,000
Large trunk exchanges	85,000	20,000	500,000
Medium international transit exchanges	8,000	2,000	50,000
Large international transit exchanges	85,000	20,000	400,000

Table 5.1   System X Operating Objectives

use of this modular approach means that it is possible to test, structure and change modules without interfering with other modules. In addition new generations of technology can be introduced into specific modules without disturbing the overall system architecture. The major modules, which are themselves built from smaller modules, are termed 'subsystems'.

Subsystems

A subsystem, which can consist of hardware and/or software, performs specified functions and interworks with other subsystems across well defined functional interfaces. Although a subsystem may be suitable for use in a number of switching systems, variations of the basic subsystem are required to cope economically with variations in sizes and facilities that are needed.

The principal hardware subsystems, most of which also have software handlers, are as follows:

— Subscriber Switching Subsystem: performs concentration of traffic from a number of infrequently used subscribers' lines onto heavily used common circuits at a local exchange;

— Digital Switching Subsystem: interconnects digital channels, with high traffic loadings, at interfaces that conform with internationally agreed standards;

— Message Transmission Subsystem: performs common channel signalling functions, with error correction;

— Signalling Interworking Subsystem: provides facilities for interworking with existing exchanges that use a diverse variety of channel-associated signalling systems. Also provides tones and recorded announcements;

— Analogue Line Terminating Subsystem: converts analogue transmission signals – speech and other waveforms – into digital form, and vice versa;

— Network Synchronisation Subsystem: ensures that an exchange operates at the same average bit rate as the synchronised network as a whole;

— Processor Subsystem: provides the data-processing facilities required for handling traffic and for controlling local and remote switching subsystems.

The software subsystems are stored and run on the processor subsystem under the control of the real-time operating system, and are outlined as follows:

— Call Processing Subsystem: controls the progress of each call on the basis of instructions sent by the caller;

— Call Accounting Subsystem: derives the charging information relating to each call;

— Maintenance Control Subsystem: diagnoses the cause of system malfunctions and provides guidance, as required, to the maintenance staff;

— Overload Control Subsystem: monitors the load imposed on the processor subsystem by other subsystems and, when necessary, attempts to avoid or minimise overloads by modifying the modes of operation of some or all of them;

— Management Statistics Subsystem: collects the basic traffic data needed for short and long term planning purposes;

— Multi-Party Connection Subsystem: enables three or more parties to participate in a telephone conversation;

— Automatic Announcement Subsystem: synthesises announce-

Hardware Subsystems

SSS   Subscriber Switching Subsystem
DSS   Digital Switching Subsystem
MTS   Message Transmission Subsystem
SIS   Signalling Interworking Subsystem
ALTS Analogue Line Terminating Subsystem
NSS   Network Synchronisation Subsystem
PS   Processor Subsystem

Software Subsystems

CPS   Call Processing Subsystem
CAS   Call Accounting Subsystem
MCS   Maintenance Control Subsystem
OCS   Overload Control Subsystem
MSS   Management Statistics Subsystem
AAS   Automatic Announcement Subsystem
MMIS Man/Machine Interface Subsystem
OS   Operating System (an integral part of the Processor Subsystem)

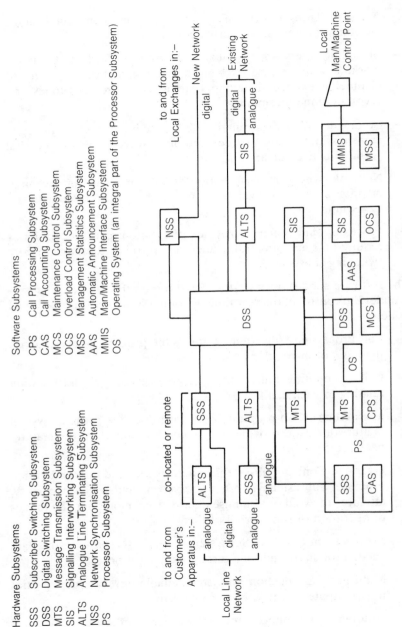

Figure 5.14   System X Local Exchange

Hardware Subsystems

DSS   Digital Switching Subsystem
MTS   Message Transmission Subsystem
SIS   Signalling Interworking Subsystem
ALTS   Analogue Line Terminating Subsystem
NSS   Network Synchronisation Subsystem
PS   Processor Subsystem

Software Subsystems

CPS   Call Processing Subsystem
MCS   Maintenance Control Subsystem
OCS   Overload Control Subsystem
MSS   Management Statistics Subsystem
MPCS   Multi-Party Connection Subsystem
MMIS   Man/Machine Interface Subsystem
OS   Operating System (an integral part of the Processor Subsystem)

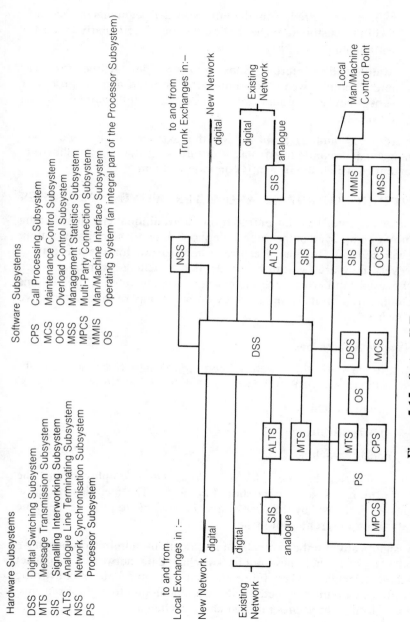

Figure 5.15   System X Trunk Exchange

ments, as required, from digitally recorded segments of speech to facilitate customer/exchange interactions, particularly those for certain supplementary services;

— Man/Machine Interface Subsystem: provides facilities for communication between the administration's staff and the processor subsystem for monitoring, controlling, and maintaining an exchange.

Figures 5.14 and 5.15 show how the System X local and trunk exchanges can be configured from the different subsystems, and illustrate the extent to which the design is common to them.

SWITCHING PRINCIPLES AND ALTERNATIVE APPROACHES

So far this chapter has concentrated on the traditional circuit switching technology employed in the public telephone network since its inception, and will continue to play a central role into the foreseeable future. However, there are two other well defined switching techniques which can be used, and which are increasingly coming to the fore. In this concluding part of the chapter we review and compare these alternative approaches.

Alternative Approaches

There are currently three well defined approaches which can be employed in the design of Public Switched Transmission Networks:

— circuit switching;

— message switching;

— packet switching.

The distinction between the *switching method* employed and the *facilities* offered by a network should be noted. The facilities are those properties perceived by the user. It may be possible to provide the same facility using different approaches.

A significant number of telecommunications administrations have decided to base their new public switched data networks on packet switching principles. Many, if not most, are also in favour of converting their present circuit switched PSTNs from analogue to digital transmission and using stored program switching exchanges.

BT has made a firm commitment to convert the existing PSTN to digital transmission and stored program switching, and long-term phased plans are in the process of being implemented. Since these new digital circuit switched networks offer a vastly improved performance in all respects compared with the analogue counterpart, at a superficial level it would appear paradoxical to be embarking on packet switching systems grafted onto existing analogue circuits.

To appreciate how this has come about it is necessary to look briefly at the history of telecommunications and parallel developments in technology over the last 15 years.

The practicability of packet switching was well established by the mid-1960s.

Although the underlying theory and practice of digitisation of speech had been well understood since the 1930s and the inherent advantages in conjunction with stored program exchanges were recognised, wholesale conversion of existing networks, using the technology currently available, presented severe technical and financial problems.

In the meantime, throughout the late 1960s and 1970s there was a growing clamour from users for improved services, more closely matched to computer requirements.

It was within this framework that the PTTs seriously began to consider packet switching as a technique for improving the existing services. A major advantage was that for quite a low capital expenditure such a network could be grafted onto the existing analogue network, and yet provide a better and more reliable service than the latter.

However, the mid-1970s onwards saw a significant change in the technical and financial relationships with the introduction of LSI and microprocessor techniques.

This has caused the PTTs to re-evaluate the economics of large-scale digitisation and, in a number of cases (as in the UK), has resulted in the announcement of firm intentions.

Although the present situation has been arrived at partly as the result of accidental influences and was not easily foreseeable, this should not be taken to imply that packet switching services will ultimately be rendered obsolescent by the new digital PSTN. The informed view is that, like PSTN and leased circuits, it is one of several alternative complementary services which differ in respect of performance, facilities offered, pricing structure, and therefore may be expected to meet different user requirements.

Circuit Switching

The chief characteristics of a circuit switched network are illustrated in Figures 5.16 to 5.18 and summarised below:

— A temporary sequence of fixed point-to-point circuits joined by switching exchanges is created;

— All the links and switches must be available for the full duration of the call or interaction;

— Following an initial call set-up delay, interaction is almost immediate (Figure 5.16);

— The called and calling parties must be simultaneously available;

— The interaction between the two parties occurs at a fixed transmission speed (Figure 5.17);

— The mechanics of the network are transparent to the users, who only need to be acquainted with the procedures for making a telephone call;

— As the load on the network increases, acceptance of calls is increasingly delayed (Figure 5.18).

We can cast further light on the discussion by referring to how people conduct a telephone conversation over the existing PSTN – although they could equally well be sitting at terminals. The way two people communi-

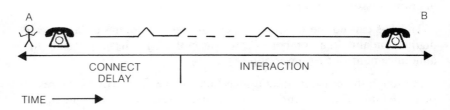

Figure 5.16　Sequence of Events in Making a Switched Call

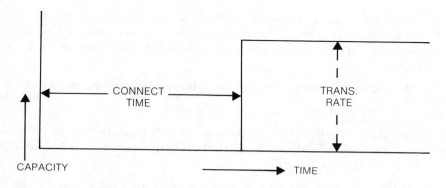

Figure 5.17   Capacity Utilisation

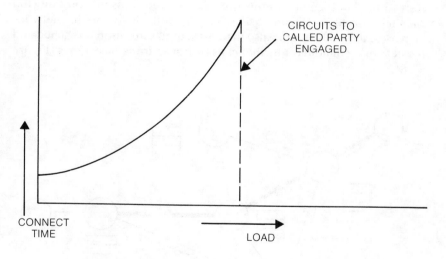

Figure 5.18   Behaviour Under Increasing Load

cate and interact depends almost entirely upon the delay inherent in the communication channel between them. This type of interaction involves:

— close conscious attention by both parties;

— minimum delays in exchanging information. Excessive delays would result in poor feedback and wandering of attention.

For a telephone call, the PSTN characteristics do not unduly restrict verbal communication. The call set-up procedure and connect time are acceptable. The direct connection permits almost immediate interaction (Figure 5.16).

But supposing one or other of the following circumstances applies:

— the called party is engaged (engaged tone);

— the network circuits and plant are heavily loaded or congested, so that one subscriber is unable to call another even though he is able to accept it.

In those cases the user will have to try again, thus increasing the call connect time. The diagrams further illustrate a number of the features described above. Following successful connection there is an immediate start to the interaction and this occurs at a fixed transmission rate (full channel capacity – Figure 5.17). As the total load on the network increases, the connect time also increases, until saturation is reached and the network will hold off further calls by transmitting busy tones (Figure 5.18).

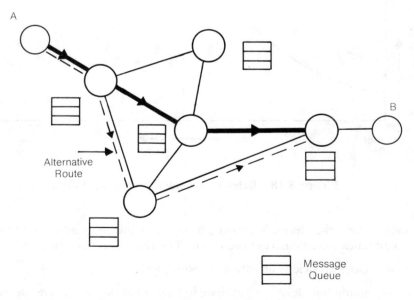

Figure 5.19   A Message Switching Network

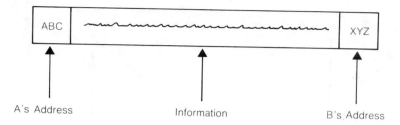

Figure 5.20   Message Format

Message Switching

Message switching is an entirely different form of communication from circuit switching. By exchanging messages the participants need not be simultaneously involved with each other, and the message transfer can take place when it is most convenient.

As with circuit switching, a message switching network comprises a number of point-to-point circuits connected by switching exchanges, each switching exchange being equipped with computer intelligence and memory within which messages are stored (see Figure 5.19). Each message contains within it the address of the destination and the address of its origin apart from the information to be transmitted (see Figure 5.20).

Each exchange inspects the address of the message's destination, and, providing that an outgoing circuit is free, forwards it on to the next exchange. If there is no outgoing circuit available, or the destination is unable to accept it, the message is stored in a queue of messages, and is subsequently transmitted when circumstances permit. For this reason the method is sometimes known as 'store-and-forward' message switching.

A message switching system using store-and-forward switching obviates the need for repeated attempts at establishing a call, by accepting the message and undertaking to deliver it when this becomes possible. There is a minimum time necessary to transfer a message through the network. This comprises the time to travel between switches at the transmission speeds of the intervening links and a minimum message handling time at each switching point, including the time taken to read a message into and out of the stores at the switches. This is illustrated in Figure 5.21.

With a store-and-forward system, an increase in the overall network

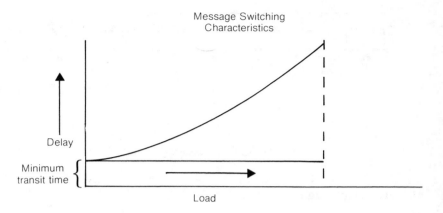

Figure 5.21   Behaviour of a Message Switching System Under Load

load naturally results in congestion, which might not be immediately apparent to the user, however, for the system continues to accept messages, at least for a while. The local switching centre usually can take and store further information, but may not be able to forward it for some time. Eventually, of course, no further messages will be accepted, until there is some relaxation of the congestion (or the destination is free to accept further messages). The upper limit to capacity is clearly set by the total storage available and the number and capacity of the transmission circuits.

Another way of looking at it is to regard the network as a large distributed set of stores which enable peak loads to be effectively spread out through increasing the transmission delay. By contrast, in the telephone network, the smoothing occurs because subscribers obtain a busy tone when they dial, and so try again later.

In the store-and-forward network, messages will be accepted (if the store at the first switch is large enough) but delivery will be delayed. In the latter case, the originator of the message is spared the task of repeatedly trying to begin a conversation with another subscriber, but the conversation will proceed more slowly as the network load increases. With the circuit switch, the start of the conversation will be delayed as the load increases, but once begun it may proceed at a speed unaffected by loading on the network.

In summary, the fundamental properties of message switching are:

— no connect time delay;

— accept, store, deliver mode of operation;

— equipment speed matching;

— retransmission on error;

— alternative routeing;

— different grades of service are possible;

— opportunities for improved network control.

In addition to the features described above, eg accept, store-and-forward, and loading behaviour, there are a number of other characteristic properties and other features which can be incorporated. The following can be carried over into packet switching networks:

— *Speed Matching:*   The store-and-forward capability enables the behaviour of the equipment and people (mainly the latter in this context) involved in an exchange to be more closely matched. The network accepts messages at the rate at which they can be prepared and delivers them at the rate at which the destination can accept them;

— *Error Retransmission:*   Each originating point, destination and switching centre can hold a copy of the message so that it can retransmit in the event of a faulty transmission being signalled. This applies over each component link of the transmission path, whereas on PSTN it can only be applied *end-to-end*;

— *Alternative Routeing:*   Since each message contains its own destination address, all messages can be treated as independent entities so far as the network is concerned. All that matters is that it guarantees to deliver a message to its correct destination irrespective of the actual physical route taken. Where more than one distinct physical route exists between two points on the network, we can turn this to advantage by arranging for the switching centres to select the best alternative in the event of congestion or failure of a circuit;

— *Different Grades of Service:*   The previous discussion assumed, in effect, that the messages in a queue are released for onward transmission on a FIFO basis. In fact it is possible to specify different grades of service, so that for example messages given a high priority would receive preference over other lower priority messages. This is a common feature in a number of existing message switching networks;

— *Improved Network Control Opportunities:* The presence of computer processing power in the switching exchanges clearly provides opportunities to exercise a level of overall control of the network and its performance which is technically impracticable within the existing PSTN. (However, this will be possible with the new System X exchanges);

— *End-to-End Multiplexing:* Because messages are individually addressed and a 'call' or interaction between two subscribers does not require a dedicated physical transmission path, it is perfectly legitimate to interleave messages originating and terminating at different addresses (see Figure 5.22). This has three main consequences. First of all it means that the network itself provides multiplexing as an inherent property instead of an add-on facility supplied outside the network through a variety of devices called multiplexers/concentrators. Two other effects are described below;

— *Flexible Connection/Interconnection:* When we use the expression 'end-to-end' we imply that the network multiplexing, in principle at least, extends to the computer and terminal line interfaces. Since the network itself helps to match the speed and response characteristics of the communicating parties and their equipment, there is no longer the same requirement for multiple line access ports distinguished by speeds and other transmission characteristics. Traffic originating at different speeds and having different transmission modes (eg synchronous/asynchronous) can share a common access line and port. Coupled with the ability to engage in simultaneous multiple conversations or interactions with either the same or different subscribers, the arrangements also provide a high level of interconnection flexibility;

— *Improved Circuit Utilisation:* The within network multiplexing clearly results in far higher circuit utilisation than is possible using traditional circuit switching.

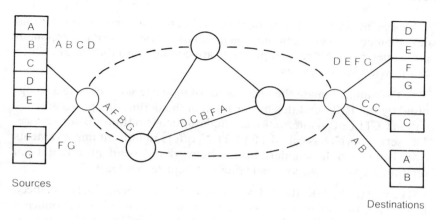

Figure 5.22   Message Interleaving and Multiplexing

Message switching principles are well established in both the public and private domains. Telegraphy and Telex are important examples of public networking, and there are numerous private systems operated by individual companies and other organisations.

The international airlines SITA network is a prime example of a very large network which provides a message switching service, in addition to the familiar seat reservation function. The SWIFT international banking network is another.

We have so far described message switching in relation to the provision of a person to person message service, which provides some message storage capability. For this type of application the storage facility is generally limited in extent, and there is no intention of providing long-term storage. If however, the transitory storage function is replaced or augmented by longer-term storage in the form of individually addressable 'mailboxes', the capability of a message system is considerably enhanced. For instance, individual users can consult their mailboxes, not only on demand, but after a considerable elapse of time. It is also practicable to use such a facility for purposes other than simple message transmission, including applications like holding conferences, either immediate or extended over time, exchange of information on co-operative ventures, and even the editing of material by geographically dispersed authors for publication.

Messaging and electronic mail services are now undergoing a rapid development. An efficient message/mailbox service is a vital component in the electronic office, and products are coming onto the market which can provide such services.

In the public domain the importance of message services is also recognised by the PTTs and this has resulted in the definition and acceptance within CCITT of an international standard for a text transmission service. The service, which is called TELETEX, offers significant improvements over Telex, and the standard itself is network independent so that it can operate across networks employing different technologies.

Turning to the UK, the Telex service has been progressively enhanced in the last two to three years, and it is also intended to introduce a TELETEX service. In addition it is planned to provide a message service on PRESTEL, also on the packet switched network together with a separate mailbox service.

The Transition to Packet Switching

The traditional message switching approach contains the germs of packet switching, subject to some important modifications. These are designed to overcome certain features which limit its application in computer communications.

Traditional message switching systems were designed primarily to meet the requirements of human users exchanging messages in text form. Messages are the units of information recognised by the users, and their length must be moderately unrestricted.

With conventional message switching systems, messages of any length are accepted in their entirety and stored as such at each switching point during their passage from switch to switch to their destination. The network takes full responsibility for maintaining the integrity of the message, and elaborate procedures are employed to ensure that this is achieved. The accent is on reliability, rather than speed, in the information transfer between subscribers, and the messages are held by the network until the recipient is ready to accept them, however long this may take. It was not originally intended that subscribers should interact rapidly with each other through a message switching network, so the type of interaction common between telephone users to overcome errors introduced by the network, or indeed their own mistakes, is not possible.

We find, therefore, that in traditional message switching networks the transit delay (transmission time plus queueing time) for a message can be of the order of minutes. This is clearly unacceptable for many terminal to computer or computer to computer applications.

Call Identification and Message Sequencing

We have noted earlier that the message interleaving and multiplexing property not only simplifies the local connection arrangements but permits multiple streams of messages to be despatched to different locations. Clearly, a computer could indulge in more than one conversation at the same time, providing the messages of one can be distinguished from those of another.

One solution is to carry both the source and destination addresses in each message, and this would distinguish the different source-destination paths. However, a computer could be engaged in several simultaneous conversations each relating to a different job. Therefore, to identify which conversation a message belonged to, it would still be necessary to include additional information in each message. Also, since different messages belonging to the same application may experience different delays, they may arrive at their destination in a sequence which differs from the original.

Implementation

It should be evident that the operations of a network of this type are far more complex than in the case of the PSTN. Substantial intelligence and appropriate software are required in the exchanges, and, although the local connection arrangements are visibly simpler, and more flexible, they have still to be implemented. If universality of access of a public switched network is to be realised, this must be done in such a way that end-to-end compatibility between widely different types of equipment is possible.

This is achieved through the adoption of the X25 and associated protocols which are described in Chapter 12.

Packet Switching Principles

A major difference between packet and message switched networks is that the data (or messages) is broken down into standard fixed maximum length packets. Large messages can be readily handled by breaking them into packets before transmission and re-assembling them at their destination. The term packet is appropriate because the data is carried within an envelope of control and error checking information.

The control field contains a number of items such as:

— the addresses of destination and origin;

— a process number indicating the facilities required at the destination by the user – this will be a specific application or a sub-address, such as another computer;

— other information to allow the user to reconstruct the data stream.

Every packet is terminated by an error checksum which is used to ensure that packets have been correctly transmitted. The checksums are verified on reception at each exchange and only if found to be error-free is a packet accepted, and an acknowledgement transmitted to the previous exchange. Only when the acknowledgement has been correctly received will the packet be deleted and transmitted to the next exchange.

Unlike a message switching network, a packet switching network is designed primarily for computer to computer communications. It has a much more rapid response which matches the internal behaviour of computers, and handles information in much the same way as does a computer. At the same time it can readily match the speed of attached computers to that of the terminal users, by virtue of its internal storage.

The improved response time is achieved by the following means:

— The fixed packet structure permits efficient handling, and the absence of indefinitely long messages prevents the blocking of transmission links and keeps the queues at switching points small. Storage at switches is made sufficient only for a few packets and the total amount of information stored in the network is low. The result is that the delay through a packet switching network is much smaller than through a normal message switching network and the rate of throughput of information can be much higher. Where message storage is required as a service to subscribers, it must be provided externally to the network, rather than as an integral part of the switches in the manner usual in a conventional message switching network.

Indeed, packet switching technology provides an efficient vehicle for message and mailbox services, and applications involving human interaction, and may be expected to displace traditional message switching technology.

In order to accommodate the lengthy messages and queues at an acceptable cost, traditional message switching systems have been compelled to use low-speed mass storage such as disks and drums. Packet switching in contrast uses fast-access memory. A time-shared computer system provides a useful analogy.

A time-shared computer system is able to serve many users apparently simultaneously because it is inherently much faster in operation than any one user and, by switching rapidly between them, is able to share its resources among them, serving each one at a rate convenient to him. This is achieved by using storage to smooth out the traffic flow: the users are allowed to fill and empty buffer stores at rates suitable for them, while the computer communicates with the same stores at very much higher speeds. The use of storage in this way provides a match between the users and the much faster computer.

The storage in this case is located within the computer and each user has a separate connection with it, but a very great advantage is gained by distributing some of the storage within the communications network that connects users with a computer, because it can be used to share high-speed communications links between users in much the same way as the computer itself is shared. This can make better use of the links; but far more important to the user is the rapid response obtained by sharing a high-speed channel rather than having sole use of a lower-speed one.

Multiplexing and Packet Interleaving

In the discussion of message switching we referred to the message interleaving property and the multiplexing capability that this provides. Packet switching networks also employ packet interleaving.

Strictly speaking the form of multiplexing used is called 'Statistical Time Division Multiplexing'.

What happens is that a user is only allocated real transmission capacity when he is sending packets. The trunk network will then allocate the maximum bandwidth it can along each link. The effect is that on the trunk network, the bandwidth used by an individual user can vary from zero (no packets to transmit) to the maximum speed of the trunk circuits (48 kbit/sec in the case of the UK Packet Switching network). The same applies in principle to the user's local access circuits up to the maximum speed of the circuit.

In application terms, if there are no packets to transmit for that application, then the capacity released could be used for packets belonging to another application or associated with another user located elsewhere.

Datagrams and Virtual Circuits

The method of operation described so far is often referred to as the Datagram mode. This means that each packet is a self-contained entity and there is no explicit relationship between successive packets, and for many categories of application this is perfectly adequate. However, there are many situations where the following requirements must be met:

— the interaction involves the transmission of multiple packets and the sequence must be preserved;

— a single computer or terminal could be involved in interactions relating to two or more distinct jobs.

To solve this what we have to do is to establish in some way a temporary 'liaison' between the two communicating applications within the computers/terminals.

The way this is done is to arrange for a preliminary exchange of packets between the two parties, equivalent to the procedure for establishing a call on PSTN. These packets contain reference numbers (logical channel numbers) and, assuming the call is accepted and information transfer takes place, all subsequent packets contain those reference numbers identifying the call to which they belong. For reasons which will become apparent this is called a 'Virtual Call'.

It should be noted that the virtual call facility can be implemented either within the network or external to it within the user's equipment.

Now that we can distinguish between packet streams in this way, it is also possible to arrange for packets belonging to a call to be delivered in the correct sequence.

In order to create, maintain and control virtual calls, packet switched networks which provide the facility employ a concept called the virtual circuit. It should be noted that the circuit is purely conceptual and there is no corresponding physical circuit. To the user, however, it has an appearance very similar to a conventional call.

A liaison can either be permanent or temporary. If the association is permanent, it is rather like a leased line running directly from one subscriber to another. Packets bearing the appropriate logical channel number are transmitted by the sender and routed by the network directly to the receiver, where they are delivered bearing the logical channel number appropriate at that end. This facility is called a Permanent Virtual Circuit.

More detailed information on the mechanics of packet switching, such as the call establishment procedure and the arrangements for connecting subscriber equipment to a packet switching network, is given in Chapter 12 in the context of X25.

6 The UK Public Network

INTRODUCTION

Since the late 1950s the UK main network has grown tenfold and has changed from a largely manual system to full automation where all customers can dial their own trunk calls. This chapter reviews the network changes and examines the future development of the network, bearing in mind that part of the future network is already installed with the provision of the first System X exchanges.

CHARGING PRINCIPLES

There are over 6000 local exchanges in the UK. The Group Charging Scheme, which has been in operation since 1958, is arranged so that call charges are common to small groups of exchanges instead of charging for calls on a point-to-point basis for each individual exchange. The 'charging groups', approximately 640, have on average about nine local exchanges each. Each charging group has a geographical measuring point called its Charge Point.

The local call area for a given exchange comprises the charging group in which it is situated, ie its 'Home Charging Group' (HCG), and all other charging groups with which it has a common boundary, ie its 'Adjacent Charging Groups' (ACG).

Calls from a given exchange to an exchange outside its HCG and ACGs are designated as trunk or main network calls (Figure 6.1).

All calls are periodically metered, ie in addition to the first meter pulse which operates the caller's meter when the called party answers, the

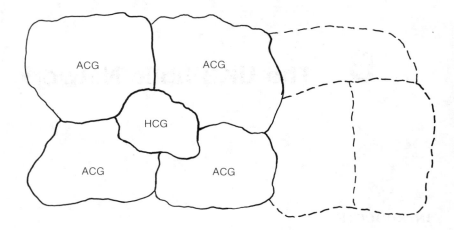

Figure 6.1 Charging Groups

meter is operated at regular intervals (periods) throughout the call. There are five metering rates:

— L or Local, for own charge group calls;

— 'a' rate for calls up to 56 km from charging point;

— 'b' rate for calls over 56 km from charging point;

— 'b$_1$' rate for 100 low-cost routes over 56 km;

— 'c' rate for calls to Channel Islands.

Call charges are also varied according to the time and day that a call is made, while using a standard unit fee, the value of which can be changed as required by British Telecom.

The charging periods are currently:

— 'peak' from 9.00 a.m. to 1.00 p.m. which attracts the highest rate of metering;

— 'standard' from 8.00 a.m. to 9.00 a.m. and 1.00 p.m. to 6.00 p.m.;

— 'cheap' from 6.00 p.m. and all day Saturday, Sunday and Bank Holidays.

Within each charging group one exchange is designated the Group Switching Centre (GSC), whose functions are to:

— act as a local exchange for telephone users within its locality;

— provide junction switching for exchanges in the HCG and to/from ACG exchanges;

— provide incoming and outgoing trunk switching facilities;

— house, if necessary, a manual board for operator assistance.

In forming the charging groups it was not possible, because of equipment and line plant limitations, to allocate a GSC to each charging group. Such charging groups are said to be 'dependent' on a remote GSC. This accounts for there being about 370 GSCs for 640 charge groups.

THE PAST

By 1933 the UK trunk network, in which all calls were set up manually, had developed to such an extent that an organised transmission plan had to be produced to:

— avoid undue delay in setting up calls;

— improve the standard of transmission performance across the network.

The 1933 plan, as it was called, was followed in 1938-9 with the start of the introduction of trunk mechanisation. This allowed controlling operators to complete the connection of a single-link trunk call without the assistance of a distant operator, thereby reducing call set-up time. Subsequent improvements in long distance signalling in the 1940s and 1950s allowed operator trunk dialling to be applied on multi-link calls.

THE PRESENT

The subscriber trunk dialling (STD) system was inaugurated in 1960 and completed in 1979. The system provides customers on the telephone network with facilities to dial all UK trunk calls automatically without the assistance of an operator. Each customer in the UK has a unique national number made up of three parts:

— trunk prefix digit 0;

— code of the distant charging group;

— subscriber's local number.

National numbers are limited, by early equipment design, to a maximum of 10 digits.

An example of a National Number is:

NOTTINGHAM 658123 (STD CODE 0602)

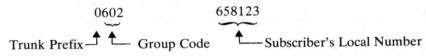

           0602   658123

Trunk Prefix—⤴ ⤴— Group Code   ⤴—Subscriber's Local Number

In Director areas local numbers have 7 digits but national numbers are kept within the 10-digit limitation by using 2-digit group codes and in the case of the largest area, London, a single digit code:

            0 1   236 2345   LONDON

Trunk Prefix   ⤴ ⤴— Group Code

            0 31   225 2345 EDINBURGH

Trunk Prefix   ⤴ ⤴ Group Code

The first digit '0' of a national number routes the call from the local exchange to the STD equipment at the GSC (Figure 6.2) called a register translator.

The register access relay set seizes a register:

— stores (registers) the rest of the dialled national number;

— applies to a translator for metering information and routeing information;

— transmits the routeing information indicated by the translator to trunk selectors setting up the connection to the required exchange;

— retransmits the stored local number;

— releases the register and leaves the connection supervised by the register access relay set.

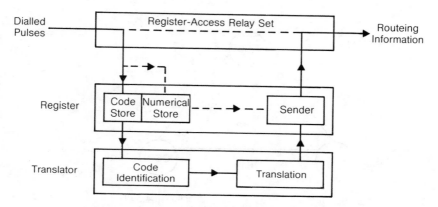

Figure 6.2   Principle of the Register Translator

2-Wire Switching Limitations

All circuits in GSCs are '2-wire switched' via selectors to local lines or to each other. Transmission losses occur both in the conversion from 4-wire to 2-wire (hybrid loss) and at the GSC in the signalling relay sets and selectors (Figure 6.3).

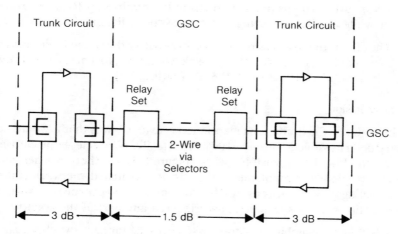

Figure 6.3   2-Wire Switching Losses

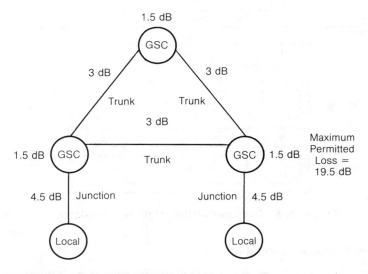

Figure 6.4   Network Transmission Losses

Another disadvantage of this method is the time taken to position selectors using 10 pps pulse trains from the originating Register Translator while a caller is waiting – known as 'post dialling delay'.

The effects of transmission loss on post dialling delay and limitations of register equipment restricted any trunk connection to a maximum of two trunk (GSC-GSC) links and 19.5 dB (Figure 6.4).

Transmission

The result of the limitations mentioned previously was that it would not have been possible to provide 100% STD facilities for telephone customers in the UK. The Transit Network (Figure 6.5) was therefore designed and installed to supplement the 2-wire switched network interconnecting GSCs and ensure that the main network provides interconnection facilities between subscribers in any part of the country.

All Transit Switching Centres (TSC) provide tandem switching capability and are known, according to their position in the network, as:

— District Switching Centre (DSC), servicing one or more GSCs in its catchment area;

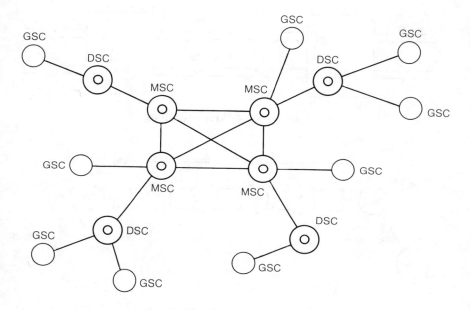

Figure 6.5   Transit Network

— Main Switching Centre (MSC), which are selected DSCs and are fully interconnected with each other.

Trunk lines are switched through each TSC in 4-wire form to keep transmission losses to a minimum (Figure 6.6).

The transmission loss from 2-wire input at a GSC to 2-wire output at a distant GSC is engineered to be 7 dB overall, irrespective of the number of TSCs in tandem (Figure 6.7).

It can be seen from the above that the loss between two local exchanges can, even with 6 trunk switching stages in the transit network, be limited to 19.0 dB. Approximately 95% of the main network (trunk) calls are 2-wire switched via:

— GSC-GSC, or

— GSC-GSC-GSC links.

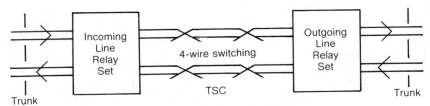

Figure 6.6   4-Wire Switching

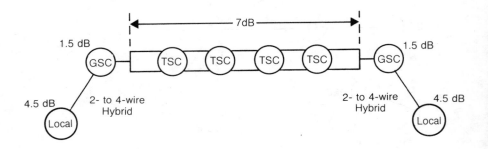

Figure 6.7   Transmission Loss

The remainder are completed via the 4-wire switched transit network, eg:

— GSC-DSC-GSC;

— GSC-DSC-MSC-DSC-GSC;

— GSC-DSC-MSC-MSC-DSC-GSC.

The existing UK network transmission plan, sometimes referred as the 1960 plan, is shown in Figure 6.8.

The maximum loss between any local exchanges (via 2 GSC-GSC links) is 19.5 dB and can be obtained by simple addition of the transmission losses. The electro-acoustic properties of a telephone instrument, local line and local exchange transmission bridge are, however, described in terms of reference equivalent (RE) or loudness ratings (LR). The use of reference equivalent permits transmission planners to gauge the subjective acceptability of transmission performance in a network. For planning purposes the individual RE values for a combination of telephone,

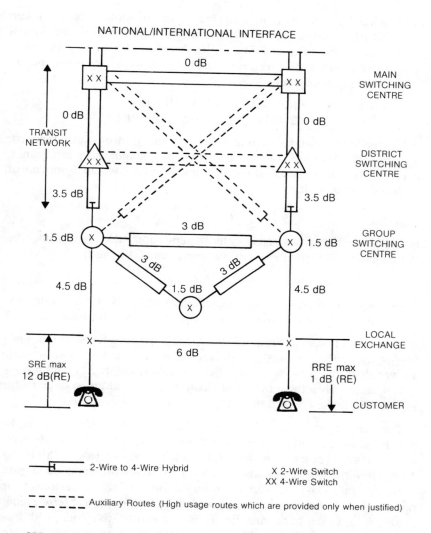

Figure 6.8   UK Transmission Plan

limiting local line of 10 dB at 1600 Hz and transmission bridge are taken as 12 dB RE (sending) and 1 dB RE (receive). The maximum Nominal Overall Reference Equivalent (NORE max) is the sum of the send reference equivalent, the maximum loss between local exchanges and the receive reference equivalent, ie:

$$\text{NORE max} = \text{SRE max} + 19.5 + \text{RRE max}$$
$$= 12 + 19.5 + 1 = 32.5 \text{ dB (RE)}$$

This is often mistakenly referred to as the transmission standard; however, the network is planned so that this 'standard' is rarely met, because 50% of users experiencing 33 dB NORE would complain of transmission difficulties.

Signalling

Post dialling delay on transit calls is kept short, thus permitting the routeing of calls through several switching units, by the use of:

— common control crossbar switching;

— high-speed inter-register signalling using tones of 80 ms duration composed of two out of six or two out of five frequencies.

To set up a transit call requires two signalling procedures. Line signalling is required to indicate signals such as seizure, called subscriber answer/clear and forward clear. These signals are worked on a link-by-link basis which allows the most economical signalling system to be installed in links, eg DC2 and AC9.

The inter-register signalling, multi-frequency No. 2 (MF2) is used to pass routeing, class of service and control information between registers. In the forward (calling) direction six voice frequencies from 1380 Hz to 1980 Hz with 120 Hz spacing are used in a two-out-of-six code to pass routeing and class of service information (coinbox, customer or operator). All information is preceded by a Forward Prefix signal (Table 6.1). In the backward direction a two-out-of-five code, with frequencies from 660 Hz to 1140 Hz, with 120 Hz spacing, is used to return signals such as congestion, number received and spare code (Table 6.2). All signals are preceded with a backward prefix signal.

MF2 uses the end-to-end principle of signalling, ie information is exchanged between the controlling (first) MF register and the last register to be seized. Voice immunity problems do not arise because all signalling is completed before customers are connected to the lines.

SIGNAL	PULSE NO	SA 1380 Hz	SB 1500 Hz	SC 1620 Hz	SD 1740 Hz	SE 1860 Hz	SF 1980 Hz
DIGIT 1	1	X	X				
DIGIT 2	2	X		X			
DIGIT 3	3		X	X			
DIGIT 4	4	X			X		
DIGIT 5	5		X		X		
DIGIT 6	6			X	X		
DIGIT 7	7	X				X	
DIGIT 8	8		X			X	
DIGIT 9	9			X		X	
DIGIT 0	10				X	X	
CLASS OF SERVICE (i) ORD	2	X		X		X	
CLASS OF SERVICE (ii) CCB	8		X			X	
CLASS OF SERVICE (iii) OPTR	3		X	X			
FORWARD PREFIX	14				X		X

Table 6.1   MF2 Forward Signals

SIGNAL	PULSE NO	E 660 Hz	D 780 Hz	C 900 Hz	B 1020 Hz	A 1140 Hz
SEND CLASS OF SERVICE	1				X	X
SPARE CODE	2			X		X
TRANSIT PROCEED TO SEND	3			X	X	
TERMINAL PROCEED TO SEND	4		X			X
CONGESTION	5		X		X	
NUMBER RECEIVED	6		X	X		
BACKWARD PREFIX	9	X		X		

Table 6.2   MF2 Backward Signals

FUTURE NETWORKS

Introduction

The elements of all telecommunications are encompassed within four areas:

— terminals;

— transmission;

— switching and control;

— signalling.

A return is slowly being made to the control features and facilities first afforded by manual systems. The control and service features of developing systems are attractive.

During the 1960s there had been a growing realisation of the importance of considering telecommunications networks as integrated systems. The traditional independent development of switching and transmission was considered by experts to have prevented the evolution of optimum engineered telecommunications systems. This independence relies on the interface and signalling engineer to provide the inter-relationship between the other components.

With the availability of digital techniques, which lend themselves to the application of large-scale integration, at low cost, the drive to integrate transmission and switching gained momentum. Digital techniques offer significant service and economic advantages to networks in a number of ways.

Digital control offers:

— high degree of flexibility;

— enhanced service features and facilities;

— faster call set-up time;

— improved reliability and quality of service.

Digital transmission can provide:

— a rugged modulation method;

— stable transmission performance;

— reduction in cross-talk and noise levels compared to analogue transmission;

— high-volume capacity;

— exploitation of 'new' transmission media, eg optical fibre;

— less dependence on skilled maintenance staff;

— reduction in circuit costs compared with analogue systems.

The digital switching area offers advantages in:

— 4-wire switching without cost penalty;

— low noise;

— stability of transmission;

— low fault rate and hence low maintenance cost;

— fast switching;

— reduced accommodation requirements;

— reduced manufacturing and installation costs;

— decrease in energy requirements.

Digital signalling provides:

— elimination of per-circuit signalling equipment;

— fast processor-processor signalling;

— increased signalling repertoire;

— improved quality of service;

— flexibility to meet new services.

It was recognised by British Telecom that development of telematics, ie telecommunications plus informatics (computing, word processing, etc) together with the move to the office of the future, would require the provision of an 'active' network capable of supporting a host of services (Figure 6.9).

The studies also took into account growth and cost trends, together with expected technological developments. The results indicated that the most economic solution to meet future requirements would be a digital

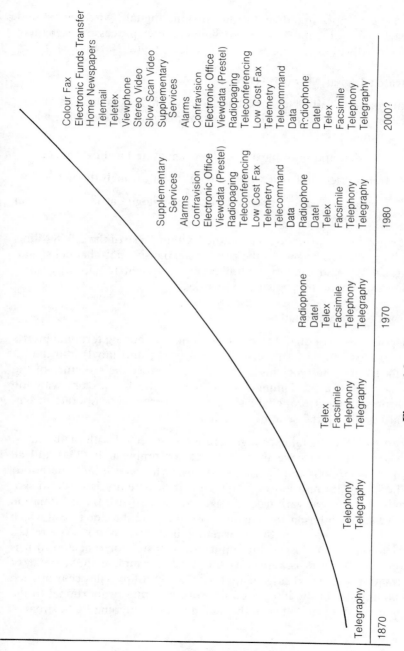

Figure 6.9 Growth in Services

network incorporating digital transmission, digital switching, stored program control and common channel inter-processor signalling (Figure 6.10): in other words, an Integrated Digital Network (IDN).

Integrated Digital Network (IDN)

The Integrated Digital Network, based on System X exchanges, is characterised by the integration of digital transmission and switching where speech signals are:

— encoded and multiplexed at the originating local exchange;

— transmitted and switched in digital form through the network;

— demultiplexed and decoded back to analogue at the destination exchange.

As signalling information is contained within TS16 of the 2.048 Mbit/s signalling, the IDN removes the need for expensive per-channel signalling relay sets and primary multiplexing equipment required by space switched analogue transmission networks.

Network Synchronisation

On a point-to-point digital transmission link the sending terminal inserts a synchronisation pattern (regarded as a frame start label) into the bit stream, so that the receiving terminal can identify the structure of the incoming bit stream. Timing information in the bit stream, with the synchronisation pattern, enables the receive terminal to operate in synchronisation with the sending terminal.

With an IDN, digital exchanges are interconnected with digital links. Each exchange will have its own 'clock' or timing unit (TU) and all outgoing bit streams and internal waveforms (for cross-point operation) will be in synchronisation with this unit. If no attempt is made to synchronise the TUs at various exchanges in the network the information rate of a signal entering an exchange will be different to the rate at which the exchange can process the information and retransmit it. As a result, information will be lost, if the input rate is faster; or repeated, if it is slower. This process is known as slip, or if a complete PCM frame of information is deleted or repeated, frame slip. Slips will occur at each switching point in the integrated network at a rate proportional to the frequency difference between the incoming and outgoing PCM streams.

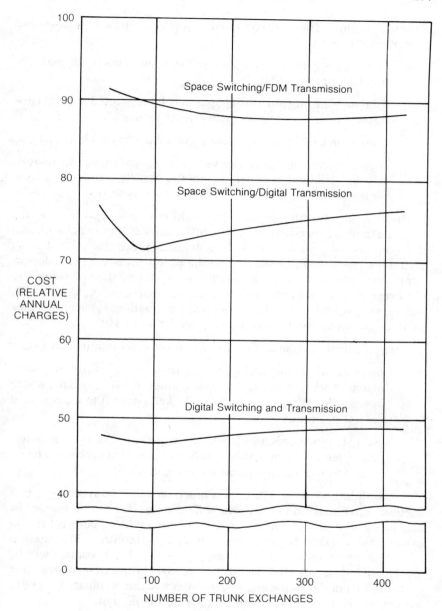

Figure 6.10   Effect of Plant Type on Network Costs

The effect of slips varies according to the service, when the slip occurs and how often it occurs:

— in speech, slip produces a noise or 'click' on a circuit, the majority of which are inaudible;

— for data transmission, throughput may be reduced due to retransmission of data blocks as errors are detected;

— one slip in a facsimile transmission could destroy a whole picture;

— slips occurring during setting up of a call could cause call failures, but the effect varies depending on the signalling system, eg common channel signalling incorporates error detection.

The planning objective for network synchronisation is expressed by the 'slip rate' and is dependent on the potential services for the network and the accuracy of exchange TUs. International proposals state that all digital international links should operate plesiochronously, ie independently but within narrow specified limits, to maintain a slip rate below one slip every 70 days. This assumes slips in a national network, like the UK, will be as good or better than this implying a national synchronous or plesiochronous network to an accuracy of 1 part in 10^{11}.

Various control methods are available for a synchronous network:

— despotic, where one timing unit controls all the other timing units in a network. An example of this is 'master-slave' working where lower order exchanges are phase-locked (slaved) to a designated central or master unit;

— mutual synchronisation, where exchange clocks are interconnected by a Synchronisation Network so that each exchange is locked to the average of all incoming clock rates.

Synchronisation of the UK IDN is based on a mutual synchronisation method. Each node in the network will be connected to other nodes by synchronisation links arranged in a 4-tier hierarchy (Figure 6.11). On synchronisation links between levels, single-ended control will be used, ie control is effective at the lower level. Within a level, control will be double-ended, ie effective at both ends. Synchronisation information recovered from the frame alignment pattern in the nominated 2 Mbit/s system will be compared with the exchange timing unit.

Control signals, eg speed up or speed down, will be returned to the

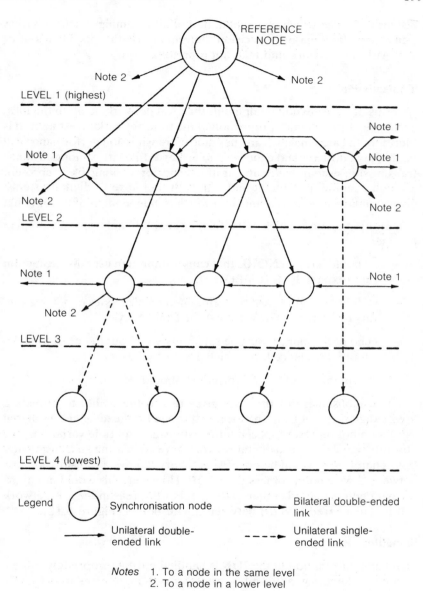

Figure 6.11   Synchronisation Network Topology

distant exchange which by examination of all incoming synchronisation signals can, by a majority decision, determine whether its TU is out of step with the network and take appropriate action.

Transmission

In terms of transmission equipment, the local network, ie up to the local exchange, forms a major proportion of the total network investment. It is therefore the area in which any upgrade in transmission performance will be the most difficult and expensive to achieve. In contrast, long-distance transmission systems have comparatively shorter working lives, represent a smaller capital investment and can, with the move to digital systems, give a nominal loss for a connection which is independent of its routeing.

Major parameters which will influence an all-digital transmission plan include:

— it should have an NORE that causes minimum user dissatisfaction (approximately 4·-18 dB(RE));

— stability margins must be maintained on all classes of connection, this being particularly critical for Datel Services;

— echo performance must be satisfactory without the need for echo suppressors/cancellors, which are costly items;

— acceptable sidetone performance should be achieved.

The establishment of the IDN gives rise to the ability to provide a 4-wire digital circuit from the local end to the local exchange. As digital signals do not represent speech information as amplitude variations, the absolute signal levels in a digital network have no bearing on transmission loss. Therefore it would be possible in theory to have a transmission loss between 2-wire points of less than 2 dB. However, this would not allow the parameters quoted earlier to be met. For this reason the UK network will be engineered to 6 dB between 2-wire points (Figure 6.12).

Signalling

Signalling information in the IDN is handled most appropriately using a common channel signalling inter-processor system, referred to as CCITT recommendation No. 7. The advantages of this type of signalling are:

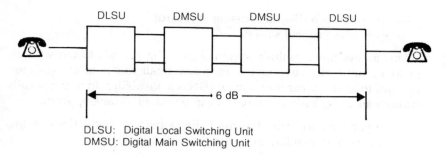

DLSU: Digital Local Switching Unit
DMSU: Digital Main Switching Unit

Figure 6.12   Digital Transmission Plan

— it provides more efficient use of processor power than the existing system;

— it increases signal repertoire;

— as signalling information is separate from normal speech time slots, it increases the range of facilities available to customers;

— inherent flexibility of software control enables changes to be easily carried out to cater for future requirements;

— the system can provide options to cater for non-telephony services thus simplifying the move to an Integrated Service Digital Network (ISDN).

Each traffic route between a pair of exchanges has its signalling carried out on a signalling module, each signalling module consisting of 2 to 4 signalling links in parallel. For security each signalling link, which can cater for up to 960 traffic circuits, should follow a different physical path. For a given direction of signalling each signalling link comprises a data link at 64 kbit/s in TS16 of a 2.048 Mbit/s digital transmission system.

Traffic Routeing

The justification of routes between exchanges is a function of the traffic carried. The increase in the basic transmission module from 12 circuits (FDM Group) to 30 circuits (2.048 kbit/s PCM) changes the justification level for provision of routes. In addition the IDN:

— reduces the switching/transmission cost ratio;

— provides a 6 dB transmission standard;
— provides fast call set-up.

This allows more multi-link routeings to be provided than with an analogue network. The move from many small routes in an analogue network to fewer larger routes in an IDN is a possibility. In routeing calls through an IDN, various strategies can be adopted ranging from:

— 'dynamic', whereby the most direct path is found through the network depending on prevailing conditions, to

— disciplined hierarchical routeing of traffic, as used in the 1960 Transmission and Routeing plan.

The dynamic routeing philosophy gives great freedom but requires strict application and monitoring. The hierarchical system, which will be used in the UK, eases management of the network and provides a firm foundation on which various routeing strategies can be built.

New Customer Facilities

The features of the IDN allow the introduction of new telephone facilities. These supplementary services, as they are termed (Table 6.3), fall into two main classes:

— independent supplementary services provided by a digital exchange for its own telephone users. The services include alarm calls, abbreviated dialling, call transfer, etc;

— cooperative supplementary services where, by the use of enhanced signalling of the IDN, services can be transferred from one exchange to another. An example would be diversion of calls to a new termination, even if that termination is on another exchange.

The development of even more sophisticated services such as teletex, fast facsimile, electronic mail, etc, will be dependent on the evolution of the Integrated Services Digital Network (ISDN).

INTEGRATED SERVICES DIGITAL NETWORK (ISDN)

Introduction

In the present BT network there are a number of discrete networks, eg Telex, Packet Switching Service, etc. Economic benefits can accrue to BT and its customers if these networks were combined into one large network.

Simple automatic call
- Dial telephones
- Push-button MF telephones

Customer line options
- Direct exchange line (analogue)
- Digital exchange line
- PBX line groups

Rapid call set up
- Abbreviated dialling

Call booking
- Automatic alarm call

Call restriction (barring)

Call diversion

Call completion
- Call waiting
- Repeat last call

Call charging
- Payphone
- Customer's private meter

Recorded information services

Operator services
- Call connect facilities
- Service bureaux

Three-party call

PBX facilities
- Direct inward dialling
- Unrestricted PBX numbering
- PBX night services

Malicious call identification

Voice guidance

Mobile customer services

Non-voice services
- Integrated services digital network (ISDN)

Table 6.3   Customer Facilities

The introduction of digital local exchanges interconnected by digital transmission provides the basis of an IDN. Although telephony services will predominate in its early years, a call routed entirely on digital line plant will have use of a 64 kbit/s path from local exchange to local exchange. However, the local path from the branch exchange to the subscriber's premises will still be analogue and this is a limiting factor on the exploitation of the full potential of IDN.

The extension of digital transmission of the IDN from the local exchange to the customer's premises will permit the development of an ISDN. Types of service considered suitable for ISDN applications are given in Table 6.4.

Interface Equipment

In the analogue network a standard interface between the two-wire line and customer terminal equipment was never really achieved. The move to an ISDN will provide the opportunity for this to happen both at the functional and physical level; it will also permit the independent development of line transmission systems. An outline of the ISDN interface arrangements is given in Figure 6.13.

It is expected that the ISDN customer interface will either closely follow the existing CCITT X series of interfaces, eg X21, or that international agreement will be achieved on a new ISDN interface standard.

Circuit Switched Data Service
(2.4, 4.8, 9.6, 48 and 64 kbit/s)

Private Digital Circuits

Facsimile Service at 64 kbit/s

Teletex Service at 2.4 kbit/s

Access to Packet Switching Service

Access to Prestel at 8 and 64 kbit/s

Slow Scan Television

Telephony Service

Table 6.4   Possible ISDN Services

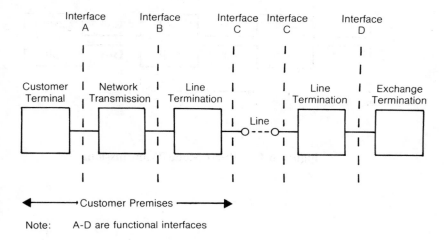

Note: A-D are functional interfaces

Figure 6.13   ISDN Interfaces

Local Line Transmission

A prime requirement of the ISDN is that it must make as much use of the existing local transmission network as possible. Duplex digital transmission techniques for use over a single pair of existing local distribution plant have been investigated.

Since the IDN will provide a 64 kbit/s capacity, an ISDN local line transmission system should provide at least the same capacity. Initial international discussions called for a total capacity of 144 kbit/s, however, economic and technical restrictions have resulted in the adoption of lower overall bit rates. In the UK an 80 kbit/s option has been chosen which will provide capacity for three channels:

— 64 kbit/s – for speech or non-voice;

— 8 kbit/s – for non-voice;

— 8 kbit/s – for signalling.

The 64 kbit/s channel and 8 kbit/s non-voice channel are independent and may be used to make simultaneous calls, for different services, to different destinations. The signalling channel provides signalling for both of the other channels.

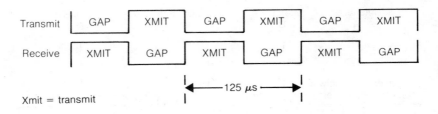

Xmit = transmit

Figure 6.14   Burst Mode Transmission

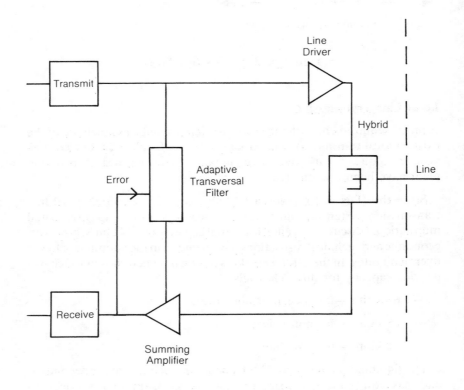

Figure 6.15   Adaptive Hybrid

The availability of those facilities at the telephone termination will have major implications for the user whether in the home or in the office. The bandwidths, simultaneous channels and common digital paths will enable speech, data, text, facsimile and static video to be handled with equal facility, on an end-to-end basis across the PSTN. The telephone therefore becomes a significant starting point for the evolution of the multifunction workstation in the office of the future.

The three channels will be multiplexed into a 10 bit 125 μs duration frame with 8 bits for the 64 kbit/s channel and 1 bit for each of the other two channels. The actual line rate will be higher than 80 kbit/s and will depend on the method of line transmission used.

One method of transmission being developed is a time division duplex technique, commonly known as burst mode. With this method information is transmitted in one direction in 'bursts' with information 'bursts' in the opposite direction being interleaved in the transmission gaps (Figure 6.14).

With this method the 80 kbit/s gross bit rate can be transmitted up to 3 km using a burst rate of 8000 kHz with 10 bit bursts. The instantaneous line bit rate will be 256 kbit/s.

Another method that could be used is based on a digital hybrid echo cancelling technique. The digital circuit subtracts appropriately delayed and attenuated parts of the transmitted signal from the received signal thereby cancelling unwanted echo which would distort the signal at the terminal (Figure 6.15).

A conventional analogue hybrid would not be suitable as it would not provide nearly enough suppression of the unwanted signal to allow operation at 80 kbit/s.

ISDN Service

A pilot ISDN service, for about 500 customers, will be provided in 1983.

7 The Data Communications System

INTRODUCTION

The book has so far been almost entirely concerned with the principles and underlying transmission technology which supports data communication. However, a *data communications system* in which terminals communicate with computers and computers with computers in order to achieve specific results, comprises much more than the transmission services.

It involves hardware components such as modems, and multiplexers, and these components can be connected together in various configurations, networks and physical architectures. But the user's view of the system, when he accesses files or application programs, will generally be different from the physical appearance. In other words, the functional architecture also needs to be considered. These are the main topics we shall cover.

TYPES OF NETWORK

Networks consist of two or more locations (nodes) which are connected together using communication links. A node may contain any number of communication and computing devices. A number of special terms are used when describing data links and networks; these are described below.

Point-to-Point

Point-to-point is the simplest and is extensively used (Figure 7.1). It may be transitory and exist only for the duration of a call on the switched

A —————————————————————————— B

Figure 7.1   Point-to-Point Data Link

network, or exist permanently as a leased circuit. Point-to-point configurations are commonly used where only a limited number of physically
distinct routes are involved, and the distances are not excessive.

Multidrop

Where a large number of locations have to be connected, and these can be
broken down into geographical clusters, the multidrop form of configuration is generally more cost-effective (Figure 7.2).

All transmissions from Node A can be received by Nodes B, C and D.
Similarly, only Node A can receive data from B, C and D, only one of
which may transmit at a time. Multidrop circuits provide a way of reducing line costs by using a single branched circuit to connect Node A to
Nodes B, C, and D respectively rather than the three point-to-point
circuits that would otherwise be required. It must be stressed that Nodes
B, C and D cannot communicate directly with each other, only with Node
A. Node A will use a protocol mechanism, known as polling, to address
each of B, C and D in turn, accepting input data from each before moving
on to the next. The mechanism is explained in Chapter 10.

Multidrop networks are mainly used to connect host computers (at
Node A in our example) to terminals or terminal clusters at several
remote locations. Multidrop configurations are only available on leased
circuits. Point-to-point and multidrop circuits are the basic network components from which other types of network can be built up.

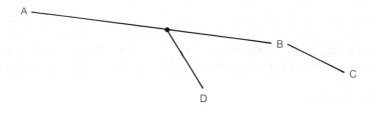

Figure 7.2   Multipoint or Multidrop Data Links

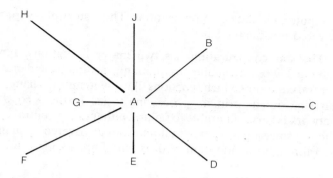

Figure 7.3   Star Network Using Point-to-Point Circuits

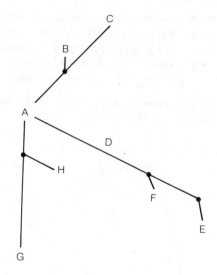

Figure 7.4   Multidropped Star Network

Star Configurations

Figures 7.3 and 7.4 depict two star configurations, the former employing point-to-point links and the latter multidropped links. In the figures, A represents a central computer site, and the other letters represent remotely situated terminals. At the present time, almost all configurations are of this type and reflect the early evolutionary stages of the computer and data communications. The historical perspective is briefly covered in Chapter 8.

The star configuration has two major limitations. First of all, the remote devices are unable to communicate directly and must do so via the central computer which functions like a switching exchange in addition to carrying out its primary processing tasks. In the second place such a network is very vulnerable to failure, either of the central computer, or of the transmission links. These limitations are overcome in mesh networks and through the adoption of distributed processing principles.

Loop Networks

There are several variations of loop networks:

— a closed-loop with the data links being provided by two-wire leased circuits. Messages are passed between the nodes in the network in one direction only; the host computer (A) controls communication using a mechanism known as 'list polling'. The failure of a single data link will halt all transmission on the loop;

— a closed-loop capable of supporting transmission in both directions. In the event that a single data link is broken, the host

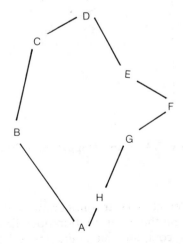

Fig 7.5   A Closed-Loop Network

computer (A) will be able to maintain contact with the two sectors of the networks. Two data links will need to be broken before one or more nodes are isolated from the host.

Mesh Networks

While star networks are suited to linking host-computers to slave terminals or computers on a one-to-many basis, mesh networks are primarily used where multiple hosts need connection to multiple slaves (Figure 7.6). (In many cases the idea of host and slave is inappropriate as the nodes connected are of equal status.)

Mesh networks are very resilient to failure, with alternative data routes being available when data link failure occurs. In many cases this resilience means that users are unaware that a network failure has occurred. Mesh networks are generally very expensive to implement and where circuit lengths are long or data volumes low, a public packet switched service may offer a cost advantage over a private mesh network.

Wide Area and Local Area Networks

Local area networks are specifically designed for the interconnection of computer systems and terminals within a single geographical site. The main difference between local and wide area network lies in the technology employed. Local area networks are characterised by:

— wide bandwidth, ie 10 Mbit/s and above;

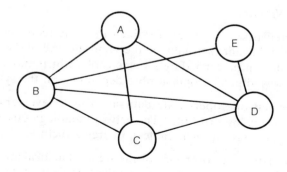

Figure 7.6   Mesh Network

— simple protocols, compared with those necessary over the longer distances of wide area networks;

— low cost and ease of installation;

— uniform method of attachment for diverse types of equipment, ie plug compatibility.

Wide Area Networks

The Public Switched Telephone Network (PSTN) is used extensively for data communications. Normal dial-up circuits are employed and consequently the quality of the circuit allocated will be variable.

Modems are currently available which will operate at 2400 bits/s full duplex using a single dial-up connection. Modems operating at higher data rates (such as 4800 bit/s) will utilise double dial-up procedures.

Depending on the distance involved and the total length of connect time, the use of the Public Switched Telephone Network on a day-to-day basis may be expensive and a leased line connection justified. However, PSTN provides a valuable standby in the event of a leased-line failure.

Packet switching principles are discussed in Chapter 5. Although packet switching has now been adopted in the public domain, it has also been implemented in a number of wide area private networks. The packet concept is also employed in a number of proprietary local area network offerings. In the public domain, the tariff structures are generally distance-independent and favour intermittent traffic patterns.

Local Area Networks

Local area networks offer a very flexible way of interconnecting computer and terminal facilities usually on the same site. All of the data traffic within the site can be carried by a single cable, which may be single or twin-coax, twisted pair or optical fibre depending on the system.

Local area networks operate at a data rate of up to several megabits per second with a very low error rate. The network topologies used are either rings (loops), or buses (linear cables), or tree structures.

Two basic data-transport mechanisms are used in local area networks, though it should be noted that the detailed implementations of these mechanisms vary widely between suppliers.

The first of these mechanisms is known as 'empty slot' or 'token passing' and is suited to ring networks. Using the 'empty slot' principle, one (or more) data packets circle the network in one direction only, being passed from hand-to-hand between the nodes. When a node needs to send a message, it waits for the arrival of an empty packet and inserts its message, together with the destination node address, into the packet before passing it on to the next node. The destination node takes a copy of the data and marks the packet as having been received but not empty; the packet completes a revolution of the ring before being 'emptied' by the original sender.

The 'token passing' principle is very similar in concept. Rather than complete packets (empty and full) permanently circling the ring, only short control messages called tokens are *permanently* present. Any node wishing to send a message has to wait for the arrival of a token, it then transmits its addressed message followed by the token. Again, the message makes a complete revolution of the ring, being acknowledged by the addressee node as appropriate, before being removed from the network by its originator.

The second mechanism allows nodes to contend for the use of the network using a technique known as 'Carrier Sense Multiple Access with Collision Detection' (CSMA/CD). A transmission from any node will be heard by all the others; however, only one node should transmit at a time, as single simultaneous transmission from more than one node could result in collision and data corruption.

Any node wishing to transmit first 'listens' to check whether another node is already transmitting (whether a carrier signal is present on the network). Once the network is free, the node will transmit its addressed message, but it will continue 'listening' to ensure that it is the only node transmitting. In the event that a collision is detected, the node will wait for a random period of time before trying again. The random nature of this delay avoids the possibility that the same two nodes will transmit repeatedly at the same intervals, with each attempt resulting in a collision and neither node ever being able to transmit successfully.

At the time of writing, a large number of local area networking products are available, many of them from computer manufacturers. In some cases, no details are provided of the internal structure of the products, and they are limited to use with the manufacturer's own data products. However, there is increasing pressure for local area network standards to

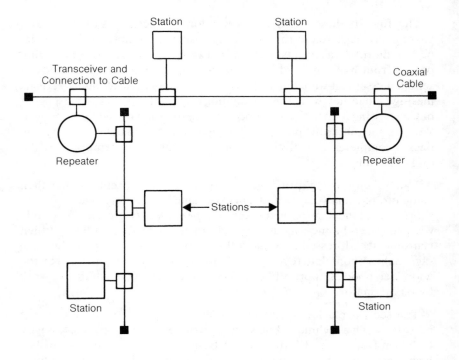

Figure 7.7   Ethernet Configuration

be published and adopted by manufacturers. The international standards bodies are currently considering this area, although it would appear that an industry accepted standard is still some way off. Ethernet (CSMA/CD) (Figure 7.7) and the Cambridge Ring (Empty Slot)(Figure 7.8), are two examples of the proprietary products.

Once the cabling for a local area network is installed, it can be regarded as a 'ring-main' which can be plugged into whenever and wherever the requirement for a terminal occurs providing flexibility and aiding portability of equipment. It also offers the very major advantage that demands for new terminals can be accommodated in a relatively short time when compared with the installation procedures required when traditional approaches are used.

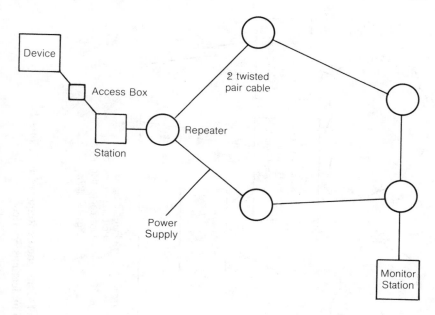

Figure 7.8   Cambridge Ring

NETWORK COMPONENTS

The availability of low-cost microprocessors has resulted in an ever widening range of network components, ranging from the long-established modem and multiplexer products, where functionality is being enhanced to a major degree, to 'black box' devices which can be programmed to perform specialist tasks such as protocol conversion.

In this chapter we will be discussing the more common communications devices and the functionality which each contributes to a network. (Figure 7.9 explains the dependency that each network component places on others in linking computers and terminals together.)

Modems

In Chapter 3 we discussed the techniques of modulation and demodulation necessary to transfer data messages over a voice quality telephone line. BT have traditionally exercised tight control over the attachment of

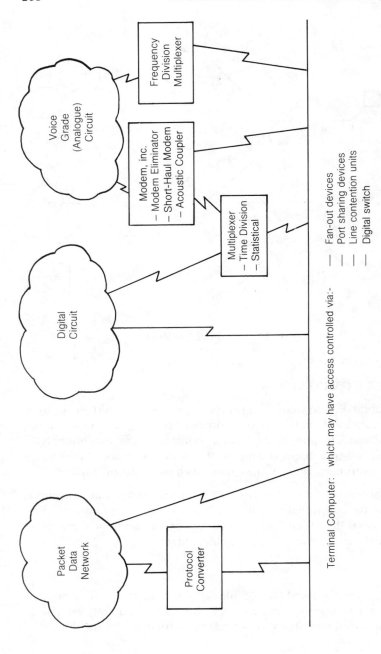

Figure 7.9   The Interdependency of Components Required to Connect Terminals to Communications Services

modems to the PSTN, and have insisted that the modem must always be BT supplied, except in circumstances where an alternative product provides a superior performance or facility than the BT product. In regard to private circuits, the regulations have been less strict. In all cases though, BT approval is required for attachment whether to the public network or to leased circuits.

However, under the telecommunications liberalisation policies stemming from the recent BT Act, it can be anticipated that the regulations governing equipment attachment will be progressively liberalised, and there should be considerably greater freedom of choice for users.

Approval and certification of equipment will be carried out by the British Approvals Board for Telecommunications which will vet equipment and certify that it conforms to standards specified by the British Standards Institution in association with BT.

A wide range of modems are available to meet varying requirements such as synchronous/asynchronous, duplex/half duplex transmission in addition to matching the circuit characteristics. The different transmission modes are discussed elsewhere in this book; here we summarise the data rates which are currently available, together with some modem variants.

MAXIMUM TRANSMISSION SPEED	TRANSMISSION MEDIUM
2400 bit/s full duplex over one line 9600 bit/s full duplex using two lines simultaneously	Public Switched Telephone Network
9600 bit/s	S3 Unconditioned Leased Line (4-wire)
16000 bit/s	Tariff T Leased Line (4-wire)
72000 bit/s	48 kHz Wideband Group

Figure 7.10   Transmission Capabilities of Modern Modems

Data Rate

Figure 7.10 lists the maximum data rates which can be achieved using the synchronous modems on the market today.

Baseband Modems

A baseband modem does not modulate or demodulate a carrier signal in the way that a true modem does. It merely takes the binary data signal and transmits it to line in a modified form, as a baseband signal. (A baseband signal, it will be recalled, is a signal containing frequencies down to DC.) The modification takes the form of pulse shaping – rounding off the square pulses to reduce the high-frequency components – and scrambling, to give the baseband signal a satisfactory frequency spectrum independent of the binary data signal.

Baseband modems require a physical pair of wires over which to transmit, since the baseband signal contains frequencies outside the normal 300–3400 Hz speech band. They are therefore only suitable for short-haul applications where an unloaded physical pair is available.

One particular application of baseband transmission is found in wideband 48 kbit/s links, for which special cable capable of transmitting the high-frequency signals has to be laid to the customer's premises. Short point-to-point links can be cabled directly, and baseband modems would be used at each end of the link. Longer point-to-point circuits are routed via 48 kbit/s circuits derived from the telephone FDM system. In this situation, baseband transmission is used for the two ends of the circuit, between the customer and the group band modem located at the nearest trunk network access point (Figure 7.11).

Acoustic Couplers

Basically, an acoustic coupler is a modem equipped with audio transducers (a loudspeaker and a microphone) so that it can interface to the telephone handset instead of to the telephone line. It can be used at low data rates where the standard modulation method is frequency shift keying.

An acoustic coupler presents a normal V24 interface to the terminal. It accepts data from the terminal and coverts it into audible high- and low-frequency tones, which are then fed to the microphone in the telephone handset. In the reverse direction, the coupler converts the audible

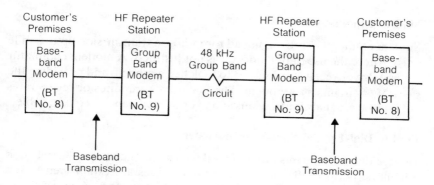

Figure 7.11   Modems in a 48 kbit/s Link

tones from the telephone earpiece into binary data signals for transfer to the terminal. Some terminals have built-in acoustic couplers.

The great advantage of an acoustic coupler is that it permits a terminal to use any convenient telephone. No wiring or other modifications are necessary. Its performance is inferior to a normal modem – the error rate is worse – but this is not a serious problem for many users.

Acoustic couplers are (reluctantly) permitted by the PTTs, and have to be approved to ensure they do not interfere with other users or with telephony plant. They are not favoured for permanent terminal installations.

Limited-Distance Modems

The modems standardised by the CCITT are designed for international and intercontinental use. Over shorter distances it is possible to achieve equivalent performance using less sophisticated modulation/ demodulation and equalisation techniques, and there is now a number of limited-distance modems offering very good price/performance ratios. Typically these modems have a range of about 50 miles, and operate up to 4800 bit/s.

Note, however, that not all 'short-haul' or 'limited-distance' modems are true modems. Many are baseband modems and can only be used when unloaded physical pairs are available, which limits their range considerably.

Modem Eliminators

Modem eliminators are employed for in-house transmission up to a mile or so, where the use of full modems is not justified. A modem eliminator is a line driver/receiver packaged to look like a modem and providing the same V24 circuits as a modem. The line driver amplifies or regenerates the interface signals for transmission over twisted pairs or coaxial cable.

Double Dial-Up and Split-Stream Modems

Double dial-up modems are designed for use on the the public switched telephone network. Two telephone connections are established to the required destination, and the two paths are then used as a 4-wire connection providing full duplex transmission (Figure 7.12).

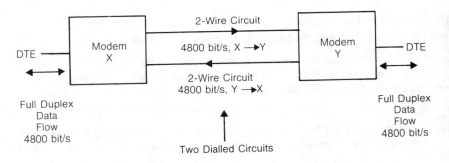

Figure 7.12   Double Dial-Up (4800 bit/s)

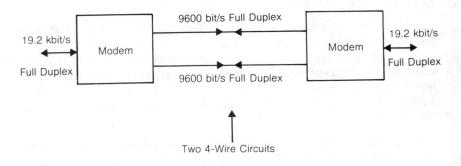

Figure 7.13   Split-Stream Modem (19.2 kbit/s)

Split-stream modems also use two separate circuits, but in this case both circuits carry data in the same direction. By transmitting at 9.6 kbit/s over two high grade leased lines operating in parallel, a split-stream modem can provide a data throughput rate of 19.2 kbit/s (Figure 7.13).

The electronic circuitry which splits the data stream and handles all the synchronisation problems can take the form of a separate unit, when it is known as a lineplexer.

Modem-Sharing Unit

A modem-sharing unit, also called a fan-out unit, allows several terminals to share one modem. All the terminals receive data from the modem simultaneously, but only one terminal can transmit at any one time. This distinguishes the device from a multiplexing modem which provides individual channels to each terminal it serves.

Modem-sharing units are economical where several co-located terminals require access to the same information and where the data traffic generated by each is low. They may be used at a computer centre to permit more than one computer port to have access to a communications link, which can be useful in circumventing faults.

Multiport (Multinode) Option

Many higher-speed synchronous (4800 to 14400 bit/s) modems incorporate a multiport option which allows the capacity of the modem to be divided between several ports; with the sum of the port data rates equalling the modem's rated speed. For example, a 9600 bit/s multiport modem can be configured with any of the following combinations of port speeds:

— 1 x 9600 bit/s port;

— 2 x 4800 bit/s ports;

— 1 x 4800 bit/s plus 2 x 2400 bit/s ports;

— 4 x 2400 bit/s ports;

— 1 x 7200 bit/s plus 1 x 2400 bit/s ports.

This in effect provides the facilities of both a modem and a Time Division Multiplexer.

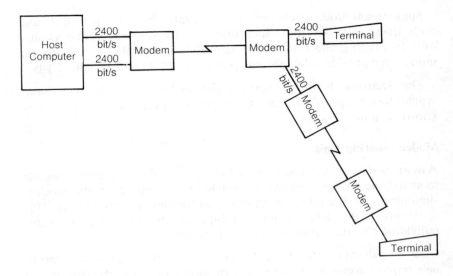

Figure 7.14

The facility can offer significant cost savings by avoiding the need for multiple point-to-point circuits. The ports can serve co-located devices, or alternatively the links may be extended to further locations as shown in Figure 7.14. In either case the overall circuit lengths can be greatly reduced.

Auto-Answer

An auto-answer option will allow a dial-up connection to be made without human intervention at the called site. It is important that the computer or terminal at the called site can handle the auto-answer modem interface.

The auto-answer has particular use in a time-sharing computer bureau operation. Here a series of modems can be installed in a 'hunting group' associated with a contiguous series of exchange lines. The bureau customer will dial the number of the first line in the hunting group and will be automatically connected to the first available modem.

Further use for the auto-answer feature is found in the retailing trade. Portable data collection units are used in supermarkets to record stock levels. At the end of the day's work the data collection terminal is connected to an auto-answer modem.

During the night, the staff at the computer centre ring each of the supermarkets in turn. The auto-answer option of the modem allows a connection to be made without supermarket staff involvement. The data transferred to the computer centre could be used, for example, to control supermarket stocks and schedule deliveries where stocks are running low. (Dialling could be automated if the computer centre was equipped with 'auto-dial' capabilities.) Overnight data transmission can be particularly economical if British Telecom's 'Midnight Line' is used between midnight and 6 a.m.

Auto-Dial

The British Telecom auto-dial facility (Data Communications Equipment 1A) allows a computer or terminal to 'dial' a telephone number. The DCE 1A has a parallel interface conforming to the CCITT V25 standard. Compatible interfaces are comparatively rare on computer and terminal systems; however, there is a growing number of 'black box' devices which allow the computer/terminal to output the dialling instructions as a serial data stream and convert those instructions to meet the requirements of the DCE 1A.

Line Conditioning

The modem supplier will specify the quality of leased circuit required for the satisfactory operation of their equipment.

All telephone circuits have the same nominal electrical characteristics; however, tolerances are applied to those nominal values in defining the guaranteed characteristics of a line. The higher the stated quality of the line, the more closely it will conform to the stated nominal values, ie the tighter will be the tolerances allowed. The term 'conditioning' is used in describing the quality of a telephone circuit.

It may be that, because of a modem's design, it requires a lower line quality than others operating at the same data rate. The use of a lower quality line will offer savings in line installation, charges and rentals.

Dial Back-Up

Where a data link is crucial to an organisation's day-to-day work, it is important that an alternative service should be available. One approach would be the provision of a dial back-up capability making use of the PSTN network.

For most data rates twin dial-up lines are required in order to provide a standby link capable of full duplex operation. It may be considered adequate to provide a degraded service using a half-duplex data link, the degradation being caused by modem turn-around prior to the transmission of each message.

Some dial-up circuits may not be of sufficient quality to support the original data rate. Many modems have controls which allow them to operate at lower speeds to cover this eventuality. For example, it may only be possible to operate a 9600 bit/s modem at its 'fall-back' data rate of 4800 bit/s.

Miscellaneous Interfacing Devices

Line Contention or Line Sharing Adaptor

Where a computer port is only able to support a single terminal at a time but cannot itself arbitrate on conflicting demands from multiple connected modems, a variation of the fan-out unit may be used. Known as a *line contention unit,* this allows a line to be shared between terminals on a first come, first served basis. The terminal user requests connection by sending a predetermined signal to the contention unit; if the computer port or line is free, the connection is made, otherwise the user is left to try again later. In general, these devices are very simple in construction so the 'dialogue' between the terminal and the unit will be rudimentary; very often there is little evidence of the success or otherwise of a request for connection until the terminal user attempts to use the computer service.

Line Access Unit

A Line Access Unit (LAU) is a diversion device which simplifies the changeover from a private circuit to alternative dial-up connections in the event of a circuit failure. The LAU may also provide the interface signals needed to change the modulation technique or transmission speed employed in the event that a circuit's quality will only support a degraded performance.

Voice Adaptor

A Voice Adaptor enables a leased circuit to be manually switched to speech traffic when it is not being used for data transmission.

Voice/Data Units

These units allow voice and data communications to be routed over the same lines. Simultaneous voice and data transmission is possible using some devices, whilst others only permit voice or data transmission to take place at any particular time.

There are two principal reasons why transmission of voice and data over a common line can be advantageous:

— to optimise bandwidth utilisation on expensive leased-line facilities;

— network management often requires voice communication facilities between a network control centre and remote sites.

Units which allow simultaneous or effectively simultaneous transmission of data and voice over one 4-wire voice band line are:

— the speech-plus-data multiplexer, sometimes referred to as the s+dx panel; available bandwidth for voice and data is fixed;

— the dynamic multiplexer which utilises the bandwidth released during the pauses in conversations for data.

The essential characteristics of each type of device and situations in which it should be considered are shown in Figures 7.15 and 7.16 below.

Multiplexers and Concentrators

The terms multiplexer and concentrator are often used interchangeably, particularly by suppliers. In general, a concentrator is a more sophisti-

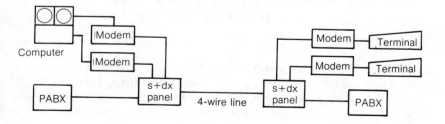

Figure 7.15   Typical Network Configuration Utilising s+dx Panels

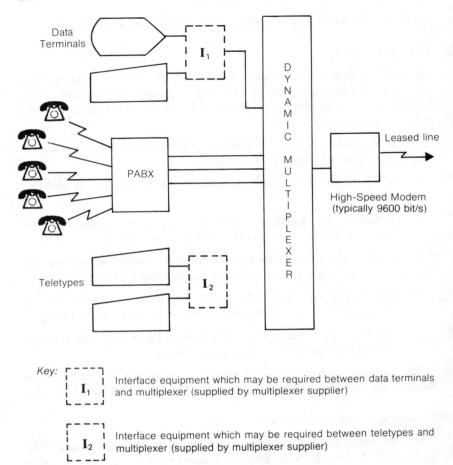

Figure 7.16 Typical Network Configuration Utilising Dynamic Multiplexer Equipment

cated device than a multiplexer, it does not offer a 'transparent' route for the data on each channel, but rather manages the terminals connected to it and communicates on their behalf with a host computer. In many cases, these concentrators are special-purpose devices tailored to a single user's requirements.

A major distinction sometimes drawn between the two devices is that a multiplexer only has the capacity to handle the sum of the transmission rates on the input circuits, ie the sum of the outputs cannot exceed the sum of the inputs.

In contrast a concentrator has buffering capability to 'queue' inputs which exceed capacity.

However, as multiplexers become increasingly intelligent, even this distinction is being eroded.

The purpose of both multiplexers and concentrators is to enable a number of devices, usually connected locally by relatively low-speed circuits, to share a more expensive, higher bandwidth circuit.

We now examine the different classes of multiplexers and concentrators and discuss the facilities which each may offer.

Most time division multiplexers employ sophisticated error detection and recovery techniques in transmitting data across a line. The very low level of residual errors which result may make the use of cheap asynchronous terminals a viable alternative to more expensive synchronous devices.

Frequency Division Multiplexing (FDM)

FDM divides the available bandwidth of a communications channel into a number of independent channels, each having an assigned portion of the total frequency spectrum. Figure 7.17 shows the frequency bands of the first four channels in a typical FDM system (UK Post Office Dataplex). The 'bearer' circuit, as the multiplexed circuit is called, has a nominal bandwidth of 3000 Hz giving 12 channels each of 240 Hz bandwidth. Four-wire circuits are used giving 12 'send' and 12 'receive' channels, enabling full duplex facilities to be given.

One of the limitations of an FDM system will be seen from Figure 7.17: ie guard bands or safety zones are needed to prevent overlapping of the electrical signals, resulting in under-utilisation of the available bandwidth.

The data signalling rate of each channel on the example system is 110 bit/s to cater for the numerous 10 character/second dataprinters in use. If all the channels were in use at once, a total of only 1320 bit/s would be transmitted which is far less than the data signalling rate capability of

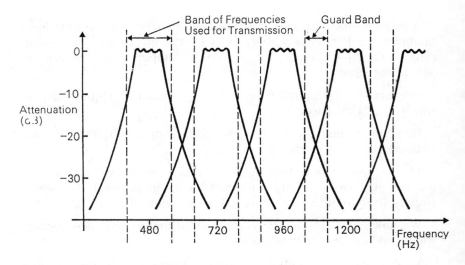

Figure 7.17   Frequency Bands of a FDM System

the bearer circuit (up to 9600 bit/s using suitable high-speed modems). More expensive filtering equipment can improve the aggregate bit rate on FDM systems but this would not be likely to exceed much above 2000 bit/s in the example case.

A further disadvantage, inherent with FDM systems, is that the error performance of some channels may be poorer than others due to the loss/frequency and group delay characteristics of the bearer circuit. For example, signals in a channel in the higher part of the frequency spectrum will be more severely attenuated than the signals in a lower channel; this problem can be largely overcome by equalisation but at added cost.

The main advantage of FDM for a user is to be found in those applications where the low aggregate bit rate is not a constraint. Where only a limited number of low-speed channels are required, the simplicity of FDM systems can give a lower cost per channel compared with the TDM systems which are discussed below. One of the reasons for this is that no modems are required between frequency division multiplexers – the multiplexers themselves performing the necessary digital/analogue conversion for transmission over the bearer circuit.

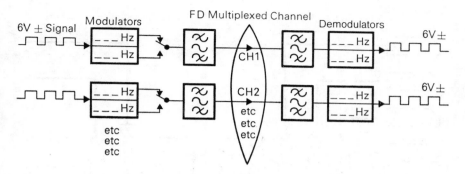

**Figure 7.18   Modulation and Demodulation of Separate Channels for a
Typical FDM System**

Time Division Multiplexing (TDM)

A time division mulitplexer works on the principle of taking data from a
number of sources and allocating each of these sources a period of time or
'time slots'. The individual time slots are assembled into 'frames' to form
a single high-speed digital data stream. PCM systems use time division
multiplexing to interleave a number of speech conversations which are
first converted from analogue into digital form. The output from data
terminals is already digital and this simplifies the time division multiplexing process. The interleaving takes two different forms, 'bit-interleaving'
and 'character- or byte-interleaving'.

Bit-Interleaved TDM

Figure 7.19 shows a simplified representation of the bit-interleaving
process. It will be seen from the diagram that, if synchronisation between
the multiplexing and de-multiplexing functions is lost, there is a danger
that bits may be delivered to the wrong outputs (when de-multiplexed).
Synchronisation is maintained by assembling the individual bits sampled
from each terminal into a frame so that nominally one frame consists of
one bit from each of the terminal inputs to the system.

A unique bit sequence termed a framing pattern is included within each
frame (or can be distributed throughout a number of frames) and must be
detected a predetermined number of times by the de-multiplexing stage
before synchronisation is assumed. Similarly, the loss of frame synchron-

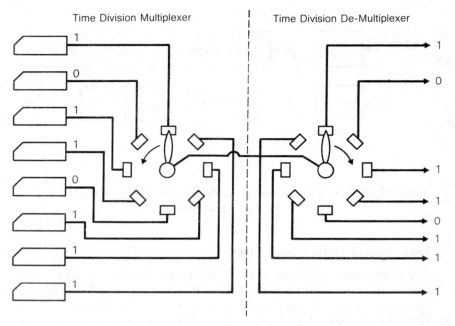

Figure 7.19   Principles of Bit-Interleaved Time Division Multiplexing Using Simple Commutators

isation is not assumed until the framing pattern has failed to be detected a predetermined number of times. If synchronisation is lost due to any factor such as a line disturbance, re-synchronisation is not assumed until this has been detected several times.

In practice, the digital output from any time division multiplexer must be converted into analogue form for transmission over telephone circuits and back from analogue to digital at the distant end. The modems used may be an integral part of the multiplexer but are more often separate as shown in Figure 7.20. Synchronous modems are used so that bit synchronisation can be maintained throughout the system.

Character- or Byte-Interleaved TDM

A character-interleaved multiplexer interleaves characters received from low-speed channels on to the high-speed bearer circuit. Each interleaved

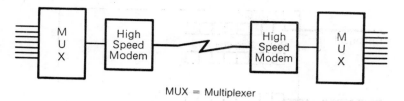

MUX = Multiplexer

Figure 7.20 Modems Required in TDM

character occupies eight bits in the frame, but this may vary depending on the code level being transmitted and the need for a status bit. The simplified elements of a character-interleaved time division multiplexer are shown in Figure 7.21. Data is received serially from each low-speed channel and assembled in a serialiser. When a complete character has been received, it is shifted in parallel form into a buffer register and then transmitted in serial form to the high-speed line at the high-speed line rate during the time slot period allocated to that low-speed channel.

The scanner operates at a speed related to each low-speed character period. For a 10 character per second terminal, scanning for transmission to the high-speed line would take place every tenth of a second. If a buffer is empty, the related byte in the transmitted frame will be padded. Each frame consists of typically nine bits per low-speed channel (this will vary in accordance with the terminal code being used) plus a synchronisation sequence and frame control information, the nature and length of which vary between manufacturers. The frame structure used in a typical character-interleaved system is shown in Figure 7.22.

The effect of lost synchronisation with bit-interleaved TDM was mentioned earlier and similar schemes have been developed in order to maintain frame synchronisation on character-interleaved TDM systems. Again this involves the use of a unique framing pattern within each frame which must be detected a predetermined number of times before frame synchronisation is assumed. Because characters rather than bits are interleaved in each frame, the frames are longer than in bit-interleaved systems. This usually means that the proportion of synchronising bits to information bits is lower with character-interleaving but the greater efficiency which results is offset to some extent by the longer time taken to re-synchronise.

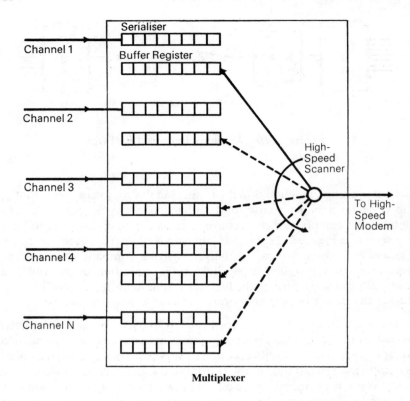

Figure 7.21   Simplified Character-Interleaved Time Division Multiplexer

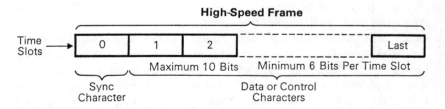

Figure 7.22   Frame Structure in a Character-Interleaved System

Because whole characters have to be assembled in a character-interleaved system, more storage has to be provided than in a bit-interleaved system and this tends to increase the costs. However, as it is unlikely that all the terminals will be in use at the same time, storage can be reduced by dynamically allocating buffers to those terminals which are actually being used. Some modern character-interleaved multiplexing designs not only reduce costs in this way but also achieve significant reductions in the size of the TDM equipment.

Character-interleaving offers a number of advantages over bit-interleaving. In particular, when used for multiplexing asynchronous terminals, they offer more efficient transmission. Start and stop elements can be simply stripped off and replaced at the de-multiplexing stage, as the units sampled are characters and not bits. This effectively compresses the data on the high-speed line and improves the aggregate low-speed bit rate of the TDM link. On ten character per second machines using ASCII or IA 5 code, three bits of the eleven bits per character are used for start/stop, and bit stripping, therefore, provides a potential saving of over 27 per cent of line time. IA 2 with its 7.5 bit structure with 2.5 bits used for start/stop provides even greater potential savings of over 33 per cent. Thirty characters per second machines use one start and only one stop element in a 10 bit character structure but bit stripping still offers an attractive 20 per cent improvement factor. In practice, the need for

Low-speed inputs		Data signalling rate of the bearer circuit	Aggregate low-speed bit rate
Example 1	8 x 110 bit/s		
	12 x 134.5 bit/s	4800	4894
	8 x 300 bit/s		
Example 2	11 x 110 bit/s		
	1 x 1200 bit/s	2400	2410
Example 3	11 x 110 bit/s		
	12 x 134.5 bit/s		
	2 x 300 bit/s	4800	4624
	2 x 600 bit/s		

Figure 7.23   Typical Examples of Mixed Input Rates Possible on a Character-Interleaved Multiplexer

synchronisation and control bytes within frames reduces the aggregate low-speed bit rate of character-interleaved multiplexers to some extent, but this is still usually between 10 per cent and 20 per cent higher than the rate of the bearer circuit; ie a 2400 bit/s circuit will typically bear some twenty-five 110 bit/s terminals – an aggregate low-speed bit rate of 2750 bit/s. The actual improvement will depend on the character structure used by the terminals and whether terminals of mixed speed are being multiplexed. However, as the proportion of synchronisation bits to information bits is usually higher in bit-interleaved systems, character-interleaving gives a significant improvement in efficiency. Typically, a bit-interleaved multiplexer will support twenty-one 110 bit/s terminals on a 2400 bit/s bearer circuit (an appropriate low-speed bit rate of only 2310 bit/s). Bit stripping is possible on bit-interleaved systems but the added logic necessary reduces their cost advantage. A major advantage of character-interleaving over bit-interleaving is that noise bursts affect fewer terminal users. A ten bit burst would affect a maximum of two terminals whereas up to 10 terminals would be affected in a bit-interleaved system. The relatively better error performance of character-interleaved systems has to be weighed against the added length of time they take to re-synchronise.

Most TDM systems can accept input from terminals using different speeds and codes but because the multiplexer system operates on a synchronous basis it is necessary to know in advance the speeds and codes to be handled and to program for them. TDM systems can also handle data from synchronous data terminals where the terminal transmission is in the block mode rather than character by character. For this type of transmission, bit-interleaving is usually employed as this provides a degree of bit sequence independence not possible with character-interleaved systems and in any case is cheaper and simpler. It should be remembered that data characters within a block do not usually include start and stop bits and thus the facility of bit stripping which is a significant advantage of character-interleaving would not be applicable.

Where a TDM system is required to handle a mixture of input speeds and codes, it is usual for groups of channels and their related computer ports to be dedicated for particular speed and code operation. Some types of multiplexer, however, can provide a facility which enables some or all channels of the system to handle terminals operating at any speed or code within a predetermined range – this facility is variously known as 'adaptive speed control' or 'automatic bit rate' (ABR) and code level selection.

To provide the facility, all messages from the terminals connected to the multiplexer must be prefixed by an agreed character which, when compared with internally programmed set characters at the multiplexer, enables the multiplexer to determine the speed and code level being employed and to adapt the channel conditions to handle that type of terminal. This facility has a particular advantage for computer bureaux operators who use the PSTN to provide contention for inputs to the multiplexer. For example, if a bureau's customers in Birmingham were to be connected to a London computer centre over a TDM multiplexed link Birmingham - London, access to the TDM multiplexer would be gained by dialling a local call in the Birmingham area. If the terminals used by the bureau's customers in Birmingham were all one speed and used the same code, they could all be given the same number to dial for access to any one of the TDM ports (see Figure 7.24). The concentration function of the PSTN can be seen in this example and, typically, a contention ratio of four terminals to one input port is used, giving high utilisation of the TDM channels. The effect of having terminals of two different speeds, 110 bit/s and 300 bit/s, can be seen from Figure 7.25.

Different ports must normally be used for the two types of terminal and separate telephone numbers provide two distinct access routes. Because 110 bit/s ports may be free while 300 bit/s ports are overloaded the efficiency of the whole system is reduced.

Although adaptive speed control overcomes this problem, we cannot obtain 'something for nothing'. The penalty, apart from slight increased cost of the multiplexer equipment, is that the channel capacity of the multiplexer system will be restricted and must be determined on the basis that all channels may need to operate at the highest required speed, ie 300 bit/s in the example in Figure 7.25; time slots are not allocated dynamically.

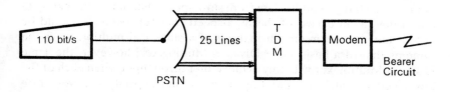

Figure 7.24   Access into a 'Local' TDM Using the PSTN as a Concentrator

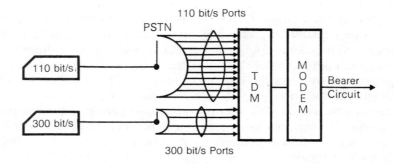

Figure 7.25   Access into a 'Local' TDM from Different Speed Terminals, Using the PSTN for Concentration

When using adaptive speed control, it is necessary for the computer ports also to be able to adapt to the required terminal speed and this can be arranged by sampling a prefix character in a similar manner to that described for the multiplexer – this adds to the complexity and cost of the computer system.

Statistical (Time Division) Multiplexers

Statistical Multiplexers extend the concept of character-interleaved Time Division Multiplexing. Rather than allocate high-speed channel capacity in a fixed manner with each low-speed channel being allocated its share whether it needs it or not, a statistical multiplexer will monitor each of the slow-speed channels at the rated speed of that channel but only use high-speed channel capacity when there is data to be transmitted. A typical configuration is illustrated in Figure 7.26.

Where the low-speed channels are lightly utilised, it is possible for the multiplexed link to handle data from slow-speed channels with aggregate data rates far in excess of the high-speed channel speed. It should be noted that the maximum throughput of a statistical multiplexer is the same as that of a basic Time Division Multiplexer; however, the Time Division Multiplexer will only achieve that throughput when each of the low-speed channels is operating at maximum capacity – a very rare occurrence in practice. A Statistical Multiplexer, on the other hand, serves more, but less heavily utilised, channels to achieve a higher average throughput across the multiplexed link.

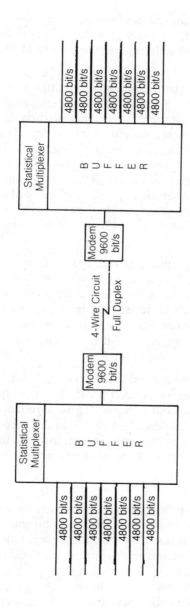

Figure 7.26 Statistical Multiplexer Application

As the combined data rates of the low-speed channels exceed that of the high-speed channel, it is possible for the data-flow from the slow-speed channel to exceed the throughput capability of the multiplexed links.

To cope with this eventuality, statistical multiplexers contain large buffers which are capable of absorbing short-term peaks in demand. However, it is important that there is a mechanism capable of suspending data-flow into the multiplexer should there be any danger of buffer overflow. One of two methods is usually used to achieve this 'flow control'. Either the multiplexer outputs the 'X-OFF' characters to the terminals via the 'Receive Data' circuit in the terminal interface, or the 'clear to send' signal in the terminal interface is dropped (when it is safe for data transfer to resume, either the character 'X-ON' is output, or the 'clear to send' signal is raised) (see Chapter 9 for explanation of the Interchange Circuits).

Most multiplexers will implement the 'hold off' signal when a given buffer reserve is reached. It is therefore important that the terminal or computer should stop outputting data before the reserve is exhausted; to this end, the input/output characteristics of the terminal/computer should be matched carefully; for example, since some computers output as many as 256 bytes after receiving X-OFF, it is crucial that the multiplexer should have enough reserve capacity.

For some types of terminals, notably printers, the flow into the terminal should be capable of being suspended if data loss is to be avoided; for example, if the printer runs out of paper. Those terminals use the same 'flow-control' mechanism as described above; in this case the multiplexers should suspend the data-flow into the terminal and then avoid data loss resulting from an overflow of the multiplexer's buffers.

Data Compression

It is common practice for intelligent multiplexers to perform editing functions such as recovering stop-bits from asynchronous data prior to transmission, and when reinstated by the multiplexer at the receiving site. This bit stripping usually offsets the overhead involved in the link protocol employed between multiplexers, making it possible for a high-speed channel operating at 9600 bit/s to carry 960 data characters per second at least, (asynchronous channels operating at an aggregate speed of 9600 bit/s carry a maximum of 96 character/sec, each 8-bit data character being assumed to have one start- and one stop-bit associated with it).

We are also now beginning to see the emergence of multiplexers which compress multiple occurrences of the same character. Depending on the data being transmitted, this feature should result in major improvements in overall throughput.

Synchronous Channel Provision

One or more of the multiplexer's ports may be designated as synchronous. The high-speed channel capacity for these ports is allocated in a fixed fashion, while the remaining capacity is shared between asynchronous low-speed channels using 'statistical' techniques. For example, an 8-channel multiplexer operating on a 9600 bit/s high-speed data link may have two 2400 bit/s synchronous ports configured. In this case, 4800 bit/s of the high-speed channel capacity is dedicated to the synchronous channels' needs, the remaining 4800 bit/s is allocated in response to demands from the six asynchronous ports.

Multiplexers have also been introduced recently which allocate the synchronous channel capacity according to demand.

Designated Printer Ports

When a multiplexed data link is being used for both printer and VDU traffic, large amounts of printer data could swamp the multiplexer buffers possibly resulting in a degraded service to the VDU users. One approach to this problem was to limit the speed of a printer channel; however, this had the disadvantage of limiting the output to the printer even when no other use was being made of the fast channel. Some multiplexers will now allow ports to be specially designated as printer ports; the service to these ports will be preferentially degraded during periods of peak load so assuring adequate VDU response times. At all other times printer data is allowed full use of the available channel capacity.

Networking and Switching Capabilities

Some multiplexer products now allow second multiplexers on a number of sites to be interconnected in a mesh network, providing channels between any two multiplexer ports in the network. An extension of this capability is that temporary connections between ports may be established by a terminal user who requests connections to a particular port or class of port.

Such a network combines the functions of multiplexers with those of the data switches discussed later.

Software De-Multiplexing

A typical configuration for a TDM system is shown in Figure 7.27.

At the computer centre, incoming data is received in a serial digital stream from the high-speed modem. It is then de-multiplexed, presenting the communications interface with a number of lower-speed digital data streams (usually but not always in serial form). The data is then re-multiplexed at the communications interface before being passed to the computer. The reverse process occurs when information is output from the computer. As further costs are incurred because of the need for individual terminations for each low-speed channel, the whole process seems an extraordinary way to set about saving costs. However, it has its merits; standard computer/communications interfacing equipment can be used which means that terminals carried over a multiplex link can be treated just as any other terminal – the line multiplexing being virtually transparent to the computer system and the terminal user. Testing arrangements are also simplified by separating the low-speed channels at the computer centre.

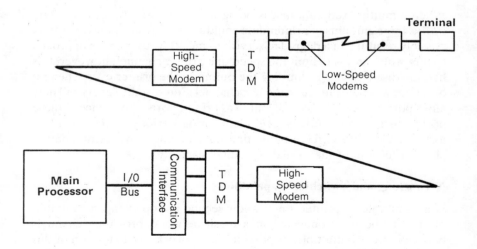

Figure 7.27   A Typical TDM Configuration

The obvious alternative to the arrangements discussed above is to dispense with the multiplexer at the computer centre altogether. The high-speed serial digital data stream can be taken from the modem straight into the communications interface where it is simply converted from serial to analogue form and passed over the high-speed input/output to the main processor. The main processor then has to de-multiplex the data by means of a special de-multiplexing software program. In the reverse direction, the computer software has to construct multiplexed frames of data for transmission via the communications interface and modems to the remote time division multiplexer. The process is termed 'software multiplexing' and there are savings to be gained through dispensing with one time division multiplexer and the low-speed channel terminations. However, the problem arises yet again that the reduction of costs in one area results in increased costs in another. The additional software required may be fairly simple, particularly when terminals of the same speed are being multiplexed. An incoming frame, for example, has only to be read into memory and a check is made for each time slot to find out whether or not a character is present. Programming can become much more complex and costly, however, when different speeds are being multiplexed. One of the most important arguments against software multiplexing is the additional work required of the central processing unit. As processing only takes place after each frame, it follows that the number of interrupts on the central processing unit will depend on the size of the frame, and character-interleaving has obvious advantages in this respect over bit-interleaving.

FDM versus TDM

Many of the arguments for and against these two fundamentally different forms of multiplexing have been discussed, but they can usefully be summarised as follows:

— The simplicity of FDM brings cost advantages when only a few low-speed channels are required. At present FDM is economic when fewer than about 10 or 12 channels are needed, the actual break even figure depending on which particular manufacturers' equipments are being compared. TDM is progressively cheaper per channel than FDM as the number required rises beyond 12;

— FDM techniques offer very little scope for cost reductions through technological development. Conversely, the reduction of logic and storage costs through the use of large scale integration (LSI) could significantly reduce the costs of TDM in the future. Whether these cost reductions will be realised depends on whether the demand for time division multiplexers warrants manufacturing the large quantities needed to justify the use of LSI techniques. As TDM requires the use of high-speed modems, the total system costs will obviously be reduced if modem costs are reduced, or the through-put on bearer circuits can be increased without significantly increasing modem costs;

— Because of the need for guard bands on FDM systems, the aggre-gate low-speed bit rate achievable is less than on TDM systems on which no guard channels are required and some data compression can be applied. This not only affects the costs per channel but also limits the ability of FDM systems to expand. For example, a TDM system over a typical leased circuit could expand to accommodate up to twenty-five 110 bit/s terminals. The most modern FDM system would be unlikely to handle more than eighteen 110 bit/s terminals. Some FDM channels may give a worse performance than others due to the line characteristics of the bearer circuit. TDM systems give a constant performance on all channels of the same speed;

— TDM systems are more flexible than FDM systems. Time division multiplexers can intermix terminals of different speed and with different synchronisation methods; system and channel configura-tion changes can also be effected more easily;

— The monitoring and diagnostic facilities on TDM are very much better than on the relatively less sophisticated FDM systems. High- and low-speed parity check facilities can also be given on TDM but not on FDM;

— One minor disadvantage of TDM systems – particularly when character-interleaving is employed – is when the low-speed termi-nals operating through the multiplexer system use echo-checking techniques for error control. With this technique, termed echo-plexing, a character entered on the terminal is transmitted to the computer and looped back to provide a local check for the user. The effective use of this technique requires the minimum possible delay between entering the character and the subsequent print out at the terminal. However, when a multiplexer system is included in

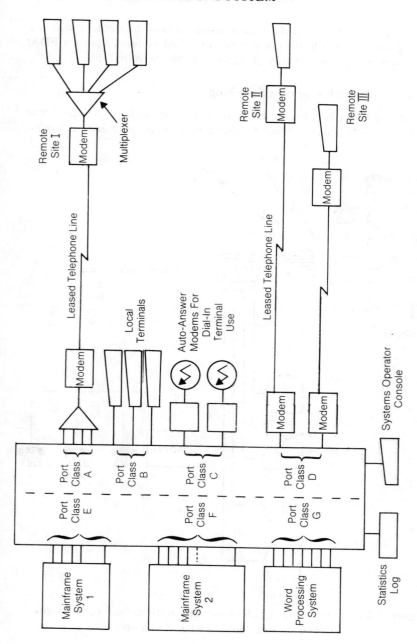

Figure 7.28 Communications Network – Historical Approach

the transmission path, transmission delays do occur which are more noticeable on some types of TDM systems than on FDM systems and may prove disturbing to the terminal user.

Integration through Common Switching

In recent years a number of large-scale organisations with significant telephony traffic have started to rationalise their wide area telecom-

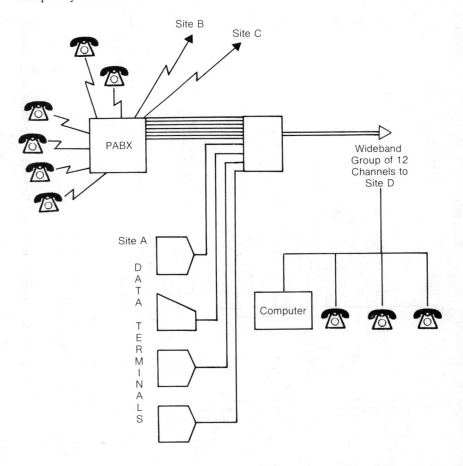

Figure 7.29　Level of Integration through Rationalisation of Circuit Provision into one Wideband Group

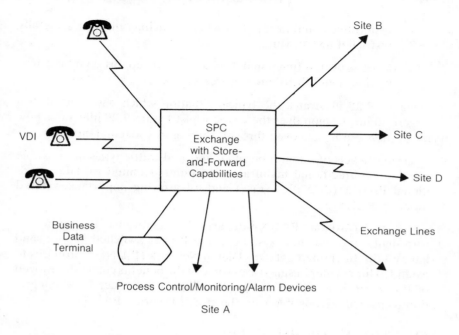

Site B

VDI

SPC Exchange with Store-and-Forward Capabilities

Site C

Site D

Business Data Terminal

Exchange Lines

Process Control/Monitoring/Alarm Devices

Site A

VDI Key:

VDI Telephone instrument acting as a voice and data input device

Figure 7.30 Extensive Integration through Sharing of Common Switching Facilities and Lines

munications and have achieved substantial economic savings through installing private wide band networks to handle all forms of traffic. Generally they have been able to justify the investment on the basis of speech alone, with the spare bandwidth available after meeting the voice requirement being utilised for data and other traffic.

The switching of traffic between user and computers and terminals is achieved through one or more methods in combination:

— traditional or shared program control PABXs serving local and wide area switching;

— mainframe computers performing a switching function generally restricted to non-voice;

— a sophisticated functional architecture to support computer networkings and distributed processing.

Figure 7.28 illustrates the typical situation which has evolved in a largely ad hoc fashion over the years; whilst Figure 7.29 illustrates how integration can be achieved through sharing of wideband circuits.

Various levels of integration of circuits and traffic types are possible using either traditional mainframe computers (limited to data), traditional PABXs (data plus voice) and, of growing importance, stored program PABXs.

The stored program PABX is of particular significance. In conjunction with digital transmission, System X, the Packet Switched Service, and later on the Integrated Services Digital Network (ISDN), it promises to extend to the smaller business user some of the benefits currently enjoyed by the larger organisation. Figure 7.30 illustrates the degree of integration which will be possible with the stored program PABXs.

FUNCTIONAL ARCHITECTURE

Introduction

Until the mid-1970s most computer users tended to have centralised Data Processing departments with mainframe computer systems. As more powerful systems evolved, organisations that had previously installed computers at subsidiary sites, concentrated their computing activities in Corporate Data Centres. Remote batch terminals incorporating cardreaders and punches together with line-printers were installed at the subsidiary site to provide access to central site services.

The main reasons for centralised computing was economics; large mainframe computers offered much cheaper processing than the smaller versions. Initially the work being done involved bulk processing; batches of input data were input to the computer and results were output either as punched cards or printed listings. By its nature, bulk data processing required extensive manual activity both before and after the computer had done its job. For example, once the user had written data onto a coding sheet, the data had to be collated, punched and verified before being input. For some applications, the time involved in the clerical procedures associated with batch data processing severely limited its effectiveness. To address these limitations, systems evolved which allowed files to be accessed directly by the user via networks of simple terminals. These on-line (or real-time) systems used expensive telephone circuits operating at comparatively slow data rates (initially 2400 bps was considered fast), to connect the terminals to the computer. Initially, on-line data processing was limited to very specialised applications (eg airline booking systems), but was eventually applied to other aspects of an organisation's activities.

While minicomputers and microprocessors had been available for a considerable amount of time, they were initially considered unsuitable by the majority of computer users. A mainframe computer user had many program development tools available to him which minimised the work involved in developing new applications, but the same could not be said for minicomputers, and the minicomputer user was involved in far more effort. This initially limited the use of minicomputers to a fairly small class of specialised users – for example, universities and research organisations; and they were also ideally suited for use as communications controllers and in process control.

Gradually the facilities available on mini- and subsequently microcomputers were improved until they could be considered attractive alternatives to the larger mainframe computer in many applications. Multiple minicomputers could be configured which provided equivalent functionality to a mainframe but at significantly lower cost.

In parallel with this trend towards multiprocessor systems, a second major component of today's distributed systems was emerging within the research and academic communities, primarily in the United States: the resource sharing network concept.

A primary design goal of the resource shared network is to provide many users with shared access to the total resources of the network, whether computers or other expensive resources such as large-scale memories.

The first major network with this capability was ARPANET which was commissioned by the Advanced Research Projects Agency (ARPA) of the USA Department of Defence. ARPANET is of great historical importance, and is regarded as the progenitor of many of the fundamental concepts in networking and advanced data communications. For example, it was the first large-scale network to employ packet switching principles, and many of the ideas underlying the structure of modern communications protocols were developed within it.

Such was the success of ARPANET, which primarily served users in the United States, that its design formed the basis for the first public packet switched network, TELENET. In its turn TELENET technology formed the basis of the UK Public Packet Switched Service and the International Packet Switched Service.

The linking together by a communications network of terminals, local computing facilities, centralised computers, and other central shared resources such as large-scale memory units and other specialised resources provides a distributed processing environment. It enables computing power to be located adjacent to where it is required, and permits remote access to more extensive and possibly expensive resources when needed.

We now briefly review some of the functional aspects and benefits of distributed computing.

Functional Distribution

Many of the advantages claimed for distributed processing are only achievable in respect of communication between remote sites. However, the ability to divide functions and applications between different devices brings advantages in both the local and remotely accessed systems. In fact, one of the earliest examples of distributed processing involved the use of a separate processor (front-end processor) to handle data communications links, a notoriously heavy user of a mainframe system's processing power. A front-end processor may undertake responsibility for many, if not all, of the tasks associated with transmitting data across the data link; for example, polling, error detection and correction, the only involvement of the mainframe computer being to supply the messages to be transmitted and to respond to interruptions caused either by the arrival of a new message, or a reported error which cannot be converted at a lower level of the system.

The concept of multiprocessor installations at a central location, not always incorporating a mainframe, has now been extended. Some of the processors involved may have software and hardware architectures specially designed to perform a particular task with high efficiency as in the case of a 'back-end' processor, whose role is to access an installation's database, or an array processor. In other cases, however, multiple processors may be configured either to cope with the volume of processing required or as a means of providing a level of service in the event of hardware failure.

When we consider remotely located systems in the context of distributed processing, a number of advantages may accrue:

— lower transmission costs;

— improved response-time at user terminals;

— a measure of autonomy for the slave site. The extent to which this is possible will vary widely from organisation to organisation, and between individual applications in an organisation. However, it is frequently possible for a local device to continue operating, albeit at a degraded level, even when the communication link is down.

Even a minimal level of added 'intelligence' at a remote user site can have a dramatic effect on the service provided to the terminal user. For example, many of the screen layouts used on Visual Display Units contain a considerable amount of narrative material; eg headings and other fields which do not vary with the data displayed but are there to add clarity. It is often possible to transmit this narrative material once only at the beginning of the day for storage in the terminal's (or terminal controller's) memory. Subsequently, whenever a particular screen layout is required, the narrative material is retrieved from the terminal's memory under the control of the host computer. This mechanism can result in a significant saving in the number of characters which need to be transmitted with subsequent reductions in response-time at the user terminal.

Alternatively the entire process can of course be located in the terminal memory.

Distributed Data

Where the bulk of the data which is accessed from a location is specific to that location and rarely if, ever, accessed from elsewhere, there are operational advantages to be gained by siting that data at the user location together with sufficient processing power to handle local requirements. There must be sufficient local demand to warrant the cost of a local processor, perhaps with groups of locations sharing a processor sited at one of them.

When databases are located at the user site, the volume of data transmitted to and from that site will be reduced. This can have a significant impact on data transmission costs because lower speed circuits may be adequate.

Distributed Network Architectures

We have seen that distributed data processing involves providing 'intelligence' at terminal user locations and, where appropriate, locating data where it is most used, whilst at the same time supplying communication paths to enable access to other locations in the network.

It will be evident that a network which provides a distributed processing environment presents major problems of control and coordination. At the same time it is essential that users – many of whom may be non-technical – should have easy and transparent access to the facilities. For example, if they are accessing a remote application, they should not be aware – apart from a short transmission delay – that it is remote, and should have the impression that it might just as well be provided by the local device.

This is the central role of functional Network Architectures, a subject we cover in more detail in Chapter 8.

For the time being we observe that, by insulating the user from the network and providing him with the facility to access for example, a file, a program etc, either at a specified location, or more generally, irrespective of the physical location of that facility and the data paths required to access it, network architectures provide a number of advantages:

— easy and flexible access for the user;

— changes may be made to the network topology in response to changing patterns in data traffic;

— data files may be moved so that the data traffic resulting from users accessing them is minimised;

— processors dedicated to particular applications may be relocated.

Thus, the bulk of the detailed raw mechanics is concealed from the user. And in advanced systems the user need only refer to a resource, whether it be a file or a program for example, by name. The system software then does the rest, such as constructing the correct physical address, or even finding a location with sufficient available resources to perform the required task.

8 The Data Communications System: Control and Coordination

INTRODUCTION

Up to this point, the book has concentrated on the principles of transmission, and how transmission circuits and other pieces of hardware can be assembled and linked together to form a *data communications system*. It should be apparent by now that in an actual system there is an enormous gulf between the communicating entities. Ultimately, these entities are application programs and data residing in dispersed devices, or a human being at a terminal, interacting with a remote application program. And yet, at the transmission level, the fundamental physical unit of transmission is an electrical signal which may be digital or analogue in form. The gulf between these two levels is not just physical but also conceptual, and in addition to the physical principles and arrangements, a whole panoply of procedures and conventions has to be introduced in order to ensure that a meaningful and disciplined exchange of information takes place, and that the intentions of the communicating entities are faithfully carried out.

This subject is the chief concern of the present and succeeding chapters.

AN EVERYDAY ILLUSTRATION

That some form of discipline is needed to ensure that devices, connected by a communications link, communicate in an intelligible fashion can be readily appreciated if we consider the familiar situation where we wish to say something of importance to just one other person.

Before we begin speaking, we first try to gain his or her attention. If in the same room, we make sure that the person is within earshot, looking

255

towards us, or giving some other indication of suitable attentiveness. We may prefix our message by calling the person's name, thumping the table or asking the person to excuse us. Whichever of the numerous methods we adopt, our aim will be to make sure that when we begin speaking the person is prepared to listen, ie is synchronised with us at the start.

As our message is important, we will strive to make the other person understand us. The first requirement is to sustain the person's attention, and we may go to extraordinary lengths to achieve this, varying our approach to suit different circumstances. Most of us are rather better at transmitting than receiving and are skilled in detecting when another's attention begins to wander. To prevent this, we may break our message up into a number of sections and ask questions periodically about what has just been said.

When we have come to the end of our important message, we are likely to give some indication that we have finished. Although this might simply involve stopping talking, in many situations we will use a recognisable end of message phrase such as 'Well that's it' or a final question such as 'now are you sure you've understood?'.

Finally, no matter how we have finished our message, we will usually wait for some kind of response from the other person before we break off the conversation.

PROTOCOLS AND THEIR FUNCTIONS

The above illustration can be made even more instructive, if, instead of the conversation taking place face-to-face, it occurs on the telephone. Now, a transmission medium (the telephone network) is interposed between the two parties, and the interaction between the user and the telephone system itself is governed by strict rules, incorporated in dialling procedures and codes, tone signals and so on.

In general, data communications is far more complex; the communicating entities are ultimately applications programs situated in devices, at least one of which is programmable. The requirement for clearly and unambiguously defined rules is a fundamental one and arises directly from the relationship between the communicating devices. Although they can communicate over a transmission link, the remote devices are essentially *autonomous* and there is no *necessary* relationship between events at each end of the link. This must be controlled by externally imposed rules, and events at each end coordinated through the exchange of control messages and signals of various kinds. When machine talks to machine, no allowance can be made for discretion and intuition. The rules must be spelled out in minute detail, clearly and unambiguously defined, and rigidly adhered to.

Definition

PROTOCOL: A set of rules agreed between two parties who wish to communicate so that a meaningful dialogue can take place.

This form of words has great generality, and it should be noted that we do not at this stage define the characteristics of either the 'parties' or what is 'meaningful'.

Historical Perspective

Since communications was first introduced into computing, data communications protocols and standards have progressively evolved in response to changing technology and the increased demands placed upon communications systems. We shall briefly review the salient features and main influences.

Telecommunications Services

In the very first data communications systems, transmission was restricted to a single location so the terminal might be in the same room as the computer, and certainly not very far away. Because the distances were relatively short, dedicated lines could be used, and there was no requirement to use the public telephone network, and the quality and conditions of attachment and use were largely within the control of the user and the suppliers. In particular, the circuits were not prone to some of the errors inherent in the public telephone network.

A major change took place when data communications was extended beyond the local environment to remote locations, and it was natural that the telephone system, being so widely available, should be an obvious choice. This had two main consequences. First of all, because of their responsibility for monitoring the integrity of the network, and the control that they exercised over attachment of equipment and the use of the network, data communications was exposed for the first time to the influence of the PTTs. Although the influences have not always been desirable, some have brought major and long-lasting benefits. Of particular significance is the long and successful standardisation experience of the PTTs under the aegis of the CCITT.

The world's telephone network as we know it today is a fitting monument to these efforts. It was inevitable that this experience would have an impact on the specification and widespread adoption of the electrical interface standards governing the attachments of computers and terminals, and implemented in the modem.

The second and less welcome result was that data communications now had to face up to a less reliable transmission medium, partly because of the longer distances, but also because of the interposition of equipment such as telephone exchanges, circuit loading elements and the like, which conferred undesirable characteristics on the line, ie from the viewpoint of data communications.

More serious attention therefore had to be given to the control of errors.

Transmission Mode

For a number of years, transmission was largely restricted to the asynchronous mode; ie sending a character at a time using simple teletype terminals. The characters were generated at a slow rate dictated by the manual capabilities of a human being, and could be printed or displayed on a terminal at a similar rate easily comprehended by the human operator. Nor was error control a major problem, since the operator could fairly easily detect an error by the garbled nature of the message, and could readily request a retransmission. Character 'echoing back' of each character transmitted also proved to be an effective way of detecting errors.

Asynchronous transmission from simple terminals is still widely employed, and is a reasonably efficient and effective way of transmitting short messages. However, this was not adequate for the transmission of large volumes of information, and so remote batch transmission was developed. This employed higher transmission speeds and there was increasing use of the synchronous mode. This had a major impact on protocol requirements. Protocols which could accommodate block and message structures were required, and it was clearly impracticable to employ the error control techniques adequate for asynchronous transmission. Far more automatic procedures were needed. The Basic Mode and, more recently, HDLC protocols were developed specifically to support synchronous transmission.

Terminal Characteristics

The continually reducing cost of processing power brought about by solid-state technology has had a marked influence on terminal capabilities and indirectly on protocols and their implementation.

The provision of more intelligence in terminals was a major factor in the widespread adoption of polling disciplines in conjunction with synchronous transmission, since these required local buffering to store blocks of information awaiting transmission, and sufficient intelligence to 'listen' to polling messages and to respond to them.

The ability to locate low-cost intelligence wherever it is required has also been a major influence in the development of sophisticated protocols like HDLC and X25, which demand substantial processing power for their implementation.

The Computer Interface

Throughout the history of data communications, the development of efficient methods for managing not only communications lines but also the whole range of directly attached peripheral devices has been a central problem to computer engineers and the designers of systems software.

In the beginning, the terminals used were all of the teletype variety operating in asynchronous mode, and because these transmit one character at a time in an unpredictable fashion, in the early computers it was necessary for the computer to give undivided attention to the terminal. With few exceptions these early computers were capable of only obeying one program sequentially from beginning to end, and the instructions for handling the terminal were therefore either embedded in the program or in a separate subroutine.

It then became evident that the time consumed in handling terminals and other peripherals constituted a significant overhead, and to overcome this the multiprogramming mainframe was developed.

This enabled a signal from a peripheral or other external device to interrupt a program currently being executed. This caused executive and operating system software to initiate the transfer and then return to the original program (or some other program) at the point previously left, while the transfer proceeded autonomously.

Various techniques were developed and much ingenuity employed in minimising the effect of external device interrupts on system overheads. These included: isolation of input/output details to autonomous units with their own storage areas; the queueing of interrupts at the periphery; and arranging for the rate of arrival of requests for service to be controlled by the computer.

This exercise of control by the central computer rather than by an externally connected device became a dominant feature of the traditional mainframe suppliers' offerings, and has exerted a significant influence on network configurations, their functional architectures, and, to an extent, some features of data communications protocols. For example, centralised control was very appropriate to star-connected systems using either point-to-point or multipoint circuits.

Mainframe versus Minicomputer

For quite a large part of the history, computer development followed two parallel paths. The original mainframe computer progressed through various generations to become the large centralised multiprogramming mainframe computer with its vast armoury of systems software. Many of these systems still being marketed in the 1970s contained within them some traces of their 1960s batch processing ancestry. Because of this they were, in some respects, not ideally suited to support data communications.

The minicomputer, in contrast, arose out of the process control environment, and from the start, process control necessitated a different approach. First of all the computer had to be capable of handling a multiplicity of external signals and responding very quickly to them. Also, the time criticalities were such that the overheads introduced by layers of sophisticated systems software just could not be tolerated. Other considerations were cost and the requirement to disperse the intelligence throughout the area of plant being controlled.

The large mainframe and the process control approaches resulted in different philosophies for handling external events such as the arrival of data on a line, or a request for attention by a terminal. Because of the time-critical constraint, process-control computers and their programs were designed to operate in a fairly direct interrupt mode.

From the start this was reflected in the structure of their executive and operating systems software which were designed specifically to handle interrupts efficiently. This was not generally true of multiprogramming executives which were really designed to maximise the throughput of batch programs. This is the main reason why the successful implementation of high-performance data communications systems required additional systems software, often of considerable sophistication, to overcome the limitations of the traditional multiprogramming approach.

Networks and Network Architectures

The majority of data communications systems in use today have been constructed out of point-to-point and multipoint circuits with control being exercised centrally. For much of the time development has been largely haphazard, with solutions being adopted on an ad hoc basis in response to changing technology and application needs.

As data communications systems became increasingly complex, together with the trend towards distributed processing and networking, equipment suppliers started to face significant problems. A pressing requirement was to maintain upwards compatibility in their product ranges, and to be able to easily assimilate new products into their data communications systems. Clearly, a more logical and coherent framework was required. What they did was to construct conceptual *Network Architectures* which, broadly speaking, comprise the body of rules specifying how the suppliers' products can be connected together and their physical and functional relationships. The architectural principles also specify the various communications protocols to be used. These may conform to international standards or may be the supplier's own version.

Protocol Functions

Because of their different purposes, protocols differ greatly in character. Some consist of little more than a vocabulary of messages for carrying out certain actions. Others describe the interaction of complex mechanisms which obey mathematical rules. Usually the protocol specification begins

by defining messages of various kinds and giving a rough idea of their
meaning. It then describes the interactions which should take place using
these messages. At each stage of the interaction there must be a number
of alternatives available to the interacting devices, and therefore the
overall behaviour is often complex. A large part of the protocol may be
concerned with the methods for recovery from errors, whether caused by
faulty operation in one of the interacting devices or faulty operation in the
system which connects them.

The functions of some particular protocols are described in the following chapters, but it will be useful here to summarise the main requirements and circumstances which they must cater for.

Link Initiation and Termination

Until entities wish to communicate, the path joining them is essentially in
a quiescent but well-defined state. By some appropriate signalling convention, one or other party must be able to 'seize' the link and initiate the
interaction. Similarly, there must also be prescribed rules for terminating
the interaction.

Synchronisation

Since the communicating entities are essentially autonomous and operate
according to their own particular rules, it is clearly necessary to synchronise the temporal sequence of events. Synchronisation will normally be
required at several levels. Because information is transmitted serially in
bits, bit synchronisation will always be necessary, and since information is
generally given a character structure superimposed on the bit stream,
synchronisation of character boundaries will also be necessary. Depending upon the form of transmission and protocols employed, the characters
may also be grouped into larger units, such as blocks, packets (in packet
switching networks), and, almost always the application program will
only be interested in the actual message, or some other structure, such as
a file, meaningful to the application.

Link Control

In relation to both the initiation of the interaction and its subsequent
progress, the question arises of the relationship between the two distant
ends. Is the relationship a subordinate one, one party being in full control,
and the other essentially passive, or can they function as equals?

The *polling* mechanism employed in multidrop configurations is an example of the first approach, and is a dominant feature of the traditional centralised mainframe philosophy. Here, to avoid *contention* between a number of devices sharing the same circuit, each device must receive an invitation before it is permitted to transmit. In a different version, on packet switched networks, the network in effect continuously polls the connected devices, which can then transmit without being invited to do so, although the network will reject the transmission if it becomes congested, or for other reasons.

In point-to-point links the relationship tends to be one of equal parties, and is becoming increasingly important in distributed processing networks.

A question of great concern is the possibility that the progress of an interaction may come to a halt because each party, following its rules strictly, is waiting for a message from the other one or, for some other reason, such as storage limitations, is unable to respond. Various mechanisms are employed for handling these situations. The imposition of a *time out* is one way, so that if one end does not receive an acknowledgement within a specified time interval, it aborts its previous transmission, thus avoiding a *deadlock situation*.

Protocol resilience is also an important consideration. The modern protocols such as HDLC and X25 which are now coming into use are very sophisticated and cater for a very wide range of possible circumstances and contingencies. Nevertheless, it is currently impossible to fully test them over the full range of possibilities – which for all practical purposes can be regarded as infinite. Accordingly, these protocols make provision for one or the other party to effect a *restart* in a situation which appears to be totally deadlocked or impossible to recover from, within the protocol.

Error Detection and Correction

Although transmission technology continues to improve and the introduction of digital transmission will lead to dramatic improvements in performance, the transmission network can never be completely error-free.

A significant part of the increased complexity of the more recently developed protocols is due to the improved error-detection and error-recovery mechanisms. An important design aim has been to place the responsibility for error detection and recovery as far away as possible from the application levels of the system. This has the advantage that the application is largely insulated from errors, and most of the time it will be entitled to assume that most of the information that it receives is error-free.

However, a price has to be paid for enhanced error control. This involves the small but finite probability that blocks of information get lost, or are duplicated, or fail to arrive at their destination in the same order in which they were despatched by the sender. Additional mechanisms have therefore to be introduced to cover these situations.

Efficiency

Since a given communications channel has a maximum capacity it is obviously desirable that the capacity should be fully utilised. As will be seen in the relevant discussion this is a major limitation of some versions of the Basic Mode Link Control Protocol.

Flow Control

In systems which employ polling, the polling mechanism exercises tight control over both the rate and the sequence of transmission. A number of factors have contributed to a requirement for more flexible flow control procedures.

These include: the trend towards greater decentralisation of control; the requirement to maintain correct sequence; speed matching and buffer control. We briefly explain the relevance of the latter item. One fairly obvious way of improving both the response at the remote ends, and optimising channel throughput, is to allow each end to transmit at whatever rate it is capable of, subject to the receiver being able to accept it. This can be achieved by providing buffer storage in the communicating devices, but this means that some form of control is required that takes cognisance of the buffer availability at each end. Advanced error and sequence control procedures also require buffers to be available.

A FORMAL FRAMEWORK

We now propose to present a more formal descriptive framework for protocols and their relationships.

Protocols as Rules

Our earlier definition referred to a protocol as a set of rules or a rule book, specifying how a particular conversation is to be conducted. Although the name is sometimes used to refer to the conversation itself, strictly speaking it is restricted to the controlling rules, as Figure 8.1 illustrates.

It should be evident that the communicating parties must use the same rules if they are to be mutually intelligible, so that standardisation is an important requirement for protocols whose effects are externally visible. However, it should also be observed that standardisation still leaves freedom to vary the form of implementation.

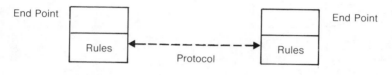

Figure 8.1

Protocol Variety and Protocol Relationships

It will probably be apparent by now that a variety of protocols are required to manage different segments of the data communications system and the communication path. Figure 8.2 provides a simple illustration.

However, before we comment upon it, some further definitions are required.

Interface

It is useful to regard an *interface* as a boundary between two regimes which may be physical or conceptual.

Protocols and interfaces have a lot in common. An interface also describes the signals that may pass and the interaction rules. When the connection between the communicating parties is a direct, or physical one, the term 'interface' is used. In its typical form an interface is defined

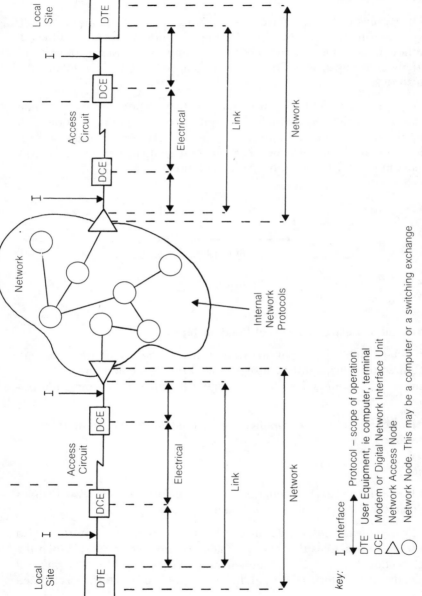

Figure 8.2 Protocols And Their Relationships

key: I Interface
      Protocol – scope of operation
DTE   User Equipment, ie computer, terminal
DCE   Modem or Digital Network Interface Unit
△   Network Access Node
○   Network Node. This may be a computer or a switching exchange

at a plug-socket connector and need not make allowance for delays and errors in the message paths.

Some interfaces are designed to work either with a local short connection or a longer communication path. The local high-speed interfaces employed by computer manufacturers for connecting peripherals are examples of the former; the CCITT V and X series interfaces governing attachment to wide area networks are examples of the latter.

DTE and DCE

CCITT devised this nomenclature for use in the context of public data networks.

DTE stands for Data Terminal Equipment, which could be a computer, a communication processor terminal controller or terminal.

DCE stands for Data Circuit Terminating Equipment which provides the interface between the DTE and the physical transmission circuit, or network.

Figure 8.2 depicts a situation where one device (DTE) wishes to communicate with another device, making use of an intervening data communications network. Merely to *transport* the information from one end to the other requires three protocols, although if the network were absent, it would reduce to a point-to-point circuit, and the network protocol would no longer be required.

The electrical level protocol is the most primitive and it governs the exchange of electrical signals between the remote modems and a modem and the DTE which it serves. The figure identifies an interface between the DTE and DCE – located in fact at the connector by which they are linked. The specification of this interface goes beyond the physical attributes of the plug and the characteristics of the electrical signals. It also entails the exchange of control messages or handshaking procedures, between the DTE and its local DCE on the one hand, and between the two remote DCEs on the other. This is shown in Figure 8.2. Although other types of interface could be shown, this has not been done, partly to avoid confusion, but also because their definitions are more abstract, and their precise locations more arbitrary.

The locations of the vertical dotted lines intended to represent the scope of individual protocols must also be regarded as somewhat arbitrary – depending upon where and how they are implemented. This is not important providing the approximate locations and division of responsibilities are noted.

The primary concern of the *link level protocol* is the transfer of messages or blocks of information, commonly having a character structure, without error, and also without loss of sequence.

The *network protocol* – or perhaps more accurately, *network access protocol* governs the exchange of information across the access link to the network, and ensures that a disciplined exchange of information takes place between a DTE and the network access point. The network can then be relied upon to transport information reliably to the remote DCE and DTE. The network itself will employ certain specific protocols, although it is usual to employ the commonly used electrical and link protocols on the links between the network nodes.

It will be evident that, starting with the electrical protocol each successive protocol is dependent upon its predecessor, in the sense that it utilises services provided by the latter.

The Protocol Hierarchy

The type of relationship just described can be observed at other levels of the communication path and derives from the natural tendency during the evolution of computer systems to group similar functions into layers.

The architecture for computer communications also follows the layered approach. When the idea of applying such an approach to data communications was first conceived, the term 'onion skin technique' was used. It was realised that the functions required to be performed in data communications can be considered separately. Data which passes one way through the system will be subject to a series of operations, which will be reversed when data passes in the opposite direction. Hence it was visualised as a series of concentric circles or hierarchical layers, which gave rise to the term 'onion skin'. The concept is now termed a layered architecture and is illustrated in Figure 8.3 which derives from the ISO seven-layered architecture model. There are other models, such as the one used on the ARPA network, and which differ in some respects. This does not mean that one way is correct, merely that there is more than one way of designing a protocol hierarchy.

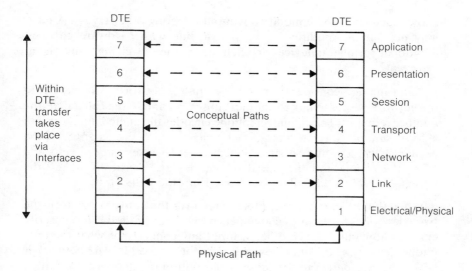

Fig 8.3   Layered Protocol Hierarchy

In Figure 8.3 the protocol layers are numbered serially starting with the physical circuit or electrical layer. The names of levels 1, 2, 3 are already familiar and are the protocols which we shall be mainly concerned with in this book, although we shall briefly comment on the significance of the other layers. One other feature which should be noted is that actual transfer of information only takes place along the physical circuit. Any intercommunication and transfer of information between successive layers occurs within the DTEs across defined interfaces.

A layered model of this kind has several interesting properties, and implementations based upon the approach confer a number of benefits. First of all, no one function or module in any particular layer needs to know how the services it requests from the lower layers are actually carried out, or is concerned with the way the services it offers are used by higher layers. It is required, however, that the way one layer requests services from a lower layer, and the form of the response, are clearly defined. This layering has a number of advantages; it separates out functions, eases design and debugging, allows separate groups of people to write separate parts, ensures clear interfaces between layers, and allows each layer to be modified without affecting other layers. A layer may need to be modified to keep it in line with hardware changes, additional peripheral devices or when the technology changes in a significant way.

As an analogy, consider the normal telephone network. A subscriber to the network wishes to talk to another subscriber and so the caller dials the number required. The calling telephone encodes the dialled numbers into a form suitable for interpretation by the telephone exchange. These exchanges use the numbers to connect together a series of circuits and when the calling and the called telephones are physically linked the exchange local to the called telephone rings the bells on it.

When the called subscriber lifts the receiver the network connects the two telephones together to allow speech to be transmitted. The subscribers may now talk to each other without any concern for what the telephone network is doing or how it is doing it. The telephone network is said to be *transparent* to the subscribers. Within the network itself there may be a hierarchy of services required for a call using a trunk circuit (Figure 8.4). The local exchanges are connected to the telephones on one

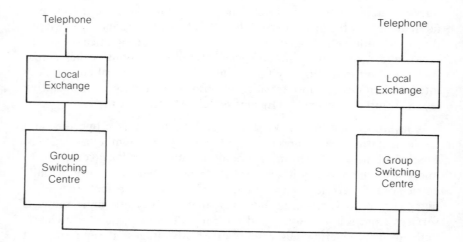

Figure 8.4 Hierarchical Nature of the Telephone Network

side and the group switching centres on the other. They are not concerned with how the group switching centres process the call or in what form the speech is transmitted along the trunk lines. The trunk circuits are transparent to the local exchanges, and also to the subscribers.

Having established a connection, the telephone network transmits the speech using its circuits. If one person using the telephone hands over to another person on the same telephone, the network is not aware of the change in the users of the circuit it has set up. Its job is to establish a connection and to ensure that it does not break down. It is not concerned with how the subscribers use the circuit so established.

To return to the consideration of data communications. We will use the word user to denote some component of the total computer system which wishes to use the communication services. Thus a user may be a person using a terminal, a program on the computer or some sort of measuring device. A user communicates with the equivalent user at the same level within another part of the network. The data is passed to the next lowest layer in the communications hierarchy and this layer, after processing it, will pass it on again. This passing from layer to layer will continue until the data has reached the receiving user in the same form that it left the sender. To the users it appears that they are communicating directly with each other: in other words, the layers below the users are *transparent*. Similarly, each layer sees the layers below it as transparent. Because corresponding entities in the same layer *appear* to communicate meaningfully *at that level* although there is no direct physical path, we can regard the path as a *conceptual* one. This is indicated by the broken horizontal lines in the diagram.

Further consideration of the model suggests that there are two fundamentally different kinds of protocol. There are those concerned with the transport of information, irrespective of its *meaning* and those by which its meaning is expressed independent of the mechanics of transport. This is illustrated in Figure 8.5 in which levels 1 to 4 are concerned exclusively with the transport function and are referred to collectively as the *Transport Service*. Levels 1 to 3 are the Data Communications Protocols with which we are primarily concerned in this book.

The Higher Level Protocols, comprising layers 5 to 7, utilise the Transport Service. This can be defined and implemented in such a way that it has no understanding of the meaning or the purpose of the

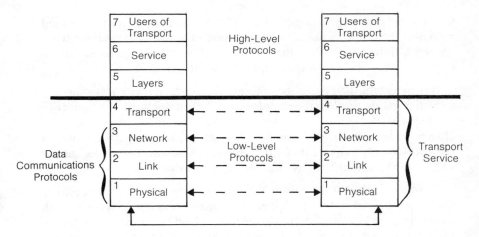

Figure 8.5 Transport Service and High Level Protocols

information which it transports, and only interprets and uses those parts of the information that it requires for its own functions. Thus, part of the communication content is undefined so that it can carry intelligence to the Higher Protocol Levels. As a matter of interest when we come to examine the structure of the HDLC transmission frame we shall see that this also has an 'onion skin' architecture, in which the uninterpreted information required by the application is surrounded by successive layers of control information required by the Data Communications Protocols. This illustrates the value of the transparency mechanism; it enables the transport user entities to behave as if they expressed their meanings to each other directly, even though they communicate via the Transport Service, and ultimately the most primitive level of all – the physical circuit.

Although the Transport Service and the Higher Level Protocols are strongly decoupled from each other, it is evident that some formal rules governing internal communications between the two regimes are required. This is provided by the Transport Service interface functions which are the primary concern of the Transport layer.

The ISO model which we have outlined is currently the subject of intensive ongoing development and refinement, particularly in regard to the layers above the Transport Service. However, actual implementations of layers 1 to 3 already exist, and as we shall see the X25 protocol for public packet switching networks has a layered structure which closely corresponds to levels 1 to 3 of the model. Several Transport Service definitions have been proposed, and one or two implemented, but there has yet to be international agreement on a standard.

TOWARDS OPEN SYSTEMS INTERCONNECTION

Open working for computers has been defined as the ability for a computer program, terminal or user of a computer to communicate meaningfully with any other program, terminal or user. In practice this means that if a user of one computer wishes to send data to or request data from another computer connected to the first computer, and there is an agreement between the owners of the two computers that this is allowed to happen, then the exchange of data can take place.

If the computers or terminals belong to the same organisation then there are relatively few problems in exchanging information, even if the computers are of different manufacture. The cost may be high in writing the software or obtaining the hardware required but the single management involved can make the necessary decisions that such a data exchange must take place. However, if the computers or terminals belong to different organisations then there must first of all be an agreement between the managements that they will allow this interconnection. Then they must agree on the form of the data and on the way the dialogue will be carried out. These agreements must be reached before any hardware or software is ordered to implement the data exchange.

The aim of open working is to provide a standard communication interface so that any computer or terminal connected to a data communications network will be able to meaningfully communicate with any other on that network.

The ability to communicate in this way is called Open Systems Interconnection. There is no compulsion for any user of that network to send or receive data from any other user; it merely allows the users to do so if they wish.

A set of protocols which permits Open System Interconnection and the relationship of these protocols to one another is described as an Open Systems Architecture. An architecture defines the functions of the various components of the system which are needed for open working to take place, the interfaces between these components and the protocols required for a component in one computer to communicate with its equivalent in another.

An architecture does not define how these functions are performed. In fact they may be implemented in a completely different way in one piece of computer equipment from the way they are implemented in another piece. For example, a large mainframe computer may be one of the machines on the network with all the architectural functions incorporated into its software. This would allow the machine to use its resources to support teleprocessing when connected to the network; but when the computer is being used in isolation and not connected to the network, these resources could, for example, be used for additional batch processing.

However, a terminal may also be connected to the network and this will seldom, if ever, be used in a stand-alone capacity. In this case, the networking functions could be implemented in hardware. What matters is that the interfaces between the functional components of the architecture and the protocols used are all agreed so that interconnection can be made and data exchanged.

We have noted elsewhere that mainframe computer suppliers had earlier recognised the value of a coherent functional framework to facilitate interconnection and maintain compatibility within their own product ranges. This resulted in the emergence of a number of *Proprietary Network Architectures*. However, whilst these offered significant benefits to individual suppliers and their customers, they did not solve the problem of interconnection in the wider context.

The fact is that continuing advances in computing and communication technology are opening up a whole new range of opportunities and novel application possibilities which, until recently, would not have been technically or economically feasible. But the potential benefits will only be fully realised if diverse products, systems and services are able to easily intercommunicate.

Both the CCITT and the International Organization for Standardization (ISO) have for a number of years been working on defining standards for the transport of data using telecommunications, and the V and X series standards (CCITT) for the electrical level, and the HDLC Link Protocol (ISO), are amongst the fruits of this work.

During work in the UK on the Post Office's Experimental Packet Switched Service it was realised that, to make most effective use of the future data communications facilities, protocols at a higher level than those provided by the telecommunications organisations were needed. The British Standards Institution studied the work and in 1976 recommended that the area of High-Level Protocols was suitable for standardisation. In 1977 ISO created a new sub-committee to examine the area of Open Systems Interconnection with a view to defining standards. In particular the sub-committee was asked to produce a reference model for an Open Systems Architecture which would help to define the areas which required standardisation. The reference model would also indicate where existing and projected standards would fit into the architecture. The result of this work is the seven-layered model which we have already outlined.

How Open Systems Interconnection can be achieved through implementation of these architectural principles can perhaps be best appreciated by considering the operation of the Transport Service layers. In functional terms this is currently the most well defined and probably least controversial part of the model.

As we have already seen, the *transparency* property enables the DTE, whether computer or terminal, to be isolated from the properties of the network (level 3), and this is achieved through the Transport layer (level 4). As seen from the application level, the Transport layer will be responsible for, amongst other things, selecting a transmission service of appropriate quality; establishing a connection between application processes; and ensuring safe transfer of information from one application process to another. The addressing of the destination is in terms of application processes at level 4, whilst level 3 is concerned with device and network addresses.

Thus, by using appropriate addressing mechanisms, a transport-level connection may span several networks, each of which may have its own level 3 implementation, and may differ in other respects. Interconnection between networks at the physical level will normally be effected by means of a *Gateway*, and this can be viewed as a special kind of network node.

Providing the architectural principles are correctly implemented, all the arrangements underlying the end-to-end connection can be concealed from the intercommunicating applications.

High-Level Protocols

At the present time, this part of the model is the subject of considerable debate and there is less measure of agreement than exists for levels 1 to 4. The debate centres mainly around the partitioning of the layers and how the specific functional components should be allocated. For this reason we do not feel that it would be appropriate to explain the roles of the Presentation and Session layers but instead will describe some of the generalised High-Level Protocol requirements which have been identified. Several of these have been implemented employing some particular functional interpretation and these include: *File Transfer Protocol, Virtual Terminal Protocol, Remote Job Entry Protocol* and *application dependent protocols.*

A File Transfer Protocol will obviously be needed to allow data in a file on one computer to be transported meaningfully across the network to another computer. To allow such a protocol to be defined where a number of different types of computing equipment are connected to the network it will be necessary to define a virtual file store. The virtual file store would contain files described by a standard set of properties and would permit only standard sets of operations. A local interface would exist to map the virtual file store properties and operations into the real file store.

On any network there may be a number of different types of terminal. A particular application will not wish to be constrained to a small number of types of terminal on an open network and so the concept of the Virtual Terminal has been developed to provide terminal independence. An application would ideally need only to communicate with this one type of terminal, conversion to the appropriate format of the actual terminal being handled locally. It is envisaged that a number of different classes of virtual terminal will be required to accommodate all the various classes of real terminals. When a human user is using a terminal to access an application program, the operations of the real terminal will undergo conversion to appropriate virtual terminal operations which will be passed to the application using a virtual terminal protocol. Before reaching the application itself the operations may undergo a further conversion into the form appropriate to the type of terminal which the application assumes it is conversing with.

A remote job entry protocol will be needed to enter jobs into the network for execution by a remote computer, the resu .s possibly being returned to the initiator. This protocol exists at a higher level than the file and virtual terminal sevices and will use the facilities of these two.

Applications protocols are considered to be the highest-level protocols. They include protocols specific to a particular industry, such as banking and airlines. They also include protocols which any one company may need in order to communicate within its own organisation.

The list of high-level protocols is by no means exhaustive but it serves to indicate the complexity needed in an architecture which must be capable of encompassing all these facilities.

Although there has been commendable progress in this area, much remains to be done, particularly in securing agreement on the higher levels. This is not surprising since it involves a very significant encroachment onto what is traditionally the supplier's territory. Even so, there is already widespread international agreement on levels 1 and 2 and on X25 at level 3 in respect of packet switched networks. And there are good grounds for believing that agreement will eventually be reached on a Transport layer and Transport Service definition. This alone would constitute a significant advance, and if widely adopted would provide an interconnection potential comparable with that currently available in the global telephone network.

9 The Electrical Interface and Physical Level Protocols

INTRODUCTION

This chapter is concerned with the conditions which must be satisfied, and the procedures for ensuring disciplined interaction between two devices or DTEs at the primitive electrical level.

The rules governing the physical interconnection of data communications equipment lend themselves to precise definition, and so it is perhaps not surprising that there was an early recognition of the advantages to be gained from international standardisation so that equipment made by different manufacturers could interact successfully across the telephone network. Another very significant factor encouraging early standardisation in this area has been the role of the PTTs and CCITT. These organisations have had long experience of standardisation, and the world's telephone network is a more than adequate testimony to the benefits deriving from the large-scale adoption of standards. And of crucial significance is the power of the PTTs to enforce standardisation in equipment to be attached to their networks. There is no doubt that the early availability and widespread adoption of standards governing physical connection and access have played a vital part in the development of data communications.

In contrast, standards serving the conceptual, as distinct from the physical level, have been slow to emerge; until very recently, suppliers have tended to go their own separate ways, and the relevant standardisation authorities such as the national standards bodies and the International Organization for Standardization (ISO) have lacked the power of the PTTs acting in concert.

The primary principal standardisation body for telecommunications is the CCITT, which does not publish standards as such, but issues them in the form of recommendations. Adoption of these is not mandatory, but the PTTs generally adopt them, partly through the acceptance of a moral obligation to do so; and because of technical convenience, since non-adoption could seriously impede interworking with other countries.

CCITT interests range over a wide area, and in addition to those covered in this chapter, it makes recommendations relating to such things as: transmission speeds and the speed multiplexing hierarchy for the public network, pulse code modulation and digital transmission, and a wide range of other engineering standards.

In this chapter we shall review the recommendations relating to attachment of digital data processing equipment to analogue networks and those relating to digital transmission networks. The former are collectively referred to as the 'V' series and the latter as the 'X' series, from the letters which prefix the number identifying the recommendation.

THE DTE-DCE INTERFACE

The boundary between the DTE and the DCE is at the connector by which they are linked. But a complete description of this boundary goes beyond the physical attributes of the connector and includes protocols governing the exchange of electrical signals. The electrical signals fall into two categories: those which perform control functions such as causing some event to happen or seeking or communicating status information to the other party; and signals which are transporting data. So far as the DCE and the communications link are concerned, the meaning and content of the data are irrelevant. The interfaces and relationships for two communicating DTEs are shown in Figure 9.1. This figure also illustrates that at the signalling level the total path comprises three segments, along each of which there has to be exchange of signals according to prescribed rules. These are: the two DTE-DCE paths and the DCE-DCE path spanning the transmission circuit.

Also shown is the end-to-end link, the control of which is the responsibility of a Link Level Protocol.

The majority of DCEs in current use are modems, but, as analogue transmission circuits are replaced by digital transmission, many of the

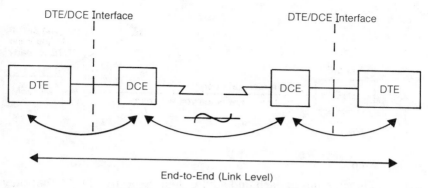

Figure 9.1 The Physical Path

modem's functions will no longer be required and they can be replaced by some kind of Network Terminating device, which is considerably simpler.

A SIMPLE EXAMPLE

Before discussing the CCITT recommendations we present a simple example in the form of a 'conversation' of the signalling interchange or 'hand shaking' procedures involved in transmitting data over the PSTN.

Step 1

The modems at each end must be advised that the data terminal equipment (DTE) is ready to operate. The modems must also be switched to the line. These two requirements could be achieved in a number of ways, but the two most common methods are shown below as steps 1(a) and 1(b).

(a) A single signal can be sent from each data terminal equipment to its associated modem.

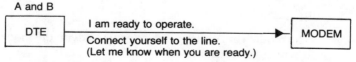

(b) The DTE can merely advise its modem that it is ready to operate. The switching of the modem to the line will not take place until it receives a signal from another source (eg a switch on an associated telephone).

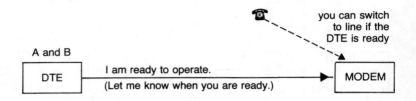

Step 2

The modems at each end advise their associated DTEs that they have switched to line and are ready to accept further instructions.

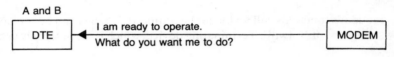

Step 3

No indication has yet been given of the direction of the transmission which is to take place. The modem at A must be conditioned to transmit and the modem at B conditioned to receive. The first action must be from the DTE at A.

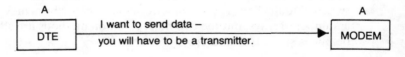

Step 4

The modem at A must send a signal to advise the modem at B that it wishes to transmit.

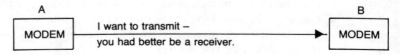

Step 5

When the modem at B is satisfied that it is receiving a satisfactory line signal from A it will advise its DTE to organise itself as a receiver.

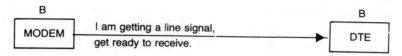

Step 6

After a pre-set time to allow the distant end time to be conditioned for receiving, the modem at A can give an affirmative response to the request to send data from its DTE.

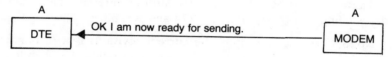

We will assume that a block of data is successfully passed from A to B. The DTE at B will assemble a receipt message and steps 3-6 will be followed again in the reverse direction beginning with a 'request to send'.

It will be seen that, even in this simplified example, a strict discipline is necessary to successfully bridge the demarcation between modems and the terminals which work with them. It will also be clear that standardisation of the interface is essential if there is to be compatibility between a wide range of different equipments.

THE MODEM INTERFACE AND THE CCITT V SERIES RECOMMENDATIONS

The interfacing functions of a modem are additional to the basic modulation-demodulation function. The various electrical signals are carried on a number of *interchange circuits* and these, together with a number of other features summarised below, comprise the specification of the interface.

Physical Attributes	Logical Attributes
Dimensions and construction of connector.	Meaning of the electrical signals on each pin.
Number of pins in connector.	Interrelationship between signals.
Electrical signals on the pins.	Procedures for exchanging information between DTE and DCE.

Table 9.1

These features have all been standardised internationally, the standards being known generally as V24 and RS232.

RS232C (the C indicating the current revision) is a recommended standard of the US Electronic Industries Association. The standard is in widespread use in America, and formed the basis of CCITT recommendation V24, which is common in Europe. RS232C defines all the features listed above. Rec V24 lists only the DTE-DCE interchange circuits and their functions; the electrical characteristics are defined in another CCITT recommendation, V28, and the connector pin allocations in an international standard (ISO 2110). However, conformity to these other two standards is usually implied when referring to a 'V24' interface. For most purposes, V24 and RS232 can be regarded as synonymous.

It is neither practicable nor necessary for our purposes to give a detailed and comprehensive account of these interface specifications, and our primary objective will be to highlight their main features, and to convey a broad picture of how they work. Those readers who are interested in a more extended treatment, and many of the details not covered here, are referred to the Bibliography.

Interchange Circuits

In a V24 interface, signals between the terminal and the modem are carried on separate interchange circuits. One interchange circuit is provided for each function. There are more than 40 interchange circuits in all, which seems excessive at first sight, but then V24 is a general-purpose interface covering a wide range of modem applications, and no single modem would use all the interchange circuits.

There are in fact 2 sets of interchange circuits, the 100 series used for data, timing and control circuits, and the 200 series used for automatic calling. Of the 100 series circuits, there is a core of 8 circuits which is common to many applications, and these are listed in Table 9.2.

The operation of these circuits can best be understood using the earlier example relating to data transmission over the PSTN. This is a simplified description aimed at giving an overall view of the procedure; a detailed description of the operation of each circuit is given later.

When a data connection is required over the PSTN, the first step is to dial the required number on the telephone in the usual way. When the call is answered and a communication path exists between the two parties, the telephone line needs to be switched at each end from the telephone to the data terminal. This is done by the modem once the data terminal has

Circuit V24	Designation	Direction	
		To Modem	To Terminal
102	Signal ground or common return		
103	Transmitted data	X	
104	Received data		X
105	Request to send	X	
106	Ready for sending (Clear to send)		X
107	Data set ready		X
108/1	Connect data set to line	X	
or			
108/2	Data terminal ready	X	
109	Data channel received line signal (ie carrier) detector		X

Table 9.2

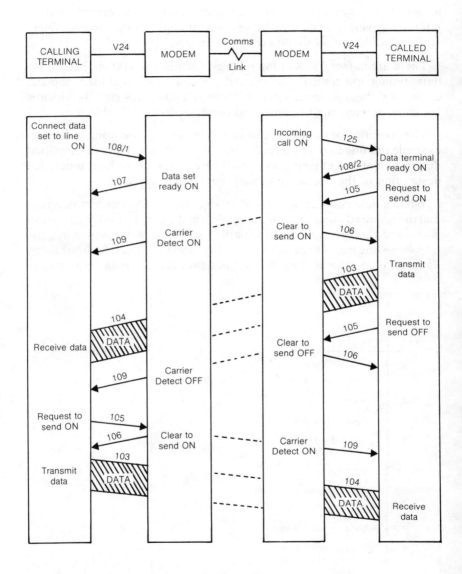

Figure 9.2   V24 Interface Procedure

turned ON circuit 108. (There are two slightly different ways of using this circuit as described later. The circuit is designated Connect Data Set to Line (108/1) or Data Terminal Ready (108/2) to distinguish the two.)

When connected to line, the modem informs the terminal by turning ON the Data Set Ready circuit 107. If the distant modem is already connected to line and is transmitting, the local modem will turn ON the Carrier Detect circuit 109 to indicate that it is detecting a carrier signal. This is often indicated by a light on the terminal. Any data that is received will be passed to the terminal over the Receive Data circuit 104. Figure 9.2 shows this sequence of events.

If a terminal wishes to transmit, it turns ON the Request to Send circuit 105. When the modem is ready to accept data for transmission, it replies by turning ON the Clear to Send circuit 106. Data can then be transmitted by the terminal on the Transmit Data circuit 103.

The one circuit not mentioned so far is the Signal Ground circuit 102. This provides the essential common return lead for all the other interchange circuits. In the future, equipment may use two common return circuits, one from the terminal to the modem, and the other from the modem to the terminal.

The 100 Series Interchange Circuits

Table 9.3 presents a list of the 100 series interchange circuits. This is to be regarded as a 'shopping list', and how many of the circuits listed are actually required will depend upon the modem used and the facilities to be provided. The table classifies the signals into categories, and for each circuit indicates whether the DCE is either the source or the recipient of the signal. If the former, then the DTE will be the recipient and if the latter, the DTE will be the source.

Each recommendation also stipulates which of the 100 series interchange circuits are needed. For example, Tables 9.4 and 9.5 show the interchange circuits which are essential for the 600/1200 bit/s modems covered by CCITT recommendation V23 when these are used on the general switched telephone network and on non-switched leased telephone circuits.

It will be seen that between 8 and 18 of the interchange circuits are necessary depending on the facilities required.

Interchange Circuit Number	Interchange Circuit Name	Ground	Data		Control		Timing	
			From DCE	To DCE	From DCE	To DCE	From DCE	To DCE
101	Protective ground or earth	X						
102	Signal ground or common return	X						
103	Transmitted data			X				
104	Received data		X					
105	Request to send					X		
106	Ready for sending				X			
107	Data set ready				X			
108/1	Connect data set to line					X		
108/2	Data terminal ready					X		
109	Data channel received line signal detector				X			
110	Signal quality detector				X			
111	Data signalling rate selector (DTE)					X		
112	Data signalling rate selector (DCE)				X			
113	Transmitter signal element timing (DTE)							X
114	Transmitter signal element timing (DCE)						X	
115	Receiver signal element timing (DCE)						X	
116	Select standby					X		
117	Standby indicator				X			
118	Transmitted backward channel data			X				
119	Received backward channel data		X					
120	Transmit backward channel line signal					X		
121	Backward channel ready				X			
122	Backward channel received line signal detector				X			
123	Backward channel signal quality detector				X			
124	Select frequency groups					X		
125	Calling indicator				X			
126	Select transmit frequency					X		
127	Select receive frequency					X		
128	Receiver signal element timing (DTE)							X
129	Request to receive					X		
130	Transmit backward tone					X		
131	Received character timing						X	
132	Return to non-data mode					X		
133	Ready for receiving					X		
134	Received data present				X			
191	Transmitted voice answer					X		
192	Received voice answer				X			

Table 9.3   100 Series Interchange Circuits by Category

(Note 2)

No.	Designation	Forward (Data) Channel One-Way System				Forward (Data) Channel Either Way System	
		Without Backward Channel		With Backward Channel		Without Backward Channel	With Backward Channel
		Transmit End	Receive End	Transmit End	Receive End		
101a	Protective ground or earth	X	X	X	X	X	X
102	Signal ground or common return	X	X	X	X	X	X
103	Transmitted data	X	–	X	–	X	X
104	Received data	–	X	–	X	X	X
105	Request to send	–	–	–	–	X	X
106	Ready for sending	X	–	X	–	X	X
107	Data set ready	X	X	X	X	X	X
108/1 or	Connect data set to line	X	X	X	X	X	X
108/2 (Note 1)	Data terminal ready	X	X	X	X	X	X
109	Data channel received line signal detector	–	X	–	X	X	X
111	Data signalling rate selector (DTE)	X	X	X	X	X	X.
114 (Note 3)	Transmitter signal element timing (DCE)	X	–	X	–	X	X
115 (Note 3)	Receiver signal element timing (DCE)	–	X	–	X	X	X
118	Transmitted backward channel data	–	–	–	X	–	X
119	Received backward channel data	–	–	X	–	–	X
120	Transmit backward channel line signal	–	–	–	X	–	X
121	Backward channel ready	–	–	–	X	–	X
122	Backward channel received line signal detector	–	–	X	–	–	X
125	Calling indicator	X	X	X	X	X	X

a May be excluded if so required by local safety regulations.

NOTE 1 This circuit shall be capable of operation as circuit 108/1 (connect data set to line) or circuit 108/2 (data terminal ready) depending on its use. For automatic calling it shall be used as 108/2 only.

NOTE 2 Interchange circuits indicated by X must be properly terminated according to Recommendation V24 in the data terminal equipment and data circuit-terminating equipment.

NOTE 3 These circuits are required when the optional clock is implemented in the modem.

Table 9.4 Interchange Circuits Essential for V23 Modems when Using the Public Switched Telephone Network (PSTN)

(Note 2)

Interchange Circuit		Forward (Data) Channel One-Way System				Forward (Data) Channel Either Way or Both Ways Simultaneously System	
		Without Backward Channel		With Backward Channel		Without Backward Channel	With Backward Channel
No.	Designation	Transmit End	Receive End	Transmit End	Receive End		
101a	Protective ground or earth	X	X	X	X	X	X
102	Signal ground or common return	X	X	X	X	X	X
103	Transmitted data	X	–	X	–	X	X
104	Received data	–	X	–	X	X	X
105	Request to send	–	–	–	–	X	X
106	Ready for sending	X	–	X	–	X	X
107	Data set ready	X	X	X	X	X	X
108/1 or	Connect data set to line	X	X	X	X	X	X
108/2 (Note 1)	Data terminal ready	X	X	X	X	X	X
109	Data channel received line signal detector	–	X	–	X	X	X
111	Data signalling rate selector (DTE)	X	X	X	X	X	X
114 (Note 3)	Transmitter signal element timing (DCE)	X	–	X	–	X	X
115 (Note 3)	Receiver signal element timing (DCE)	–	X	–	X	X	X
118	Transmitted backward channel data	–	–	–	X	–	X
119	Received backward channel data	–	–	X	–	–	X
120	Transmit backward channel line signal	–	–	–	X	–	X
121	Backward channel ready	–	–	–	X	–	X
122	Backward channel received line signal detector	–	–	X	–	–	X

a   May be excluded if so required by local safety regulations.

NOTE 1   This circuit shall be capable of operation as circuit 108/1 (connect data set to line) or circuit 108/2 (data terminal ready) depending on its use. For automatic calling it shall be used as 108/2 only.

NOTE 2   Interchange circuits indicated by X must be properly terminated according to Recommendation V24 in the data terminal equipment and data circuit-terminating equipment.

NOTE 3   These circuits are required when the optional clock is implemented in the modem.

Table 9.5   Interchange Circuits Essential for V23 Modems when used on Non-Switched Leased Telephone Circuits

If neither 108/1, 108/2, nor 105 are implemented in a particular application, the modem will need to be strapped to see an ON condition on the missing circuit.

Notes on the 100 Series Interchange Circuits

Some explanatory notes on the thirty-seven 100 series interchange circuits defined in the recommendation are given below. Although it is hoped that these will be helpful to the reader in understanding the functions of the various circuits, they should not be taken as being a substitute for the recommendation itself.

Because the data communications equipment (DCE) referred to in the recommendation is usually a modem, the term modem has been used in the explanatory notes on this series. The ON and OFF conditions referred to are logical conditions; ON is given the binary value 0 and is expressed by a positive voltage; OFF is given the binary value 1 and is expressed by a negative voltage.

Circuit 101 – Protective ground or earth

This circuit was used to extend the protective earth condition from the DTE to the modem but it is no longer specified.

Circuit 102 – Signal ground or common return

This circuit is the common earth return for the signals on all the interchange circuits (except 101). At the modem, this circuit may be connected to circuit 101 by a wire strap.

Circuit 103 – Transmitted data (DTE ⟶ modem)

Data signals transmitted from the DTE to the modem are passed over this circuit.

When no data is being transmitted, circuit 103 is held in the OFF condition (binary '1'). The DTE cannot transmit data on this circuit unless an ON condition (binary '0') is present on all the following circuits, where these are implemented:

Circuit 105 – Request to send
Circuit 106 – Ready for sending
Circuit 107 – Data set ready
Circuit 108/1/108/2 – Connect data set to line/data terminal ready.

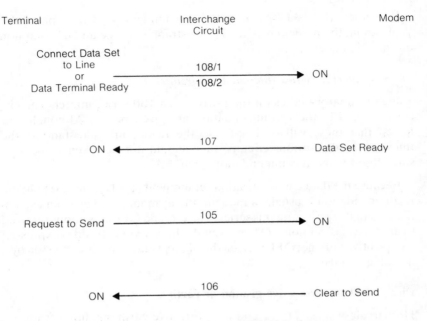

Figure 9.3   V24 Initial Handshake

This condition is the result of the handshaking procedure shown in Figure 9.3. Transmission of data continues until one of these circuits is turned OFF. Normally the terminal would switch OFF either 105 to signify that it had finished transmitting and was ready to receive or 108/1, 108/2 to signify the end of a call.

Circuit 104 – Received data (modem ⟶ DTE)

Analogue signals received from the line are converted into digital signals and transmitted from the modem to the DTE on this circuit.

NB   To prevent spurious signals being sent to the DTE due, for example, to excessive noise on the line this circuit may be held in the OFF condition until an ON condition on circuit 109 indicates that a signal within appropriate limits is being received from the line (see circuit 109 below). This procedure is termed 'clamping'.

Circuit 104 may also be clamped to binary 1 in half-duplex operation wherever the terminal is transmitting, ie whenever 105 is ON. This prevents the transmitted signal being fed back to the terminal. Removal of this clamp may be delayed for up to 175 ms after 105 is turned OFF, to allow for completion of transmission and to protect the terminal from false signals such as synchronisation sequences.

Circuit 105 – Request to send (DTE ⟶ modem)

When the DTE wishes to send information, it applies an ON condition on this circuit causing the modem to assume the transmit code. The OFF condition signifies that the DTE does not wish to transmit.

Circuit 106 – Ready for sending (modem ⟶ DTE)

Replies from the modem to the DTE, in response to a request to send, are passed on this circuit. An ON condition indicates that the modem is ready to accept data from the DTE on circuit 103 (transmitted data).

The delay between an ON condition being applied by the DTE to circuit 105 and the answering ON condition being sent from the modem to the DTE is termed the 'ready-for-sending delay'. This delay is built into the transmit modem to give time for a distant modem to condition itself to receive signals from the line.

There are a number of factors which can influence the ready-for-sending delay which is required, and the number of times that this delay occurs:

— If automatic calling and answering are used, a time allowance is required to allow the calling condition to be detected at the receive modem; the detection of the calling signal (typically ringing current) allows the call to be automatically answered. For example, on the 600/1200 bit/s modem designed to CCITT recommendation V23, the initial ready-for-sending delay is between 750 and 1400 ms; after the call has been established, this time is reduced to between 20 and 40 ms.

— If uninterrupted transmission is maintained in one direction (simplex) or in both directions simultaneously (duplex), there are no ready-for-sending delays after the first one. Users are, however, encouraged to switch off circuit 105 (request to send) whenever there are breaks in transmission to reduce the power loading of carrier circuits; in these circumstances, whenever transmission restarts, there is further ready-for-sending delay.

— If the modems and/or the lines cannot give duplex facilities and a half-duplex method of transmission is adopted, it is necessary to 'turn round' the modems at each end whenever there is a change in the direction of the transmission. Two ready-for-sending delays are therefore incurred for each change of direction. To avoid this delay, many applications use full duplex 4-wire circuits even though the data flow is essentially half-duplex.

However, this procedure does not make optimum use of the full duplex channel capacity. As we shall see later, this limitation can be overcome using the recently introduced HDLC Link Control protocol.

— Some modems require longer ready-for-sending delays than others. Generally speaking, the slower, asynchronous or unlocked modems merely require a carrier to be on the line for a brief period (typically 20-40 ms) to ensure that the receive modem is receiving it at the right power level.

The ready-for-sending delay is, therefore, the same whether the request to send is the first one in a transmission or one which occurs subsequently. The higher speed modems (over 2400 bit/s) are usually synchronous and may employ adaptive equalisers. An 'initial training pattern' is sometimes sent which enables the receive modem to synchronise with the transmit modem and to allow time for the adaptive equalisers in the receive modem to adjust to the line conditions. Subsequent training patterns between blocks may be considerably shorter as the timing and equalisation elements in modern modems will remain stable and will require little adjustment once they have been set.

Circuit 107 – Data set ready (modem ⟶ DTE)

The signals on this circuit indicate to the DTE that the modem is ready to receive its next instruction. The transmission of line signals for equalisation, etc, will not take place unless this circuit is switched on.

Circuit 108 (DTE ⟶ modem)

There are two options for the use of this circuit to meet different user requirements:

108/1 – Connect DTE to line

This circuit gives the terminal direct control over switching the modem to the telephone line, for connections set up over the PSTN. The call is dialled with circuit 108/1 OFF, and when the call is answered the circuit is turned ON by the terminal. The ON condition will immediately connect the modem to line; this results in circuit 107 (data set ready) being switched to ON. An OFF condition on 108/1 disconnects the modem from the line when data on circuit 103 has been transmitted.

108/2 – Data terminal ready

This circuit provides the terminal with indirect control over switching the modem to line. An ON condition on this circuit from the DTE informs the modem that the data terminal is ready to operate. It is not in itself an instruction to connect the modem to line and before this can be done a subsidiary signal is necessary. This signal may be given by an operator pressing a 'data' button on the telephone associated with the modem.

This alternative would also be implemented when the modem has automatic answering facilities. Under this arrangement a terminal ready to receive incoming calls maintains 108/2 ON, so that when a call is received and Calling Indicator circuit 125 is turned ON, the modem is automatically switched to line. This happens at the end of the first cycle of ringing tone (see description of 125) and is indicated to the terminal by circuit 107 coming ON. Circuit 108/2 cannot be permanently strapped on, because the DTE needs it in order to clear down PSTN calls.

Circuit 109 – Data channel received line signal detector (modem ⟶ DTE)

An ON condition on this circuit indicates to the DTE that the received signal is within the appropriate limits. These limits are specified in the CCITT recommendations for the type of modem being used. For example, V23 (600/1200 bit/s) will apply an ON condition on circuit 109 when a signal greater than 43 dBm is received. This circuit may be 'clamped' to circuit 104 to avoid false signals being passed to the DTE.

Circuit 110 – Data signal quality detector

Data signal quality detection is a method of error control whereby the line signal is checked for certain characteristics which are likely to cause errors. An ON condition on this circuit indicates that there is no indication from the line signal that an error has occurred. An OFF condition indicates that there is a reasonable probability that the distortion detected on the line signal will cause an error.

Circuit 111 – Data signalling rate selector (DTE ——▶ modem)

When modems offer a choice of two fixed data signalling rates or a choice between two ranges of data signalling rate, the selection is usually made at the DTE. An ON condition on circuit 111 from the DTE directs the modem to adopt the higher rate, or range of rates and an OFF condition indicates that the lower mode is selected.

Either (but not both) circuit 111 or circuit 112 can be used for data signalling rate selection.

Circuit 112 – Data signalling rate selector (modem ——▶ DTE)

This is an alternative to circuit 111, choice of data signalling rate being made from the modem.

Circuits 113, 114, 115, 128

These circuits provide alternative ways of maintaining bit synchronisation in synchronous mode operation. For convenience we describe their operation under the separate section headed synchronisation.

Circuit 116 – Select standby (DTE ——▶ modem)

When standby communication facilities are provided, such as a standby exchange line, this circuit may be used for selection between the normal and standby facilities. For example, some modems operating at 2400 bit/s over leased lines offer fall-back operation at 1200/600 bit/s over PSTN. Circuit 116 is used to select normal or fall-back operation. For the latter circuit 111 would be used to determine whether to operate at 600 or 1200 bit/s.

Circuit 117 – Standby indicator (modem ——▶ DTE)

The signals on this circuit indicate to the DTE whether the normal or standby facilities which have been selected are conditioned to operate. For both circuits the ON condition is used for standby, and the OFF condition for normal operation.

Circuits 118 to 124 inclusive

Used only when backward channels are provided by the modems. A backward or 'supervisory' channel operates at a lower data signalling rate (typically 75 bit/s) than the data channel and is intended to be used for the return of short supervisory or error control messages. The interchange circuits used are equivalent to other circuits described above except that they are associated with the backward channel rather than the data channel.

Circuit 118 – Transmitted backward channel data (DTE ⟶ modem)

Equivalent to circuit 103 (transmitted data).

Circuit 119 – Received backward channel data (modem ⟶ DTE)

Equivalent to circuit 104 (received data). This circuit may be clamped to circuit 122 just as circuit 104 may be clamped to circuit 109.

Circuit 120 – Transmit backward channel line signal (DTE ⟶ modem)

Equivalent to circuit 105 (request to send).

Circuit 121 – Backward channel ready (modem ⟶ DTE)

Equivalent to circuit 106 (ready for sending).

Circuit 122 – Backward channel received line signal detector (modem ⟶ DTE)

Equivalent to circuit 109 (data channel received line signal detector).

Circuit 123 – Backward channel signal quality detector (modem ⟶ DTE)

Equivalent to circuit 110 (data signal quality detector).

Circuit 124 – Select frequency groups (DTE ⟶ modem)

Signals on this circuit are used to select the desired frequency groups available in modems designed for parallel data transmission.

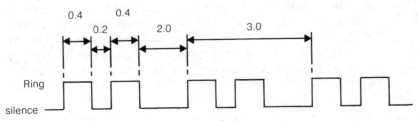

Figure 9.4   UK Ringing Tone (times in seconds)

Circuit 125 – Calling indicator (modem ⟶ DTE)

An ON condition on this circuit notifies the DTE that a calling signal is being received from the line. This circuit is used for automatic answering and alerts the terminal to an incoming call. The circuit reacts in sympathy with the ringing current, turning ON during rings. Figure 9.4 indicates the UK ringing tone. Its use in conjunction with 108/2 is described above.

Circuit 125 is independent of the other interchange circuits, and remains operational during modem testing.

Circuits 126, 127 (DTE ⟶ modem)

Circuit 126 Select Transmit Frequency.
Circuit 127 Select Receive Frequency.

Select Transmit Frequency Circuit 126 Terminal to Modem
Select Receive Frequency Circuit 127 Terminal to Modem

These circuits were designed for the standard 200/300 baud V21 modem, which uses different transmit frequencies for the two directions of transmission. Usually on PSTN connections, however, the choice of frequencies is made automatically by the modem, depending on whether it is the called or calling party, and these circuits are not required. On some multipoint applications control of the modem frequencies by the terminal may be required, but often circuit 126 will be used to control both transmit and receive frequencies and circuit 127 will not be implemented. For both circuits, an ON condition signifies the higher and the OFF condition the lower frequency.

Circuit 128 – Receiver signal element timing (DTE ⟶ modem)

Use of this circuit is described under Synchronisation.

Circuit 129 – Request to receive (DTE ⟶ modem)

Signals on this circuit are used to control the receive function of modems used for parallel data transmission. The ON condition causes the modem to assume the receive mode.

Circuit 130 – Transmit backward tone (DTE ⟶ modem)

An ON condition on this circuit conditions the modem to transmit a single tone on the backward channel. A potential use of this circuit is in a system using push button MF telephones. The in-station modem could be conditioned to transmit a single tone as an audible acknowledgement to a person listening on the telephone that data had been received correctly.

Circuit 131 – Received character timing (modem ⟶ DTE)

Any signals on this circuit provide the DTE with character timing information. This information cannot normally be provided. Most modems transmit and receive data serially bit by bit and do not know when characters begin and end. The circuit is only used in conjunction with parallel modems which accept data from the line and pass it to the DTE a character at a time.

Circuit 132 – Return to non-data mode (DTE ⟶ modem)

An ON condition on this circuit instructs the modem to return to a non-data mode (eg a telephone) without losing the line connection to a remote station.

Circuit 133 – Ready for receiving (DTE ⟶ intermediate equipment)

This circuit is optional when there is intermediate equipment between the DTE and the modem (eg error control equipment to CCITT recommendation V41). An ON condition on circuit 133 is an indication to the intermediate equipment that the DTE is ready to receive a block of data on circuit 104 (received data).

Circuit 134 – Received data present (intermediate equipment ⟶ DTE)

This circuit is only used when error control equipment is provided between the modem and the DTE. The intermediate equipment notifies the DTE on circuit 134 which of the bits in a block transferred on circuit 104 are information (ON condition on circuit 134) or supervisory (OFF condition on circuit 134).

Circuits 140, 141, 142

These circuits enable loopback tests to be carried out, in which the transmitted data is looped back so that it appears on the received data path. This provides an effective means of fault isolation. On a simple point-to-point connection, there are four locations at which loopback can be conveniently arranged to supply helpful diagnostic information, and these are shown in Figure 9.5.

The method of operation is as follows:

Loop 1 checks the terminal, loop 3 the local modem, and loop 2 the remote modem. These loops may be activated by a switch on the modem, or via a terminal-modem interchange circuit. Loop 4 (which is only possible on 4-wire circuits) is for PTT use only. The circuits provided in V24 are:

Terminal to Modem:

Remote loopback circuit 140

— activates loop 2 in Figure 9.5

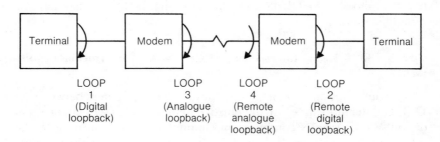

Figure 9.5   Loopback Points

Local loopback circuit 141

— activates loop 3 in Figure 9.5

Modem to Terminal:

Test indicator circuit 142

The modem switches this circuit ON in response to a loopback command from the terminal on circuit 140 or 141. Circuit 142 is also switched ON when the modem is tested from a remote location. Data transmission is impossible when circuit 142 is ON.

As data networks have grown in complexity, the need for adequate monitoring and diagnostic aids has grown in importance. Many modem manufacturers now provide centralised network control equipment, which is able to communicate with all the modems on a network. With such equipment it becomes possible to monitor the V24 interface circuits at each modem, perform loopback tests, switch in standby modems, change over to spare circuits or alter data transmission rates – all remotely. Communication can take place over the modem's low-speed secondary or backward channel, or over a separate dialled connection, and so can occur while data is being transmitted on the main channel.

The 200 Series Interchange Circuits

The 200 series of interchange circuits are all related to the operation of automatic calling over the public switched telephone network. A similar interchange of circuits is provided for automatic calling over the Telex network; these are covered in CCITT recommendation V2.

Automatic calling over the PSTN involves a disciplined interchange of responsibility between the DTE (which is computer-related equipment of some kind) and the automatic calling equipment provided by the telecommunications authorities.

Both automatic calling and automatic answering present particular problems in connection with the transmission of data on the public telephone network. This arises partly because the speech network was not designed for transmitting data, and also because of the need to ensure that, on the one hand signals are not generated which interfere with the operation of the network, and on the other, both nationally and internationally agreed signalling schemes are adhered to.

| Circuit | Designation | Direction | |
		To terminal	From terminal
201	Common return		
202	Call request		X
203	Data line occupied	X	
204	Distant station connected	X	
205	Abandon call	X	
206	Digit signal 2^0		X
207	Digit signal 2^1		X
208	Digit signal 2^2		X
209	Digit signal 2^3		X
210	Present next digit	X	
211	Digit present		X
213	Power indication	X	

Table 9.6   200 Series Interchange Circuits in V24 for Automatic Calling

A good illustration is echo suppression and echo suppressor disablement on long distance (eg transcontinental and transoceanic) circuits. Echo suppressors are introduced on long distance circuits to minimise the effects of echo, in which a person talking hears an echo of his own voice. For data transmission the effect is not so serious as the countermeasures. These take the form of echo suppressors, which, although preventing echoes on speech circuits, also prohibit full duplex data transmission. Modern echo suppressors are therefore fitted with a disabling mechanism which can be activated by a signal from a remote modem. By international agreement a signal frequency of 2100 Hertz is used, both for answering and echo suppressor disablement.

There are twelve interchange circuits in the 200 series: four for data, seven for control and indication, and the common return circuit. These are listed in Table 9.6.

Method of Operation

The automatic calling unit allows calls to be set up over the PSTN without manual intervention. The unit is interposed between the DTE and the modem and is connected to both.

The DTE passes the digits to be dialled to the automatic calling unit, and the unit converts these to dial pulses (or to multifrequency tones for telephone networks so equipped). Having sent all the digits, the unit causes the modem to transmit a calling signal to line to announce the fact that the call is being originated automatically. The calling signal comprises short bursts of 1300 Hz or other binary 1 tone repeated every $1\frac{1}{2}$-2 seconds.

The automatic calling unit relies on detecting a 2100 Hz answering tone before it will connect the calling DTE to line. If no such tone is received within a specified period the unit advises the DTE to abandon the call.

The procedure for making a call is illustrated in Figure 9.6 which is based on CCITT recommendation V25. The DTE turns ON the Call Request circuit 202 causing the automatic calling unit to go 'off-hook', which is indicated by the Data Line Occupied circuit 203 coming ON. When dial tone is received the unit invites the DTE to 'Present next digit' via circuit 210. The DTE presents the first digit to be dialled in parallel form on the 4 circuits 206-209, coded as shown in Table 9.6 and informs the unit by turning ON the Digit Present circuit 211. After dialling the first digit, the unit turns 210 OFF. The DTE responds by turning 211 OFF, and then the unit turns 210 ON to request the second digit. The procedure is repeated until all digits have been sent, which is signified by the DTE placing the End of Number code on circuits 206-209. Delays between digits, to allow for a second dial tone for example, can be introduced by presenting the Separation Control Character SEP between digits.

The calling tone is transmitted for a preset time between 10 and 40 seconds, and in the absence of 2100 Hz answering tone the unit turns ON the Abandon Call circuit 205, to which the DTE must respond by turning 202 OFF.

If the call is answered, the unit detects a 2100 Hz tone from the distant modem. This is allowed to persist for 450-600 ms to ensure that any echo suppressors have been disabled, after which the unit transfers control of the line from circuit 202 to circuit 108/2. The 2100 Hz tone lasts for 2.6-4.0 seconds, and about 75 ms after it ceases, circuit 107 is turned ON indicating that the unit has completed its calling procedures. Receipt of carrier from the distant modem causes the Distant Station Connected circuit 204 to be turned ON, after which the automatic calling unit plays

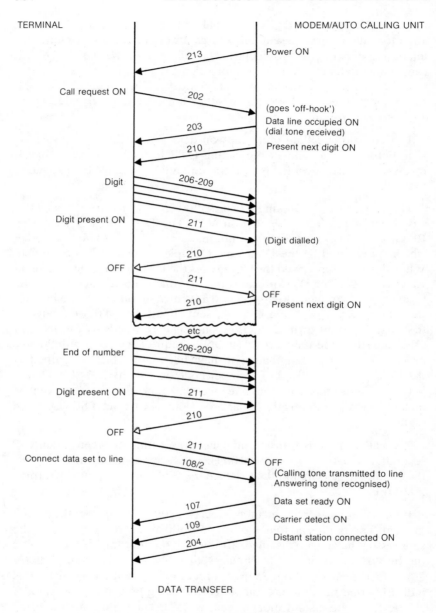

Figure 9.6   V25 Call Establishment Procedure

no further part. Circuit 202 can then be turned OFF by the terminal and control of the connection is vested in circuit 108/2 as for a normal call.

The US standard for automatic calling is RS366, and it uses the same circuits as CCITT recommendation V25, although the circuit designations differ slightly.

Recommendation V25 also defines the procedures for automatic answering. Many modems have automatic answering facilities today, and for those that do not, the PTTs can supply automatic answering devices to interpose between the terminal and the modem.

When an incoming call is received, an auto-answer modem signals to the terminal over the Calling circuit 125, and assuming 108/2 is ON, goes 'off-hook' on completion of the first ringing cycle. The modem waits for 1.8-2.5 seconds and then transmits 2100 Hz tone for 2.6-4.0 seconds. Like the modem at the calling end, the calling modem turns on the Data Set Ready circuit 107 about 75 ms after the 2100 Hz tone ceases.

SYNCHRONISATION

In the preceding chapter we noted the requirement to ensure the proper time synchronisation of transmitted elements between the two ends of a communications link.

For both asynchronous and synchronous transmission bit synchronisation is maintained either within the modem or the terminal. In asynchronous transmission, character synchronisation is also achieved within the terminal. All other synchronisation requirements, including character synchronisation in synchronous transmission, and block and message synchronisation, are the responsibility of Link Level Protocols and higher protocols.

We consider the asynchronous and synchronous cases separately.

Asynchronous Case

In asynchronous transmission, characters can be sent and therefore received at any time. The human operator types characters at an indeterminate rate, and there will also be periods when no characters are being typed. Similarly, the terminal may receive a few characters from the remote computer, and there may be an interval, during which the user thinks about the message. In each case neither party knows when the next character is going to arrive and how many characters there will be.

Bit synchronisation is achieved as we have said, by a clocking mechanism common to both ends, either within the modem or the terminal. In fact, the traditional teletype machine maintained bit synchronisation by means of synchronous drive motors in the send and receive machine.

Character synchronisation is achieved by framing each transmitted information character between a start bit and one or more stop bits, the format being depicted in Figure 9.7. Synchronisation is achieved in the following way.

During a quiescent state, when there are no characters to transmit, the voltage is kept at −V (usually 12 volts). Depression of a key indicates that a character is ready for transmission, and this causes the voltage level to be changed to +V which it maintains for a one bit time duration, and this is called the start bit. Following the start bit, the bits which make up the character are then transmitted by using the appropriate voltage level, +V for a '0' and −V for a '1', the voltage level being maintained for one bit time duration on each occasion. When all the character bits have been sent, the transmitter then transmits a stop signal, by holding the voltage at −V for at least one bit duration.

The start bit serves to warn the receiving device that a character can be expected, and the receiver uses the −V to +V transition to start a local clock to read in the character bits. The stop bit is not directly concerned

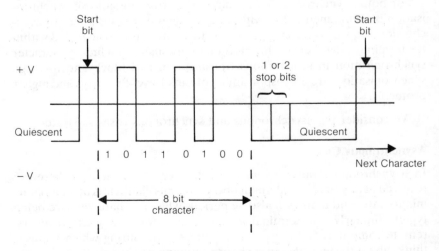

Figure 9.7   Asynchronous Character Framing

with marking the end of the character. By making it –V, it ensures that the –V to + V transition will be properly recognised regardless of what the last character bit was. Also, on mechanical terminals, two stop bits are used to allow the mechanical parts to prepare for the next character, whereas for teletype compatible VDUs one might be adequate. The bit duration is determined primarily by the transmission speed.

The Synchronous Case

In synchronous operation the data to be transmitted is clocked into the modem from the terminal at a steady rate. The clock which provides this timing may be located within the modem or may be external to the modem, in the terminal. The modulated waveform transmitted by the modem contains timing information which allows the destination modem to clock out the data to its terminal at the same steady rate.

There are four V24 interchange circuits for conveying clock signals between modem and terminal.

Circuit 113   Transmitter signal element timing – DTE source
(to modem, clock in terminal)

Circuit 114   Transmitter signal element timing – DCE source
(to terminal, clock in modem)

These two circuits are used to time the data sent to the modem on the Transmit Data circuit 103. Either terminal timing (circuit 113) or modem timing (circuit 114) would be provided but not both. Usually data is transmitted to the modem under control of the modem clock, using the Transmit clock timing circuit 114. External transmit timing is used in applications where modems are connected back-to-back, and timing is derived from one single source.

Circuit 115   Receiver signal element timing – DCE source
(to terminal, clock in modem)

Circuit 128   Receiver signal element timing – DTE source
(to modem, clock in terminal)

These two circuits are used to time the received data on circuit 104. The Receive clock signal on circuit 115 tells the terminal when to sample the received data on circuit 104. This timing is derived from the incoming modulated signal and is therefore synchronised to the timing used at the transmitter.

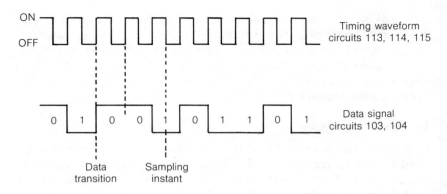

Figure 9.8   Relationship of Timing and Data Circuits

Circuit 128 is rarely implemented. It enables the terminal to clock in the received data on circuit 104 in its own time. This circuit could be used in conjunction with a synchronous modem which had asynchronous standby facilities.

On the timing circuits, the ON to OFF transition nominally coincides with the centre of the data bits on the transmit or receive circuits, and the OFF to ON transition with transitions in the data signals (Figure 9.8).

Timing from the modem clock is normally provided to the terminal whenever the modem is powered up, although signals may be suspended for short intervals during modem testing. Receive data clock on circuit 115 may not be available when the Carrier Detect circuit 109 is OFF.

DIGITAL DATA NETWORKS AND THE CCITT X SERIES RECOMMENDATIONS

Analogue transmission circuits and the associated transmission modems are going to be around for some considerable time to come. However, most of the world's PTTs and Telecommunications Administrations have made the commitment to eventually convert their networks to digital transmission. The process will inevitably take time and in a number of countries it is unlikely to be before the end of the century. But digital networks are beginning to emerge, and, in the UK in particular, plans are well advanced, and it is anticipated that within the present decade there will be substantial penetration of digital services.

In response to this trend CCITT are actively engaged in preparing recommendations governing the attachment of equipment to digital networks, and to the new range of services and capabilities that they will be able to provide.

Interfaces for Digital Services

The services to be provided on the new public data network include digital leased lines, circuit switched services and packet switched services. At the lowest level – the level of the DTE-DCE interchange circuits – the interface is the same for all services, and is somewhat simpler than a V24 interface. This is because many of the functions are performed at the logical rather than the physical level.

In a digital network, the DCE is not a modem as it would be in an analogue network, but a form of coder/decoder, which takes the binary data from the DTE and converts it to a form suitable for digital transmission along the line. It is essentially an unintelligent device.

The intelligence is distributed between the network switching exchange or network access node, and the DTE, although the intelligence required in the latter will vary, depending upon the characteristics of the

Circuit	Name	Direction	X20	X21
G	Signal ground or common return	—	X	X
Ga	DTE common return	to DCE	(X)	(X)
Gb	DCE common return	to DTE	(X)	
T	Transmit	to DCE	X	X
R	Receive	to DTE	X	X
C	Control	to DCE		X
I	Indication	to DTE		X
S	Signal element timing	to DTE		X
B	Byte timing	to DTE		(X)
	Cable screen			

(Brackets indicate optional features)

Table 9.7   X20 and X21 Interchange Circuits

service accessed, and the facilities required. Thus, to set up a call on the network the DTE must communicate directly with the exchange or network access node. The DTE-Exchange protocol is one component of the DTE-DCE interface specification.

There are two basic interface specifications, defined in CCITT recommendations X20 and X21. X20 is designed for start/stop terminals and provides full duplex transmission up to 300 bit/s. X21 is designed for synchronous terminals, and provides full duplex operation up to 48 kbit/s. (X25, the interface to a packet switched network, is a three-level user-to-packet network interface protocol; it uses X21 at its lowest level.)

With these new interfaces, the DTE is directly responsible for all aspects of call establishment and disconnection. A handshake protocol is defined in which the DTE inputs the number (address) of the party to be called, together with details of any special facilities, and the data exchange responds with instructions and call progress signals. Call establishment time is less than one second.

X20 DCEs employ the electrical characteristics of Rec V10 (= X26); they may be connected to DTEs using V10, V11 or V28 electrical characteristics. X21 DCEs employ V11 (= X27); below 9600 bit/s the DTE may use V10 or V11 electrical characteristics, but above 9600 bit/s only V11 DTEs (with cable termination in the load) are permitted. Both use a selection of interchange circuits from Rec X24 (the equivalent of V24), and a 15-way D-shape connector.

Recognising the need for the new networks to cater for the existing population of V24 terminals, CCITT has developed alternative versions of the two basic standards; they are known as X20 *bis* and X21 *bis*. They employ V24 interchange circuits with the traditional electrical characteristics and connectors, and thus make the digital network DCE look like a modem to the terminal. They do not offer all the facilities of the full X20 and X21 interfaces.

10 Link Level Protocols: Basic Mode

INTRODUCTION

The primary role of a Link Level Protocol is to ensure the *disciplined* and *reliable* exchange of information between autonomous pieces of equipment, over a channel which is inherently unreliable. This means ensuring that the information reaches the correct destination address, and that effective flow control, block and message synchronisation and error control procedures exist.

This is in marked contrast to the role of the electrical interchange circuits and signalling arrangements described in the preceding chapter. At this level the primary concern is the establishment, maintenance and termination of the *physical* link in terms of electrical signals representing streams of otherwise undefined binary bits, rather than conceptual structures such as characters, blocks and messages. Also, whilst the DTE, relying solely on the interchange circuit signals can derive useful information about the status of the physical links, the scope for detecting and diagnosing the cause of errors is strictly limited. Both additional information and additional functions are needed for this to be carried out effectively. These functions are supplied by the Link Level Protocol.

However, if the Link Level Protocol was designed to do no more than detect an error on each and every occurrence and then report this to a higher level – perhaps the application itself – this would result in gross inefficiencies apart from causing much irritation to a user at a remote terminal. An important design principle therefore, is that the protocol – and for that matter Higher Level Protocols – should not only detect errors, but should, so far as practicable, recover from them without recourse to higher levels. For some categories of error this goal can be almost completely satisfied, but there will be certain categories which, by their nature and semantic content, can only be resolved at higher levels, and possibly only in the application itself.

In this chapter and in Chapter 12 we describe the main features of two Link Control Protocols, Basic Mode and HDLC (High-Level Data Link Control), both of which were developed to support synchronous transmission. We shall have little to say about asynchronous transmission, since the requirements are far simpler and do not necessitate the sophisticated procedures required in the synchronous case. However, asynchronous applications have tended to adopt the control character designations and block formats used in Basic Mode.

We shall start with an account of Basic Mode, and then in the next chapter review the various approaches to error detection and recovery before tackling HDLC. This follows the order of historical development, and has the merit that if the reader understands the limitations of Basic Mode, he is likely to more readily appreciate the significance of the main features of HDLC.

BASIC MODE

Background

The International Organization for Standardization (ISO) began studying data link communications control protocols in 1962. This resulted in the development of a standardised character-oriented protocol known as Basic Mode. This was based on the ISO Standard 7-bit Alphabet which had ten characters allocated to transmission control. Initially, meanings were assigned to each of these codes (eg start of text, end of text, end of transmission), and then the Basic Mode protocol was defined in terms of the various characters within the overall information flow.

The development of this definition spanned a period of fifteen years during which the proposed standard evolved through a series of enhancements. Throughout this period many manufacturers, under pressure from user requirements for data transmission equipment, anticipated the form of the eventual standard and implemented their own proprietary versions. These versions were neither compatible with one another nor were they aligned with the standard.

Protocols developed in this period have therefore become widely known as *Binary Synchronous (Bisync),* following the terminology adopted by IBM, *Character Structured*, or *Basic Mode protocols*. The net result therefore has been a vast proliferation of terminal-oriented protocols using ideas gleaned from the Basic Mode protocol standard. In general many proprietary implementations have been sufficiently 'individual' to prevent connection of terminals obtained from one manufacturer to equipment from another. However, a group of manufacturers emerged (the so-called 'plug compatible' manufacturers) who specifically set out to service this market area. One major mainframe manufacturer is estimated to have developed about fifty distinct terminal-specific protocols over this fifteen year standardisation period.

In common with all character-oriented protocols, in Basic Mode all the control information is carried over the data link by discrete transmission control characters selected from the ISO 7-bit code. There are now a number of ISO and ECMA standards covering different aspects of basic mode.

Transmission Block Formats and Control Characters

Transmission Block Format

In Basic Mode the data to be transmitted is usually formed into fixed length blocks and sections of the block are identified by the use of special control characters. The block is the physical unit, but the logical unit such as a message can extend over more than one block. The format for a single isolated block is represented in Figure 10.1.

Figure 10.1 A Simple Basic Mode Block

Control Characters

The ISO 7-bit alphabet and other alphabets such as ASCII and EBCDIC provide a wide range of control characters, but the ones listed below are the most important for our purposes.

ACK   Positive acknowledgement confirming satisfactory receipt or responding affirmatively to a poll.

NACK   Negative acknowledgement, signifying an error in a received message, or the inability of a device to respond to a poll with data.

ENQ   Request for a response, ie 'have you anything to send?'.

EOT   This signifies the end of the transmission of a series of texts or messages. In some variants it may also be used to clear or reset the link.

ETB   End of Transmission Block. Indicates the end of a physical block of data where this may not coincide with the logical format.

SOH   Start of Header. Indicates the start of the header if one is present at the beginning of the block.

STX   Indicates the end of the header (if present) and the beginning of the actual text.

ETX   End of Text. Indicates the end of the text which started with STX.

SYN   Synchronous Idle. This character provides a sequence of synchronising bits. SYN characters will normally precede data blocks, but also may be embedded in the data or sent continuously as 'idle' characters during intervals when no data is being transmitted.

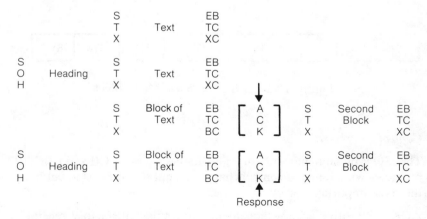

Figure 10.2   Typical Message Formats

DLE   Data Link Escape. This character can be used for two purposes. One is to assign alternative meanings to a continuous set of following characters, and thus enabling additional control characters to be created. In this mode it operates in a similar way to ESC in the full alphabet. The more common use is to facilitate the transmission of data containing unpredictable bit patterns, which might include control characters, which, when interpreted according to the conventions would make orderly communication impossible. This is discussed more fully below.

Block and Message Text Formats

Some typical message formats are shown in Figure 10.2.

Data Blocks and Messages

SOH, STX, ETB and ETX are used as information framing characters and there must, therefore, be at least two in all information messages or blocks transmitted. In the simplest case, it may only be necessary to indicate the beginning and end of a text. Assuming that the complete message can be accommodated in a single block we have:

S	S	S		E	B
Y	Y	T	TEXT	T	C
N	N	X		X	C

The BCC or block check character is a longitudinal parity check which starts the check at STX and ends at the character immediately preceding BCC. This is described more fully in the next chapter.

If a heading was required and the message was transmitted in a number of blocks, the first block might have the following sequence:

S	S	S		S	E	B
Y	Y	O	HEADING	T	TEXT	T	C
N	N	H		X	B	C

Each intermediate block must begin with STX to give:

S	S	S		E	B
Y	Y	T	TEXT	T	C
N	N	X		B	C

and the final block must indicate the end of the message:

S	S	S		E	B
Y	Y	T	TEXT	T	C
N	N	X		X	C

Control Messages and Responses

Special formats are defined for control and supervisory messages and the response to them. The following are typical examples, although variations may be encountered in practice.

Positive Acknowledgement

A		S	S
C	(PREFIX)	Y	Y
K		N	N

Negative Acknowledgement

N		S	S
A	(PREFIX)	Y	Y
K		N	N

Selection or Polling

E		E	S	S
N	(ADDRESS)	O	Y	Y
Q		T	N	N

The ACK and NACK responses respectively are used to signify that a block has been either received correctly or is in error. They are also used to respond to a request from a master station to transmit an information block to a slave station. ACK indicates that the slave station is able to receive the block; NACK would indicate inability to receive.

Provision is made in the ISO standard for a status prefix to ACK, NACK and EOT to define or qualify the meaning of the sequence, ie the terminal's status or address, but the ISO standard does not define the content.

EOT is employed for two main purposes: to clear the previous link establishment phase or relationship, or as a response from a polled terminal that it has nothing to send. In either case control of the link is returned to the nominated master station of the link.

The polling and selection sequences for use in multipoint configurations are identical, the address/prefix information indicating to the addressed terminal whether the sequence is an invitation to transmit or an invitation to receive.

Transparent Mode Control Procedures

The procedures discussed so far rely on the fact that the line control is sensitive to a number of control characters. This means that none of these control characters, with the exception of SYN (synchronous idle), may be allowed to appear in the heading or text of a message. This presented no special problems so long as the coding and error detection methods specified in the original ISO standard applied. These required the 7-bit information characters to be carried in an 8-bit octet, the eighth bit being a parity bit which was used to construct the Block Check. However, a major extension to the standard allows information transfer without code restrictions.

The extension drops the use of the character parity bit to allow all the bits in each octet of the information to be used as data bits. This destroys the 'matrix' error protection method of the Basic Mode and a 16-bit check sequence is used in place of the 8-bit block check character to provide error protection. The generator polynomial for the block check sequence is:

$$X^{16} + X^{12} + X^5 + 1$$

and the highest order bit is sent to line first (see next chapter).

In Basic Mode, 'code transparency' is achieved through the use of DLE sequences for all the transmission controls. Hence, DLE.STX means start of text; DLE.ETX means end of text, etc. Single transmission control characters such as STX and ETX then become meaningless to the data link and can be sent in text, thus achieving code transparency.

Naturally, DLE.STX, etc, could also occur in text so a simple rule is used that, whenever a DLE is detected in the text by the transmitter, it adds an extra DLE. Hence, DLE.STX would be sent as DLE.DLE.STX; DLE as DLE.DLE; DLE.DLE as four DLEs, and so on. The receiver removes one DLE from each pair of DLEs and restores the text to normal but the double DLE indicates that the sequence is not a real transmission control. A single DLE prefix to a transmission control character identifies a true control sequence.

Synchronisation

In the preceding chapter we discussed how bit synchronisation is achieved in the modem. However, depending upon the facilities provided, and in particular, whether the modem supplies timing information to the DTE, it may be necessary for the latter to clock in the incoming bit streams. Assuming that bit synchronisation has been achieved, in the modem, additional synchronisation mechanisms were found to be necessary during the development of Basic Mode. These arose partly from technical limitations in respect of electronic timing accuracy, and also the inherent character structure of the protocol.

Character Synchronisation

Unlike the terminals used in the start/stop systems described earlier, a terminal on a synchronous system has no clear indication of the beginning and end of each character and this must be achieved in some other way.

The most common way of achieving character recovery is to use SYN characters at the beginning of each block transmitted. Figure 10.3 shows the unique bit pattern used in the SYN character of the ISO 7-bit alphabet and how these characters enable a receive terminal having the necessary logic to establish (or recover) character timing. It can be seen that none of the characters shifted left in Figure 10.3(a) is duplicated in Figure 10.3(b). Also, it is not possible for bits in a following or preceding character to form the same combination as SYN. It is possible, therefore, to logically detect SYN characters if any of the shifts numbers 1 to 5 occur, identify whether it is shifted left or right and by how many bits. The necessary adjustments can then be made. This process is often referred to as 'character framing'. Only 2 SYN characters are required for this purpose and in practice it is usual to transmit SYN characters continuously during idle periods. For this reason the character is sometimes referred to as 'synchronous idle'.

In some variants of BASIC MODE and where long block lengths are used, it is also common to transmit further SYN characters within the block or at regular intervals.

(a)

SYN = 0 1 1 0 1 0 0

	b1	b2	b3	b4	b5	b6	b7
	0	1	1	0	1	0	0
1	1	1	0	1	0	0	F
2	1	0	1	0	0	F	F
3	0	1	0	0	F	F	F
4	1	0	0	F	F	F	F
5	0	0	F	F	F	F	F

F = bit from following
character

(b)

	b1	b2	b3	b4	b5	b6	b7
	0	1	1	0	1	0	0
1	P	0	1	1	0	1	0
2	P	P	0	1	1	0	1
3	P	P	P	0	1	1	0
4	P	P	P	P	0	1	1
5	P	P	P	P	P	0	1

P = bit from preceding
character

Figure 10.3 Character Synchronisation

The block prefix SYN character has a parallel in the 'flag' sequence which precedes and delimits a frame in the HDLC protocol. However, as we shall see, the latter is employed somewhat differently and to greater effect.

Message Synchronisation

This requires little comment. It is really not so much a matter of synchronisation in the earlier sense, but, in terms of an application, determining the beginning and end of meaningful pieces of text, and the location of headers, etc.

As we have seen, this is achieved through the use of control characters such as STX, ETX.

Basic Mode in Operation

Basic Mode was designed for two-way alternate operation between a 'Master' station and one or more 'Slave' stations on a physical point-to-point or multipoint data link. No provision is made for slave stations to communicate with each other, and it was designed primarily for terminals connected in star configurations using point-to-point or multipoint circuits and with a high degree of centralised control.

Transmission is character-oriented using the ten Transmission Control Characters (TCCs) in the standard 7-bit code set to identify significant events in the flow of information and to signal commands, responses and status information.

The Master station is responsible for scheduling the data flow in the link by 'polling' or 'selecting' slave stations, using specific address characters. Polling authorises the addressed slave station to transmit to the Master station and selection instructs the slave to accept data.

Transmission is always one block at a time, and the transmitter retains a copy of the block just transmitted until it receives a positive acknowledgement of correct receipt (ACK) by the receiver. The receiver, on receipt of a block, recalculates the block check character, and if there is disagreement between the calculated and transmitted values, it returns a NAK response to the transmitter.

Transmitting information synchronously in Basic Mode is obviously more complex than transmitting characters asynchronously. As far as possible every eventuality must be catered for, as the following examples illustrate:

— First it is necessary to establish a connection and for one or other of the parties to 'seize' control of the link. But supposing each tries to do this simultaneously.

— Supposing a terminal goes down or through lack of storage space or time it is unable to receive a message. How can the situation be retrieved with minimum disruption?

— The main purpose is to transfer data securely, so that in the process, data must not only be error-free, but neither must it be lost.

— The error correction technique employed in Basic Mode requires that blocks in error should be retransmitted. The question arises: how long should the transmitter continue retransmitting a block in error before giving up?

— Finally, the exchange has to be terminated decisively, unambiguously and to the mutual satisfaction of both communicating parties.

As Figure 10.4 illustrates, Basic Mode is inherently a *half-duplex* protocol because each block transmitted must be followed by an ACK/NAK response before the next block is transmitted. This means that even

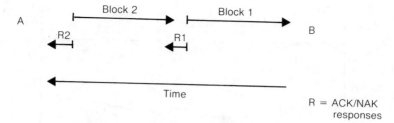

Figure 10.4   Half-Duplex Message Flow

on a link which physically offers full duplex transmission, the protocol cannot effectively support simultaneous transmission in the two directions. However, in practice full duplex physical circuits are frequently employed in order to minimize the transmission delay resulting from modem turnaround time, which would otherwise occur for every block transmit/response interaction on a half-duplex link.

Since the capacity used by the response messages is small in relation to that required for data blocks, for many applications this represents an inefficient use of duplex transmission. This aspect will be pursued in more detail when we come to discuss error detection and flow control.

We shall now briefly describe the principal modes of operation, and indicate how some of the contingencies and conflicts referred to above are handled and resolved.

Modes of Operation

Three classes of operation are catered for:

— Contention;

— Polling;

— Conversational.

Contention

Contention is the approach adopted for point-to-point links, which may be private circuits or switched paths established on the PSTN. The essential feature of this mode of operation is that neither end of the link has permanent control over the dialogue. Figure 10.5 illustrates a typical sequence.

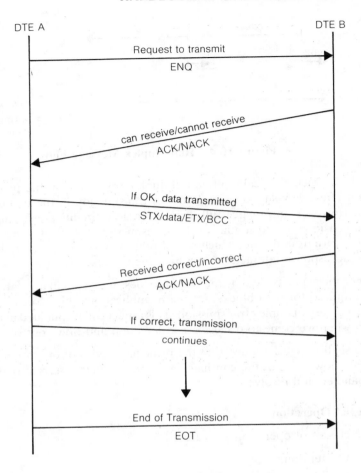

Figure 10.5   Point-to-Point Operation

Consider the question raised earlier of what happens if both ends send ENQ at the same instant, ie each end is contending for the link. This is resolved by assigning a priority to each station, the one with highest priority being referred to as the primary and the lower priority one, as the secondary. The primary/secondary concept is more fully developed in the HDLC protocol, and corresponds to the master/slave relationship. The functional distinction can be achieved in various ways. One common way is to bias the time out/retry limits (see below) in favour of the primary. Another way, either independently or in combination with the preceding method, is to constrain the functional implementation of the protocol in some way – perhaps by restricting the commands it is permitted to use – in the designated secondary, so that it can only function as a secondary.

Polling

In polling, the primary station is very much in permanent control and is intended for use in multipoint configurations using private circuits.

In a multipoint environment, the control station either polls or selects the tributary stations. Polling is an 'invitation to send' transmitted from the control station to a specific tributary station. Selection is a 'request to receive' notification from the control station to one of the tributary stations instructing it to receive the following messages. These capabilities permit the control station to specify the transmitting station and to control the direction of transmission. Each station in the data link is assigned a unique station address, which is used to acquire the station's attention during either polling or selection. Once the station's attention is acquired and it responds affirmatively, message transmission can begin.

Therefore, all transmissions for this type of operation are regulated by the control station by means of polling and selection. By sequentially polling each tributary station, the control station directs the incoming message traffic. The outgoing traffic is regulated from the control station by selection of the desired tributary station to receive the message. All transactions are between the control station and the selected tributary station.

The initialisation phase for multipoint operation is accomplished by the control station transmitting the following sequence:

EOT (Polling or selection address) ENQ

This sequence ensures that all monitoring tributary stations are now in a control or 'listening' mode and thus prepared to receive either a poll or a selection from the control station. The polling or selection sequence transmitted while in control mode designates the station that is to transmit or receive data. This sequence can also define the specific device required if the station has several available.

We do not propose here giving detailed examples. It is sufficient that

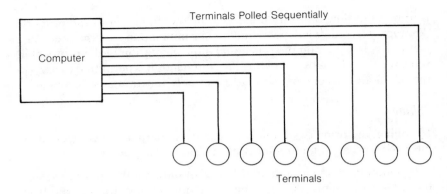

Figure 10.6   Roll Call Polling

the general principles are understood. In practice, polling can take three forms depending upon such factors as the physical design of the network and the distances involved.

Roll Call Polling (Figure 10.6) involves the computer in inviting each terminal, in turn, to take over as the master station, in order to transmit information to the computer. The polling sequence is commonly pre-determined by a polling list of terminal addresses, but in most systems provision is made for the sequence to be changed to take account of changing priorities or traffic volumes.

Drop Polling (Figure 10.7) is a variation on roll call polling in that the computer polls a controller which in turn serves the terminal connected to it. The controller can transmit one or a number of messages as a result of each poll.

Compared to roll call polling, drop polling is generally more efficient, the number of 'no traffic' signals being usually fewer. It needs fewer lines and computer access ports, but increases the vulnerability of the system to line failure. Because each controller can usually handle several terminals expansion is simpler involving an additional local line to the controller instead of a separate extended line back to the CPU as in roll call polling.

Hub Polling (Figure 10.8) also involves controllers or concentrators. In this case, however, the line is configured on an omnibus basis. Usually the last controller on the line is polled by the computer. If it (the controller)

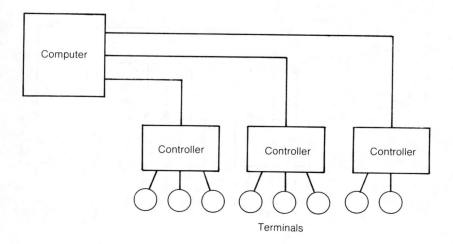

Figure 10.7   Drop Polling

has any message to transmit, it transmits it to the next to last controller which retransmits it and adds on its own messages. The whole is forwarded to the next controller in the link, each controller augmenting the train of information with its own messages.

This polling method is used in situations where long distances are involved and line costs need to be kept to a minimum. Mainly for this reason it has been used in airline reservation systems.

However, because of the relatively short distances involved, hub polling is unlikely to offer any circuit cost benefits within the UK.

Conversational Mode

In an interactive or conversational mode, where there is a frequent exchange of relatively short messages, the rigid adherence to the ACK/ NAK procedure could constitute a significant overhead with adverse effects on the response times experienced by the terminal user.

This simple extension to the ISO standard defines the rules for the interchange of messages in a conversational mode. The rules permit an information message to replace an ACK sequence. This option can only

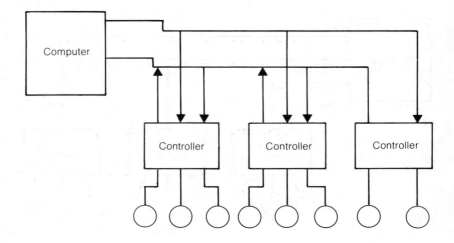

Figure 10.8   Hub Polling

be invoked after an ETX termination (not after an ETB termination) and cannot be used in place of a NAK sequence. When the option is used, the STX or SOH opening character equates to ACK.

Time-Outs and Retries

We have noted above that the normal course of events involving alternate transmission and acknowledgement can be disturbed for a variety of reasons. These include:

— transmitted block contains an error;

— a block is completely obliterated; this could arise from a transient power failure; both information blocks and control messages such as ACKs and NAKs could be equally affected;

— two devices are contending for the link at the same time.

Where a block received is in error, at least the recipient is aware of the situation and can request retransmission by issuing a NAK. However, when a block is completely obliterated, recovery must be initiated by the transmitter.

In order to satisfy this need for recovery it is necessary to incorporate both a time-out and a retry mechanism into a data link communications control protocol.

The simplest implementation of a retry mechanism would be to repeat every message until a positive acknowledgement is received. This would establish that the message has been received satisfactorily by the other party. This assumes a transient communications problem, in general an unwarranted assumption. A limit is therefore defined, set high enough to prevent premature disconnection and low enough to establish that further communication is likely to be unprofitable within a particular time period. Typical values for this limit range from three to fifteen retries per message.

Where messages may be completely lost, the retry limit needs to be reinforced by a time-out mechanism. Such a mechanism is initiated when a message is transmitted. It defines a reasonable period (typically from five to thirty seconds) during which the recipient must transmit a reply. If no reply is received by the transmitting party during the time period, the retry mechanism is brought into force.

The time-out mechanism also provides one solution to the contention problem. If one end of the link is defined as the primary, and the time-out threshold before an ENQ is transmitted is set to a lower value for the primary than for the secondary, this will ensure that, providing the primary persists, it will 'get in first'.

The number of retries required versus the total number of messages transmitted gives an indication of communications link performance. A deteriorating link is shown by an increasing requirement for retransmission. This may permit engineering action to be initiated in a controlled manner before final breakdown occurs.

Limitations of Character-Oriented Protocols

Although Basic Mode protocols and the family of character-oriented protocols to which it belongs, have served data communications well over the years, they suffer from a number of limitations. The chief ones are:

— a master/slave relationship is inherent in the protocol;

— the protocols are orientated towards centrally controlled systems. These have sometimes proved unsuitable for interconnecting intelligent devices because of considerable redundancy in the protocols to allow for the lack of intelligence at the remote terminal;

— a number of different block types are required for various purposes such as:

  — information transfer;

  — positive acknowledgement;

  — negative acknowledgement;

  — requests for retransmission;

  — busy indication (ie inability to process further information transfers at present).

In order to extend and enhance the protocol, other types may also be required:

— the monolithic structure of blocks and text sequences with control sequences being embedded in the text strings results in strong interdependencies between the various components. The weak separation of functional components and the lack of a direct correspondence between function and structure make it difficult to organise protocols into well-structured hierarchies. This has an adverse effect on the structure of the hardware and software components which implement protocols and system architectures;

— use of the same message coding to convey several meanings introduces context sensitivity when trying to interpret activity on a link;

— implicit protocol enforcement of the data structure of the information transfer (typically into characters, messages or files). Ideally, these distinctions should be reserved for a higher level, and the information carried should be handled transparently;

— additional procedures are required to transmit binary data by using extended control sequences. Thus an additional untidy appendage is required to provide code transparency;

— error protection is restricted to the data field, whereas block headers are unprotected;

— the protocols operate in half-duplex mode and therefore make inefficient use of duplex transmission links.

Most of these limitations were identified quite early on, and, over the years considerable effort has gone into the design of link protocols which would overcome these deficiencies. The result of this work is HDLC (High-Level Data Link Control) which is now coming into use, and eventually may be expected to displace character-oriented protocols typified by Basic Mode.

In order to gain a reasonable understanding of HDLC, it is essential that the limitations of Basic Mode are appreciated, and also why Basic Mode cannot be satisfactorily modified to support full duplex transmission. We consider this latter aspect in the next chapter on error detection and error control methods, before reviewing HDLC in the subsequent chapter.

11 Error Control and Efficiency Considerations

INTRODUCTION

In this chapter we consider the nature of transmission errors and the various approaches to combating the problem, particularly at the Link Protocol level.

As Figure 11.1 illustrates, even a simple data communications system comprises a number of components, and each component can be a source of errors, some being more error-prone than others. Protection against transmission errors must therefore be seen in perspective as only part of a solution to a total systems problem.

The recognition of the inevitability of errors in any part of a data communications system is the first step towards a remedy. The next steps are to evaluate the likely costs of errors and to examine the probability of their occurrence. A very high degree of error control can be applied to any part of a system, although it should be emphasised that the cost of guarding against errors must not be allowed to exceed the cost of allowing them to occur. Errors can be expected on data communications links and the nature of these and the available means of error control are discussed in this chapter. Much attention has been given to this interesting subject in recent years and initial fear of transmission errors has been replaced to some extent by an enthusiasm to control them. There is, however, a need for consistency of approach to the problem. Residual error rates can now be reduced to infinitesimal proportions but it is unrealistic to design for a residual error rate of say, 1×10^{14} in this area without protection to the same degree in other equally important parts of a system.

The level of protection deemed necessary must also be related to the nature of the applications and the penalties of producing faulty informa-

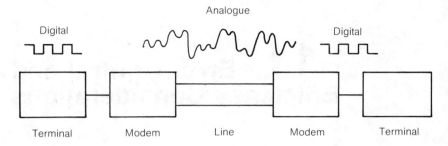

Figure 11.1   The Elements in a Data Communications System

tion. Clearly errors in a system producing plain language transmission (where errors are largely self-evident) need only a rudimentary form of error check, to give an acceptable level of error performance. On the other hand an air traffic control system concerned with human safety can afford very few errors in its data transmission system. Such a system will have been designed using normal data transmission equipment and lines, which in themselves might have an unacceptable level of error performance. The systems designer, however, would have built into the system error control techniques to reduce these errors to an acceptable level.

Thus, some systems might tolerate an error rate of 1 bit in 10^3, others might necessitate 1 in 10^9 or better.

THE NATURE OF ERROR

We shall briefly comment upon the definition and measurement of error, and then review the respective contributions of the main system components before considering transmission errors in particular.

Definition and Measurement

An error in a data transmission system means usually that where, say a binary 1 has been sent, a binary 0 has been received. The other way in which errors can occur are where bits are lost, but this will have a catastrophic effect on the block being transmitted, easily recognised by the receive terminal.

Error rates are quoted usually as one error in so many bits (1 in 10^4 or 1 in 10,000 bits) but clearly the situation of 1 bit in error being followed by 9999 'good' bits is very unlikely so that an error rate as quoted above really means that 'given a representative sample then the probability will be that 1 bit in 10^4 will be in error'. In computer systems such 1 bit errors are common but on data transmission lines errors tend to occur in bursts.

The Operator

Although data communications links are prone to errors, they are by no means the worst offenders; sadly the people within a system are not beyond reproach. Terminal operators in an on-line system are often the weakest link in an otherwise reliable installation and very high keying errors indeed are to be expected – particularly, it seems, in the critical early days of operations. In batch processing systems, the very best operators dedicated to a particular task such as card punching produce a high proportion of errors.

In a field study involving more than 1000 operators of IBM card punches and bank proof machines in 20 different installations in the USA it was found that experienced punched card operators averaged between 1600 to 4300 key strokes per undetected error, experienced bank proof machine operators averaging 3500 cheques per undetected error. The study revealed the interesting facts that the least accurate operators make ten times as many errors as the most accurate, and that fast operators tend to make fewer errors.

These figures emphasise the inevitability of human error and indicate an upper limit of error performance in the order of 2×10^4 characters. This, of course, is way beyond the reach of most on-line terminal operators who may be performing a variety of tasks in very different conditions to the punch room. In many on-line systems, a good performance is regarded as being nearer 1 in 100.

The Computer

Like anyone else, the computer professional may be fallible. Many residual program bugs are lurking now in computer systems seemingly ready to pounce at the most critical moment and then retire to await their next opportunity. The development of appropriate tools to enable the production of error-free programs is a long-standing goal of software engineers. Computers themselves can make mistakes and the transient errors such as the dropped bit caused perhaps by dust particles on a magnetic tape or disk are familiar to computer programmers and operators.

Other Hardware Components

Hardware components with mechanical parts are in general more error-prone, particularly as the parts progressively wear out, than electronic components. Furthermore the advent of solid-state electronics has brought about vast improvements in reliability.

Thus, visual display terminals may be expected to be inherently more reliable than traditional teletypes, and for similar reasons modems are also relatively error-free.

Whilst terminals can cause an error in transmitting to the modem, and the same with computers, these errors are clearly the fault of the terminal or the computer. Modems have no facility to validate received data; they are designed to transmit a binary 1 or 0 and to recognise and register the receipt of a binary 1 or 0. If the send modem transmits a binary 1 and the receive modem registers a binary 0 then an error has occurred due possibly to a fault in the modem but more likely to transient line conditions. These 'mistakes' made by the receive modem are due in the main to impulsive noise on the line, the duration of the noise burst determining the number of bits in error.

Other causes of errors are the intermittent short duration disconnections on circuits. These short breaks (in the order of milliseconds) may not interfere with speech communication but have a marked effect on data.

Most modems have a 'carrier detect' facility which, when a circuit is broken, tells the terminal that 'carrier' has failed. This operation can come into effect immediately or a delay or 'hold over' period (of up to $1\frac{1}{2}$ seconds) can be built in. In either event the transmitted block will be corrupted, but if carrier detect fails, the receive terminal will 'time out' and stop looking for incoming data. If the 'hold over' period is not exceeded then retransmission is easily established. The advantage of this 'hold over' facility enables synchronisation to be partly maintained whereas following a 'time out', full synchronisation has to be re-established (and this can take some time with high-speed dynamically-equalised modems).

Transmission Errors

Background

The only statement that can be made with certainty about transmission errors is that they will occur. How often they will do so and what the distribution of errors will be on a particular circuit is a forecast which the bravest communications engineer would not attempt. The factors affecting circuit quality are numerous and varied, and as we have seen in earlier chapters, the transmission of digital data along analogue paths raises additional problems which do not apply to the same extent when speech is transmitted along such paths.

The following discussion, and the statistics which are quoted, relate to analogue transmission, which will continue to be an important transmission vehicle for some time to come, until it is completely displaced by digital transmission. The rate at which this is occurring varies in different countries, but in the UK the conversion program is well advanced, particularly on the trunk circuits.

Experience to date provides very firm evidence that digital transmission, together with stored program switching (as on System X), results in a massive improvement in transmission quality. For example, the noise amplification is virtually eliminated, as is impulsive noise directly caused by electromechanical exchange switching. Therefore, within the UK context, progressive improvements in quality may be expected with increasing penetration of digital technology.

Error Characteristics

Private circuits can be provided with defined characteristics which indicate the distortions on the line which are unlikely to be exceeded. To what extent errors result from these imperfect line conditions will depend largely on the modems and transmission techniques used. All telecommunications authorities are naturally reluctant to quote guaranteed error rates on their networks because of these factors and because inevitably some circuits will give a poorer performance than others. Table 11.1 shows, however, the maximum bit error rates recommended by CCITT for different types of connection. These show only the maximum average number of error bits to correct bits and, while being useful to telecommunications engineers for maintenance purposes, they are not very helpful either to designers of error control systems or to systems analysts.

Transmission errors in fact pose different problems for three different groups of people. The telecommunications engineers – and here modem manufacturers are included – must study the transmission problems which are likely to cause errors so that circuits can be engineered and

Modulation rate (bauds)	Connection	Maximum bit error rate
1200	switched (when possible)	10^{-3}
1200	leased	$5\text{-}10^{-5}$
600	switched	10^{-3}
600	leased	$5\text{-}10^{-5}$
200	switched	10^{-4}
200	leased	$5\text{-}10^{-5}$

Table 11.1   Maintenance Limits for Errors on the PSTN and Leased Terms (CCITT Green Book, Vol. VIII 1973, Recommendation V53)

modems designed to minimise their effects. In addition, the telecommunications engineers, through their PTTs, have the added responsibility of providing as much information as possible regarding the frequency and distribution of those conditions on their networks which are likely to cause errors and to recommend means of controlling them.

The designer of an error control system is primarily concerned with the control of errors with a view to providing the maximum protection against them with the minimum amount of redundant information. The prime interest is the distribution or pattern of errors as well as the frequency with which they are likely to occur; the designer will conduct laboratory and field experiments as well as using CCITT statistics in order to obtain the required information.

The systems analyst working on data communications systems apparently has the easiest transmission error control problem. Indeed the problem may be ignored altogether in the belief that the level of protection which he needs against this type of error can be readily obtained. This is understandable, for, with modern data communications systems, retransmission of blocks in error takes place automatically and the presence of transmission errors is rarely evident. The systems analyst could be forgiven for wondering what the fuss is all about and concentrating on other more pressing or exciting tasks. If the communications hardware has already been purchased and manufacturers' communications control software is being used, there may be very little the systems analyst could do about transmission errors anyway. However, a knowledge of data transmission error control may help a systems designer in a number of ways.

By considering carefully the effects of errors in a proposed system, the analyst can determine the proper degree of protection required and try to select an error control method which will give him the necessary residual error rate with the minimum redundancy. From then on, the systems analyst can regard errors as delays, delays which can increase costs or lengthen response times or both. These delays can be reduced considerably by careful attention to the block sizes and the error control procedures used. Later in this chapter, different types of error detection and correction codes will be discussed and the throughput of information in the presence of errors will also be considered. Before examining these subjects, it is useful to clarify what is meant by the various terms used to describe errors and to have some idea what causes them.

First of all, let us consider the term 'error' itself. This could not be easier, for the nature of computer data is such that the symbols 0 and 1 are mutually exclusive. If, therefore, a binary '1' is received when a binary '0' has been transmitted, an error has occurred. This is described as a single bit error if the bits on either side are received correctly. Errors also occur in groups and a two bit error group, for example, is two consecutive erroneous bits with correct bits either side. Table 11.2 shows the recorded distribution of error groups found on a series of tests on a looped private circuit in the UK using FSK modems at 1200 bit/s.

The results of these tests, which were conducted using a 4082 bit pseudo-random pattern, cannot be regarded as typifying those to be

Number of 1 bit errors	584
Number of 2 bit errors	204
Number of 3 bit errors	73
Number of 4 bit errors	43
Number of 5 bit errors	16
Number of 6 bit errors	9
Number of 7 bit errors	5
Number of 8 bit errors	3
Total number of error groups	937

Table 11.2   Distribution of Error Groups from Tests on a Private Circuit in the UK at 1200 bit/s (CCITT White Book, Vol. VIII. Supp. 15)

found on other private circuits, but they serve to illustrate the fact that a variety of error groupings can be expected. In this case, only 62 per cent of the error groups were found to be single bit errors, the average number of bits in an error group being 1.68.

Line disturbances also cause bursts of errors to occur. An error burst is defined by CCITT as a group of bits in which two successive erroneous bits are always separated by less than a given number (X) of correct bits, the definition going on to state that the last erroneous bit in a burst and the first erroneous bit in the following burst are accordingly separated by X or more correct bits. Such precise definition is necessary in international communications but can pose problems of understanding. The reader may be relieved to learn that CCITT have not so far attempted to define an 'erroneous bit'. Burst errors, in fact, are not as incomprehensible as they sound and are extremely important. If errors are to be detected, it is necessary to find out more about the way in which they are distributed. To say that an average error rate is, for example, 1 in 10^4 tells us very little, for errors will certainly not be conveniently slotted into a stream of data 1 every 10,000 bits. Error groupings, as in Table 11.2, are helpful but give no indication of the distances which separate the errors – a key factor in the design of effective error detection and correction codes. The analysis of data in terms of error bursts is very useful and fairly simple. Consider the small block of data shown in Figure 11.2.

An error burst must begin and end with an error but may or may not contain other error bits; the term therefore describes a 'span' rather than a number of errors. We could, therefore, consider first of all the span E1 to E2 as being a four bit burst. However, if we were to require the transmission of four error-free bits (ie X) to indicate the end of an error burst, we would have considered the burst to be terminated by E3. The block in fact contains an eight bit burst E1-E3. This is followed by a three bit burst E4-E5.

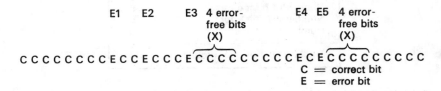

Figure 11.2   Analysis of a Block for Burst Errors

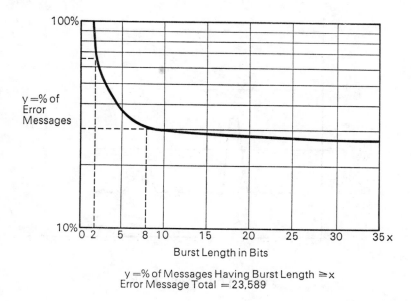

Figure 11.3   Error Burst Size Distribution (CCITT Blue Book, 37/22)

Figure 11.3 gives a typical graph of error burst size distribution.

Impulsive Noise

Transmission errors are caused by a number of factors but impulsive noise is probably the major problem. The main source of impulsive noise is switched connections through automatic telephone exchanges.

The electromechanical switches in the exchanges cause vibrations which create movement on contact surfaces resulting in noise peaks or spikes with typical peak to peak values of 100 milli-volts. There is also some evidence to suggest that the quality of the final selectors in the called exchange exerts a considerable influence on the level of impulsive noise. Noise power is normally expressed in dBm0 which refers to the ratio of the noise power at a point in the transmission path to the test level measured at that point (expressed in decibels). The maximum number of noise peaks which occur during any period of 15 minutes on *private* circuits is published in the relevant PTT circuit specifications. For exam-

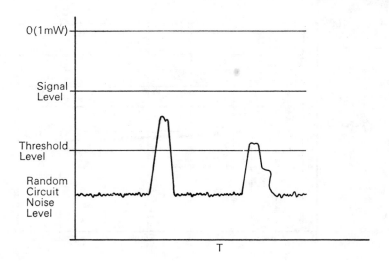

Figure 11.4   Noise Peaks

ple, on a BT schedule D circuit, a threshold level of – 21 dBm0 is set which must not be exceeded more than 18 times in any period of 15 minutes (see Figure 11.4).

Signal Power and Transmission Errors

As the most important factor affecting transmission error performance is the ratio of impulsive noise power to the signal power, it would obviously be advantageous to increase the signal power of the modems used on telephone circuits. Unfortunately, there are limits which must be observed and these have been agreed internationally (CCITT recommendation V2). The reasons for this are, firstly, to avoid overhearing or cross-talk which can be caused in the local cable network by excessive signal power and, secondly, because the multi-channel carrier systems used on the networks have design tolerances which limit the power values of individual channels.

The CCITT has recommended a maximum send level of –10 dBm0 from subscribers' equipment into simplex private circuits and –13 dBm0 for duplex circuits. BT stipulates a send level not exceeding –13 dBm0 on all private circuits. An inland private circuit to schedule D specification and an international circuit to M102 specification conform to CCITT recommendations regarding impulsive noise levels. Noise levels exceeding a threshold level of −21 dBm0 are measured and a count is made of the number of times the noise exceeds the threshold level. On private circuits, the signal to noise power level at the noise threshold point is therefore 8 dB (signal level −13 dBm0, noise level −21 dBm0). The count should not exceed 18 during any 15 minute period.

In the UK, prior to liberalisation, modems attached to the PSTN had to be provided by the Post Office and were adjusted on installation so that the sending level is −10 dBm0 at the Group Switching Centre. This complies with the international agreement (CCITT recommendation V2) that systems transmitting continuous tones should have the power level of the customer's equipment adjusted so that on international calls the level of the signal at the international circuit input shall not exceed 10 dBm0 for simplex systems or −13 dBm0 for duplex systems. Calls connected on the PSTN are not only more subject to impulsive noise and interruptions than private circuits but the ratio of the level of these disturbances to the signal power is likely to be very much higher because of the greater attenuation of the signals. It follows from this that the error rate of calls over the PSTN will be considerably worse than on a private leased circuit.

Telephone Traffic and Transmission Errors

The incidence of errors on telephone circuits tends to follow the same pattern as that of the exchange traffic. The typical telephone traffic graph is shown in Figure 11.5.

This close correlation between busy hour traffic and data errors is an international phenomenon and can be seen clearly by comparing Figure 11.5 with Figure 11.6 which shows the distribution of erroneous blocks transmitted on the PSTN in Chile.

The error peaks are due to the additional impulsive noise introduced by automatic selectors in automatic telephone exchanges during busy periods.

The same effect can be seen on private circuit connections. The tests referred to earlier on a private circuit in the UK (CCITT White Book, Vol. VIII, Supp. 14) show a different distribution but the influence of peak traffic can be seen clearly in Table 11.3.

The results shown here, and other tests throughout the world, suggest

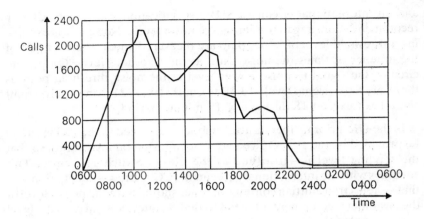

Figure 11.5   Telephone Call Distribution

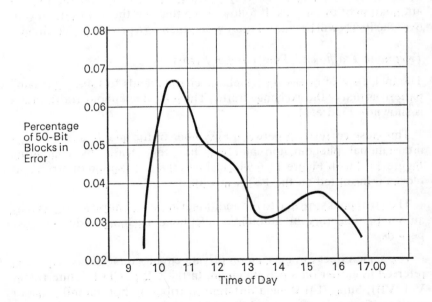

Figure 11.6   Time Distribution of Erroneous Blocks on the PSTN in Chile

9.00 – 10.00 hrs	1 bit in	75,343
10.00 – 11.00 hrs	1 bit in	14,378
11.00 – 12.00 hrs	1 bit in	46,014
12.00 – 13.00 hrs	1 bit in	1,277,811
13.00 – 14.00 hrs	1 bit in	12,876,768
14.00 – 15.00 hrs	1 bit in	79,529
15.00 – 16.00 hrs	indeterminate, better than 1 bit in	6,425,000
16.00 – 17.00 hrs	1 bit in	10,261
17.00 – 17.30 hrs	indeterminate, better than 1 bit in	2,140,000

Table 11.3   Bit Error Rates against Time of Day. Tests on a Private Circuit in the UK (CCITT White Book, Vol. VIII, Supp. 14)

Monday	1 bit in	1,647,283
Tuesday	1 bit in	1,272,290
Wednesday	1 bit in	55,770
Thursday	1 bit in	3,006,290
Friday	1 bit in	647,140

Table 11.4   Variations in Bit Error Rates Monday to Friday. Tests on a Private Circuit in the UK (CCITT White Book, Vol. VIII, Supp. 14)

that the error performance of data links in traffic off-peak periods will yield better results than in the busy periods. This is particularly true of calls on the PSTN where there is the added incentive to use off-peak periods because of reduced call charges.

There may be a wide variation of bit error rates over different days of the week and again there are indications that this is probably due to variations in telephone traffic density. Table 11.4 shows the results found on the UK tests (CCITT White Book, Vol. VIII, Supp. 14).

Although over 300 million bits were transmitted during these tests, they were conducted over a period of only three weeks and it would be unwise, therefore, to draw any other conclusions from these figures alone except that considerable variations in error rates from day to day may be experienced. The figure for Wednesdays is interesting and, although considerable efforts were made to find the reasons for the relatively poor performance on that day, no convincing explanation could be found. The perversity of errors being so great on Wednesdays during these tests is further evidence that average bit error rates are not to be trusted.

Short Breaks in Transmission

A problem which occurs in all telephone networks is that of short interruptions in transmission during which the line signals may be lost completely. Table 11.5 shows the results of an investigation during a two-week period in January 1966 on a channel with a total length of 200 miles.

The channel measured was set up on a through-supergroup over three old-type coaxial systems. The majority of causes for the interruptions were identified and it is expected that with the more modern design features of newer systems and the improved maintenance procedures which have been and are continuing to be introduced that the incidence of short interruptions will be reduced. However, it is most unlikely that these breaks will ever be eradicated and data will not be transmitted during the periods they are present. With modern error control procedures, the majority of these shorter breaks will result in the blocks of data in which they occur being retransmitted and data will not be lost but delayed. Longer interruptions may cause further delays if synchronisa-

Duration of interruption (milliseconds)	Total number of interruptions	Number of interruptions whose cause could not be identified
<10	4	4
10-20	16	7
20-50	21	3
50-100	7	0
100-300	20	1
300 to 1 minute	25	1
>1 minute	7	2
TOTALS	100	18

Table 11.5   Distribution of Durations of Interruptions Recorded on a 200-Mile Channel During Two Weeks

tion is lost and some systems will register a failure if a number (typically 3) of retransmissions is unsuccessful. Unless each block of data is clearly identified, there is a danger that a line interruption may result in a message being lost – particularly when continuous automatic retransmission methods are used.

Echoes

In speech conversations over long distance circuits, a person's voice may be returned or echoed back. These echoes are due to reflections which can occur whenever there is a change of impedance in the line such as a 2- to 4-wire conversion through hybrid transformers.

This talker echo effect is a nuisance when measured in tens of milliseconds, and above 500 ms will|inhibit speech altogether; some long distance circuits are fitted with echo suppressors to prevent echoes being returned but these can be disabled when the circuit is used for data transmission as it may be essential to have the return channel open for duplex transmission.

Echoes have a different effect on data transmission. The problem is that data transmitted may be followed by a delayed replica of itself (listener echo) which may interfere with the operation of the data receiver. Delays of fractions of a millisecond may be significant and, if the echoes are of sufficient amplitude, errors may be produced.

On schedule D circuits, for example, the maximum level will be 20 dB. On the public switched telephone network, some connections may have a signal to listener echo ratio of worse than 15 dB.

ERROR DETECTION AND CORRECTION METHODS

The methods used to date fall into one or other of the following categories:

— Information feedback;

— Forward Error Control (FEC);

— Decision feedback, sometimes referred to as Automatic Retransmission on Request or ARQ methods.

The first of these is generally used in asynchronous transmission, and the others in synchronous transmission.

FEC methods are in fact little used, but are included for completeness. ARQ methods, of which the Basic Mode ACK/NAK procedure is an example, are by far the commonest.

Information Feedback Systems

This method is widely employed for single bit error detection in low-speed asynchronous data transmission. In Figure 11.7 the data entered on the keyboard does not directly activate the local printer but is transmitted from the keyboard down the line to the receiving end which loops the signal back on the other half of the duplex pathway. When this returning signal reaches the originator it drives the printer and displays the character received. If this received character does not agree with that depressed on the keyboard an error is assumed to have occurred during transmission. The human operator is visually doing the error detection by comparing the known keyed input against the printed output 'fed back' from the receiver to the originator. The technique is sometimes referred to as 'echoplexing'.

Forward Error Control (FEC)

Unlike ARQ systems, forward error control (FEC) systems attempt to correct errors at the receiver without employing retransmission procedures. Sufficient redundancy must therefore be carried in the blocks so that not only is the presence of an error detected but also its location

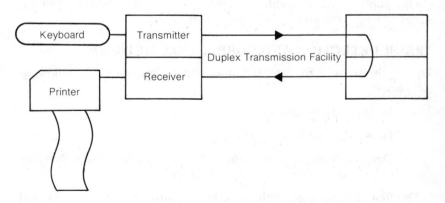

Figure 11.7   'Echoplexing' in Asynchronous Transmission

within the block. Once the position of an error is known, correction is achieved simply by inverting the erroneous bit from 1 to 0 or vice versa.

The technique relies upon the use of special coding schemes which entail carrying additional redundant bits in the block.

Principles

Many complex coding schemes have been developed for forward error correction. The most common of these is the Hamming single bit error correcting code which is perhaps the simplest method used for error correction and, therefore, provides a useful introduction to the subject.

A Hamming code can be constructed for any group of data to give error correction of any one bit in the group which is detected as being in error; it can, therefore, be applied to a character or a block of information. The checking bits which are used occupy pre-determined positions within the data field, the positions being all those with the value of 2^n. For example, in a protected data field of 15 bits, the checking bits occupy the bit positions 1, 2, 4 and 8 as shown in Figure 11.8.

In Figure 11.9 an 11 bit data message (10101011001) is shown which is to be protected by four check bits.

Bit positions 15, 13, 11, 9, 7 and 3 contain binary 1s and the binary values of these bit positions are added using modulo 2 arithmetic to produce the Hamming bits (see Figure 11.10).

Bit position	15	14	13	12	11	10	9	2^3 8	7	6	5	2^2 4	3	2^1 2	2^0 1
	I	I	I	I	I	I	I	X	I	I	I	X	I	X	X

I = Information bit
X = Hamming or check bits

Figure 11.8   Position of Hamming Bits in a Protected 15 Bit Data Field

Bit position	15	14	13	12	11	10	9	8	7	6	5	4	3	2	1
	1	0	1	0	1	0	1	X	1	0	0	X	1	X	X

Figure 11.9

Bit position	Binary value	
15	1 1 1 1	NB: Modulo 2 addition
13	1 1 0 1	(addition without carry)
11	1 0 1 1	produces even parity
9	1 0 0 1	
7	0 1 1 1	
3	0 0 1 1	
	0 1 0 0 ← Hamming bits	

Figure 11.10   Hamming Bits Produced from a Modulo 2 Addition

Bit							X			X		X	X
position	15	14	13	12	11	10	9	8	7	6	5	4	3	2	1
Data field	1	0	1	0	1	0	1	0	1	0	0	1	1	0	0

X = Hamming bits

Figure 11.11

Bit position	Binary value	
15	1 1 1 1	
13	1 1 0 1	
11	1 0 1 1	
9	1 0 0 1	
7	0 1 1 1	
4	0 1 0 0	
3	0 0 1 1	
	0 0 0 0 ← modulo 2 result	

Figure 11.12

Bit							X			X		X	X
position	15	14	13	12	11	10	9	8	7	6	5	4	3	2	1
Data field	1	0	1	0	0	0	1	0	1	0	0	1	1	0	0

↑
error

X = Hamming bits

Figure 11.13

Bit position	Binary value			
15	1	1	1	1
13	1	1	0	1
9	1	0	0	1
7	0	1	1	1
4	0	1	0	0
3	0	0	1	1
11	1	0	1	1

← modulo 2 sum indicates bit position 11 in error

Figure 11.14

The full 15 bit field is shown in Figure 11.11, the lowest order Hamming bits being inserted into the lowest order bit positions.

At the receiver, the binary value of each bit position containing a 1 bit is added using modulo 2 arithmetic. If there have been no errors, the result should be zero as shown in Figure 11.12.

If a single bit error occurs in transmission, the position of the error will be indicated by the modulo 2 sum. For example, assuming an error in the 11th bit position in Figure 11.11, the data would be received as shown in Figure 11.13.

At the receiver, the binary values of positions 15, 13, 9, 7, 4 and 3 would then be added as shown in Figure 11.14.

The modulo 2 sum in Figure 11.14 indicates that the 11th bit position is in error and the bit is then inverted from 0 to 1. If two bit errors occur, the position of the errors cannot be determined from the modulo 2 result, although, as this will not be zero, the presence of a double error will be indicated. The code can correct single bit errors and detect double errors but some multiple errors will escape detection.

Comments on FEC Methods

In general ARQ methods are considered to be superior to FEC methods. As we shall see, using the former, residual error rates can be reduced to very low levels when efficient error detection codes are allied to simple control procedures. If a code is required simply to detect errors, systems using redundant parity bits will be able to detect a very high proportion of the many different error patterns which can be expected on telephone circuits. The fraction of undetected error patterns will be only $1/2^r$ irrespective of the length of the error detection code used where r is the number of checking bits in the code. A code using eight checking bits is, therefore, capable of detecting all but 1/256th of all the error patterns which can possibly occur. The effectiveness of the codes can be further increased by careful design to give maximum protection against those error patterns which are most likely to occur. Comparatively few error patterns are correctable when using parity checking. This fraction will be no better than $1/2^k$ where k is the number of information bits in a block – regardless of the algorithm used. It follows from this that unless the error characteristics of a channel are such that only a very small number of error patterns are present, the residual error rate will be high when using FEC. Forward error correction is usually used, therefore, when a return channel is not available as in simplex transmission and more efficient ARQ methods are not possible. Typically, they are designed to correct single or two bit errors but will detect other error patterns and give an error indication at the receiver when these occur.

The general effect of FEC is to reduce the error rate of a channel but the high proportion of checking bits to information bits also significantly reduces the transfer rate. The transfer rate of an FEC method can be given as:

$$\frac{Rk}{n}$$

where R = the data signalling rate;
       k = the number of information bits transmitted;
       n = the total number of bits transmitted.

A general comparison between the throughput efficiency of an ARQ system and a FEC system cannot be made, as the output from a FEC system will in general contain a much higher proportion of uncorrected errors than the output from an ARQ system.

ARQ Methods

The common feature of ARQ methods is the calculation by the transmitter of some function of the contents of the block, which is transmitted with the block, and recalculated by the receiver. The calculated value is compared with the transmitted value, and, if the two agree, then a positive acknowledgement (ACK) is sent back to the transmitter; otherwise a negative acknowledgement (NAK) is despatched, and this in turn triggers a retransmission of the block in error.

An unlimited number of functions can be calculated for use as a check value, but the ones which have found most favour are:

— the block check count (BCC) as used in the Basic Mode protocols;

— the CCITT cyclic polynomial as used in extensions to Basic Mode and which is standard in HDLC.

To date the first of these has been the most extensively favoured technique, but the cyclic polynomial is becoming increasingly important as HDLC starts to displace Basic Mode.

Parity Checking and the Block Check Count (BCC)

The standard practice in Basic Mode and similar character-oriented protocols is to provide checks at two levels.

First of all an eighth parity bit is added to each 7-bit information character. The convention in the Basic Mode standard is that this should be chosen so that the total number of 1 bits in the character is odd. This technique will detect errors in a single bit position, and is illustrated in Figure 11.15. It should be noted that although the single bit error is detected, it is not possible to determine its location.

In addition to the character or vertical parity check, it is also possible to define a single parity bit for each row of the block corresponding to specific bit positions of the constituent characters. This longitudinal parity check supplies the Block Check Character, which is added to each transmitted block. Figure 11.16 shows how this is calculated.

The BCC is composed of 7 bits plus a parity bit which is the parity of the BCC character not the summation of the parity bits in the block of text, and is accorded odd parity.

The longitudinal parity sense is arranged to be even. The opening STX or SOH is excluded from the longitudinal parity summation but all succeeding characters including STX in a block started by SOH and the ETB or ETX ending character are included. SYN characters if they occur are excluded as a special case because they could be introduced after the formation of the block or text in some systems.

This two co-ordinate parity check provides a powerful error detection

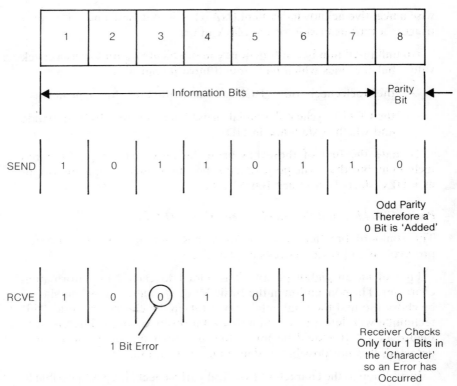

Figure 11.15   Character Parity Checking

capability. All block errors with an odd number of error bits can be detected as well as all two bit errors and some other even bit errors. Compensating errors are reduced but rectangular co-ordinate error patterns will remain undetected as indicated in Figure 11.16.

The Cyclic Polynomial Technique

Some of the most powerful codes in current use are known as Cyclic Codes or Cyclic Redundancy Codes (CRC Checks). Cyclic coding involves a calculation at the transmitting station in which the block of data to be sent is treated as a pure binary number and is then divided by a predetermined number defined by a polynomial expression. This produces a remainder which forms the check digits which are then transmit-

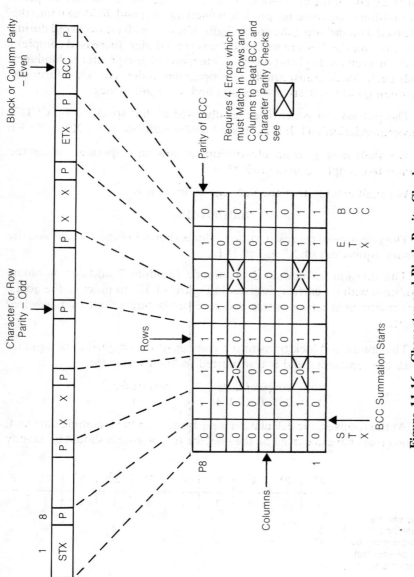

Figure 11.16 Character and Block Parity Checks

ted at the end of the data block. At the receiving end the terminal repeats the division using the same predetermined number and dividing it into the received data including the check digits. If no errors have occurred during transmission the division will produce no remainder. Increased complexity of the cyclic code gives powerful detection but also greater redundancy with each block transmitted. The optimum codes are a compromise between good burst error detection and low redundancy.

The polynomial which is generally used is that specified by CCITT recommendation V41. It is expressed symbolically as: $X^{16} + X^{12} + X^5 + 1$.

We shall now give an illustration of how this operates, using the somewhat simpler polynomial $X^2 + 1$.

We shall assume that the message to be sent is

$$1001001010$$

The polynomial representation of this is shown in Figure 11.17 and the binary equivalent of $X^2 + 1$ is 101.

The division in modulo 2 arithmetic (modulo 2 addition is binary addition with no carries) is given in Figure 11.18. In practice the actual arithmetic at the transmitter and receiver is carried out by hardwired logic.

The complete block transmitted consists of the original data together with the remainder and is transmitted to line as follows:

$$\textit{original data} \qquad \textit{remainder}$$
$$1\ 0\ 0\ 1\ 0\ 0\ 1\ 0\ 1\ 0 \qquad 1\ 1$$

At the receiver, the calculation is performed on the incoming data and, if no errors have occurred on the line, the received data should be exactly

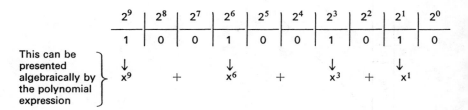

Figure 11.17

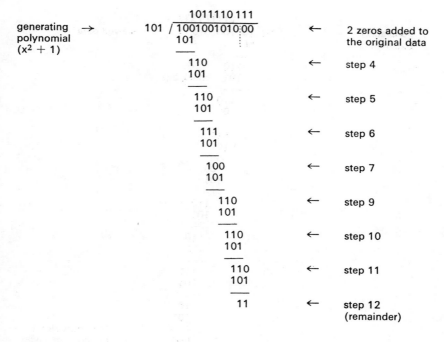

Figure 11.18

divisible by the generating polynomial as shown in Figure 11.19.

If the calculation at the receiver produces a remainder other than zero, this indicates that an error has been detected in the received data and the receiver requests a retransmission.

Through theoretical studies and subsequent practical experience this has been proved to be a very powerful error detection technique. For example, it has been found from computer simulation that when using a block size of 260 bits (including service bits and check bits) an improvement factor in the order of 50,000 is achieved. On a circuit with a mean error rate of 1 in 10^4 the residual error rate would, therefore, be in the order of 2 in 10^9, the 16 redundant bits comprising only 6.1 per cent of each block. All odd numbers of errors within a block would be detected, also any one error burst not exceeding 16 bits in length and a large percentage of other error patterns.

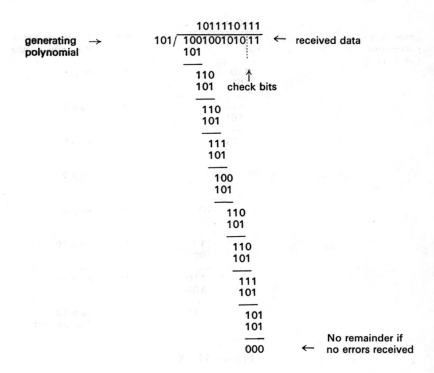

Figure 11.19   Division at the Receive Terminal of the Received Data by the Generating Polynomial

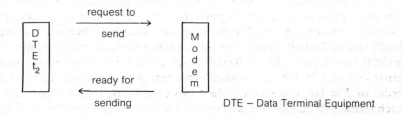

Figure 11.20   Ready-for-Sending Delay

Efficiency Considerations

The various features of a Link Control Protocol have a significant influence on the efficiency of a data communication channel. These include such things as the block size, and the error detection and correction arrangements. We consider these aspects below and give some numerical illustration.

Block Size

The size of the block used is often determined by the operational requirements of a system or the hardware used rather than the need to optimise the throughput of transmission links. In most cases, the blocks transmitted are of variable length although the upper limit is usually conditioned by the type of message or by terminal characteristics such as buffer capacity. On alphanumeric display terminals, for example, the maximum block size is likely to be determined by the size of the buffer although the block sizes actually transmitted will vary considerably depending on the size of the input and output messages.

From an error control point of view, blocks should ideally be of fixed length; the actual length being determined by the probabilities of errors occurring and the nature of the error bursts likely to be encountered. There is, therefore, a conflict between the need for efficient transmission of information and other important design considerations. In on-line systems, it is difficult to reconcile these differing requirements and compromise is necessary.

There are advantages in using large blocks. Firstly, as we shall see, where synchronous transmission is employed with half-duplex control procedures, a significant period may elapse between blocks transmitted. This period is constant whether blocks are long or short and the larger the block the less time is wasted. Secondly, with a large block the proportion of redundant data to information may be smaller for a given degree of protection than with a smaller block.

There are, however, disadvantages in using large blocks. First of all, these have to be retransmitted when necessary and this increases the local buffer storage requirement. However, with the declining costs of memory and intelligence, this factor is reducing in importance.

This might not be costly with paper tape or magnetic tape terminals where the tape readers can be reversed to the beginning of a block.

However, on buffered terminals the increased buffer capacity required by using long blocks might outweigh other savings. The second factor is that the probability of errors increases proportionately with the block length; allied to this is the fact that the retransmission of each block takes longer. Some examples of the effects of these different considerations are given later.

Throughput Efficiency

The throughput efficiency of a system in an error-free situation is given by the equation:

Equation (1)   where   E = the throughput efficiency
                               B = the block length in bits
$$E = \frac{\dfrac{B}{R}}{\dfrac{B}{R} + T}$$
                               T = the total round trip delay
                               R = the input data rate (bit/s)

The losses due to parity bits or to control and synchronisation bits within blocks are ignored in this equation as these factors are independent of those given and their relatively minor effect is best calculated separately. Also excluded is the effect of erroneous return messages as the probability of these being in error is much smaller than in the relatively longer message blocks.

It will be seen from (1) that the duration of T is the critical factor in determining throughput efficiency. The total round trip delay T is the time delay between the end of transmission of one block (block n) to the beginning of transmission of the next (block n + 1). 'T' may include:

1 *The loop propagation time of the line:* this is the time taken for a signal to travel the length of the circuit and back again. Generally, propagation time increases with distance; within the UK, loop propagation times rarely exceed 15 ms but on intercontinental circuits via satellites may be in excess of 540 ms.

2 *Modem propagation delay:* additional delays are introduced when a signal passes through filters, equalisers and other components in a modem. This delay is in the order of a few milliseconds for each modem and in the examples which follow is added to the loop propagation time of the line to give the 'total propagation delay'.

3 *Transmitter and receiver delays:* when the last bit of the last character in a block is received, the data terminal equipment at the receive end will check the accuracy of the received block and assemble a receipt message. When the receipt message is returned, the data terminal equipment at the transmit end must interpret the meaning of the received message and initiate the appropriate action. The delays introduced by these two operations are usually small and are ignored in the examples which follow in this chapter.

4 *The time taken to transmit the return message:* this message may be simply a binary '0' condition for a positive acknowledgement or a binary '1' condition for a negative acknowledgement (CCITT recommendation V41) in which case no time allowance need be added to the loop propagation time. However, message receipts are usually in the form of special characters (ACK and NAK) which may be accompanied by SYN and other control characters. In some cases, these messages comprise 32 bits and the time taken to transmit them will depend on the bit rate of this return channel. For example, 32 bits on a 75 bit/s supervisory channel would take 427 ms.

5 *Modem turn-around times:* On 2-wire circuits, there are two ways of providing a return channel. One is to have a frequency division multiplexed, narrow band, low-speed simultaneous channel. The other is to reverse the direction of transmission after each block; this requires the modems at each end to 'turn-around' and introduces delay. This delay will vary considerably between modems. The most significant factor is the time which elapses between the data terminal equipment signalling 'request to send' (on circuit 105 on the CCITT V24 interface) and the modem returning 'ready for sending' (on circuit 106 on the CCITT V24 interface). This is termed the 'ready-for-sending delay' (or 'response time of circuit 106' in the appropriate CCITT recommendations) (see Figure 11.20).

Modems with data signalling rates above 2400 bit/s may be provided with adaptive equalisers – these become necessary where the modem has to automatically adapt to the range of different circuit conditions to be met on the PSTN. Early modems of this type had extremely long turn-around times of two seconds or more because the equalisers in these modems had to re-adapt to the line conditions each time the direction of transmission changed. Modern modems use adaptive equalisers which have a fairly long initial period of adjust-

ment during which time a long 'training pattern' of signals is transmitted: this may be up to two seconds depending on the conditions
found on the particular PSTN connection. The equalisers store their
settings so that subsequent training patterns can be very much shorter in duration – in some modems less than 100 ms. Each time the
modems turn-around, this short training pattern must be sent before
data can be transmitted; the duration of the short training pattern is
included in the modem turn-around times.

The total round trip delay (T) has been defined as being the time delay
between the end of transmission of one block (block n) to the beginning
of transmission of the next (block n + 1). It is useful to consider the
progressive build up of T in an example of an idle-RQ system on a circuit
with half-duplex facilities.

(a)   The last bit in the last character of a block will pass through two
modems and over the transmission link. In Figure 11.21, $t_1 + t_2 + t_3$
is the time delay between the last bit being transmitted from A and
received at B, ie the propagation delay between the modem interface
at A and the modem interface at B.

(b)   After the last bit is received, the terminal at B will check the
block and assemble the return message. This delay we will term t_4.

(c)   The terminal at B will then signal request to send to the modem
at B and the modem will turn-around (delay t_5).

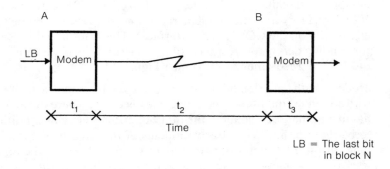

LB = The last bit
in block N

**Figure 11.21   Propagation Delay Between the Modem Interfaces at A
and at B**

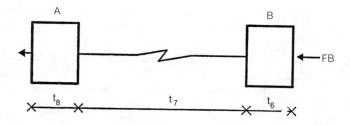

Figure 11.22 Propagation Time Between the Digital Interfaces at B and at A

(d)   In Figure 11.22, $t_6 + t_7 + t_8$ is the time delay between the first bit of the receipt message (FB) being transmitted from B and received at A, ie the propagation time between the digital interface at B and the digital interface at A.

(e)   The time for the receipt message to be returned will depend on the length in bits of the return message and the data signalling rate at which it is transmitted (delay t_9).

(f)   After the last bit of the message receipt arrives, the terminal at A will interpret the meaning of the message and determine the appropriate action, ie decide whether to retransmit block n or transmit block n + 1 (delay t_{10}).

(g)   The terminal at A will then signal a request-to-send to the modem at A and the modem will turn-around ready to transmit the first bit of the next block (delay t_{11}); the modem at B will have turned round before t_{11} is completed.

It will be seen from this that the total round trip comprises delays t_1 to t_{11} added together. The total propagation time can also be seen to be the sum of the loop propagation time of the line ($t_2 + t_7$) and the propagation times of the two modems ($t_1 + t_8$ and $t_3 + t_6$).

There are various ways of organising the retransmission of erroneous blocks in ARQ systems and we now review these.

Idle-RQ

This is the commonest method and is the one described in the discussion of Basic Mode protocols. Reference to Figure 11.23 shows that the

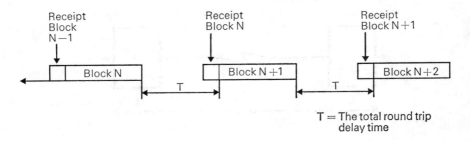

T = The total round trip
      delay time

Figure 11.23   Simple Half-Duplex Error Control (Idle-RQ)

requirement to transmit a block and then wait for a positive acknowledgement before transmitting the next block, or retransmitting the same
block again causes longer gaps (T) when the data blocks are being
transferred, and for that reason it is sometimes referred to as Idle-RQ.

Since the communications channel is usually the slowest part of a
communication system, any inefficiency in its use impairs the performance of the whole system. If T is small compared with the total transmission time of a data block the reduction in efficiency may be quite small,
but on wideband or long distance channels it will become increasingly
inefficient as the block transmission time approaches the idle time.

Consider now an idle-RQ system where a simultaneous 75 bit/s return
channel is available and thus modem turn-around times can be ignored.
In the first case error-free transmission is assumed so that the effect of
errors on throughput efficiency may be seen in better perspective later.

Example 1 **Throughput efficiency (E) of an Idle-RQ system with a simultaneous return channel**

Equation (1)   E = Efficiency

$$E = \frac{\dfrac{B}{R}}{\dfrac{B}{R} + T}$$

Block length (B) = 1000 bits
Input data rate (R) = 1200 bit/s
Length of receipt message = 16 bits
Data signalling rate of simultaneous
      return channel = 75 bit/s
Total propagation delay = 25 ms

T = 25 ms for total propagation delay + the time taken for the 16 bits
      message receipt at 75 bit/s

$$T = 25 + \left(\frac{16}{75} \times 1000\right) ms$$

$$T = 238 \text{ ms}$$

$$E = \frac{\left(\frac{1000}{1200}\right) \times 1000}{\left(\frac{1000}{1200}\right) \times 1000 + 238}$$

$$E = \frac{833}{833 + 238}$$

$$E = 77.77 \text{ per cent (933 bit/s)}$$

In considering throughput in the presence of errors, the additional consideration is the number of blocks in error relative to the total number of blocks sent. We can now extend equation 1 to allow consideration of throughput in the presence of errors so that:

Equation (2)

$$E = \frac{\frac{B}{R}(1 - P(e))}{\frac{B}{R} + T}$$ where $P(e) =$ the block error probability

Example 2 **Throughput efficiency of an Idle-RQ System with a simultaneous 75 bit/s return channel showing the effect of errors**

Using the basic data for example 1, we now assume that 1 block in 100 has to be retransmitted because of detected errors.

$$P(e) = 0.01$$

$$E = \frac{833(1 - 0.01)}{833 + 238}$$

$$E = \frac{824.6}{1071}$$

$$E = 76.99 \text{ per cent (923 bit/s)}$$

These figures are for maintenance rather than planning purposes. Nevertheless, they do indicate that even if errors occur in a purely random fashion no more than 1 bit in 20,000 at 1200 bit/s on a leased circuit, a maximum of 5 in 100 thousand bit blocks, would be in error. Because of the clustering effect of error bursts, the proportion of erroneous blocks would probably be a good deal less than this in practice. It will be seen that from the simple example above that errors have a relatively minor effect on throughput efficiency with blocks of this size when compared to the total round trip delay T. Although it is obvious from equation (1) that increasing the block size will improve the throughput efficiency in the absence of errors, the presence of errors imposes a restraint as the block error rate will increase with block size. There is therefore an optimum block size for any given bit error rate and total round trip delay T to give maximum throughput efficiency.

However, it will be remembered that there are other factors which influence block size, and the throughput efficiency of some idle-RQ systems, particularly where variable block lengths are used, may be very low indeed.

In examples 1 and 2, a simultaneous 75 bit/s narrow band return channel was used for message acknowledgements. Consider now (example 3) data being transmitted over the PSTN at 2400 bit/s: assume that no simultaneous return channel is available and the modems, therefore, have to be 'turned-round'. Two reversals per block will be required, one to establish the return channel and one to re-establish the forward channel.

Example 3 **The effect of modem turn-around times on the throughpu efficiency of an Idle-RQ System**

Assume, for convenience, an error-free connection.

$$E = \frac{\dfrac{B}{R}}{\dfrac{B}{R} + T}$$

Block length (B) = 1000 bits
Input data rate (R) = 2400 bit/s
Length of receipt message = 16 bits
Total propagation delay = 25 ms
Data signalling rate of return
  channel = 2400 bit/s
Modem turn-around time = 75 ms

T = 25 ms for total propagation delay + time taken for 16 bits at 2400 bit/s + (modem turn-around time) × 2

$$T = 25 + \left(\frac{16}{2400} \times 1000\right) + 150 \text{ ms}$$

$$= 25 + 6.6 + 150 \text{ ms}$$

$$T = 182 \text{ ms}$$

$$E = \frac{\left(\dfrac{1000}{2400}\right) \times 1000}{\left(\dfrac{1000}{2400}\right) \times 1000 + 182}$$

$$E = \frac{417}{599}$$

$$E = 69.6 \text{ per cent } (1670 \text{ bit/s})$$

Example 4 **The effect of increasing data signalling on throughput efficiency of an Idle-RQ System**

There are a number of problems involved in using higher speed modems on two-wire connections. First of all, as the data signalling rate increases, the time to transmit each block (B/R) is reduced and T becomes proportionally bigger. Let us assume that the same conditions apply as in example 3 except that R is increased from 2400 to 4800 bit/s.

$$E = \frac{\left(\dfrac{1000}{4800}\right) \times 1000}{\left(\dfrac{1000}{4800}\right) \times 1000 + 178}$$

NB: T is reduced slightly because of the reduction in time required to transmit the 16 bits return message.

$$E = \frac{208}{386}$$

$$E = 54 \text{ per cent } (2590 \text{ bit/s})$$

It can clearly be seen from this example that it becomes increasingly important to use longer blocks as the data signalling rate increases. However, the problem arises that as the length of the block becomes greater the block error probability rises also. Another problem is that the adaptive equalisers used on some high-speed modems may increase the modem turn-around times and throughput efficiency may suffer.

It has been found from customer experience in the UK using the Datel 2400 dial up service, transmitting at 2400 bit/s, that maximum throughput efficiency is apparently achieved with block sizes in the order of 1000 bits, although the evidence is by no means conclusive.

The above calculations have been presented primarily to demonstrate the inter-relationship of the more important factors which determine throughput efficiency. Costs have been ignored for the sake of clarity but it will be seen that if the throughput efficiency is known, the cost per bit or cost per thousand bits can be calculated for different circumstances.

Despite its limitations Idle-RQ is simple and reliable and has been employed in the vast majority of communications-based systems until recently. A major factor which influences the total round trip delay in the UK is modem turn-round time and this is widely avoided by using duplex facilities on four-wire private circuits. However, as we have seen, with higher speed transmission, half-duplex operation particularly on poor quality circuits can still restrict throughput efficiency to very low levels. There is a problem too on long distance circuits. While loop propagation times are normally short on circuits within one country, on intercontinental circuits they may be extremely long and idle-RQ becomes unsuitable. For example, let us assume a half-duplex intercontinental connection via a satellite with a total propagation delay of 540 ms with the other data as in example 3; the throughput efficiency would then be an optimistic 37 per cent on a circuit with no errors at all.

Continuous RQ

It will now be clear that much greater efficiency could be obtained if we could devise a procedure for transmitting in full duplex mode on duplex channels.

Some indication of the effect on throughput efficiency can be gained by subtracting modem turn-round time from T in example 3 above, and the calculation repeated. This is done in example 5 resulting in an efficiency of 93 per cent. The class of continuous RQ techniques was developed for this purpose.

Example 5 **Effect of full duplex facilities on throughput efficiency**

$$E = \frac{417}{599 - 150} \text{ (from example 3)}$$

$$E = \frac{417}{449}$$

E = 93 per cent (2229 bit/s)

In this approach, the data blocks are transmitted continuously over a duplex link with the objective of minimising idle time.

The procedure works like this. A number of data blocks are transmitted in succession by the transmitter without waiting for individual block acknowledgements. At the receiver they are processed and acknowledged as in Idle-RQ. However, by the time the transmitter gets an acknowledgement, it will generally have transmitted further data blocks, so that acknowledgements will lag behind the transmitted data blocks. This is illustrated in Figure 11.24.

In this mode of operation a number of difficulties arise. First of all, at the transmitter each block transmitted but not acknowledged needs to be stored in case retransmission is required. Secondly at the receiver, if a block is found to be in error, then a number of subsequent blocks may be received before the block in error can be retransmitted, and this may disturb the sequence of the data blocks. Therefore in order to control sequence and to maintain correspondence between blocks and their respective acknowledgements, it is necessary to include in each block a unique block sequence number.

In continuous RQ there are two different techniques for handling retransmission; Go-Back-N, and Selective Retransmission.

— *Go-Back-N* In this scheme, when the receiver sends a NAK, indicating that the block with the corresponding sequence number must be retransmitted, the sender transmits that block, and then continues transmitting subsequent blocks, even though they may already have been transmitted. The procedure is illustrated in Figure 11.25.

Following receipt of the erroneous N + 1 block the receiver ignores blocks N + 2, N + 3, N + 1 since they are out of sequence, and waits for the retransmitted block N + 1 to arrive. When block N + 1 has been transmitted, the transmitter continues with blocks N + 2, N + 3, and so on. Each end is able to keep track of the situation by reference to the block sequence numbers.

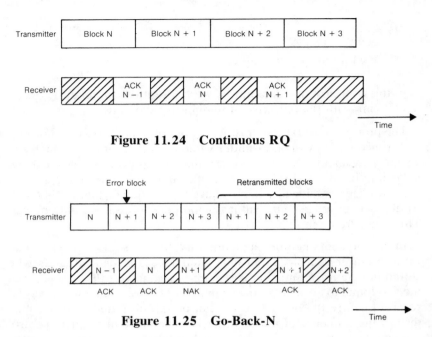

Figure 11.24   Continuous RQ

Figure 11.25   Go-Back-N

— *Selective Retransmission* A deficiency of the preceding approach is that some blocks are unnecessarily retransmitted, thus wasting channel capacity. In contrast in Selective Retransmission, illustrated in Figure 11.26, the transmitter only retransmits block N + 1, the block in error, whilst the receiver accepts blocks N + 2, N + 3, even though N + 1 has to be retransmitted and will therefore be out of sequence when it is received. After retransmitting block N + 1, the transmitter continues with blocks N + 4, N + 5, etc.

Both approaches have their respective advantages and disadvantages. Selective Retransmission makes more efficient use of channel capacity compared with Go-Back, but entails a re-sequencing operation at the receiver. Both methods introduce a buffering requirement exceeding the single block storage requirement of Idle-RQ. Go-Back requires buffering at the transmitter to enable retransmission, and Selective Retransmission requires it at the receiver to enable the correct sequence to be re-established.

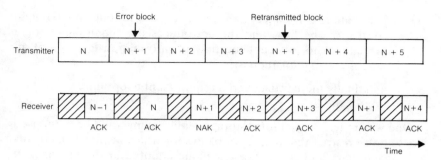

Figure 11.26 Selective Retransmission

We have covered ARQ and its ramifications in some detail, first of all because the basic ARQ principles are utilised in the HDLC protocol, and secondly because it provides a useful background for understanding HDLC which was designed to overcome the limitations inherent in character-oriented protocols.

Flow Control

The discussion of Continuous RQ was incomplete in several aspects. First of all, unrestricted transmission of blocks could overwhelm the capacity of the receiver to process them. Secondly, if large amounts of data are being transmitted, the sequence numbers themselves could also become correspondingly large, and could quite easily exceed the space allocated to them in the block. These considerations introduce the requirement for an efficient *flow control procedure,* the chief functions of which are:

— to maintain the correct sequence of data end to end between transmitter and receiver;

— to ensure that transmission rates match the processing capacities of the two ends. This includes both processing capability and buffer storage provision;

— in addition some mechanism will be required for one end to inform the other end that it is congested, and that no further information, apart from perhaps control information is to be transmitted, until the congestion has cleared;

—   in certain circumstances it may be necessary for one end to regain
    control of the link, and this introduces the requirement for a
    mechanism to interrupt the flow of information to transmit an
    urgent message or request;

—   and finally there is the overall requirement to optimize the utilisa-
    tion of the link.

One way in which the buffer storage requirement could be minimised
would be to restrict the number of blocks for which acknowledgements
are outstanding, and this is the technique adopted in the Go-Back-N
technique, N being the number of outstanding blocks.

A further refinement to keep sequence numbers down to a manageable
size is to interpret sequence numbers in a modulo arithmetic. This is
equivalent to dividing the sequence number by the modulus number and
using the remainder as the actual sequence number.

Thus, is an arithmetic using a modulus of 8, sequence numbers would
continuously cycle round the values 0, 1, 2, 3, 4, 5, 6, 7. The limited
number of values does not constitute a limitation, since in HDLC where
this is employed, the combination of sequence numbers with the modulus
provides the basis for an efficient method of flow control.

12 Protocols: HDLC and X25

INTRODUCTION

We conclude our discussion of protocols with a review of HDLC and X25, the former being a link level protocol, and the latter a network access protocol for use with packet switched networks.

HDLC

Historical Background

HDLC stands for High-Level Data Link Control, a description which is really a misnomer, because it is a *Link Level Protocol* and should not be confused with the *High-Level Protocols* proper.

The essential features of HDLC such as the frame structure and its nested construction or 'onion skin' architecture had their origins in the work of a BSI (British Standards Institution) Committee in 1968. ISO had been studying protocols since 1962, and a major result of this work was the Basic Mode Protocol. The BSI ideas were taken up within ISO, and the study of data link control procedures continued in association with the evolution of a model for overall Communications Systems Architecture and resulted in the standardisation by the ISO of a more sophisticated method of data link control, known as 'High-Level Data Link Control Procedures' (HDLC).

The HDLC standards are much sounder – as standards – than the earlier Basic Mode standards. They were evolved by what is termed 'prospective standardisation' – the planning of standards before many conflicting systems became established in the market. Taken together, they specify a powerful and sophisticated group of facilities, which are

371

very widely used. Although they have great versatility to cover a wide spectrum of applications, at their core lies a relatively simple set of procedures; for the great majority of systems these will suffice, and will thus readily permit interworking.

Overview

The HDLC family has the following characteristics.

HDLC was originally designed for two-way simultaneous operation between a 'Primary' station and one or more 'Secondary' stations on a physical point-to-point or multipoint data link. No provision is made for secondaries to communicate with each other.

The primary station is responsible for scheduling the data flow in the link by authorising secondaries to transmit. This may be on a one-for-one response basis or a long-term delegation which applies until terminated by the primary.

All transmissions are in 'frames'. Transmission is bit-oriented which means that any sequence of any number of bits can be transmitted in a frame. Each frame has an address field, a link control field, and space for an information field. All frames carry a Frame Check Sequence (FCS) using the CCITT cyclic polynomial sequence for error checking. When the frame contains only link control information, the information field has zero length.

In frames from the primary (Command Frames) the address identifies the station or stations which are authorised to receive the frame. In frames from the secondaries (Response Frames) the address identifies the secondary of origin.

The control field provides for two independent numbers (modulo 8) for sequencing the forward and reverse flow of frames in the link.

There are three components to HDLC:

— the frame structure;

— the elements of procedure;

— the classes of procedure.

The first specifies the common 'Frame Structure', including the error checking and bit sequence transparency mechanisms and the size and position of the Address and Link Control fields.

The 'Elements of Procedure' specify the commands, the responses and the sequencing information which can be coded into the control field for link control and error recovery purposes.

The 'Classes of Procedure' define various modes of operation of a link (master-master, master-slave, etc); each class uses an appropriate selection of the commands and responses defined in elements of procedure.

HDLC Variants

The introduction of link protocols using the standardised frame format is increasing and all of the major manufacturers support it, either as HDCL or under their own acronym:

SDLC   —   IBM Synchronous Data Link Control

BDLC   —   Burroughs Data Link Control

ADCCP   —   American National Standards Institute (ANSI) Advanced Data Communications Control Procedure

HDLC Frame Structure

Figure 12.1 shows the uniform frame structure. Each flag sequence identifies both the start of one frame and the end of the previous frame. More than one flag sequence can be used if a longer time interval is needed between frames. If the transmitter has no information to send, it

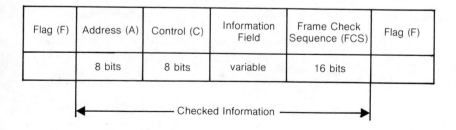

Flag (F)	Address (A)	Control (C)	Information Field	Frame Check Sequence (FCS)	Flag (F)
	8 bits	8 bits	variable	16 bits	

◄─────────────── Checked Information ───────────────►

Figure 12.1 HDLC Frame Structure

may transmit either continuous 1s or flags. It may also abort the transmission of a frame (to save time when retransmission is called for) by sending at least seven continuous 1s.

Each frame begins with an Address Octet and a Control Octet, followed by a data field (which may be omitted) and closes with a 16-bit Frame Check Sequence. The address field has 256 combinations but no rigid rules are specified for allocating addresses to secondaries. The contents of the control field are defined in the Elements of Procedure Standard which is discussed later. A mechanism is provided for extending the length of the address and control fields but they are always a multiple of octets.

The Frame Check Sequence is applied to all fields of the frame excluding the flag sequence. The information field can contain any number of bits – subject to some upper limit set by the system, and in any code.

As shown in Figure 12.1, the address and control fields normally consist of one octet but they can both be extended to two if required.

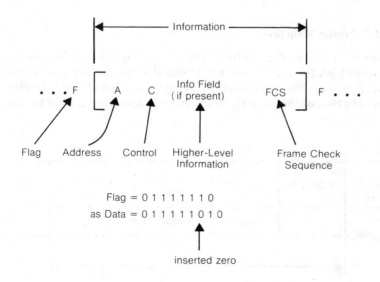

Figure 12.2   Bit Stuffing and Transparency

Code Transparency

The flag pattern could occur in the combined A, C, information and FCS fields and Figure 12.2 shows how transparency is achieved. If the transmitter finds a sequence of five adjacent 1-bits, an extra 0-bit is inserted before transmitting the next real data bit. To keep the system simple a 0-bit is inserted even if the data bit following the five adjacent 1s is already a 0. The receiver can thus be sure that a 0 which follows five adjacent 1-bits has been artificially inserted and the process, known as 'bit stuffing', ensures that the receiver can distinguish the true frame delimiters.

Bit-oriented operation is obtained by passing the incoming bits (including the stuffed 0s), in sequence, past an 8-bit 'window'. As each new data bit is received, the window is opened to see if the last 8 bits are a flag sequence. If not, the window is closed until the next bit is received. When a flag is framed in the window the receiver accepts it as a frame delimiter. If the following octet is not another flag the receiver assumes that a frame has commenced and it removes any stuffed zeros from this and the ensuing bit stream until another flag appears in the window, at which point it assumes that the previous 16 bits (unstuffed) are the Frame Check Sequence. Hence, the frame length between flags can be any number of bits equal to or greater than 32. Frames with less than 32 bits between flags are discarded. The inclusion of the Frame Check Sequence prior to the end of frame delimiter implies a short FCS buffer in the receiver, so that the traditional cyclic check summation can be correctly phased, but this does not pose a difficult implementation problem.

It will be evident that, compared with the procedure employed in the character-oriented protocols, this is far tidier and is a well structured method for securing code transparency.

Synchronisation

In a two-way simultaneous character-oriented system (eg Basic Mode), the loss of character synchronism can be disastrous because it becomes impossible to identify the delimiters which separate data, commands and responses. Recovery is a painful process involving time outs and total resynchronisation in both directions. The bit-oriented HDLC system is superior because frame synchronism is restored whenever a flag is detected. The loss of a flag, the simulation of a flag, or the loss of octet

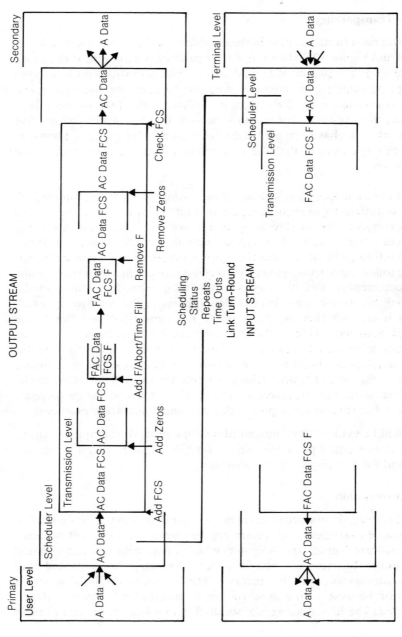

Figure 12.3   Architectural Concepts

synchronism during a frame, is recovered, quite simply, by the error control system and is indistinguishable from a simple frame error.

Implementation

Figure 12.3 shows how the 'nested' architecture facilitates a structured approach to constructing and dismantling a frame. However, most of these functions are implemented by custom-built integrated circuits.

The receiver follows a logical sequence of operations on the incoming data. The first step is to identify the flags which mark the beginning and end of a frame. All the data between the flags is subjected to an inserted 0-bit removal process, in order to recover the original data. The frame check sequence (FCS) is applied and this permits transmission errors in the address, control or information fields, or the FCS itself to be detected. (If a flag is corrupted, the receiver will assume, erroneously, that the 16 bits preceding the next flag it detects are the FCS, and this will yield an invalid check result.) If the frame is error-free, the address and control fields are examined and can be checked for procedural errors. Only if the frame is valid will the receiver proceed to deal with the information bits.

Elements of Procedure

The Elements of Procedure are concerned largely with the use of the Control field controlling the data link.

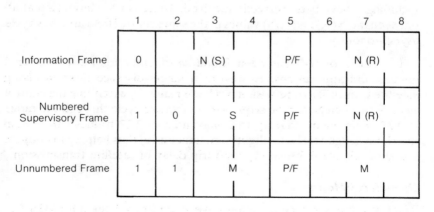

	1	2	3	4	5	6	7	8
Information Frame	0		N (S)		P/F		N (R)	
Numbered Supervisory Frame	1	0	S		P/F		N (R)	
Unnumbered Frame	1	1	M		P/F		M	

Figure 12.4   Basic Control Octet Coding

The basic single octet control field has three possible formats which are shown in Figure 12.4. The format type is contained in bits 1 and 2. We shall describe the Elements of Procedure under the following headings:

— Sequence Numbers;

— Operational Modes;

— Information Frames;

— Numbered Supervisory Frames;

— Unnumbered Command and Response Frames.

Sequence Numbers

Both Information Frames and Numbered Supervisory Frames carry either one or two sequence numbers in the control field. These are referred to as the N(S) and N(R) sequence numbers and normally cycle through the values 0 to 7. In an information frame, the control field contains both N(S) and N(R). Every information frame transmitted by a station is given a send sequence number, starting at N(S) = 0 for the first I-frame transmitted. N(R) is the sequence number of the next information frame which that station expects to receive. N(R) also serves as an acknowledgement to the other station, the implication being that all I-frames with numbers up to and including N(R − 1) have been received correctly. For example, N(R) = 6 implies that all frames up to and including 5 have been correctly received. There is no relationship at all between the N(R) and N(S) values in the same control field and they cycle asynchronously.

The range of 0-7 has been found satisfactory for most terrestrial circuits and applications. However, in longer-distance links involving satellite transmission, provision has been made, by extending the control field to two octets, for the sequence numbers to cycle through the range 0-127. This means that up to a maximum of 127 frames can remain unacknowledged (ie be in 'flight' simultaneously) thus helping to mitigate the approximate 0.5 second round trip delay of satellite transmission.

Operational Modes

The following operational modes have so far been defined for HDLC:

Normal Response Mode (NRM) –	in which the secondaries are strictly disciplined to transmit only when specifically instructed to do so. This is aimed at the control of multipoint links;
Asynchronous Response Mode (ARM) –	in which a secondary is free to transmit information until the mode is changed;
Asynchronous Balanced Mode (ABM) –	in which a secondary temporarily assumes an equivalent role to the primary until the mode is changed;
Normal Response Mode Extended (NRME) –	extended version of above;
Asynchronous Response Mode Extended (ARME) –	extended version of above;
Asynchronous Balanced Mode Extended (ABME) –	extended version of above.

Information Frames

The first of these types of frame, the information format, is used for transmitting information. As we have seen, an important property is the 'piggy-backing' of acknowledgements for multiple frames onto a single information frame, rather than the one for one ACK and NAK procedure of character-oriented protocols.

Numbered Supervisory Frames

Supervisory format frames are used to acknowledge correct reception of all information frames up to and including the one numbered N (R–1) and to convey control signals.

Supervisory frames never contain an information field, and therefore do not require an N(S) number. An N(R) number is present, and has the same significance as for an information frame. Bits 3 and 4 of the control field are coded to provide four controls.

Receive Ready (RR)   – a combined acknowledge and proceed signal. N(R) identifies the next required frame;

Receive Not Ready (RNR)   – also an acknowledgement specifying the next required frame but with a warning that the station is temporarily unable to receive it;

Reject (REJ)   – indicates that a frame has been received in error. N(R) identifies the number of the frame at which retransmission should start;

Selective Reject (SREJ)   – indicates that a specific frame has been received in error and requests the retransmission of that frame only. This mechanism introduces more complex sequencing problems and is only intended for sophisticated systems, such as satellite links.

Each of the above can serve either as commands or as responses.

Unnumbered Command and Response Frames

Unnumbered frames contain no sequence numbers and the five bits 3, 4, 6, 7 and 8 can be coded to provide 32 supervisory functions. Unnumbered frames can contain an I-field but this cannot be sequence number checked unless a separate numbering system is included in the I-field by the user. Unnumbered commands and responses are used for link housekeeping functions such as mode setting, status signalling and problem reporting.

Set Normal Response Mode (SNRM)

Set Asynchronous Response Mode (SARM)   – sets the link into a specific operational mode but also performs a link reset function;

Set Asynchronous Balanced Mode (SABM)

Reset (RSET)	– performs a pure link reset function without changing the link operational mode;
SNRME SARME SABME }	– extended versions of SNRM, SARM and SABM;
Unnumbered Acknowledgement (UA)	– reports that the secondary has accepted the SNRM, SARM or SABM command;
Unnumbered Information (UI)	– signals an information frame without a sequence number;
Unnumbered Poll (UP)	– requests transmission from the addressed secondary without specifying the restart point;
Command Reject (CMDR)	– reports that the secondary is unable to obey a command from the primary either because it does not include the command in its repertoire, the command is illogical, the frame is too long or the sequence numbering is wrong. The rejection frame is extended by 3 octets of information which repeat the rejection control field, declare the send and receive counts and indicate specific reasons for rejection;
Frame Reject (FRMR)	– has the same effect as CMDR but FRMR can be used either as a command or a response;
Exchange Identity (XID)	– allows for address identity to be exchanged. This may be extended later to include agreement of optional elements to be used;

Disconnect (DISC)	– restores the link to a disconnected mode. SNRM, SARM or SABM must be sent to restart;
Request Disconnect (RD)	– requests disconnection;
Disconnect Mode (DM)	– reports that the secondary has obeyed the disconnected command;
Set Initialisation Mode (SIM)	– a command which initialises the link. Use may be extended later to embrace more sophisticated link initialisation functions such as program load;
Request Initialisation Mode (RIM)	– requests initialisation of the link;
Test	– accompanies a special test message frame.

The Poll/Final (P/F) Bit

All frames contain a P/F bit in bit position 5 of the control field. It is referred to as the P bit in command frames (ie frames sent by the primary) and the F bit in responses (ie frames sent by the secondary).

Originally the P/F bit was designed to allow the primary to instruct a secondary to respond and, in the reverse direction, for the secondary to indicate the final frame in a sequence.

This procedure, therefore, has an obvious application in multipoint operation using the Normal Response (NRM) Mode.

However, its use has now been extended to distinguish repeated sequences from original sequences for error control, known as 'check pointing'. Discipline is exercised by following the rule that in Asynchronous Response Mode or Asynchronous Balanced Mode a response with F set to 1 must be sent when a command is received with P set to 1. A second command with P set to 1 should not be sent until a response with F set to 1 has been received.

Flow Control

The procedures described above provide the basis for an efficient and resilient method for flow control and error control. It is beyond the scope of this publication to give a detailed and comprehensive account of how this operates; a brief description of some of the principles must suffice.

In addition to the N(S) and N(R) sequence numbers carried in the frames, the two ends also maintain sequence counts or state variables.

Send State Variable V(S)

The Send State Variable denotes the sequence number of the next in-sequence I-frame to be transmitted. V(S) can take on the value 0 through 7. The value of V(S) is incremented by one following each successive I-frame transmission, but it is not allowed to exceed the N(R) of the last received frame by more than the permitted maximum number of outstanding frames (k). We have seen that under normal conditions (k) has the value 7.

Receive State Variable V(R)

The Receive State Variable indicates the sequence number of the next in-sequence I-frame to be received. Thus V(R) can take on the values 0

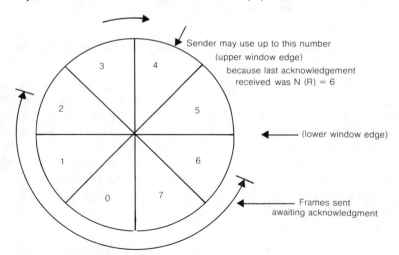

Figure 12.5 The Window Mechanism

through 7. The value of V(R) is incremented by the receipt of an error-free, in-sequence I-frame whose N(S) equals V(R).

When a station has an information frame to transmit (ie one not already transmitted, or having to be retransmitted) it will transmit it with an N(S) equal to its current V(S), and an N(R) equal to its current V(R). At the end of the transmission of the I-frame, it will increment V(S) by one.

If V(S) is equal to the last value of N(R) received plus k, the station will not transmit any new information frames.

The number of frames (k) which can be outstanding before an acknowledgement is received is sometimes referred to as the 'window', through which the values of N(R) recycle. The window is progressively 'closed' by the transmission of each information frame, until, after the seventh it is shut, and so no more information frames can be sent in the channel, until an acknowledgement is received. Figure 12.5 illustrates the mechanism. This shows that:

—   the last acknowledgement N(R) received was 6, thus acknowledging satisfactory receipt of frames numbered up to 5;

—   frames numbered 6, 7, 0, 1 and 2 have been transmitted but are awaiting acknowledgement;

—   two slots are still available and frames with sequence numbers 3 and 4 can be transmitted without any further acknowledgement being received.

Several commands and responses are provided to initialise the link and to indicate whether the station is able to receive frames. For example if temporarily embarrassed for space to receive frames, a 'response not ready' (RNR) frame may be sent. This indicates that no more information frames should be sent. To enable acknowledgement of received frames, this also carries an N(R) number. The instigator removes the hold condition by the transmission of a 'response ready' (RR) frame with the appropriate address.

Classes of Procedure

The frame structure standard is quite rigid and fully definitive with the one simple exception of address allocation.

However, the Elements of Procedure Standard contains many operational modes and command/response options and it is not possible to guarantee compatibility between systems by using this standard alone. When this was recognised, the ISO decided to specify two Classes of Procedure Standards, one for multipoint link control and one for point-to-point operation. These are sometimes referred to respectively as the *Unbalanced* and *Balanced Classes of Procedure*.

Unbalanced Class

In the unbalanced class of procedure, one station (designated the primary) has total responsibility for control of the link. The link may be point-to-point or multipoint supporting one primary station and a number of secondary stations. Only the primary station can issue commands and these always contain the address of the secondary for whom the command is destined. Responses sent by a secondary always contain the address of the secondary.

Two modes of operation are defined: the Normal Response Mode in which a secondary can only transmit after receiving permission to do so from the primary; and the Asynchronous Response Mode in which a secondary may transmit without receiving explicit permission from the primary. Only one secondary at a time may be in the asynchronous response mode.

The standard gives a basic repertoire of commands and responses for this class of procedure together with 10 optional functions which can either extend or restrict the basic repertoire to alter the characteristics of the procedure. The optional features supported must be stated in any implementation of the standard. Typical of the additional optional functions described is the command and response for initialising a remote station.

Balanced Class

The characteristic of the balanced class of procedures is that the stations at either end of the data link are Combined Stations which perform as both primary and secondary stations. This standard was developed in consultation with CCITT, since this is the class of procedure that applies to the DTE-DCE interface on a public data network, where equal control of the link is required at either end. The operational mode is known as the

Asynchronous Balanced Mode (ABM); either station may send commands at any time and initiate responses without receiving permission from the other station. Commands contain the recipient's address. Responses contain the sender's address.

The standard specifies:

— the addressing scheme;

— the basic repertoire of commands and responses for this class;

— twelve optional functions to modify the basic repertoire (achieved mainly by the addition or deletion of commands and responses in the basic repertoire);

— operating procedures.

A welcome inclusion in this standard deals with conformance, ie the extent to which an implementation conforms to the standard. The twelve options are rigorously numbered, and a description of the class of operation must indicate the options provided; eg class BA 2, 3 is the balanced asynchronous mode class of procedures with optional features 2 and 3 (for improved performance and single frame retransmission) implemented.

A station conforms to the balanced class of procedures (with optional functions) if it implements all commands and responses in the basic repertoire as modified by the optional functions.

X25: A NETWORK ACCESS PROTOCOL FOR PUBLIC PACKET SWITCHED NETWORKS

Historical Background

In the early 1970s several experimental packet switched networks were being designed by the French and British PTTs and by research and commercial organisations. As early as 1968, the need for network standards had been recognised and CCITT had set up a small working party to study digital networks, and by 1972 this became a full study group – CCITT Study Group VII. By 1974, public networks were being designed in the USA, France, the UK and elsewhere.

This provided the impetus for reaching agreement on a packet switched network access standard, and, following the preparation of a draft recommendation, a final recommendation was approved by CCITT in 1976.

Overview

The X25 Recommendation defines the interface between Data Terminal Equipment (DTE) and Data Circuit Terminating Equipment (DCE). On our earlier definition the DCE is, strictly speaking, the equipment that converts DTE signals into a form in which they can be transmitted over a physical circuit. However, in the sense used in X25 it refers to the access node or the Packet Switching Exchange (PSE) to which the DTE is connected, but on this interpretation the DCE also includes the modem on the subscriber's premises. Figures 12.6 and 12.7 illustrate the arrangements. (Figure 12.7 is reproduced from Sloman, 1978.)

It is essential to recognise that X25 is a *network access protocol*. It makes no assumptions about the way in which the network functions, other than that the packets involved in an interaction between two DTEs are delivered in the order in which they enter the network. Therefore, providing the two DTEs employ equivalent implementations of X25, they should be able to intercommunicate satisfactorily, and the network should appear *transparent* to them.

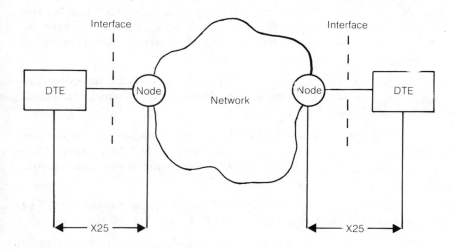

Figure 12.6   Applicability of X25

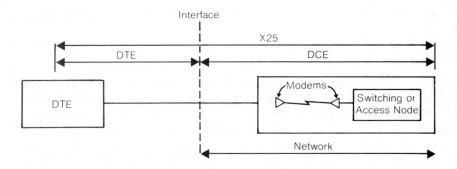

Figure 12.7   The X25 Interface to a Packet Switched Network

X25 applies only to DTEs connected by a synchronous transmission circuit and which have sufficient intelligence to implement the X25 protocols. During the development of the standard it was realised that there would be a requirement to connect simple terminals with limited intelligence, accessing via asynchronous circuits whether leased or PSTN. A set of associated standards, X3, X28 and X29 were accordingly developed to meet these requirements. Central to X25 is the concept of the *virtual circuit* and a corresponding *virtual call* which enables the network access circuit capacity to be split into *logically* separate channels, the packets corresponding to a number of different calls being multiplexed onto the same, physical circuits.

This capacity sharing extends across the network and then onto the access circuits of the destination (or destinations) to which the virtual calls are addressed.

The X25 specification merely defines the technique for accessing the network, and there are other interpretations which have been implemented, which are not included in the official recommendation. These include:

—   as a node-to-node protocol within the network. A number of PTTs have implemented networks in this way;

—   the highest level of X25 (Level 3) used as an end-to-end protocol between two computers or DTEs.

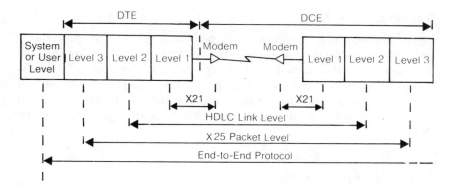

Figure 12.8   Protocol Relationships in X25

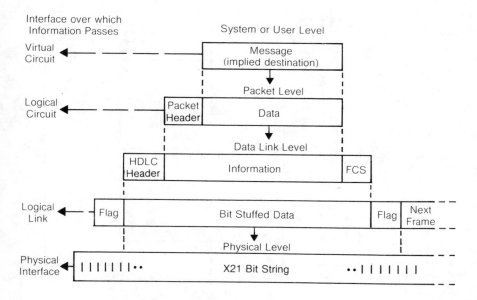

Figure 12.9   Hierarchical Information Flow

The Structure of X25

X25 comprises three distinct and independent levels, and the procedures
at one level utilise the functions of the level immediately below, but are
independent of the manner in which the latter are implemented. There is
a close correspondence between these three levels and levels 1, 2 and 3 of
the 7-layered architecture. Indeed, the structure of the ISO 7-layered
model, particularly in the lower layers, has been strongly influenced by
X25.

The three levels in X25 are:

— the physical interface;

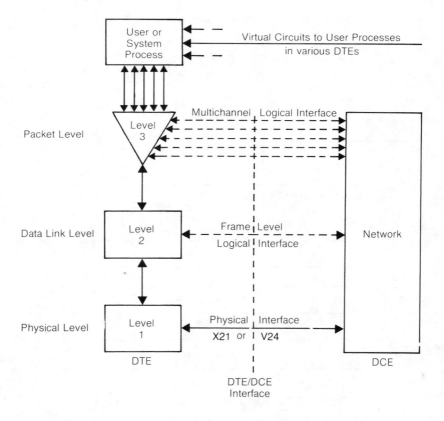

Figure 12.10   Logical Structure of the X25 Interface

—   the link control or link access protocol;

—   the packet level protocol.

X25 specifies the protocols for exchanging information between corresponding levels in the DTE and the DCE. Figures 12.8, 12.9 and 12.10 (reproduced from Sloman, 1978) illustrate the relationships between the levels. A packet is transported in the information field of an HDLC frame, and each level accepts information from a higher level and adds header or trailer information before passing it to a lower level. The 'packet' as such accordingly remains uninterpreted except at the packet level (level 3). Figure 12.10 illustrates how the logical structure of X25 maps onto the physical configuration.

Level 1– The Physical Interface

For the physical interface X25 utilises the X21 standard, or, until digital circuits are more widely available, X21 bis for the interim period. The important characteristics of this level are that it provides a bit-serial, synchronous, full duplex, point-to-point circuit for digital transmission. The physical arrangements are depicted in Figure 12.11.

Level 2 – Link Control

The aim of level 2 is to provide an error-free transport mechanism for packets generated at level 3 across the DTE-PSE link. It uses the frame structure and procedures of the High-Level Data Link Control (HDLC) protocol to achieve error control and flow control.

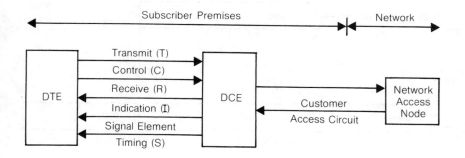

Figure 12.11   X21 Physical Interface

It utilises the Asynchronous Balanced Mode (ABM), although in the CCITT Recommendation for X25, this is referred to as LAPB, for historical reasons, which need not concern us here. The two are compatible, and it may be recollected that under ABM either station may send commands at any time and initiate responses without receiving permission from the other station.

The level 3 packet occupies the information field of the HDLC frame (Figure 12.12). Level 2 treats all level 3 packets in exactly the same way; it does not inspect the packet, and is not concerned with the ultimate destination or logical channel number of the packet. The only concern of level 2 is to convey the packet across the terminal-PSE link, uncorrupted by errors.

The flow control performed at level 2 applies to the DTE-PSE links and extends across all logical channels since the latter have no individual identities at level 2.

The address field in the HDLC frame carries one of two values: commands contain the recipient's address, and responses contain the sender's address. The address field does not contain the address of the destination DTE, which is specified in the header of the packet contained in the information field of the frame, but is not required at level 2.

Level 3 – The Packet Level

The packet level of X25 defines the packet types and transitions which occur when various types of packet are transmitted or received. It does

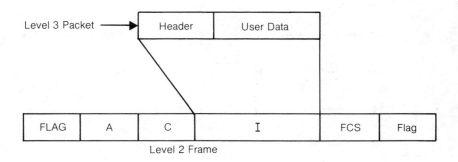

Figure 12.12   X25 HDLC Frame Format

not however completely specify how all the control information carried by packets should be interpreted. This depends on whether a particular implementation is designed to support end-to-end control between DTEs or local control across the DTE–DCE interface. The local control interpretation is the one most favoured by many PTTs, particularly in Europe, and this is the one we concentrate on.

This level also performs a multiplexing function by converting the single channel provided by level 2 into a number of logical channels, and makes provision for independently controlling the flow of information on each logical channel. Error recovery, which may entail clearing and re-initialising the channel, can be applied either to a single channel or to all of them.

The method of flow control and error recovery is very similar to the method employed in level 2, and there is also a similarity between some of the commands and responses of the two levels.

In summary, X25 level 3 provides the following facilities:

— multiplexing of logical channels onto a single data link;

— error and flow control across the local interface between DTE and DCE (not end-to-end);

— guaranteed packet sequencing;

— interrupt facilities;

— error recovery by reset and flushing out of packets;

— virtual calls end-to-end between DTEs;

— permanent virtual circuits between DTEs;

— virtual circuits which perform end-to-end addressing;

— packet size conversion between DTEs.

Packet Formats

There are a number of distinct packet types and formats defined to support information transmission and a variety of control functions. The schematic in Figure 12.13 identifies the main types and the significance of the packet fields.

The maximum length of the data field can be specified at call establishment time or at subscription time, depending upon the particular network. In a number of countries and particularly in Europe, the preferred maximum is 128 bytes. If the maximum packet size differs at each end, thus resulting in a lack of correspondence not only between packet sizes but also between the counts of packets transmitted and those received, the protocol can assume responsibility for packet fragmentation

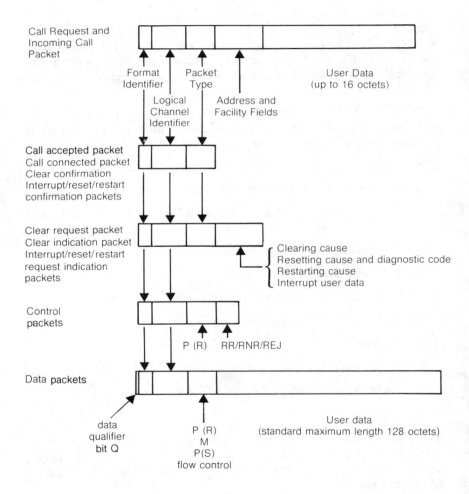

Figure 12.13   X25 Packet Formats

and reassembly. The more data indicator (M) is utilised for this purpose.

The qualifier bit (Q) is used for transmission between an X25 DTE and the PAD supporting asynchronous DTE access, and distinguishes between packets destined for the remote DTE and those packets which are directed to the PAD to modify its mode of operation.

The address field comprises 14 digits. The first twelve are for use by the network administration, and on public networks, are used nationally to address each individual DTE which is connected to the network, and internationally to identify different countries and individual networks within countries. The two remaining digits are for optional use by the subscriber, and could for example address a specific application or process within the DTE. This optional address field will pass transparently through the network.

The facilities field is used by the DTE during the call establishment phase to specify amongst other things, the network facilities required, where optional user facilities are provided by the network.

Logical Channels and Virtual Circuits

An X25 terminal can support several virtual calls simultaneously, by

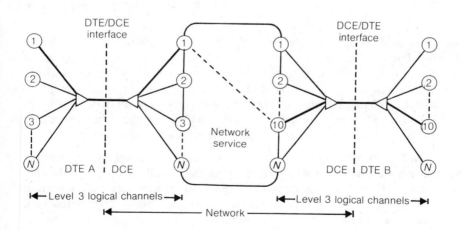

Figure 12.14 Virtual Circuits and Logical Channels

means of packet interleaving. Each call is allocated a logical channel number, and all packets related to that call carry that channel number. The logical channel number is in fact in two parts – a logical channel group number < 15, and a logical channel number < 255, giving a total of 4096 possible channels.

Both the DTE and its supporting DCE use the same logical channel number.The logical channels define two-way associations or liaisons between two DTEs and are illustrated in Figure 12.14. These liaisons are called *virtual circuits,* or, more accurately switched virtual circuits (SVC), and a call established on a virtual circuit is referred to as a *virtual call.* The logical channel numbers associated with each virtual circuit may have different values in the two DTEs, since the channel numbers are allocated independently at each end of the link.

For example, in Figure 12.14 the path 1-1-10-10 comprises a virtual circuit which associates logical channel 1 in DTE A with logical channel 10 in DTE B. However the logical channel numbers are usually chosen from opposite ends of the number range, to avoid collisions.

The major difference between a switched physical circuit and a switched virtual circuit is that the latter is only allocated circuit capacity or bandwidth when packets are being transmitted. Another type of circuit is the *permanent virtual circuit,* which is a permanent association. It is allocated a permanent logical channel at each DTE, and is analogous to a conventional leased circuit.

As we have already observed, the X25 specification merely defines a set of procedures for accessing the network. This allows some freedom of choice of the internal switching and routeing techniques employed within the network. There are basically two approaches. The first employs switched virtual circuits based upon logical channels, all packets belonging to a call being uniquely associated with it. In the other approach, packets are transmitted as independent entities or *datagrams.*

Networks offering the virtual circuit facility use level 3 of X25 internally between the network switching nodes. At call set-up time, adaptive routeing is used to select a physical path, taking into account congestion conditions and availability. Thereafter, for the duration of the virtual call, data packets follow a fixed end-to-end path. This approach is favoured by the PTTs, and has been implemented on a number of national networks.

In the datagram technique, each individual packet contains full source and destination addresses, and is an independent entity which does not depend upon an initial call set-up phase. Therefore, individual packets can take any route through the network, allowing adaptive routeing to be used from packet to packet. Because the datagram avoids the call set-up overhead, it is particularly suitable for certain categories of application.

Thus there is a wide class of applications which are characterised by very 'bursty' traffic patterns – consisting perhaps of no more than the exchange of two simple short messages. Credit enquiry and electronic funds transfer are typical examples. Accordingly some PTTs have introduced a facility which simulates the datagram within the virtual call environment.

Virtual Call Establishment.

The procedure for establishing and terminating a virtual call is illustrated in Figure 12.15.

A virtual call is set up by sending a Call Request packet to the network. This contains the address of the called party and details of any facilities required on the call, and may also contain a limited amount of user data. The network routes this packet to the called party, who responds with a Call Accepted packet; the network then sends a Call Connected packet to the caller. This completes the call set-up phase, and the call then enters the data transfer phase in which both parties can exchange packets containing data. Either party can clear the call by sending a Clear Request packet and, on receipt of a Clear Confirmation packet, a terminal reverts to the idle or 'Ready' state.

Both the calling and called DTE addresses are required to set up a virtual call, and, although the called DTE does not strictly require to know its own address, and this could be stripped off by its serving DCE, inclusion of the address does provide an opportunity for the network to check for incorrect addressing. Each DCE also arranges for incoming packets to be allocated the correct local channel number before onwards transmission to the DTE.

Permanent virtual circuits are treated as a special type of virtual call; there is no call set-up phase and the logical channel is permanently in the data transfer state.

The Clear Indication packet may contain the reason for the clearing, eg DTE out of order, network congestion, number busy, remote or local error.

Flow Control At Level 3

Since the primary purpose of level 2 is to provide a reliable transport mechanism using error-prone circuits, the virtual circuits at level 3 should be comparatively error-free. Therefore the emphasis at level 3 is on controlling congestion. Flow control is generally interpreted as a local function, and the acceptance of data packets by the serving DCE does

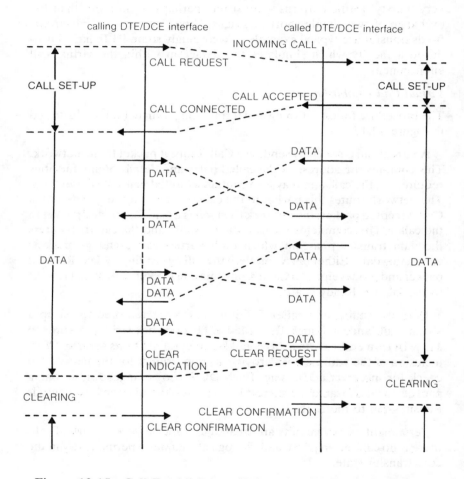

Figure 12.15   Call Establishment, Data, and Call Clear Phases of a Virtual Call

not imply that the destination DTE has agreed to accept them, but merely that the network has sufficient storage to hold the packets and await their acceptance by the remote DTE.

An independent 'window' flow control mechanism analogous to that of level 2 is applied on each logical channel.

Every data packet transmitted contains a Packet Send sequence number P(S) which cycles repeatedly from 0 to 7. Some networks may also provide the extended scheme in which sequence numbers can cycle from 0 to 127. The first data packet sent across the DTE-DCE interface in a given direction carries the send sequence number 0, and P(S) is then incremented by one for each subsequent packet sent in that direction. The number of packets or window size that can be sent before an authorisation is required from the receiver is negotiable, up to a maximum of 7 (or 127 when extended).

Both window size and maximum packet data field length are flow control parameters agreed at subscription time with the network administration. However there is an optional user facility by which flow control parameters can be altered on a per call basis.

An authorisation from the receiver takes the form of a Packet Receive sequence number P(R) contained in an incoming packet. In the absence of an incoming data packet, a special control packet known as a Receive Ready packet is used to carry P(R). As noted earlier, receipt of a P(R) value at a terminal only conveys an indication of how many data packets the network is prepared to accept, and does not necessarily imply that previous packets have been received correctly at the distant terminal. However some networks are expected to use the (R) value as a form of end-to-end acknowledgement.

The principal flow control commands are:

— Receive Ready (RR);

— Receive Not Ready (RNR);

— Reject (REJ).

These operate in a similar way to their counterparts at level 2.

Provision is made for priority interrupt packets to carry data from DTE to DTE, and these are not bound by the normal flow control procedures.

An interrupt packet may overtake earlier packets and will be acknowledged by an interrupt confirmed packet. Only one outstanding unacknowledged interrupt is permitted in each logical channel.

The principal error recovery mechanisms are RESET and RESTART, and these can be initiated from either end. They will usually be involved as a result of either a sequence error detected at level 3 or an error detected at a higher level – possibly in a Higher Level Protocol. An error at a lower level which perhaps resulted in a link reset at level 2 does not automatically have an effect at level 3. In such an event, a restart at level 3 might be necessary, but this would have to be explicitly requested.

RESET reinitialises a specified Virtual Circuit or Permanent Virtual Circuit in both directions and flushes out any data or interrupt packets in transit.

The RESTART function operates in a similar manner to RESET but is applied to all virtual circuits and permanent virtual circuits. Parallelling the Call Establishment procedure, the two functions are initiated by issuing a REQUEST, which becomes an INCOMING INDICATION at the remote DTE; and it is then followed by a CONFIRMATION returned to the originating DTE.

The PAD and the X3, X28, X29 Recommendations

The PAD facility was developed to enable unintelligent DTEs operating in asynchronous mode to access other DTEs connected through a full X25 interface. PAD stands for Packet Assembly Disassembly and it is associated with and located at the Packet Switching Exchange or access node.

The PAD Functions

The primary function of the PAD is to accept the serial character strings generated by a start-stop DTE, and to convert these into the packet formats specified by X25 level 3 on behalf of the DTE. The packets are then despatched across the network to the Packet Switching Exchange serving the destination X25 DTE to which they are delivered under the normal X25 arrangements.

Packets flowing in the reverse direction, on reaching the Exchange serving the start-stop DTE, are converted into character strings acceptable to the DTE.

A separate set of procedures contained in recommendations X3, X28 and X29 govern the operation of the PAD and specify the interfaces between the PAD and the start-stop DTE on the one hand, and the X25 DTE on the other. The interrelationships are shown in Figure 12.16 and the recommendations are described briefly below.

X3

This recommendation defines the basic functions of the PAD. The start-stop DTE not only has limited intelligence, but terminals vary widely in their characteristics, and also the remote DTE may only recognise and be able to converse sensibly with terminals having specified characteristics.

The PAD is therefore provided with a set of parameters, the values of

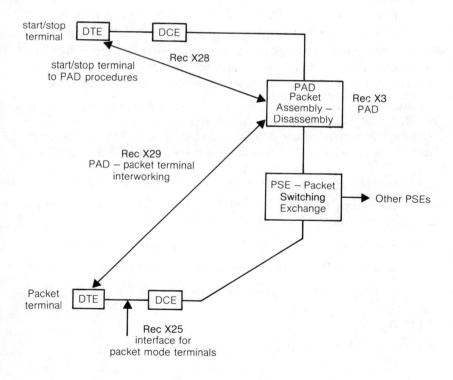

Figure 12.16   X3, X28, X29 and X25 Relationships

which can be set either from the terminal or the remote DTE which is being accessed. So far 18 parameters have been defined and they relate to such features as:

— whether echo checking is required;

— selection of the Data Forwarding characters (these are the characters which must be inserted by the terminal to define packet boundaries, and instruct the PAD when to assemble and forward a packet);

— auxiliary device control signals to activate a locally attached device at the remote terminal such as a cassette or diskette drive;

— specification of terminal format effectors such as line feed or carriage return;

— padding delay requirements to allow the terminal time to effect a line feed (applicable mainly to mechanical terminals).

Thus, the PAD can in effect supply some of the terminal handling functions, and also enables a 'foreign' terminal to simulate the characteristics of a terminal recognised by the remote packet mode DTE.

Initially the parameters can be set to one of a number of 'standard profiles', but their values can be altered or negotiated between the start-stop terminal and the PAD or the remote X25 DTE at logging on time or during a call. The procedures are specified in X28 and X29.

X28 – Interface Between the Start-Stop Mode DTE and the PAD

The recommendation specifies the protocol to be used between a start-stop terminal and the PAD. It lays down procedures for:

— establishing a call to the PAD from the start-stop terminal;

— setting the PAD parameters to the required values;

— exchanging data between a start-stop terminal and the PAD.

Access to the PAD

Access to the PAD can be:

— via the public switched telephone network using Rec V21 modems;

— over analogue leased lines, using Rec V21 modems.

Where digital data services exist, access will also be possible:

— over digital leased lines, using a Rec X20 or X20 bis interface, or

— over the circuit switched data network, using a Rec X20 or X20 bis interface.

(The Rec X20 bis interface is compatible with the Rec V24/RS232 interface, thus allowing existing terminals to use the new digital data services.)

Where digital data services exist they can be expected to provide a more reliable link than analogue circuits, and with increasing System X penetration, there should be substantial improvements in call establishment time for dialled calls (< 2 secs).

PAD Initialisation

Having accessed the PAD, the start-stop terminal sends a Service Request signal. This enables the PAD to detect the data rate and code used by the terminal, and to set the PAD parameters to an appropriate initial setting.

Provision is made for a password to be required at this stage, to prevent unauthorised usage.

Procedures are given whereby the start-stop terminal user can change and /or read out the values of the PAD parameters.

Virtual Call Set-Up to the Destination Packet Terminal

The start-stop terminal user indicates to the PAD the address of the packet terminal to be called, together with the facilities required on the call. The PAD sets up the virtual call, and then prepares to carry out the packet assembly/disassembly function during the data transfer phase.

During the data transfer phase the start-stop terminal can recall the PAD (ie escape from the data transfer phase and enter into a control phase) in order to alter the PAD parameters, reset or request the status of the virtual call, send an interrupt to the packet terminal, or clear the call.

X29 – Interface between a Packet-Mode DTE and the PAD

This protocol is essentially the same as the X25 protocol used for connection to other packet-mode terminals, and call establishment and flow control follow normal X25 procedures. However, it has extra procedures to accommodate the presence of a PAD. When a packet-mode terminal is called by a non packet-mode terminal the intervening PAD sets the value of particular bits in the first octet of the Call User Data field of the Call Request packet to indicate that PAD assistance is being given. In general these bits qualify the use for the following 3 octets in identifying any additional protocol to be used on the call. The first 4 octets together form the Protocol Identifier Field, and are followed in the Call Request packet by up to 12 octets of user data.

In the reverse direction, the packet-mode terminal may communicate with the PAD by means of qualified data packets (in which the Q bit discussed under X25 is set to 1). The information in such packets is identified by the Q bit value as being for use by the PAD, and not for passing to the non packet-mode terminal. This procedure allows the packet-mode terminal to read, and in certain cases set the values of, the PAD parameters described under Recommendation X3.

A particular coding of bits 8 and 7 of the first octet of the Protocol Identifier Field allows the identification of non-CCITT protocols to be used on a virtual call. This opens the way for an organisation such as the International Organization for Standardization to standardise terminal to terminal protocols and their individual identification by this mechanism.

The coding of the above bits is:

bits 8 and 7 = 0 0 for CCITT use
= 0 1 for national use
= 1 0 reserved for international user bodies
= 1 1 for DTE-DCE use

In addition to the facility for reading and setting the PAD parameters, two other types of message can be sent from the packet-mode DTE to the PAD. It can cause a 'Break' signal to be sent to the start-stop terminal, and it can request the call to be cleared down.

Packet Switched Network Facilities

In addition to the basic facilities such as the Virtual Call, X25 can be used to support the provision of a range of other facilities and services. Depending upon the network administration, some of these may be present amongst the basic offerings, but in general they are supplied as options. The user must specify which optional facilities he requires, and they will generally incur additional charges.

Over 20 such options have been defined, and they include:

— Abbreviated Address – for Datagrams, allows short forms of addressing. The network maps this to the full network address;

— Datagram Queue Length Selection – allows selection of the length of the queue of Datagrams and Datagram Service Signals awaiting delivery to a terminal;

— Datagram Service Signal Logical Channel – allows a logical channel to be dedicated to the reception of service signals;

— Fast Select – allows more than the normal amount of data to be carried in a Call Request packet. Data can also be carried by a Call Accepted packet and in a Clear Request packet;

— Closed User Group – allows a user to communicate with other terminals in the same Closed User Group but prevents communication with other terminals. The overall effect is to create the security of a private network within a public network;

— Reverse Charging and Acceptance – two complementary facilities allowing the request and acceptance of reverse charge calls;

— Non-Standard Default Packet Sizes – allows selection of other than the normal default maximum packet size of 128 octets;

— Flow Control Parameter Negotiation – allows selection of maximum packet size and window size across the network interface.

13 Aspects of Network Design and Management

INTRODUCTION

In the preceding chapters we have been largely concerned with the basic principles, the underlying transmission technology, and the fundamental concepts of data communications systems. It is only in the preceding chapter that we started to consider how all the components might be assembled together to provide a system which meets the applications requirements for which it was designed. We now turn our attention to the subject of network design and we shall discuss some of the more important aspects which have to be considered.

Once a properly designed system is installed and operational, it is also of paramount importance to ensure that it consistently supplies the level of service for which it was designed. It is a fact that communications-based systems are decidedly more vulnerable to performance shortcomings than are batch processing systems. This arises partly because of the change in expectations which arises when batch applications are transferred to a real-time environment; lead times are reduced and a whole range of company activities and procedures are modified to take advantage of the vastly improved response times and processing power.

It is therefore not sufficient to have a well designed system, but it must also be effectively managed, not only in terms of the management skills which are employed, but also in regard to the resources and facilities provided, both within and external to the system, to support the management function.

A comprehensive discussion of each of these two subjects is beyond the scope of this book, and we shall therefore confine ourselves to a review of the more important issues.

NETWORK DESIGN

The most difficult part of the network design process involves defining the scope of the problems to be solved. The basic demands on the network will depend on the computer systems design. Increasingly, with the advent of distributed processing techniques, the network is a vital component in the system's functionality. It is therefore vital that the designs of both computer systems and data networks should be co-ordinated closely. While it will be possible to quantify the load that an individual transaction places on the network (this is a function of computer system design), it will be very difficult to forecast the numbers of transactions which will need to be supported per day or how that load is distributed between the sites in the network. The crucial demand on any network design is that it should meet the peak loads placed on it.

The very best forecasts of network loadings will inevitably prove to be inaccurate in practice. It is important, therefore, that once installed, the system and network should together maintain as much information as possible on the network's use. This will allow the network design to be reviewed on a regular basis with a view to maintaining the service to the users in the most cost-effective manner possible.

Acceptance by the user is a vital ingredient in the success of data communications systems.

The level of success achieved will depend upon the extent to which the total system meets the user's needs; however, the network has its part to play in delivering data to the user in a manner which is timely, available and reliable. We will now go on to look at how the choice of network components can provide a cost-effective solution to network requirements in respect of:

— performance;

— reliability and availability;

— cost;

— expandability.

Performance

The data transmitted through a network will be of two basic types. Where bulk data is being passed between nodes without direct human involvement, other than issuing the commands to start the transfer, short-term delays in delivering the data may not be important, and can be tolerated; for example, it will be needed at the central site in time for the beginning of overnight processing at 6 p.m. The second category of data being transferred involves on-line applications with interactive transactions running on a question-answer basis on a user terminal. In such applications, 'response time' is a major concern. Although there are several definitions, 'response time' is commonly defined as the elapsed time from depressing the SEND key on the terminal, to receiving the first character of the response. In general, response time consists of four elements:

— time taken to propagate the user's request through the network to the computer;

— time taken to execute program code on the central processor;

— time taken in accessing the data required from file (or database) storage devices;

— time taken to propagate the computer system's response through the network to the terminal.

Network design, as opposed to distributed system design, can only affect two of these elements of response time: the propagation times to and from a remote site. For example, where a dedicated data link is used in connecting a computer system to a terminal, the propagation time will equate to the time taken to *transmit* the question and its answer. However, where the link is used to serve multiple devices at either or both ends, a contention situation arises and users have to queue for service. As already discussed the characteristics of the link protocol used have an important bearing on transmission efficiency.

Queues of messages waiting for service can build up on various points in the system: waiting for circuits to be available; a disk access arm to be free; a CPU program to be released, and so on. Queue formation is inevitable and must be allowed for during the design of the system. A whole body of 'Queueing Theory' exists which can be utilised for predicting queue sizes and the effect on response time under various assumed traffic levels and system capacities.

The average communications component of response time is found to have an exponential relationship with the level of utilisation of the link. Figure 13.1 shows how the average response time varies with the transac-

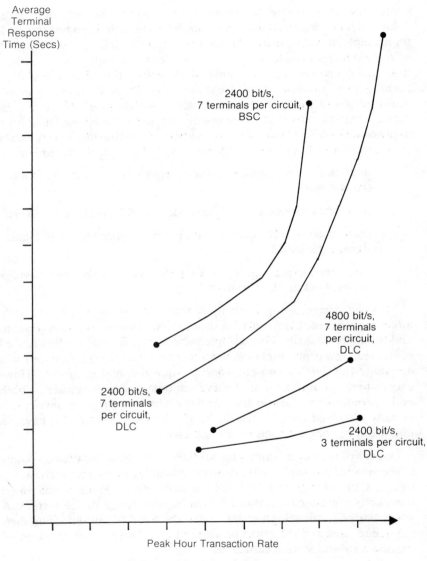

Average
Terminal
Response
Time (Secs)

2400 bit/s,
7 terminals per circuit,
BSC

4800 bit/s,
7 terminals
per circuit,
DLC

2400 bit/s,
7 terminals
per circuit,
DLC

2400 bit/s,
3 terminals per circuit,
DLC

Peak Hour Transaction Rate

BSC = Half-duplex Bi Sync protocol
DLC = Data link control, full duplex protocol

Figure 13.1   Graph of Performance Versus Peak Hour Transaction Rate

tion rate a data link is asked to service. If we are to maintain reasonable response times for terminal users the peak transaction rate must be restricted to the part of the graph before it starts steepening and average response time rises rapidly.

On the steep portion, not only are response times likely to be extended beyond acceptable limits but they would also tend to be sensitive to quite marginal variations in the level of line utilisation.

Reliability and Availability

Reliability

An important aspect of network design lies in the estimation of the likely levels of reliability, both in terms of the quality of the data transferred between nodes and in the non-availability of the systems as a result of network component failure.

We have discussed the nature of errors in transmission systems, and their detection at some length in Chapter 11. There, we noted that so far as practicable, transmission errors should be detected and corrected low down in the system and as remote as possible from the application itself, and that one important function of a Link Protocol was to convert an inherently unreliable link into one which was reliable. Nevertheless, there will be errors which arise which can only be resolved, or only manifest themselves within the application itself. The design of procedures for recovering from this category of error is perhaps one of the most difficult and complex parts of data communications systems design.

By the time the error is detected, it might already have had a widespread impact. For example, individual transactions might have got out of sequence, files may have been updated in the wrong sequence, and so on. In the meantime, the terminal user may well be wondering what has gone wrong, although certainly expecting to recommence at the point where he left off. This is where the difficulties really start, because it may be necessary to 'backtrack' to a point preceding the error.

In designing recovery procedures, therefore, very careful attention is paid to ensuring that this is achieved with the absolute minimum of disruption, that the terminal user is kept fully informed, and that the recovery process occurs as 'gracefully' as possible.

Availability

The usefulness of a system is a function of the time it is available for use relative to the time when it is required for use. The measurement of usefulness, termed availability, can be calculated, for individual components and complete systems, from the expression:

$$\text{Availability (A)} = \frac{\text{MTBF}}{\text{MTBF} + \text{MTTR}} \quad \begin{array}{l}\text{(mean time between failures)} \\ \text{(mean time to repair)}\end{array}$$

A typical data transmission link is made up of several components, modems, terminals and circuits. The availability for the system can be arrived at by considering each discrete component as an element in a series electrical circuit (Figure 13.2).

The availability of each of these components will be a factor in the overall link availability as each is mutually dependent on all other components for the functioning of the link.

Example 1 – availability of a component (ac)

$$ac_1 = \frac{\text{MTBF}}{\text{MTBF} + \text{MTTR}} \quad \begin{array}{l}\text{where MTBF} = 200 \text{ days} \\ \text{MTTR} = 2 \text{ days}\end{array}$$

Then $ac_1 = \dfrac{200}{202} = 0.99009$

A component will have an availability of 0.99 or be usable for 99% of the time.

Example 2 – availability of a link

If this availability is applied to all components $(1 - 5)$ that form the complete transmission path (Figure 13.2) the then availability for the link will be:

$$\begin{array}{rl} \text{Availability (A)} = & ac_1 \times ac_2 \times ac_3 \times ac_4 \times ac_5 \\ A = & 0.99 \times 0.99 \times 0.99 \times 0.99 \times 0.99 \\ A = & 0.9510 \text{ or } 95\% \end{array}$$

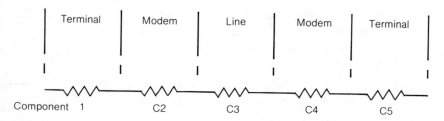

Figure 13.2   Schematic (Component) Representation of a Data Transmission Link

In a year of 365 days there is a probability that the circuit will be unavailable for 5% of the time, ie 18.5 days during the year.

Example 3 – availability of two components in parallel

If we chose to duplicate a component we would improve the overall availability, because if one component fails, its duplicate (or standby) will be there to replace it.

$$A = 1 - \left[(1 - ac_1) \times (1 - ac_2) \right]$$

where A = availability of the similar 2 components in parallel

c_1 = primary component

c_2 = spare or standby component

The composite availability of two components, each with an individual availability of 0.99 or 99% will be:

$$A = 1 - \left[(1 - ac_1) \times (1 - ac_2) \right]$$

$$A = 1 - \left[(1 - 0.99) \times (1 - 0.99) \right]$$

$$A = 1 - (0.01 \times 0.01)$$

$$A = 1 - 0.0001$$

$$A = 0.9999 \text{ or } 99.99\%$$

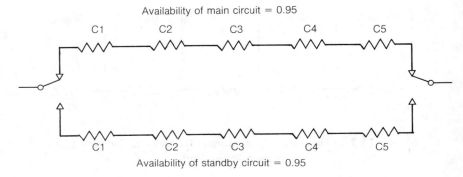

Figure 13.3   Availability of Parallel Circuits

The same methodology can be applied to the duplication of a whole circuit, where each circuit has an availability of 95% as shown in Figure 13.3.

Example 4– availability of parallel circuits

$$A = 1 - \Big[(1 - a(\text{main circuit})) \times (1 - a(\text{standby circuit}) \Big]$$

Based on the availability of each circuit (main and standby) of 0.95 or 95% as shown in Figure 13.3, then:

$$A = 1 - \Big[(0.05) \times (0.05) \Big]$$
$$A = 1 - 0.0025$$
$$A = 0.9975 \text{ or } 99.75\%$$

A further improvement in the overall availability can be achieved by duplicating each component and providing full flexibility between them as shown in Figure 13.4.

Example 5– availability with full flexibility (see Figure 13.4)

In Example 3 we calculated the availability of a component when that component is provided with a standby. This was shown to be 0.9999. Working on the same figure and with full flexibility we have:

$$A = ac_1 \times ac_2 \times ac_3 \times ac_4 \times ac_5$$
where ac_1 to ac_5 includes a spare component

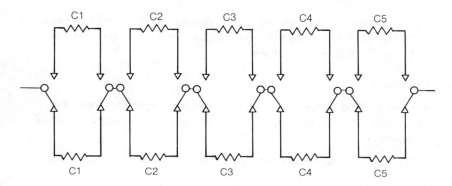

Figure 13.4   Availability when Full Flexibility between all Components is Provided

A = 0.9999 x 0.9999 x 0.9999 x 0.9999 x 0.9999

A = 0.9995 or 99.95%

These examples illustrate that by the selective duplication of the most vulnerable components, it is possible to achieve improved protection against failure for the overall system, without necessarily having to duplicate the whole.

When considering communication lines in this context it is usual to access availability of the circuits using the standard formulae, given earlier:

Availability (A) = $\dfrac{\text{MTBF}}{\text{MTBF} + \text{MTTR}}$

From a UK national survey it has been found that the average number of faults reported each year on amplified circuits (over 40 kilometres) is 2.2. The average out-of-service time per fault reported is 15 hours. (NB This 15 hours time includes nights and weekends when customers may not require to use the circuit.)

For unamplified circuits (under 40 kilometres) the out-of-service time is similar to that quoted above, the average fault rate, however, drops to 0.26 faults per circuit each year.

It would not be practicable to use these figures directly to calculate MTBF + MTTR for circuits, but useful estimates can be made as illustrated in the following example:

Example 6

A point-to-point circuit, over 40 kms which is required for use 8 hours a day, 5 days a week, 50 weeks a year. An estimate of the circuit availability is required.

This can be assessed on the basis of a fault rate of twice the national average.

Therefore:

$$\text{MTBF} = \frac{\text{No. of hours} \times \text{No. of days/week} \times \text{No. of weeks/year}}{\text{Anticipated No. of faults per annum}}$$

$$= \frac{8 \times 5 \times 50}{2 \times 2.2 \text{ faults per annum}} = \frac{2000}{4.4}$$

MTBF = 454.5 hours

The average Mean Time to Repair equals 15 hours per fault but assuming that only 8 of these hours will be in normal operational hours:

$$\text{Then A} = \frac{454.5}{454.5 + 8}$$

$$\text{A} = \frac{454.5}{462.5} = 0.9827 \text{ or } 98.27\%$$

It can be assumed that the availability of this circuit will be over 98%. By providing a duplicate circuit the availability will be increased to 0.9997 or 99.97%. In these circumstances the use of a standby exchange line can provide an effective and cheap alternative to the duplicate private circuit, but the availability for the switched telephone network is far more difficult to assess as the average fault rate of 0.8 faults per annum for each telephone is low. Many faults, particularly dialling failures, are not reported to the UK PTT.

This approach depends upon the suppliers offering MTBF and MTTR figures and their confidence in those figures (eg a well known modem supplier quotes MTBF as $2\frac{1}{2}$ years of 24 hours/day operation and states that in practice it could be exceeded by 25%). In the absence of suppliers' MTBF and MTTR figures, users may sometimes obtain valued experience of the equipment from other users.

Expandability

The demands placed on a network by the computer systems that it serves are likely to exceed the network design loadings for a variety of reasons:

— under-estimation of demand during initial design;

— growth in an organisation's business followed by an increase in transaction rates;

— implementation of new applications;

— provision of service to new users;

— extension of service to users in new locations.

It is therefore important to ensure that the system has sufficient spare capacity to cope with anticipated expansion of workload, and, in both the physical and functional sense, has the potential for easy expansion of capacity.

Anticipating future business needs, even over say a five-year timescale, is by no means easy, particularly in a world which is expecting such rapid rates of technological and socio-economic change. But, at the very least the design of the system should take into account the corporate long-term plans, so far as these are known or can be prudently revealed.

Shortcomings in the performance of the system and its components may be more difficult to rectify. For example, if a data link operating at 2400 bit/sec is found to be insufficient, a higher-quality voice circuit may be required to support modems at the higher data rate required. When designing the network it is important to take account of any uncertainties about the performance of individual network components and perhaps 'over-configure' where a shortfall might have crucial side-effects.

MAJOR CAUSES OF FAILURES

Impulsive Noise

Undoubtedly the prime cause of failures is excessive impulsive noise generated by electromechanical switching equipment carrying telephone traffic. Vibration, another by-product of telephone traffic, causes poor (dry) joints or weak contacts to fail or generate noise which, as well as affecting the dialled connections (audible clicks to telephone users – corrupted bits to data users) can be induced into adjacent circuits which could be private wires carrying data. Retransmission can give systems some cushioning up to the design limit of retries. In a multiterminal arrangement, putting the terminal which is constantly returning NAKs into a down-graded polling routine can prevent the system becoming congested handling only retries and NAKs. As some noise is transient the down-grading of the polling routine enables the rest of the network to handle data and hopefully when the troublesome terminal is polled again the noise could have subsided resulting in a satisfactory exchange of data.

The ultimate option is to take the line out of service and report it to the PTT as faulty.

Circuit Disconnections

Breaks in the circuit are the second highest cause of failures. These can range in duration from a few milliseconds, resulting from main transmission system changeovers or maintenance working parties accidentally disturbing a link, to several hours or more when cables have been physically damaged. Some devices such as modems with a Hold Over facility and intelligent multiplexers can sustain short duration breaks without affecting the users but longer breaks cause the modems to lose carrier and if the break exceeds the modem's 'hold over' time, the receiving modem will time out and produce a failure. The user with a long duration break either utilises an alternative or standby route or reports the line break to the PTT and waits for restoration.

Changes in Circuit Parameters

The electrical parameters of scheduled circuits can gradually alter, or drift over a period of time, resulting eventually in failures. Where a modem is operating near the limits of a scheduled circuit any worsening of the parameters dramatically affects its performance. Drifting of overall loss or attenuation is unlikely by itself to cause a failure unless the signal is so severely weakened as to alter its relationship with the background noise. Changes in loss/frequency performance especially with high-speed transmission where the modem is utilising most of the bandwidth available could lead to failures if the compensating capacity of the dynamic equalisers in the modem is exceeded. Some modems have built-in warning lights indicating that the equaliser is working to its limits and giving the user notice that the performance of the circuit is deteriorating. Similarly variations in group delay are compensated for by equalisation.

Echoes, or inter-symbol interference, where the signal is surrounded by lower power replicas of itself are compensated for by tap delay equalisers which tap off the replica delay and invert it and recombine it with the signal to cancel out the original echo.

DIAGNOSTICS

An ability for the user to test and monitor the performance of the components as well as the overall link can produce drastic reductions in the time taken to locate and rectify faults. Whether or not to obtain specific test equipment is initially blurred by the increasing amount of equipment, particularly modems, now available with in-built diagnostic facilities, the often bewildering range of proprietary measuring sets, as well as the cost which can range from tens of pounds to tens of thousands of pounds.

One of the requirements of the UK PTT with regard to the use of proprietary test equipment is that it shall be permitted for attachment and used at specific test points. Typical points where this could be logically carried out are either at the line modem interface, the line terminating point (eg the Case 200A on individual lines or rack mounted line terminating equipment in multi-line situations) or at the terminal/modem interface (V24 interface).

Various routines can be devised for obtaining knowledge of the performance of each link in the chain, the information obtained being directly related to cost of the equipment involved. A simple approach is the use of high impedance headphones at the line termination point monitoring the audio signals being sent or received without disturbing the transmission. With practice, the various signals can be recognised and trouble can be identified by the absence or marked change of signal.

Using the in-built diagnostic facilities of the modems normally involves line looping whereby the transmitted data is returned to its point of origin. Looping can be behind the local modem checking its modulation and demodulation, at the remote end of the line (before its enters the distant modem) which checks the line as well as the local modem and looping behind the distant modem which checks both modems and the line. Some modems need physical switch operation at each location; other more sophisticated modems can effect the looping from a central site. An interface tester which checks on the conditions across the V24 interface is a useful arbiter between the modem and the terminal and/or their maintenance support.

The ultimate level of diagnostics is the use of test equipment specifically designed to test either the modem (data test equipment) or the line parameters (transmission test equipment). These cover a multitude of test facilities and may be mounted in a network control console. A final word of caution: sophisticated test equipment needs regular calibration to ensure accuracy and the staff using this apparatus need to use it frequently to be able to expertly interpret the readings obtainable.

MAINTENANCE

Broadly, this divides into areas where it is necessary to call in the supplier's maintenance support immediately or situations where, because of the availability of on-site diagnostics, patching facilities and spare equipment, the restoration can be effected within an organisation and any subsequent rectification by the supplier is not so time critical.

Proprietary Equipment Supplier Maintenance

The majority of equipment suppliers enter into a graded maintenance service contract with their customers and respond to a site within a specified time period. The shorter the time period, the higher the cost, with a possible variation that the service engineer telephones the affected site and talks the user through some diagnostics equipment changeout. Depending upon the number and geographic location of the supplier's maintenance depots, coverage will vary and users will have catered for this in their initial purchase decision.

UK PTT Maintenance

Currently the UK PTT do not offer graded maintenance but they classify data transmission exchange lines and private circuits for Emergency (E) treatment which caters for service attention out of normal hours (week days after 1700 hours and weekends). Users are given a fault reporting number which may be the normal '151' or the number of the trunk maintenance control centre. A '151' call will initially trigger off testing of the PSTN, unamplified private circuits and possible reference to a Datel test centre for repair of UK PTT modems. The longer distance circuit faults are dealt with by the trunk maintenance control centres who can also refer UK PTT modem faults to the Datel test centres. In all cases the circuit number or exchange line number is the reference key for their procedures and documentation and should be quoted on reporting and on any subsequent progressing.

MINIMISING EFFECTS OF NETWORK FAILURES

Failures are inevitable but various precautionary or cushioning measures can, without undue cost, minimise the effects of the failure.

Geographic areas served by multipoint networks can also contain a spur from another multipoint serving an adjacent area. In the event of a common serving section or multiple spur failure, the data can be physically entered on the adjacent circuit.

Lines tend to fail at the local distribution ends and these can be duplicated (from exchange to users' premises) at a much smaller cost than complete end-to-end duplication.

Where two or more circuits are required to be used as back-up to each other, ask the UK PTT for separate routeing in the main network. Thus a failure of a main system may only take out one instead of both circuits.

The PSTN can, subject to speed and quality considerations, be used as a back-up to a private circuit.

If the data transmission link is over the PSTN, users can cater for the loss of exchange facilities by renting out-of-area exchange lines from an adjacent exchange at a distance related cost. It is vital to ensure that such lines are wired direct as a back-up rather than via the normal serving exchange.

Shared or standby equipment, such as modems, can be valuable at a central site and possibly additionally held near a group of outstations. In a central location the standby could serve as a diagnostic.

If the central site has a standby power facility, ensure that the transmission equipment is also served by this supply. The mains outlets at the base of modem racks should be on a different feed from the modems to avoid casual appliance faults affecting the rack of modems.

In all areas of duplication it is vital that some regular use of the standby lines or equipment is organised either using on alternate days or by a rota. This ensures that users are aware of any failure of the standby *before* it becomes necessary to use it as a fallback to the main operation.

NETWORK MANAGEMENT

As we have noted, the availability of the system may be crucial to the day-to-day operations of an organisation, and an unreliable service can quickly lead to dissatisfaction among its users. The role of data communications management is to ensure maximum availability and responsiveness of the system. We shall briefly examine some of the techniques and tools which are available.

Diagnostic Tools

Built-in Diagnostics

In Chapter 9 we described the diagnostic capabilities using loopback techniques which are built into many *modems*. These facilities can be invaluable in isolating simple line faults and discontinuities in transmission.

The modem is equipped with a test pattern generator which creates a 'pseudo-random' bit sequence. Various test modes allow the local modem to be tested either alone or in combination with the telephone circuit and remote modem. In these tests the test pattern is transmitted, then reflected back from one of three locations. When the 'reflection' has been passed through the testing modem's demodulation circuitry, it is compared with the pattern originally transmitted.

By examining the performance of each combination in turn it is possible to identify the circuit segment or component which is at fault.

Some *multiplexers* are also equipped with diagnostic capabilities very similar to those present in modems, and various sections of the multiplexer-modem-multiplexer path can be tested.

Additionally, tests are available which exercise individual low-speed channels. These tests are invoked from the terminal connected to the low-speed channel resulting in a test message being output to the terminal. This test message may be derived from either the local or the remote multiplexer so providing further evidence of the conditions along the path.

Stand-Alone Diagnostic Tools

The *break-out monitor* is interposed in any 25-way D-socket connection in the link. It allows the state of each of the circuits in the interface to be examined, enabling the state of a circuit and the quality of the signal to be checked.

The *on-line data content monitor* also monitors the activity in a 25-pin V24 interface. However, the monitor allows the data transferred to be displayed on an oscilloscope in character format. As an alternative, the data may be recorded on magnetic tape for subsequent analysis and investigation. This type of equipment may be particularly helpful in multiple supplier situations in allocating responsibility between the different parties.

Protocol testers are fairly sophisticated devices and are designed specifically to exercise and test the protocols which are employed by the system.

Other Management and Diagnostic Aids

The tools discussed are generally concerned with testing conditions at the electrical or link level, and although they may be applied regularly as part of the preventive maintenance procedures, they have general limitations:

— they are most suitable for taking instantaneous snapshots at discrete intervals of time;

— they generally record events at too low a level of detail;

— they are not very effective for maintaining a continuous record of events and summarising this in a form which presents an overall view of network performance and highlights those components which require attention.

These facilities can be provided as:

— systems software located in a mainframe computer or front-end processor;

— specialised network management consoles.

The majority of computer manufacturers supply performance recording and analysis software located either in the mainframe computer or the communications processor, and associated with the line-handling software. They collect accumulative statistics on such items as:

— traffic activity on each nominated link and terminal;

— polling activity for each terminal;

— frequency of transmission faults;

— number of retries before correct transmission achieved;

— terminal faults.

Either independently of, or in association with network control consoles, these can be very helpful in planning preventive maintenance. For example, circuits experiencing retries exceeding a given threshold may be a symptom of progressive deterioration, indicating that some remedial action, such as notifying BT, is required.

For large extended networks such as those operated by the multi-site corporations, the banks and the airlines, network management is a complex and costly task.

The requirements of these large networks encouraged the development of general-purpose *management consoles* which provide a wide range of monitoring and testing functions. The reduction in costs brought about by microprocessor technology is enabling equivalent products to be introduced into the market place at a price attractive to the smaller network operator. Essentially these systems comprise two components: a central control facility and a 'wrap-around' unit which is co-located with each of the modems in the network and in some cases shares a cabinet with it. Network control systems generally utilise a sideband on the network's circuits for communication between the various network components. The 'wrap-around' unit is capable of monitoring either the line or terminal sides of the modem in response to requests input to the Central Control Facility and passes information back for display there. Network control systems combine the capabilities of all the diagnostic aids described previously with the exception of the Data Content Monitor; however, the loopback testing carried out by the network control system is totally independent of any network component. It is also possible to switch to standby network components using the systems.

In short then, a network control system allows the selective testing and swift detection of errors and malfunctioning in any part of the network.

Many of the products on the market also incorporate a display which provides a dynamic indication of the state of the network at any instant.

Nevertheless, notwithstanding these facilities, the job of a network controller requires skill and understanding in order to be able to utilise them to maximum effect.

Falling somewhere in between systems software and the general-purpose products, there is an increasing tendency to build *network diagnostic functions* into both proprietary network offerings and the new public data networks. This is made possible because of the increased intelligence which is available in the terminals, and in the network components, such as switching nodes. Thus, public packet switched networks are provided with a centralised network monitoring capability which can detect and interpret a wide range of incidents, and report these back to the subscriber. For example, on the UK packet switched network, it is claimed that the network administration could in principle detect a power-down situation on an X25-connected terminal possibly before the user became aware of it.

14 Into the Future

INTRODUCTION

No book of this type would be complete without an overview of current trends and a look at the future. Before doing so we make the observation that to do this within the confines of data communications as traditionally understood, would not only be unduly restrictive, but more seriously would ignore the central and fundamental role that communications technology is destined to play in the Information Technology Revolution. Therefore the discussion takes place within this wider context.

Crystal gazing is always a hazardous process. It is inevitable that much of what is stated in this chapter could be upset by unanticipated changes in technology. We can confidently expect the rapid rate of change of recent years to be maintained. Trends which were barely discernible or even non-existent a few years ago, are now fairly well established, and the major uncertainties concern the pace of development and the nature of its ramifications and impacts.

INFORMATION TECHNOLOGY

The principal hallmarks of the first Industrial Revolution were the replacement of muscle power by machines, the discovery and exploitation of new raw materials, accompanied by vastly improved transport services.

The new Industrial Revolution is primarily about Information in all its forms, and its processing, storage and dissemination. Whilst we have very definitely stepped across the threshold of this new technology, its full and widespread impact is yet to come. But the first stirrings are already discernible: the proliferation of personal computers; the emergence of electronic mail services; the introduction of robots in factories . . . are

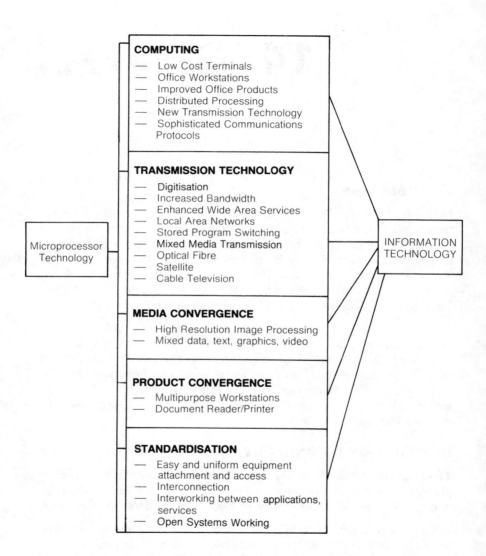

Figure 14.1   Convergence of Computing and Telecommunications

examples. In contrast to the early Industrial Revolution examples, the robots are not only replacing muscle power, they are also making decisions previously performed by people. Instead of physically transporting a message in an envelope and delivering it through a letter-box, we shall increasingly be sending messages in the form of electrical impulses along wires, and of course, if this were extended to a person working at home rather than in an office, compare the energy savings through replacing the energy equivalent of a couple of gallons of petrol with the few thimblefuls needed to transmit the information required. The implications in an increasingly energy-conscious age are obvious.

TECHNOLOGY CONVERGENCE

This vast expansion of opportunities on a scale which could exert a profound influence on the shape of the future (so that we feel some justification for calling it a new Industrial Revolution), has been brought about by the convergence of two previously disparate technologies – computing and telecommunications. This convergence operates at a number of levels and in several directions. Figure 14.1 depicts the principal threads of this convergence and Figure 14.2 expresses it in a more dynamic form by showing the main motivating forces (and possible constraints).

We shall now comment upon some of the technological influences.

SOME MAJOR INFLUENCES

Microelectronics

The importance of microelectronics hardly requires comment and its influence is all-pervasive. Apart from making terminals or workstations of widely varying sophistication available on every desk a feasible proposition, it has a number of other impacts which should be noted:

— it accelerates the trend towards dispersal of intelligence and distributed processing;

— it makes it technically and economically practicable to support the new network connection and transmission standards such as X25 and HDLC, and the Higher Level Protocols currently under development;

— its influence on Communications Network Design and transmis-

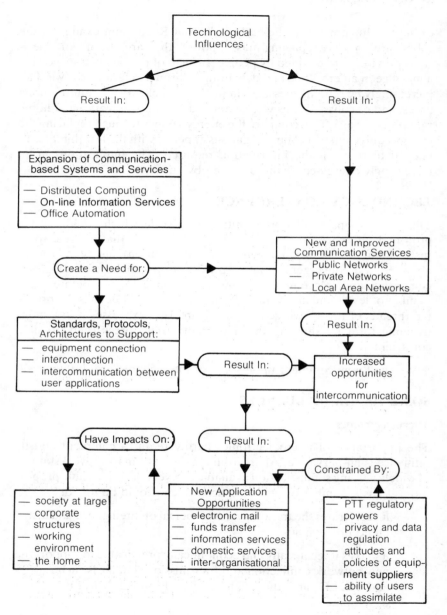

Figure 14.2   Computing and Communications Interdependencies

sion technology is dramatic. It is now economically feasible to build more intelligence into communication networks to provide better control, improved performance and additional services which would not otherwise be practicable. For example, the technical and economic justification and many of the performance features of Public Packet Switched Networks, digital transmission, the System X Switching Exchanges, the new generation of digital PABXs, and local area distribution networks rely heavily on microelectronics.

Communications Technology

Transmission and Switching Technology

It bears repeating that the bulk of the world's transmission networks were designed and laid down primarily to carry speech, and in the early days of telephony it was elected to transmit the signals in an analogue form. This form of transmission is not only inappropriate for communication between computing devices which operate wholly digitally, but it imposes physical constraints on performance and also has a number of design implications, such as the effectiveness of various kinds of multiplexing which can be employed, and the mechanism for network control signalling. For these reasons digital transmission is the preferred technology for data transmission networks, whether they are public switched, or private using leased circuits, and a number of PTTs are either constructing such networks or are planning to do so.

We have noted earlier the implications of microelectronics for switching exchange design. The move towards digital transmission is also being accompanied by the design and introduction of stored program switching exchanges, both public and private. These replace the original Strowger exchanges and the more recent hardwired electronic crossbar version.

The use of stored program control in conjunction with microelectronics enables very high switching speeds to be attained, and the flexibility and power of program control permits a wide range of additional facilities and services to be incorporated which would otherwise be technically very difficult and costly to provide.

It is evident that very significant improvements in the quality of basic transmission services will result from these developments and other proven technology, notably satellite transmission and fibre optics.

Telecommunications administrations in most advanced countries, and certainly in Europe and America, are either planning to modernise the public networks or are already in the process of doing so.

In the United Kingdom the British Telecom's System X programme, and its ISDN (Integrated Services Data Network) extension, represents one approach. The end result of this programme will be a fully integrated digital network capable of transmitting text, data, speech, slow scan video and facsimile, with equal facility.

In parallel with System X and ISDN developments in the public switched network, BT are introducing private digital circuits in order to extend the benefits of digital transmission to the business community at an early stage before the completion of switched network modernisation. These circuits will be offered in speeds ranging from 2.4 bit/sec through 64,000 bit/sec up to 8 megabit/sec. Apart from traditional point-to-point applications, the 2 and 8 Megabit/sec circuits can be used to interconnect the new generation of PABXs, thus enabling organisations to construct their own private switched digital networks.

Fibre Optics and Optoelectronics

The rapid development of optical fibre as a transmission medium is a major achievement of the last few years. The earlier technical problems associated with its installation and jointing have been largely solved, and costs may be expected to progressively reduce.

BT have now embarked on a major programme to replace the trunk network by optical cable, and from 1984 all trunk circuit replacements will be optical cable.

There is also continuing research to further enhance optical fibre performance. For example, BT have been able to demonstrate the transmission of light pulses at a rate of 140 million/sec over a distance of 102 km (63 miles) without intermediate pulse generation. This corresponds to nearly 2,000 simultaneous telephone calls over a single optical fibre. In another experiment conducted outside the laboratory, pulses have been transmitted along 31.5 km (21 miles) at a rate of 650 million/ sec. This is a digital signal rate of 650 Mbit/s, equivalent to nearly 8,000 simultaneous telephone calls.

The potential of fibre optics – or 'optoelectronics' – does not end here. Intensive research is now being conducted in conjunction with thin film technology on the development of optical switches to replace conventional electronic solid-state switches. These would not only eliminate the need to convert from the optical to the electrical regime, but they also hold out the promise of faster switching speeds. They would have an application beyond transmission and switching, in the design of even faster computers.

Satellite Communications

Although fibre optics provides the technical capability to introduce wide bandwidths into the public network, it is clearly going to be some considerable time before such bandwidths could be made available on the public switched network and internationally. Communications satellites provide that capability. There is also a unique distinction to be drawn between satellite technology and terrestrial transmission; the former provides a more or less infinitely flexible network configuration because it operates in a broadcast mode. Thus, any location within the satellite reception 'shadow' can receive information if it is suitably equipped to receive it.

At the present time, economic and technical considerations favour satellites for high-volume transmission over transoceanic or transcontinental distances. A point worth noting is that, if the capital costs are ignored, transmission costs are largely distance-independent, since the transmission medium itself is virtually a 'free' resource, in sharp contrast to terrestrial or submarine circuits.

Thus we find that the commercial applications which are currently operational or being planned include: bulk data transmission; high-speed facsimile; newspaper printing, simultaneous at a number of locations; and other applications requiring large bandwidth, such as video conferencing.

Local Area Communications Requirements

Access to efficient external public services is only one aspect of the total corporate communications requirement, the other being the internal requirement. There are currently three distinct approaches to the physical distribution of communications services within the restricted geographical area of an office building or factory: Local Area Networks; the new stored program digital PABXs; and the sophisticated central switch employing a high-performance computer.

Under the influence of digital technology and stored program control, the PABX is undergoing a major transformation, and its role is being extended beyond its basic switching function and public network interfacing role. PABX will be able to provide such functions as: terminal and other remote device support; protocol conversion; and specialised gateways giving access to a wide range of alternative services.

The Local Area Network concept forms another radically different approach, but it is too early to form a satisfactory judgement of which, if any, approach will predominate. Although at the present time it is fair to say that these various approaches are following more or less independent development paths and can be regarded as independent solutions, it would be incorrect to assume that they are mutually exclusive. In practical situations in the future, each may have a role to play, either independently or in concert.

Media Convergence

Digitisation of information – its representation, storage, transmission and switching – is the common thread. Convergence of data and text is a reality and the merger with speech is well advanced, at least insofar as store and forward *uninterrupted* speech is concerned. Although forecasts for automatic speech recognition, and its direct translation to text, vary markedly, the available evidence, particularly from Japan, indicates that progress is well advanced.

Digitisation is also starting to have a dramatic impact on image processing, and arises from the practicability of employing high-resolution bit representation at the input and output stages. Thus: on input – facsimile, OCR and photocopying lead to the Image Scanner; and on output – facsimile, plotter and copier would result in the Image Printer. To match this trend, higher resolution VDU screens are under development, at least in black and white, and the large reduction in memory costs over recent years is making it economically feasible to provide the local memory backing to support higher screen resolutions, and advanced facilities.

From being a somewhat intractable representation to handle using traditional technology, it seems likely that image and graphics information is destined to undergo rapid development over the next few years, and to occupy a more central role in information processing. Much of the new technology in this area has originated in the image processing requirements of the space satellite reconnaissance programmes, and of body scanning in medicine, and we are now seeing its extension more generally. A few facts and figures may help to place its significance in perspective.

It is now practical to scan an A4 page at a resolution of 4 million pixels, a pixel being the basic information element (square cell) into which the page surface is divided. Typically, an A4 page would be divided into 2,200 rows of such pixels. Relative to the page size, a single pixel occupies an area about half a full stop(.), and during the scanning process, its level of 'greyness' is assessed from black to white, and 254 levels of grey in between. A similar but more elaborate procedure is employed for colour. Thus scanning at this high-resolution bit level provides a common denominator for images in all their forms, from text, through line graphics to full colour. In combination with digital transmission and videodisk storage technology, the way is open to completely revolutionise the handling of traditional paper-based information.

As an example, a system has recently been announced in which document images can be stored automatically and retrieved within 1 second. The information can also be stored in long-term archival memory. The latter is a 'juke-box' construction containing 64 disks and occupies about the same floor space as an office desk.

However, the juke box has a capacity of approximately 1.5 million A4 pages, which, using conventional methods, would require a row of cabinets 60 metres long and 2.8 metres high. Each stored document image can be located within about 5 seconds, displayed on a VDU screen, and, if required, transmitted to another location.

Storage Technology

For many purposes, systems delivered over the next few years will continue to rely upon the familiar magnetic products including rigid disks, floppy disks and so on, for non-volatile memory.

As we have seen, another technique which holds out great promise, particularly for large-scale archiving purposes, is the videodisk. The exciting feature of this medium is its amazing capacity: up to 10 billion bits on a 30 cm disk has been quoted. In fact, some cost projections make the videodisk a good candidate to replace paper and microfilm: for a given amount of information, it may eventually be cheaper to use a videodisk than paper. Another advantage of this recording technique is the feasibility of disk duplication at low cost per disk when mass produced, so that one could see the use of prerecorded videodisks to distribute databases, dictionary, technical or economic information.

Terminal and Workstation Design

Under the influence mainly of microprocessor technology, the terminal has progressed from an unintelligent device to the stage where intelligent terminals are now available with powerful computing facilities. By taking advantage of the local intelligence, and by introducing common digital representation and transmission of information, the terminal can be transformed into a device which is able to support an extended range of functions. The idea is that instead of having a range of individually specialised devices for each function, these can be provided in one unit, the multifunction workstation. Products with this capability are now starting to appear, and further significant development can be expected. The functions provided could include:

— word processing and other text preparation aids;

— storage and retrieval of both personal and corporate information;

— conventional telephony;

— speech store and forward;

— facsimile transmission;

— communications support, to permit access to remote resources and services. These could be situated on the same geographical site or external to the organisation. The remote services accessed could include, for example, archival memory, large-scale computing power, information database services, and electronic mail services.

It is now within the bounds of technology to develop this capability so that these functions are accessible from the workplace or location of a single individual.

Whilst the multipurpose workstation concept can be realised without according a central role to the telephone, the enhanced capability which it will gain from the planned ISDN indicates that the telephone itself constitutes an important point of departure for the evolution of the multipurpose workstation.

Distributed Processing

Historically an outgrowth of traditional data processing, distributed processing concepts provide a natural and sympathetic framework for the construction and evolution of the new generation of information systems. The features of interest include: support for local stand-alone intelligence as well as distributed resources; provision of efficient communications services; support for resource sharing and access to common services; greater reliability than with centralised configurations; and finally, flexibility to meet changing needs.

The manner in which these concepts are being applied to office and administrative systems is illustrated in Figure 14.3. This shows user workstations connected to a network to which are also attached various shared resources, eg main storage, printers and 'servers' which provide commonly used services, eg electronic mail, word processing and the like. In addition 'gateways' are shown which provide the interfaces and access points to external networks and remote services.

The diagram is a conceptual description and no more. For example, with the exception of the workstations, it does not follow that for each function represented there is a corresponding physical box; there is some freedom of choice as to where some functions are implemented, but this does not undermine the essential validity of the approach.

Standards

It has been evident for some considerable time that the full development of communications-based systems has been hampered by the lack of a coherent body of standards designed to offer the following benefits:

— to simplify the connection of a wide range of terminals and other equipment to communications networks;

— to facilitate interworking between heterogeneous types and makes of equipment;

— to facilitate end-to-end interworking between devices connected to different communications networks employing different rules and under different ownership;

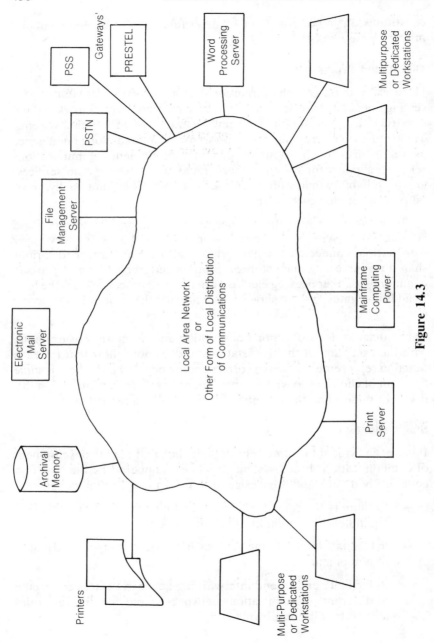

Figure 14.3

—   at the applications level to support generalised services such as file transfer, text transmission, electronic mail and so on.

The requirement becomes even more urgent when we consider the particular characteristics of office systems. The office system comprises a wide range of equipment, much of it highly specialised, and outside the mainstream of traditional data processing, and in practice this creates a multiple-vendor situation. Interworking is the very essence of the new environment, and so full compatibility or support for interworking between diverse elements becomes crucial. This is evident when we consider the kinds of activity in which an individual user may wish to engage:

—   to access a common service, eg document preparation, available locally;

—   to access a communications-based service or facility available externally, whether accessible from the public network, or provided within some other private network, or by some external value added service;

—   to transmit or receive messages or other information using the optimum transmission service selected from a range of alternatives which may be available. As above, the transmission path may span several networks;

—   to input or receive information in a variety of forms (text, data, voice, image) with the possibility of converting between them at some points.

Although suppliers able to satisfy most if not all of the product range (and thus able to deliver complete systems) will undoubtedly arise, there is lurking in the background the danger that either lack of standards or an unwillingness to adopt them could result in a repetition of the 'locked in' experience which has categorised and bedevilled the traditional mainframe-dominated marketplace. In the new environment it is even more important that users should have wide freedom to select alternative products and possess the flexibility to adapt to changing technology at minimal cost and disruption.

As explained in earlier chapters, the interconnection of systems and terminals requires a highly sophisticated set of common conventions or 'protocols' and, in order to avoid specific adaptations it is desirable that international standards be agreed upon and applied. Until quite recently, the progress of standardisation in communications has been relatively slow, but this is now changing and within the last two or three years, the standards-making bodies have made rapid progress in defining requirements and in developing concepts and specific standards. This can be appropriately illustrated by reference to: X25 for public packet switched networks (and by extension to private packet switched networks); the generalised transport service concept; and Open Systems Interconnection.

The X25 Standard

This now exists, has gained international acceptance and is being implemented in supplier equipment.

Generalised Transport Service

An appreciation of the importance attached to the Transport Service can be gained from a brief consideration of some of the benefits which it is intended to offer:

— it insulates the application programs from the idiosyncracies of different networks and transmission services, so that an applications program need not be aware that a packet switched network, a circuit switched network, a leased circuit, or a satellite link, is being used;

— the destination addressing structure permits composite communication paths spanning multiple networks (which may be public or private or a combination of the two) to be established and maintained.

Much progress has been achieved, general definitions now exist and have been implemented, and it is probably only a matter of time before agreement is reached at least within Europe.

Open Systems Working

From the users' viewpoint the ultimate goal is for an application in one device to be able to access remotely an application in another device, irrespective of the details of the underlying mechanisms. This is the objective of the seven-layered model architecture under development within ISO.

The principles currently being evolved are intended to provide a coherent framework for all the communications components which may be present in standard, de facto standard or local versions. Thus, by using it and including the appropriate component standards, then users can agree to intercommunicate *if they so wish.*

The development of Open Systems Working standards is probably one of the largest standardisation projects undertaken so far. This is recognised, and a period of five to ten years has been mentioned for the main goals to be attained.

Fitting It Together

In this overview we have ranged over a number of technological trends. Individual elements of the technology now exist, others are coming into place, and some will take a considerable time to be fully implemented. The various threads of convergence will not come together simultaneously; this is inevitable in view of the fluidity of the technology and the broad front of advance.

APPLICATION OPPORTUNITIES AND AREAS OF IMPACT

It is beyond the scope of this book to review the impact of the developments we have been describing, and the ensuing revolution in information processing. Here we shall restrict ourselves to general comment illustrated by reference to one or two specific areas. Figure 14.4 attempts to summarise the overall impact, showing examples of some of the main application opportunities which will either be created or expanded. It also indicates the areas of impact – in fact, virtually the full cross-section of society and its institutions.

In a number of applications the fundamental role of communications is readily apparent. These include: electronic mail; electronic conferencing in various forms; and news distribution. In all of these, communications bridges space and time, by enabling information to be transmitted almost instantaneously, and with the addition of memory in the form of mailboxes, it neutralises the effects of time zones as well.

Perhaps less obvious are the impacts on medicine, and on the office and the manager or professional worker. In medicine, the use of electronic implants as artificial pace makers is now fairly commonplace, and several instances have been reported recently where the implant has been equip-

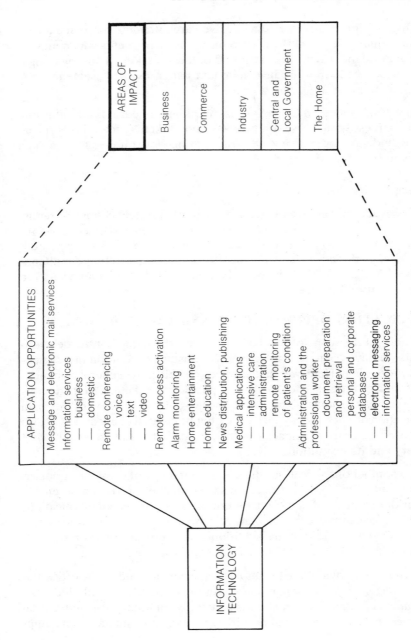

Figure 14.4 The Impact of Information Technology

ped with communications capability. By plugging in to the nearest tele-phone, it has been possible to monitor a patient's condition remotely and transmit signals which modify the behaviour of the pacemaker.

At a more mundane level, the maintenance of comprehensive medical records has resisted attack largely on account of the varied form of the information, ranging from longhand, through typescript to photographic images, ie X-ray photographs. The solution is now within the realm of possibility, and the bit image scanner will clearly play a major role.

The impact on business and commerce is expected to be very wide-spread, in both overall corporate terms, and at the administrative levels, whether amongst traditional office workers or the managerial and profes-sional categories.

Although in the sixties and seventies great hopes were entertained for the introduction of computers into commerce, it is a fact that those earlier expectations have never been completely fulfilled. That both batch pro-cessing and subsequently communications-based systems have had an enormous impact in specific well-defined application areas cannot be denied. But it is now recognised that there is a significant area which has so far failed to benefit in any significant way from traditional mainstream computing and data processing, and that is the office and administrative environment.

Apart from the introduction of the telephone, typewriters, photo-copiers and the like, the overall nature of the work and the activities performed by individuals has hardly changed over the last hundred years or so.

Major benefits in the form of increased productivity and quality of work have already been achieved in regard to typing and document preparation principally through the introduction of word processing equipment. However, it is now generally accepted that the area offering the greatest potential benefits is at the level of the manager and profes-sional worker, and their direct secretarial support.

A number of studies and investigations have established the reasons why traditional data processing is not wholly suited to the needs of the manager and professional worker. The significant finding is that a sub-stantial proportion of a manager's work entails communication in some form, whether by telephone, attending meetings or issuing memoranda. Another characteristic is the large element of informality and the relatively unstructured and unpredictable tasks which have to be performed. These features are manifested in the manager's working day, involving continual switching between tasks, with decisions often requiring access to information in a form which cannot be foreseen in advance. The new information technology which is now emerging is peculiarly well adapted to these requirements.

In education, computer-assisted learning has been with us for some time, but other consequences could be even more dramatic. It is accepted by many authorities that the potential of the average human brain is rarely fully utilised. It is by no means fanciful to suggest that the ability to access vast memory banks of knowledge and information, aided by the organising and computational power of computers, could release this latent capacity and expand the human mind.

The man in the street or at home will be increasingly affected by the progress of information technology. Shopping from home is already available in a limited fashion, and the sophistication of television games provides an insight into the educational potential.

Much has been said about the sociological impacts. There are those who forecast a Utopia, or alternatively an Armageddon, arising from the process of technological change. But technology is ethically neutral, and we should try to see it in an objective perspective.

Information Technology is destined to change the nature and pattern of employment. At the same time, properly applied, it should also provide greater creative opportunities for individuals, reducing the drudgery of some activities and leading to more leisure time. Ultimately the choice rests with society.

IN CONCLUSION

The primary concern of this book has been data communications (or the communication of information). We have seen in this concluding chapter that it forms an essential component in the Information Technology Revolution. The massive edifice of concepts and technical apparatus which has been described provides the essential underpinning for the emerging vastly expanded role of communications. To reach this stage has taken perhaps a little over 100 years and a history of almost continuous development.

The history makes fascinating reading: the early beginnings with the electric telegraph which soon put the pony express out of business; the varying opinions about the future of the telephone, represented by the quotations at the beginning of this book; the somewhat whimsical connection between a certain Kansas undertaker called Strowger and the automatic telephone exchange . . . In any event, the established and emerging technology represents a remarkable human achievement.

Appendix 1

Glossary of Data Transmission Terms

Acoustic Coupler

A portable device which couples its built-in modem to the telephone line via the telephone handset; there is no hardwired connection to the line.

Amplifier

Device which increases the power of an electrical signal.

Amplitude

Loudness, strength or volume of a signal.

Amplitude Modulation

A modulation technique in which the amplitude of a signal is the characteristic varied to transmit intelligence.

Analogue Transmission

Transmission of a continuously variable signal (usual transmission method for telephone lines) as opposed to a discretely variable signal (as in digital transmission).

Asynchronous

A transmission method where the signals employed may be of variable duration (eg Morse code).

Asynchronous Transmission

Transmission in which each character is preceded by a start signal and followed by one or more stop signals. A variable time interval can exist between characters. The start signal triggers off the receiver and following receipt of the character the stop signals switch off the receiver in readiness for receipt of the next character.

Attenuation

Decrease in magnitude of current, voltage or power of a signal in transmission (signal loss or fading).

Audio Frequencies

Frequencies that can be heard by the human ear when transmitted as sound waves. (Maximum human audibility range 16 – 20,000 Hz.)

Bandwidth

Range of frequencies available for signalling in a communications channel. The difference between the maximum and minimum frequencies on that channel.

Baud

Unit of discrete signalling speed per second; the modulation rate. Baud = Bits per second when two-state signalling is used. Because of the baud rate limitations over speech circuits, multi-level signalling is used to obtain high bit rates on these circuits.

Bit

Abbreviation of binary digit. Signal element of transmission in binary notation either '0' (OFF) or '1' (ON).

Bits Per Second

(Bps) Transmission rate possible on a circuit. (Bit rate) (Bit/s).

Block

A group of characters transmitted as a unit.

Buffer

A storage device used to accommodate a difference in rate of flow of data or time of occurrence of events when transmitting from one device to another.

Carrier (Frequency) System

A means of deriving several channels over a single link by causing each channel to modulate a different 'carrier' frequency and demodulating at the distant end to obtain the original signal.

Channel (Communication)

An information path capable of transferring data in both directions. Channels are derived by multiplexing and do not in general correspond to physical circuits.

Character	Letter, figure, number, punctuation or other sign contained in a message; usually represented by one byte.
Check Bit or Check Character	A bit or character associated with a character or a block for error detection purposes.
Circuit Switching	Conventional interconnection where a two-way fixed bandwidth circuit is allocated exclusively to the parties concerned for the duration of the call.
Circuit (2-Wire)	A circuit having a pair of conductors over which both send and receive transmissions take place.
Circuit (4-Wire)	A circuit where the send and receive directions each have a separate pair of conductors.
Common Carrier	National organisation which has the authority/responsibility to provide public telecommunications services in its own country.
Datel	Generic title of UK PTT data transmission services.
Demodulation	Process whereby the original signal is recovered from a modulated carrier. The reverse of modulation. In data transmission it is the conversion of a received analogue signal into a digital form.
Differential Modulation	A modulation technique where the coding options are related to the previously received signal, eg phase angle of the received signal related to the phase angle of the preceding signal.

Digital Transmission
This is where the data characters are coded into discrete separate pulses or signal levels.

Duplex Transmission
Transmission in both directions simultaneously.

Equalisation
Means of improving circuit quality by equalising different distortions.

Error Detection and Feedback System (ARQ)
A system employing an error detection routine and so arranged that the receiver on identifying an error initiates request for retransmission of the corrupted data.

Error Rate
The probability, within a given sample size of bits, characters or blocks, of one being in error.

Frequency Division Multiplexing (FDM)
A multiplexing method deriving several channels by slicing a given bandwidth into a number of narrow bandwidth channels. (Frequency Slicing.)

Frequency Modulation For Data Transmission
A widely used low-speed modulation method using different frequencies to represent binary 1 and 0.

Frequency Shift Keying (FSK)
See Frequency Modulation.

Gaussian Noise (White Noise)
Background noise present in communication channels due to the electrical disturbance of electrons.

Half-Duplex Transmission
Transmission in both directions but not simultaneously.

HDLC
A link level protocol using a frame and bit structure as opposed to character protocols.

Hertz (Hz)

The international standard measurement of frequency (originally expressed in cycles per second).

Impulsive (Black) Noise

Peaks of noise (usually of short duration and high amplitude) which corrupt the data signals.

Isochronous

Transmission where all signals are of equal duration and are sent in a continuous sequence.

Modem

DCE or Data Circuit Terminating Equipment which effects the conversion from digital to analogue (modulation) and analogue to digital (demodulation) thus enabling a digital signal to be transmitted over an analogue path.

Modulation

Process whereby a carrier frequency is modulated or altered by the information signal to be carried. Reverse of demodulation. In data transmission the conversion from digital to analogue.

Multiplexing

The process of combining separate signal channels into one composite stream (see Frequency Division Multiplexing and Time Division Multiplexing).

Multi-Level Signalling

The process of packing bits into a baud to achieve high-speed data transmission.

Multipoint Circuit

A network configuration with a central site and several outstations connected by a common serving section (American – Multidrop).

Parallel Transmission

The simultaneous transmission of the bits making up a character. Usually only an in-house facility because it requires a wire or communication channel for each bit. (Also known as bit parallel or character serial.)

Parity

A means of error detection usually by adding an additional parity bit to a character or block so that the sum of the binary 1s is either odd or even. Conventionally, ODD parity is a feature of synchronous systems and EVEN parity a feature of asynchronous systems.

Phase Modulation

A modulation technique in which the phase angle of the signal is the characteristic which is varied to represent the data being sent. Often combined with amplitude to effect multi-level signalling.

Point-to-Point

Simple network configuration with a communication facility from one location to another.

Port

Input/output connection.

Pulse Code Modulation (PCM)

A method of transmitting analogue speech in a digital form over a transmission link. The speech bandwidth is converted into a 64 kbit/s bit stream.

Quantising Noise/Error

A distortion with PCM due to the difference between the quantisation levels used and the actual signal being sampled.

Residual Error Rate

The undetected error potential after error detection/correction processes have been carried out.

Serial Transmission

The sequential transmission, on a bit-by-bit basis, of the bits making up a character.

Sideband

The resultant upper and lower frequency bands around a carrier frequency produced in modulation.

Simplex Transmission

Transmission in one direction only. (No return path.)

Tandem

Network configuration where two or more point-to-point circuits are linked together with transmission effected on an end-to-end basis over all links.

Time Division
Multiplexing (TDM)

A multiplexing method deriving several channels by allocating the transmission link for a limited time (time slicing) to each channel. Statistical or intelligent TDM devices further improve the number of channels obtainable.

Transparent

Originally referred to a system which imposes no restrictions on the code or bit pattern used. Increasingly it is being extended to encompass transparency at higher functional levels.

Appendix 2

Abbreviations

AC	Alternating Current
ACK	Acknowledgement (positive)
ADCCP	Advanced Data Communications Control Procedure
A/N	Alphanumeric
ANSI	American National Standards Institute
ARPA	Advanced Research Project Agency
ARQ	Automatic Retransmission on Request
ASCII	American Standard Code for Information Interchange
ASR	Automatic Send-Receive
AT & T	American Telephone and Telegraph Corporation
BCC	Block Check Character
BCD	Binary Coded Decimal
BSI	British Standards Institution
CANTAT	Canada Transatlantic Telephony Cable
CCITT	The International Telegraph and Telephone Consultative Committee
CCP	Communications Control Programme
CCU	Communications Control Unit
CEPT	European Conference of Postal and Telecommunications Administrations
COMSAT	Communications Satellite Corporation
CPU	Central Processor Unit
CRT	Cathode Ray Tube
CTA	Circuit Terminating Arrangement
dB	Decibel
DC	Direct Current
DCE	Data Circuit Terminating Equipment
DDS/DDN	Digital Data Service/Network
DTE	Data Terminal Equipment
EBCDIC	Extended Binary Coded Decimal Interchange Code
EDU	Error Detection Unit
ENQ	Enquiry
EOT	End of Transmission
EPSS	Experimental Packet Switching Service
ETB	End of Transmitted Block
ETX	End of Text

FAX	Facsimile
FCC	Federal Communications Commission (USA)
FDM	Frequency Division Multiplexing
FEC	Forward Error Control
FSK	Frequency Shift Keying
HDLC	High-Level Data Link Control
Hz	Hertz (Cycle per second)
IA 5	International Alphabet Number 5, Synonymous with ISO 7-bit code
INTELSAT	International Telecommunications Satellite Consortium
I/O	Input/Output
ISD	International Subscriber Dialling
ISO	International Organization for Standardization
ITU	International Telecommunications Union
kHz	Kilohertz
LSI	Large Scale Integration
MCVF	Multi Channel Voice Frequency
MF	Multi Frequency
MHz	Megahertz
MODEM	Modulator/Demodulator
MTBF	Mean Time Between Failure
MTTR	Mean Time to Repair
NAK	Negative Acknowledgement
NTU	Network Terminating Unit
PABX	Private Automatic Branch Exchange
PAM	Pulse Amplitude Modulation
PAX	Private Automatic Exchange
PBX	Private Branch Exchange
PCM	Pulse Code Modulation
POS	Point of Sale
PSE	Packet Switching Exchange
PSS	UK Public Packet Switched Service
PSTN	Public Switched Telephone Network

PTT   Postal, Telegraph and Telephone Authority

QAM   Quadrature Amplitude Modulation
QSAM   Quadrature Sideband Amplitude Modulation

RBT   Remote Batch Terminal
RJE   Remote Job Entry
ROM   Read Only Memory

SDLC   Synchronous Data Link Control
SITA   Société Internationale de Telecommunication
                       Aeronautique
SOH   Start of Heading
STD   Subscriber Trunk Dialling
STX   Start of Text
SWIFT   Society for Worldwide Interbank Financial
                       Telecommunications
SYN   Synchronous Idle

TDM   Time Division Multiplexing
TXE   Electronic Exchange
TXK   Crossbar Exchange

VDU   Visual Display Unit
VSB   Vestigial Sideband

Appendix 3

International Alphabet Number 5

This alphabet largely supersedes the International Alphabet Number 2 for data communications purposes. The accompanying table illustrates its construction and the character assignments. The brief notes which follow summarise the functions of the control characters.

							0	0	0	0	1	1	1	1
							0	0	1	1	0	0	1	1
						Column	0	1	0	1	0	1	0	1
Bits	b_7	b_6	b_5	b_4	b_3	b_2	b_1 Row	0	1	2	3	4	5	6	7
	0	0	0	0	0	NUL	(TC_7) DLE	SP	0	(@)	P	`	p
	0	0	0	1	1	(TC_1) SOH	DC_1	!	1	A	Q	a	q
	0	0	1	0	2	(TC_2) STX	DC_2	"	2	B	R	b	r
	0	0	1	1	3	(TC_3) ETX	DC_3	£	3	C	S	c	s
	0	1	0	0	4	(TC_4) EOT	DC_4	$	4	D	T	d	t
	0	1	0	1	5	(TC_5) ENQ	(TC_8) NAK	%	5	E	U	e	u
	0	1	1	0	6	(TC_6) ACK	(TC_9) SYN	&	6	F	V	f	v
	0	1	1	1	7	BEL	(TC_{10}) ETB	'	7	G	W	g	w
	1	0	0	0	8	FE_0 (BS)	CAN	(	8	H	X	h	x
	1	0	0	1	9	FE_1 (HT)	EM	)	9	I	Y	i	y
	1	0	1	0	10	FE_2 (LF)	SUB	*	:	J	Z	j	z
	1	0	1	1	11	FE_3 (VT)	ESC	+	;	K	([)	k	
	1	1	0	0	12	FE_4 (FF)	IS_4 (FS)	,	<	L		l	
	1	1	0	1	13	FE_5 (CR)	IS_3 (GS)	–	=	M	(])	m	
	1	1	1	0	14	SO	IS_2 (RS)	.	>	N	^	n	–
	1	1	1	1	15	SI	IS_1 (US)	/	?	O	_	o	DEL

Notes on the control characters

ACK – *Acknowledge* – A transmission control character transmitted by a receiver as an affirmative response to the sender.

BEL – *Bell* – A character for use when there is need to call for human attention; it may control alarm or attention devices.

BS – *Backspace* – A layout character which controls the movement of the printing position one printing space backward on the same printing line.

CAN – *Cancel* – A character used to indicate that the information it accompanies is in error.

CR – *Carriage return* – A layout character which controls the movement of the printing position to the first printing position on the same printing line.

DC₄ – *Device control* – A device control character used to interrupt or turn off ancillary devices (STOP).

DEL – *Delete* – This character is used primarily to erase or obliterate erroneous or unwanted characters in punched tape. DEL characters may be inserted into or removed from a stream of data without affecting the information content of that stream. DEL characters may serve to accomplish media-fill or time-fill but then the addition or removal of these characters may affect the information layout and/or the control of equipment.

DLE – *Data link escape* – A transmission control character which will change the meaning of a limited number of contiguously following characters. It is used to provide supplementary data transmission control functions and bit transparency. Only graphics and transmission control characters can be used in DLE sequences.

EM – *End of medium* – A control character which may be used to identify the physical end of the medium, or the end of the used, or wanted, portion of information recorded on a medium. The position of this character does not necessarily correspond to the physical end of the medium.

ENQ – *Enquiry* – A transmission control character used as a request for a response from a remote station. The response may include station identification and/or station status. When a 'who are you' function is required on the general switched transmission network, the first use of ENQ after the connection is established shall have the meaning 'who are you' (station identification). Subsequent use of ENQ may, or may not, include the function 'who are you', as determined by agreement by the users.

EOT – *End of transmission* – A transmission control character used to indicate the conclusion of the transmission of one or more texts.

ESC – *Escape* – A functional character which may be used to extend the standard character set of the code table. It is a warning or non-locking shift character which changes the meaning of the next single following code combination. The precise meaning of the character following 'escape' requires prior agreement between the sender and the recipient of the data. Where required the character following 'escape' may extend the 'escape' sequence.

'Escape' sequences are used primarily to obtain additional control functions which may provide amongst other things graphics or graphic sets outside the standard set. Such control functions must not be used as additional transmission controls.

'Null' and 'delete' and the ten transmission controls must not be used in defining 'escape' sequences. Where they appear in an actual 'escape' sequence they shall retain their standard meaning and be disregarded in the interpretation of the 'escape' sequence.

The use of certain 'escape' sequences will be the subject of further Recommendations.

ETB – *End of transmission block* – A transmission control character used to indicate the end of a transmission block of data where data is divided into such blocks for transmission purposes.

ETX – *End of text* – A transmission control character which terminates a text.

FF   – *Form feed* – A layout character which controls the movement of the printing position to the first predetermined printing line on the next form.

FS   – *File separator* – See unit separator (US) for definition.

GS   – *Group separator* – See unit separator (US) for definition.

HT   – *Horizontal tabulation* – A layout character which controls the movement of the printing position to the next in a series of predetermined positions along the printing line.

LF   – *Line feed* – A layout character which controls the movement of the printing position to the next printing line.

NAK – *Negative acknowledge* – A transmission control character transmitted by a receiver as a negative response to the sender.

NL   – *New line* – A layout character which controls the movement of the printing position to the first printing position of the next printing line.

NUL – *Null* – A character whose sole purpose is to accomplish media-fill or time-fill. Null characters may be inserted into or removed from a stream of data without affecting the information content but then the information layout and/or the control of equipment may be affected.

RS   – *Record separator* – See unit separator (US) for definition.

SI   – *Shift-in* – The shift-in character means that the code combinations which follow shall be interpreted according to the standard code table.

SO   – *Shift-out* – The shift-out character means that the code combinations which follow shall be interpreted as outside of the standard code table until a shift-in character is reached. However, all the control characters (colums 0 and 1) and delete will retain their standard interpretation. The shift-out character is reserved primarily for extension to the graphics.

SOH – *Start of heading* – A transmission control character used as the first character of a heading of an information message.

SP – *Space* – A normally non-printing graphic character used to separate words. It is also a layout character which controls the movement of the printing position, one printing position forwards.

STX – *Start of text* – A transmission control character which precedes a text and which is used to terminate a heading.

SUB – *Substitute* – A substitute character used to replace a character which is determined to be invalid or in error.

SYN – *Synchronous idle* – A transmission control character used by a synchronous transmission system in the absence of any other character (idle condition) to provide a signal from which synchronism may be achieved or retained between data terminal equipments.

US – *Unit separator* – Terminates an information block called a 'unit'. Similarly, 'record separator' (RS), 'group separator' (GS), 'file separator' (FS) terminate information blocks called 'record', 'group', 'file', respectively. The four information separators are in the hierarchical ascending order US, RS, GS, FS. An information block must not be split by a higher order separator, eg a 'record' may contain a number of complete 'units', but may not contain a part of a 'unit'.

VT – *Vertical tabulation* – A layout character which controls the movement of the printing position to the next in a series of predetermined printing lines.

Appendix 4

International Alphabet Number 2

Notes on International Alphabet Number 2

Most code combinations can have two meanings. Use of the 'Letters' shift character indicates that subsequent codes are to be interpreted as letters (first column shown); use of the 'Figures' shift character indicates that they are to be interpreted as figures or other non-alphabetic characters (second column). Line feed, Carriage Return and Space are common to both cases.

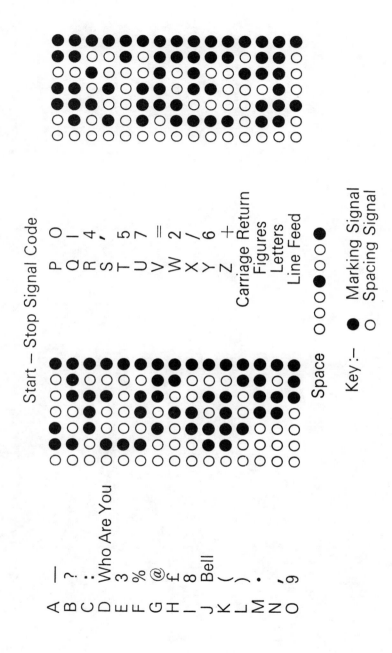

Appendix 5
Bibliography

Bleazard G B, *Why Packet Switching?*, NCC Publications, 1979

Boulter R A, Network Synchronisation, *Post Office Electrical Engineers' Journal*, Vol 70, April 1977

Brown R, *Telecommunications*, Aldus Books, 1969

Buckley D J, Main Transmission Network: Planning of Digital Transmission Systems, *Post Office Electrical Engineers' Journal*, Vol 72, April 1979

Cole R, *Computer Communications*, Macmillan, 1982

Davies D W, and Barber D L A, *Communication Networks for Computers*, John Wiley & Sons, 1976

Davies D W, Barber D L A, Price W C and Solomonides C M, *Computer Networks and their Protocols*, John Wiley & Sons, 1979

Dean P, Packet Switched Data Networking, *Guides to Computing Standards*, No. 22.6, The National Computing Centre, 1981

Gee K C E, *Introduction to Open Systems Interconnection*, NCC Publications, 1980

Gee K C E, *Local Area Networks*, NCC Publications, 1982

Gee K C E, *Proprietary Network Architectures*, NCC Publications 1981

Harris L R F and Davis E, System X and the Evolving UK Telecommunications Network, *Post Office Electrical Engineers' Journal*, Vol 72, April 1979

Harrison R, Telephony Transmission Standards in the Evolving Digital Network, *Post Office Electrical Engineers' Journal*, Vol 73, July 1980

Houldsworth J, Basic Mode Data Link Control Procedures, *Guide to Computing Standards*, No 22.4, The National Computing Centre, 1980

Houldsworth J, High Level Data Link Control Procedures, *Guides to Computing Standards*, No 22.6, The National Computing Centre, 1980

Martin J, System X, *Post Office Electrical Engineers' Journal*, Vol 71, January 1979

Moore B W, Progress to Common Channel Signalling, *Post Office Electrical Engineers' Journal,* Vol 74, October 1981

Pritchard J A T, *Quantitative Methods in On-Line Systems,* Publications, 1979

Ross H McG, Fundamental Aspects, *Guide to Computing Standards,* No 22.1, The National Computing Centre, 1981

Scott P R D, *Introducing Data Communications Standards,* NCC Publications, 1979

Scott P R D, *Modems in Data Communications,* NCC Publications, 1980

Sloman M G, X25 Explained, *Computer Communications,* Vol 1, No 6, December, 1978

Smol G, Hamer M P R and Hills M T, *Telecommunications: A Systems Approach,* George Allen and Unwin, 1976

Walker R R and Morgan A J, The Electret: A Possible Replacement for the Carbon Microphone, *Post Office Electrical Engineers' Journal,* Vol 72, April 1979

Willis G, Modem Interfaces and Connectors, *Guides to Computing Standards,* No 22.2, The National Computing Centre, 1980

Willis G, Modems, *Guides to Computing Standards,* No 22.3, The National Computing Centre, 1980

CCITT material is published by the International Telecommunications Union in Geneva and can be obtained from:

International Telecommunications Union
Place des Nations
1211 Geneva
Switzerland.

Index